George Francis Houck

The church in northern Ohio and in the diocese of Cleveland from

1749 to 1890

George Francis Houck

The church in northern Ohio and in the diocese of Cleveland from 1749 to 1890

ISBN/EAN: 9783742835703

Manufactured in Europe, USA, Canada, Australia, Japa

Cover: Foto ©Lupo / pixelio.de

Manufactured and distributed by brebook publishing software
(www.brebook.com)

George Francis Houck

The church in northern Ohio and in the diocese of Cleveland from

1749 to 1890

St. John's Cathedral, Cleveland, O.

THE CHURCH

IN

NORTHERN OHIO

AND IN THE

DIOCESE OF CLEVELAND

FROM 1749 TO 1890.

FOURTH EDITION.

(Revised and Enlarged.)

BY THE REV. GEORGE F. HOUCK,

CHANCELLOR OF THE DIOCESE OF CLEVELAND.

CLEVELAND:

SHORT & FORMAN, PRINTERS.

1890.

PREFACE TO THE FIRST EDITION.

On entering a large city the eye is filled with the evidences of the material struggle for life—some of them grand, some of them dismal. One cannot but reflect on that incessant activity which has upreared the vast mart. And yet, above all the massive or elegant structures that symbolize the various successes, pursuits and ambitions of man, there towers the cross of the Catholic church.

Passing out into the country, in the more modest village, and amid surroundings nearer to the God of nature, still we find the upreared shaft, reminder of mankind's redemption.

These temples, lowly or superb, are the evidences of the civilization that builds beyond time, and yet preserves all that is worth preserving in time. But the temples are not self-upreared, and back of this the civilization on which depends the security of the temporal, there have been architects and builders at work—their master, the Supreme Architect of the universe, and their prime domain, the spiritual. In this domain there is the perfection of order. From the lowliest church to the great cathedral divine authority overrules. There is unison, guidance, from parish to diocese, until all centre at Rome, where is the Church.

"Ubi Petrus, ibi ecclesia."

Those then who have mastered a diocese, from the building priest to the artchitect bishop, have founded more, and more lasting, than the teeming city, whatsoever the wonders of its construction or the myriads of its population. Self-interest built the city, self-sacrifice the diocese. Empires decay; religion remains, rooted in the hearts of man.

The pages that follow will give the reader an idea of how a diocese is constructed. The men who most largely figure in this volume are also heroes of battle-fields, but their victories were bloodless, won under the banner of the Prince of Peace. God knows there are wounds to be received in that field.

We who reap what those pioneer priests sowed can, in the historical sketches that follow, learn something of what it meant, of hardships, of fatigues, of disgusts and crosses, to make firm foundation of Catholicity in Northern Ohio and the Diocese of Cleveland.

Our contemporaries who are still building and supervising, they too have history to make, their Catholic imprints to leave on Time; and their road, if less rugged in one way, is as arduous in another as that of their priestly predecessors. Equal the merit of those who blaze the road, or those who lay the highway. The cross assumes many shapes.

The author of this volume—to him a labor of love—is a priest of the Diocese of Cleveland. Here was he born, here ordained, here has he ministered. To this diocese of his affections he dedicates this delineation of her ecclesiastical growth.

If its reading will conduce to reflection on what it means to live for God, the transcendent merit of laboring with eye upturned to heaven, ever facing the grand edifice of Eternity, he will have attained sufficient object.

By those of the laity whose sturdy Catholic parents figure in this work, it will be particularly treasured.

And the value of thus collating facts of early Catholic history, the advantage of this volume to the future historian on a larger scale, commends itself at once to the discerning reader.

MANLY TELLO.

September 10, 1887.

PREFACE TO THE SECOND EDITION.

The exhaustion of the first edition of "The Church in Northern Ohio and in the Diocese of Cleveland," as also a demand for a second edition, are a pleasing evidence of the growing interest among our Catholic people for information on church history, whether diocesan or general.

Though this work does not pretend to be a complete history of Catholicity in this fair and prosperous portion of the Church, it contains in succinct form the historical data and the "blazed trees" that, it is hoped, will aid and guide the future historian, who will best appreciate the dry-as-dust labor and accompanying usefulness of the "Biographical Notices," "Tables of Churches," etc. The time has not yet come to write such history, for the reason that those who helped to make it are either too recently dead or still among the living.

For valuable assistance rendered to this work I thank the Right Rev. Bishops Machebeuf and De Goesbriand, who were among the pioneer priests of Northern Ohio; also Mr. John Gilmary Shea, LL. D., the Reverends M. Healy, S. Bauer, N. Roupp, J. J. Doherty, Z. Druon, F. Westerholt, A. Martin, F. Ankly, and others.

G. F. H.

December 15, 1888.

PREFACE TO THE THIRD EDITION.

Grateful for the kind reception given the first and second editions of "The Church in Northern Ohio and in the Diocese of Cleveland," the author sends this unpretentious volume, with some changes and additions, on its third tour amongst an appreciative Catholic public.

March 20, 1889.

CONTENTS.

ILLUSTRATIONS.

HISTORICAL SKETCH

—OF—

CATHOLICITY IN NORTHERN OHIO

—AND IN THE—

DIOCESE OF CLEVELAND.

PART I.

NORTHERN OHIO.

1749–1847.

The learned Catholic historian of the Church in the United States, John Gilmary Shea, LL. D., in an interesting article contributed to the *Catholic Universe*, September 15, 1881, says that the first trace of Catholic missionaries having visited the territory now within the limits of Ohio, is found as early as 1749. It was then that the Jesuit Fathers, Potier and Bonnecamp, came to evangelize the Huron Indians living along the Vermillion and Sandusky rivers, in Northern Ohio. He also states that the first permanent chapel within the confines of the present state of Ohio, was erected near Sandusky in 1751, by the Jesuit Father de la Richardie, who, with his companions, had come from Detroit and Canada to the southern shore of Lake Erie.

A part of the Huron tribe was brought by Father de la Richardie, in 1751, to Sandusky, where, under the name of Wyandots, they soon took an active part in the affairs of the West. They were also conspicuous in the last French War, and at its close were implicated in the conspiracy of Pontiac, though long checked by the influence of Father Peter Potier, S. J. During the exciting times of the war these missionaries were driven from Sandusky, Father Potier being the last Jesuit missionary among the western Hurons. He died in July, 1781. The Indian missions in and near Sandusky thence depended entirely on the priests attached to the French Posts in Canada and Michigan. Although the Wyandots at Sandusky were thus cut off in great measure from all spiritual care and instructions they kept the Faith. When white settlers began to come into the state, the Wyandots attracted the attention of the Protestant "missionaries," who appeared to be bent rather on undoing what the Jesuit missionaries had done, than on combatting Paganism in its stronghold. A Presbyterian preacher named Joseph Badger made an attempt to "evangelize" the Wyandots, but met with a firm opposition from their chiefs, one of whom it is said, put to death a member of his tribe because he had apostatised. The Methodists next attempted what the Rev. Badger failed to do, and with better success. The old members of the Wyandot tribe having died, their children, who had not been properly instructed, followed the new religious "guides" and so were lost to the Church.*

Traces of these Indian missions have been found recently near the Sandusky river at Fremont and near the Portage river at Port Clinton, in the form of plain silver crosses, such as are known to have been used by the French Canadian missionaries.

When the Society of Jesus was suppressed, and Canada lost to the French, the above mentioned Indian missions were abandoned. From 1751 to 1795 no record is found of any further effort made in Northern Ohio to continue the missionary work begun by the Jesuits. In the early part of 1796 the Rev. Edmund Burke† was sent by Bishop Hubert, of Quebec, from Detroit to the northwestern part of Ohio, near Fort Meigs, just built by the British government on the east bank

*Shea's Am. Cath. Missions, p. 203.

†See "Letter from John Gilmary Shea, LL.D.," p. 246. Rev. E. Burke was born in Ireland about 1743: died at Halifax, as Vicar Apostolic of Nova Scotia, Dec. 1, 1820.

of the Maumee river, near the present site of Perrysburg, Wood county. Here he resided about one year, ministering to the few Catholic soldiers in the fort, and endeavoring with little success, to christianize the Ottawa and Chippewa Indians in the neighborhood—the latter work having been for long one of his aims as a missionary priest. Father Burke left this unpromising charge about February, 1797. From that time, and until 1817, no priest was stationed in Northern Ohio, and in fact none in the entire territory of the present state of Ohio.

During this period of about twenty years a number of Catholic families came from Maryland and Pennsylvania and settled in Columbiana county, some as early as 1812, and others a few years later in Stark and Wayne counties.

In 1814 the saintly Dominican Father, Rev. Edward Fenwick, was sent by Bishop Flaget, of Bardstown, Ky., to look after the spiritual interests of the Catholics, sparsely settled in Southern and Central Ohio, with a view to provide them with regular pastoral attendance. In 1817 he paid his first pastoral visit to the few Catholic families settled in the northeastern part of the state—Columbiana and Stark counties. It is therefore from last mentioned year that Catholicity in Northern Ohio really dates its beginning.

As this narrative is to be confined to the territory of Northern Ohio—the present Diocese of Cleveland—in recording the establishment, growth and progress of the Church, it will deal with such facts relating thereto as far as the subject demands, and the narrow limits of a sketch will permit.

I.

THE DOMINICANS.

Columbiana and Stark counties are the cradle of Catholicity in Northern Ohio, and the Dominicans its first missionaries. As to the early labors of these pioneer priests in Northern Ohio it is to be regretted that the records are sadly deficient. In fact, as the writer was informed by the Very

Rev. Provincial of the Dominicans in the United States, no records were kept by the Dominicans, either by themselves while attending to their scattered missions, or at their convents in Kentucky, and in Perry county, Ohio, whence they were sent to Northern Ohio. This account of their early labors must therefore necessarily be incomplete. The information here given was gathered from historical sketches of congregations under their pastoral care, and although meagre, it is hoped it will not fail to prove of interest to the reader.

As above stated, Rev. Father Fenwick, the pioneer priest of this state, made his first visit to Northern Ohio in 1817, and found a number of Catholic families settled near Hanover, and near the present village of Dungannon, in Columbiana county; also at Canton, Stark county. In 1818 he came again, accompanied by his nephew, the Rev. N. D. Young, who had been ordained the year previous. Arrangements were now made for regular visits. In December, 1818, Father Fenwick was directed to establish a convent of his Order near Somerset, Perry county, Ohio, on a tract of land given the Dominicans for that purpose by Mr. P. Dittoe, a fervent and generous Catholic.

This convent was the residence of the Dominican Fathers who attended at regular intervals, the missions entrusted to their pastoral care in Columbiana, Stark, Mahoning and Wayne counties. Rev. Fathers Fenwick and Young were soon joined by others of their Order, each of whom had charge of one or more missions in Northern and Central Ohio. The following is a complete list of their names, viz: Revs. Vincent de Raymacher, Charles P. Montgomery, John A. Hill, John G. Alleman, Joseph S. Alemany, P. Fochenkress, J. O'Meara, Thomas H. Martin, A. Fahey, Thomas McGrady, D. J. O'Leary, A. F. Van de Weyer and Richard P. Miles. Wherever they labored they did so with zeal and success, and left their impress on all the missions under their charge. Hardships and difficulties and disappointments they bore cheerfully. They laid the foundation of religion deeply, so that their successors might, as they did, build solidly thereon the edifice.

Among them, Fathers Fenwick, Young and Hill were markedly successful. Their names are intimately associated with the early Catholic history of Northern Ohio; the first two as founders of the flourishing congregations in Columbiana and Wayne counties, and Father Hill as the founder of St. John's, Canton, where his remains now rest.

Bishop Flaget finding it impossible to attend to the vast territory under his jurisdiction, petitioned the Holy See for relief. The result was the erection of the Diocese of Cincinnati, embracing the states of Ohio and Michigan, and the appointment of Father Fenwick as its first Bishop. Reluctantly he accepted the burden, and was consecrated at Bardstown, Ky., January 13, 1822. Till his death in 1832, he loved to visit the field of his early missionary labors and was always most cordially welcomed by his former co-laborers and parishioners.

The Dominicans gradually gave up to secular priests their pastoral charges in the above named counties till, in 1842, they withdrew entirely, St. John's, Canton, being their last mission in Northern Ohio.

II.

THE REDEMPTORISTS.

Meanwhile the central portion of Northern Ohio, especially the counties of Huron, Erie, Sandusky and Seneca, had received a considerable influx of Catholics, principally from Germany.

In 1832 several Redemptorist Fathers came from Austria to the United States, under direction of their Provincial and at the earnest invitation of Rt. Rev. Edward Fenwick, to take charge of the Indian and the few Catholic German missions in Michigan, then under his jurisdiction as Bishop of Cincinnati. Disheartened at meeting with little or no success in their priestly labors in Michigan they asked to be relieved of this fruitless mission. As soon as their request was granted by their Provincial. Bishop Purcell, successor to Bishop Fenwick, offered them the pastoral charge of the missions in Crawford, Huron, Erie, Seneca and Wyandot counties, with residence at Peru, Huron county, where, since, 1829, a congregation of Catholic Germans had been organized. Rev. F. X. Tschenhens was accordingly sent, in 1834; later he was joined by the Rev. Fathers Czakert, Haetscher, Prost and Saenderl. Soon these good and zealous priests found as little consolation here as did their brethren in Michigan. Their appeals to the generosity of their people in Peru, for the erection of a new and much needed church, and for other parochial wants, met with no response. The spirit of the congregation was bad; insult and abuse the return given the priests for their labors and self-sacrifice. This was most painful to good Father Tschenhens, who had in a particular manner interested himself in the spiritual welfare of his congregation. However, in spite of ill-treatment he and his faithful co-laborers continued to discharge their duty, hoping against hope for a change of spirit. Father Tschenhens now took personal charge of the scattered missions in the adjoining counties, visiting at regular intervals, on horseback, and often over almost impassable roads, Sandusky, Norwalk, Liberty, Tiffin, Bucyrus, Wolf's Creek (now New Riegel), McCutchenville (no longer existing as a mission), and occasionally Canton. Whilst he was thus engaged Father Czakert, and his associates above mentioned, attended Peru and the neighboring missions.

No change for the better taking place in the spirit of the congregation at Peru, the Redemptorist Fathers asked their Provincial for permission to give up this charge. Their request was granted, and on Low Sunday, 1839, the Rev. Father Prost announced to the congregation that he and his brethren intended to leave them, giving as a reason for so doing, the continued unkindness and ingratitude shown the Fathers in return for their labors among the people entrusted to their pastoral care.

All the Redemptorist Fathers left as announced, with the exception of Rev. F. X. Tschenhens, who a few months later followed his associates to Pittsburg, where they founded a convent and the present very flourishing congregation of St. Philomena.

In 1841, at the earnest solicitation of Bishop Purcell, Father Tschenhens again took charge of the congregation at Peru, which had been without a priest for months, owing to dissensions which caused the removal of the secular priest in charge, the Rev. Joseph Freigang. Father Tschenhens was assisted by the Redemptorist Fathers, Revs. J. N. Neumann and L. M. Alig, remaining from June, 1841, to November, 1843. Meanwhile he also attended Tiffin and a few other missions in Seneca and Wyandot counties. With last mentioned date ended the labors of the Redemptorists in Northern Ohio.

III.

THE SANGUINISTS.

The number of Catholics and missions so rapidly increased that Bishop Purcell was obliged to seek for more priestly help outside his diocese. Whilst on his return home from a visit to the Eternal City, in 1843, he chanced to meet at Havre a band of missionary priests, members of the Society of the Most Precious Blood (also and better known as Sanguinists), who were on their way to the United States to devote themselves to the pastoral care of their German brethren in the Faith. He informed them of the great and pressing need of priests for his diocese, and kindly invited them to come to his assistance. The invitation was accepted, and in January, 1844, the Very Rev. Father Brunner, Provincial of the Sanguinists, accompanied by Rev. Fathers Meier, Wittmer, Van den Broek, Capeder, Ringele and Jacomet, arrived at Peru and took charge of St. Alphonsus' congregation as successors to the Redemptorists. They also accepted charge of the missions attended by their predecessors, besides attending to the Catholic Germans in Cleveland, and the scattered missions in Lorain, Medina, Wayne, Portage and Stark counties.

The advent of these devoted priests was hailed with delight wherever they were sent. Their labors were signally blessed.

Religion flourished in all the missions under their vigilant care, so that the healthy growth of Catholicity in Northern Ohio may be justly, and in a large measure, ascribed under God to the untiring zeal of these excellent priests. December, 1844, Father Brunner established a convent for this Society at New Riegel, in 1845 one at Thompson, and in 1848 another at Glandorf, each of which places became a center of Catholicity for the surrounding country, and from which the neighboring missions were regularly attended. In 1847 the congregation of Peru, completely changed in spirit by the prayerful labors of the Sanguinist Fathers, was resigned by them. It was then placed in charge of secular priests, and has since so remained.

IV.

THE SECULAR CLERGY.

Thus far this sketch has dealt chiefly with the labors of the clergy belonging to the religious orders. The secular clergy are no less deserving of special mention, for they too labored in this part of the Lord's vineyard amid trials, difficulties and hardships, often side by side with their brethren already mentioned, and more often alone in the scattered and wide-spread missions of Northern Ohio. And their labors have borne fruit a hundred fold. They did yeoman's service; they blazed the way for those who succeeded them, and laid the foundation for many missions that have long since developed into strong, vigorous and prosperous congregations.

The first secular priest to do missionary work in Northern Ohio was the Rev. Ignatius J. Mullon, a learned and pious clergyman. He was stationed at the Cathedral in Cincinnati between 1824 and 1834, and was repeatedly sent by his Bishop to the missions in Stark and Columbiana counties, also to Tiffin and Fremont, remaining for longer or shorter periods in each place. His first visit to Northern Ohio was shortly after his ordination, in 1824. Rev. Francis Marshall was the next secular priest, doing pastoral work at Chippewa, (near Doylestown) in 1827. In 1830 Rev. John M. Henni was appointed resident pastor of St. John's, Canton, remaining till 1834. During this time he also attended missions in Columbiana, Stark and Wayne counties. Next in point of time was the Rev. Edmund Quinn, first resident pastor of St. Mary's, Tiffin, 1831-35. His mission covered all of Northwestern Ohio. In 1833 Rev. W. J. Horstmann came to Northern Ohio and founded a colony on land he purchased in Putnam county from the government. Here also he established St. John's congregation, Glandorf. Rev. James Conlan had charge of missions in Columbiana and Mahoning counties, and the eastern portion of Stark county, from 1834. In 1835 Rev. Matthias Wuertz was appointed pastor of St. John's, Canton, and attended Massillon, Louisville, Navarre, and several stations in Stark and Wayne counties. He remained till 1845. Rev. John Dillon was the first resident pastor of Cleveland, from 1835 to 1836, and during this short time attended stations in Summit and Lorain counties. Rev. Basil Schorb, a native of Pennsylvania, was appointed resident pastor of Chippewa in 1837, and had charge of Canal Fulton, Massillon, Canton, Liverpool, Randolph and Wooster. He left Ohio in 1843. Rev. George Boehne was on the mission in Putnam county, notably Fort Jennings, from 1841.

Rev. Patrick O'Dwyer had pastoral charge of the Catholics of Cleveland from 1837 to 1839, and commenced their first church in 1838.

Between 1838 and 1840 the Rev. Michael McAleer did pastoral duty at Canton, Dungannon and Navarre. From 1839 to 1847, the Rev. Joseph McNamee was resident pastor of St. Mary's, Tiffin. For several years he also had charge of all the stations and missions in Northwestern Ohio, covering the same territory as his predecessor, Father Quinn.

Rev. Projectus J. Machebeuf had charge of the missions in Sandusky, Henry, Ottawa, Wood and Lucas counties from 1839, till he was transferred to Sandusky, as first resident pastor, in December, 1840. From Sandusky he attended missions in Sandusky, Erie and Huron counties.

In 1840 the Revs. Amadeus Rappe and Louis de Goesbriand came to Ohio. The latter was sent by Bishop Purcell to take charge of St. Louis' congregation, Louisville, Stark county. Father Rappe resided about six months at Chillicothe. In 1841 he was sent to Toledo, where he organized St. Francis de Sales' congregation, and attended all the missions and stations in Lucas, Paulding, Williams, Defiance and Henry counties. In 1846 he was joined by Father de Goesbriand, who shared with him the privations and labors connected with this difficult charge. Father Rappe remained at Toledo till his elevation to the Episcopacy in 1847.

Rev. Peter McLaughlin was resident pastor at Cleveland from 1840 to 1846. Shortly after his arrival he had the interior of St. Mary's church, on the Flats, completed. The church was dedicated June 7, 1840. Father McLaughlin also attended missions in Lake, Lorain and Summit counties.

Rev. Maurice Howard was on the mission in Northern Ohio about ten years. He came in 1842. Among his charges were Doylestown, Cleveland and Tiffin. He also attended missions in Wayne, Summit, Richland, Portage, Medina, Mahoning, Lake, Huron and Geauga counties.

In 1843 Rev. John J. Doherty was appointed pastor of St. John's, Canton, where he remained about five years. He also attended Massillon, Canal Fulton and Navarre.

In 1844 the Revs. John H. Luhr and John O. Bredeick were assigned charges in Northern Ohio. Father Luhr was first stationed at St. John's, Canton, October, 1844. In 1845 he organized St. Peter's, Canton, whose pastor he was till 1847. Father Bredeick was the founder of Delphos, and of St. John's congregation, same place. In 1845 Rev. Peter Peudeprat arrived from France and was sent to Sandusky as assistant to Father Machebeuf, where he remained till the following year, when he was appointed pastor of St. Louis' church, Louisville, Stark county.

From 1844 to 1846, Rev. Cornelius Daley was first resident pastor of St. Vincent's, Akron, and from 1846 to 1847 pastor at Doylestown. Rev. Philip Foley was stationed at Massillon in 1846, and attended Wooster, where he directed the building of the first church, commenced in 1847 and finished two years later.

Besides the above mentioned secular priests the following were also on the mission in Northern Ohio; Revs. Michael A Byrne, at Cleveland, 1845-47; J. Freigang, at Peru and Norwalk, 1840-41; H. Herzog, at Ft. Jennings, 1840; J. Hoffmann, at St. John's, Canton, with charge of Louisville and Doylestown, 1836-37; H. D. Juncker, at Canton and Tiffin, 1836-37; J. Kearney, who attended East Liverpool and Wellsville from Steubenville, 1845-46; F. X. Roth, at Avon, 1845-47; E. Thienpont, at Tiffin, 1834-35; J. V. Conlan, at Dungannon, in 1847.

Very Rev. Stephen T. Badin and Very Rev. Edward T. Collins also visited some of the missions in Northern Ohio between 1835 and 1837, the former ministering to the Catholics at Canton, Canal Fulton, Fremont and Tiffin, the latter to those of Dungannon, Toledo and along the Maumee river.

This brief narrative contains the names of all the secular priests who, at any time between 1824 and 1847, were either stationed in Northern Ohio, or attended missions located therein. As this sketch would hardly permit more than the mere mention of their names, the reader is referred to the biographical notices* of these priests, many of whom are deeply enshrined in the memory of those who knew them and their disinterested work in the cause of religion.

The following is a complete list of secular priests stationed in Northern Ohio, October, 1847, when the Diocese of Cleveland was erected: Revs. G. Boehne, Glandorf; J. O. Bredeick, Delphos; James Conlan and J. Vincent Conlan, Dungannon; Louis de Goesbriand, Toledo; John J. Doherty, St. John's, Canton; Philip Foley, Massillon; Maurice Howard, Cleveland; J. B. Jacomet, assistant, St. Peter's, Canton; John H. Luhr, St. Peter's, Canton; Projectus J. Machebeuf, Sandusky; Casimir Mouret, Doylestown; Peter Peudeprat, Louisville; Amadeus Rappe, Toledo—in all, fourteen secular priests.

Of the above mentioned priests only the following are living (April, 1890): The Rt. Rev. L. de Goesbriand, present Bishop of Burlington; the Rev. John J. Doherty, pastor of St. John's, Honesdale, Pa., and the Rev. J. B. Jacomet, residing at Thompson, Seneca county, O.

---

*pp. 84 et seq.

V.

CHURCHES.

As heretofore stated, Father Fenwick came to Northern Ohio for the first time in 1817, visiting among other places in Columbiana and Stark counties, the few Catholic families settled near the present village of Dungannon. Here also, under his direction, in 1820, was built the first church in Northern Ohio. It was a small brick building, dedicated to St. Paul the Apostle, and served its purpose till 1849, when the present church in Dungannon was erected. Three years later the Catholics in Canton also built a brick church, dedicated to St. John the Evangelist. It was replaced in 1872 by the present very beautiful church. Until 1829, the above were the only two churches in Northern Ohio, when a third was built at Chippewa, near the present village of Doylestown. It was primitive in style, small in size and built of logs. In 1831 two more log churches were erected, one at Randolph, Portage county, the other between Lawrence and Canal Fulton, in Stark county. In 1832 a small brick church (St. Mary's) was opened for divine service at Tiffin. It was built under direction of the Rev. Edmund Quinn, and was enlarged by a frame addition built during the pastorate of Father McNamee in 1845. In 1833 three log churches were erected, viz.: at Glandorf, Putnam county; Navarre (Bethlehem), Stark county, and at New Riegel (Wolf's Creek), Seneca county. In 1834 the Catholics of Peru built a frame church under the direction of the Redemptorist Father, Rev. F. X. Tschenhens, who had it dedicated to St. Alphonse, the founder of the Redemptorists. In 1835 a brick church was built at Louisville, Stark county, and another (frame) at La Porte, Lorain county. In 1836 a frame church was erected at Shelby Settlement, Richland county, and another the following year at McCutchenville, Wyandot county, eight miles south of Tiffin. In 1839 a log church was erected at Thompson, Seneca county. Cleveland's first church (frame) was begun in 1838, and opened for

ST. PAUL'S CHURCH, NEAR DUNGANNON, O.

[The first Catholic Church erected in Northern Ohio.]

divine service in 1840. During the latter year the Catholics of East Liverpool, Columbiana county, erected a neat brick church.

Five churches were added to the above list in 1841. Father Rappe secured by purchase two Protestant frame meeting houses, one of them unfinished. They were located at Toledo and Maumee. The first was dedicated to St. Francis de Sales. Log churches were erected at La Prairie, Sandusky county, and New Washington, Crawford county; also one of wood, near Norwalk, dedicated to St. Peter. The last mentioned church, and the one at Maumee, are still in use.

In 1842 churches were built at Sandusky (Holy Angels'), Abbeyville, Landeck, Liberty, Liverpool, Sheffield, and St. Stephen's Settlement, the first of stone, the last of wood; the others were log churches.

In 1844 a log church was erected at Delphos by Father Bredeick, and frame churches at Massillon (St. Mary's), Akron (St. Vincent's), Defiance (St. John's), and Fremont (St. Ann's). At French Creek an old frame building was bought and fitted up for church purposes; it served as such till the erection of the present edifice in 1849.

In 1845 brick churches were built at Canton (St. Peter's), and New Berlin, Stark county; Providence, Lucas county; Tiffin (St. Joseph's), Seneca county. During the same year a frame church was also built at Harrisburg, Stark county. In 1846 a log church was erected at Bismarck (Sherman), and one of same kind, in 1847, at New Bavaria (Poplar Ridge). Total number of churches built or bought between 1820 and October, 1847, was 42, viz: stone, 1; brick, 9; frame, 15; log, 17.

VI.

RELIGIOUS COMMUNITIES.

July, 1844, a community of Sanguinist Sisters was established at Wolf's Creek (New Riegel) by the saintly Father Brunner. The convent, the first in Northern Ohio, was a log house. The community numbered but three sisters: Mother Mary A. Albrecht, Sister Rose and a novice.

December, 1845, Father Brunner also founded a community at Thompson, and here, as at Wolf's Creek, a log house was the convent building and contained a chapel. As soon as the sisters were established in their respective convent homes at Wolf's Creek and Thompson, they at once began the perpetual adoration of our Lord in the Blessed Eucharist, as directed by their Rule. They and their successors have ever since continued, day and night, the observance of this part of their Rule, as a reparation for the insults and outrages committed against our blessed Lord in the most Holy Sacrament of the Altar.

In 1846, at the invitation of the Rev. Father Rappe, five Sisters of Notre Dame came from Cincinnati to Toledo, there to establish a convent and a select school. Father Rappe secured for them a small frame house on Cherry street, near the present site of St. Francis de Sales' church. This they fitted up for their convent and academy.

They were part of a colony that had come from Namur, Belgium, to Cincinnati, with Father Rappe. The superioress of the Toledo community was Mother M. Louise, who died in 1886 at Cincinnati, where she had founded the present flourishing community in 1840. Another member of the Toledo community was Sister M. Aloysius, an accomplished Prussian lady, who later was appointed superioress of the Sisters of Notre Dame, at Roxbury, Mass. She became celebrated for a time through her testimony in court at Boston, in connection with the infamous committee appointed in 1854 by the anti-Catholic legislature of Massachusetts to pry into the convents of Boston and neighborhood. Her testimony made the members of that vile committee so odious in the eyes of decent and fair-minded Protestants that their outrageous "prying" was never repeated.

In 1848 the sisters of the Toledo community returned to Cincinnati, owing to lack of support. As Toledo at this time was but a small village and extremely unhealthy, and the number of boarding pupils and day scholars attending the sisters' academy very limited, it was thought best by the superioress of the Mother House at Cincinnati, to recall the sisters, four of whom returned, the fifth having fallen a victim to the dread Maumee fever.

VII.

BISHOPS FENWICK AND PURCELL.

The Rt. Rev. Edward Fenwick was consecrated first Bishop of Cincinnati, January 13, 1822, and had as part of his jurisdiction the whole of the state of Ohio. When he took charge of his diocese there was but one church in Northern Ohio (near Dungannon,) and no priest resided within that limit of territory. At the time of his death, September, 1832, there were six churches, viz.: near Dungannon, Doylestown and Canal Fulton, and at Canton, Randolph and Tiffin. Of resident priests there were three—at Canton, Dungannon and Tiffin.

Very Rev. F. Reze administered the diocese from the time of Bishop Fenwick's death till the advent of Rt. Rev. John B. Purcell, who at the age of thirty-three years was consecrated second Bishop of Cincinnati, October 13, 1833. He had jurisdiction of Northern Ohio till October, 1847, during which time Catholicity made wonderful strides in this part of the state. A large influx of emigrants necessitated the building of churches and the establishing of missions and stations in nearly every county in Northern Ohio, notably in Columbiana, Erie, Lorain, Lucas, Portage, Putnam, Sandusky and Seneca counties. It is true these churches were not remarkable for architecture, material or size, but they served their purpose and accommodated the faithful who frequented them with perhaps more fervor and piety than do their descendants the beautiful and costly temples since erected in their stead. Bishop Purcell visited Northern Ohio at frequent intervals, and always with gratifying results. But he soon found his vast diocese too large for his personal attention. As early as December, 1841, in an interesting communication to the *Catholic Telegraph*, describing one of his visits to Northern Ohio, he writes: "It would require the constant attention of two bishops and a hundred priests * * * to preserve the faithful, convert the erring, reclaim the sinful, found schools, and build churches necessary over such an extensive territory."

He petitioned the Holy See to be relieved of part of his jurisdiction. His petition was heard, and as a result the present Diocese of Cleveland was erected in 1847. Father Rappe, "the missionary of the Maumee," was appointed the first bishop of the new diocese, and consecrated as such at Cincinnati by Bishop Purcell, October 10, 1847.

PART II.

Diocese of Cleveland.

1847-1887

I.

TERRITORY OF THE DIOCESE OF CLEVELAND.

The territory assigned by the Holy See to the Diocese of Cleveland, April 23, 1847, was "all that part of the state of Ohio lying north of 40 degrees and 41 minutes." As this line intersected several counties, it was thought best by the bishops of the Dioceses of Cincinnati and Cleveland to petition the Holy See to establish the limits between these two dioceses by county lines, as appears from the following agreement published in the *Catholic Telegraph*, January 11, 1849:

"In order to prevent any misunderstanding or uncertainty with regard to the extent of jurisdiction, as defined only by the geographical line of 40 degrees and 41 minutes, the Rt. Rev. Bishops of these two dioceses have agreed among themselves, and they direct us to publish, that the counties of Mercer, Auglaize, Hardin, Marion, Morrow, Knox, Tuscarawas, Carroll and Jefferson, which belong to the Diocese of Cincinnati, shall constitute the northern boundary of the Diocese of Cincinnati; that all counties north of those just named, shall compose the Diocese of Cleveland. Holmes county, for the greater part south of the line above traced, is by mutual consent assigned to the Diocese of Cleveland. Any new counties that may hereafter be formed by the authority of the legislature, will belong to that diocese in which the larger portion of them will be situated. Application will be made as early as possible to the Holy See to sanction this arrangement."

When the Diocese of Columbus was erected, in 1868, Holmes county was included within its jurisdiction. All the other counties embraced within the above described limits have since been under jurisdiction of the Diocese of Cleveland, viz.: Allen, Ashland, Ashtabula, Columbiana, Crawford, Cuyahoga, Defiance, Erie, Fulton, Geauga, Hancock, Henry, Huron, Lake, Lorain, Lucas, Mahoning, Medina, Ottawa, Paulding Portage, Putnam, Richland, Sandusky, Seneca, Stark, Summit, Trumbull, Van Wert, Wayne, Williams, Wood and Wyandot, in all thirty-three counties, comprising about one-third of Ohio. The territory of the diocese extends from the west line of Pennsylvania to the east line of Indiana, and from the southern shore of Lake Erie about seventy-five miles south.

II.

BISHOP RAPPE—1847-1870.

In order to present in succinct form the growth and development of the Diocese of Cleveland, its history will be given chronologically, and by decades of years. Besides the erection of churches and the founding of religious, charitable and educational institutions, only the more important events in connection with the history of the diocese will be mentioned; to do more would exceed the limits of this sketch. In giving dates of the erection of churches, reference is had only to *first* churches built by congregations. In many cases these were built long after such congregations received attendance as stations, as will be shown in the "list of churches, etc." This remark holds also for institutions of charity, etc. Where notably fine, large and costly churches have replaced former structures, these will also receive due mention.

A.—1847-1857.

The Rt. Rev. Amadeus Rappe took possession of the Diocese of Cleveland as its first bishop a few days after his consecration, which had taken place at Cincinnati, October 10, 1847. On his arrival at Cleveland, his episcopal city, he found but one church, a frame building, located on Columbus street, corner of Girard. It had been dedicated June 7, 1840, to "Our Lady of the Lake," since 1849 known as St. Mary's church, on the Flats.

October, 1847, Rev. Maurice Howard was the only priest stationed in Cleveland. Besides having pastoral charge of the church on the Flats, he also attended a number of missions in Cuyahoga and neighboring counties. Within the limits of his diocese the Bishop found forty-two churches, attended by twenty-one priests, of whom seven were members of the Sanguinist society. The Catholic population of the diocese was estimated at this time to be about 10,000.

There were also two small convents of sisters of the same society, viz.: at New Riegel and Thompson, and an academy and convent at Toledo belonging to the Sisters of Notre Dame, whose Mother House was at Cincinnati.

For some months the Bishop resided in a rented house near the Haymarket. In 1848 he bought several lots on Bond street, corner of St. Clair, on which were located a large brick building and several frame houses. The brick building was fitted up as his episcopal residence.

Within a very short time after Bishop Rappe's arrival in Cleveland, he impressed all with his indefatigable zeal and great earnestness. As early as March, 1848, the *Cleveland Herald*, a secular paper, at no time during its long existence over-friendly toward Catholics, published in its issue of March 16th, the following item concerning Bishop Rappe, and his work in the cause of total abstinence, of which he had been for some years a practical and consistent advocate:

"Bishop Rappe is just what every man who has important enterprises in hand should be, a real workingman. His labors too, are for the benefit of others -the present and future--the temporal, social and moral improvement of the people of his charge. Strict sobriety, industry and economy are virtues which he inculcates with hearty good will—the sure stepping stones to individual, family and associated success. Temperance supports the superstructure and now over five hundred cold water men are enrolled in the Cleveland Catholic Temperance Society."

January, 1848, he appointed as his vicar-general the Very Rev. Louis de Goesbriand, who had been his co-laborer in Northwestern Ohio for two years. Father de Goesbriand was stationed in Cleveland, and had as his assistant the Rev. M. Kreusch, C. PP. S., the Rev. Maurice Howard having been sent to Tiffin as pastor of St. Mary's.

During the same year Bishop Rappe opened a small seminary in a one-story frame building, formerly a *stable*, back of his residence on Bond street. Father de Goesbriand was its first superior. Among the young men first to apply for admission as seminarists were Messrs. James Monahan, A. Berger, Peter Kreusch, Thomas J. Walsh, M. O'Sullivan, E. W. J. Lindesmith, F. McGann, N. Roupp, W. O'Connor, and F. M. Boff, all of whom became priests. In 1849 the Rev. A. Caron succeeded Father de Goesbriand as superior of this humble seminary.

The Catholic population of Cleveland rapidly increased shortly after the erection of the diocese, owing to a large immigration from Ireland and Germany. The Bishop finding it of imperative necessity to build a church for the accommodation of his growing flock (estimated in 1848 at about 4,000) in the episcopal city, proposed to make the new church his cathedral, and to assign St. Mary's on the Flats to the Germans.

Sunday, October 29, 1848, the cornerstone of the present cathedral was laid. The *Cleveland Herald* of October 30, 1848, makes mention of the ceremony in the following item:

"The ceremony of laying the cornerstone of the cathedral on Erie street was witnessed yesterday by a very large concourse of people. At one o'clock a numerous procession was formed at St. Mary's church and marched to the site of the cathedral. The ceremonies were conducted by Bishop Timon of Buffalo, Bishop LeFevre of Detroit, and Bishop Rappe of Cleveland, assisted by Vicar-General de Goesbriand of Cleveland, Rev. P. J. Machebeuf, of Sandusky, Rev. J. H. Luhr of Canton, and the students of the theological seminary in this city. An eloquent address was delivered by Bishop Timon, and a discourse in German by Rev. Mr. Luhr.

"The cathedral, when completed, will be a noble edifice and an ornament to the city. The dimensions will be 170 feet by 75, rising 50 feet from the water table to the eaves. The building is to be of brick, and the style of architecture will combine strength with beauty."

In November, 1848, the first diocesan synod was held, with fifteen priests in attendance. The second synod was held in 1852, and the third in 1854.

September, 1849, Bishop Rappe went to Europe, his object being to solicit aid in his native France for the new cathedral then in process of erection; also to secure priests and sisters to aid him in his work. During his absence the Very Rev. Father de Goesbriand, V. G., administered the diocese. The Bishop succeeded in obtaining generous assistance from his countrymen, and in securing several priests and seminarists, as also a band of devoted Ursulines, for whom the present convent on Euclid avenue had been purchased from Judge Cowles in 1849. Bishop Rappe returned from Europe in August, 1850. Besides visiting his diocese he also superintended the building of the cathedral, and had the great satisfaction of having it *consecrated*, and opened for divine service, November 7, 1852.

As above stated, Bishop Rappe was a strong advocate of total abstinence, having seen and felt the disastrous results of intemperance whilst engaged on the mission in Toledo and along the Maumee valley. In March, 1851, he published a vigorous pastoral letter on this subject, of which the following is an extract:

"Among the evils which prevail, and of which the progress and consequences are most alarming, is one which we have observed for years, and more especially during our last visitation; it is one which fills with sorrow the hearts of your pastors and counteracts all their efforts to promote your spiritual welfare; it is one which is more frightful than any calamity which could befall you; which threatens not only to put an end to all decent observance of the Sunday, but to eradicate piety and to destroy every sentiment that elevates and ennobles the Christian soul, to bring inevitable ruin upon reason, honor and fortune—*the drinking shop*, the sink wherein all that is good is buried."

During the months of July and August, of the same year, on invitation of the Bishop, Father Mathew the apostle of total abstinence, delivered a series of lectures and sermons in Cleveland and other important cities and towns in this diocese. Thousands took the pledge of total abstinence from Father Mathew. His labors, as those also of Bishop Rappe in this regard, were blessed with most gratifying results.

October 30, 1853, Father de Goesbriand was elevated to the Episcopacy as first Bishop of Burlington, Vt., which important position he still holds with eminent success. The Rev. James Conlan succeeded him as vicar-general, and acted as such till 1870.

Between 1847 and 1857 churches were erected in the following places: 1848—Delaware Bend, Six Mile Woods; 1849—Marshallville, Wooster; 1856—Archbold, Painesville; 1851—Fostoria, Independence, Sheffield; 1852—Cleveland (cathedral), Lima, Summitville; 1853—Rockport (St. Patrick's), Sandusky (St. Mary's), Toledo (St. Mary's), Youngstown (St. Columba's); 1854—Cleveland (St. Patrick's), Elyria, Massillon (St. Joseph's), Toledo (St. Joseph's); 1855—Galion (St. Joseph's); 1856—Berea (St. Mary's), Berwick, Cleveland (Immaculate Conception, *i. e.*, the Church of the Nativity, built in 1848 as a "chapel of ease," and situated in the rear of the present cathedral, was removed thence to Superior street near Lyman), Findlay, Napoleon. The total number of churches erected during this period was twenty-six.

Whilst directing and encouraging the organization of missions and congregations and the erection of churches for their accommodation, Bishop Rappe also provided for the care of orphans and the education of the young, all under charge of devoted sisters. To this end he authorized the establishing of a convent of Sanguinist Sisters at Glandorf, in 1848. In the fall of 1850 the Ursuline Academy on Euclid avenue, Cleveland, was opened and has ever since enjoyed the patronage and confidence of the public, Catholic and Protestant. The same is to be said of the Ursuline Academy, established at Toledo in 1854. St. Mary's Orphan Asylum for girls and St. Vincent's Asylum for boys were founded in Cleveland (1851), the former in charge of the Ladies of the Sacred Heart of Mary, the latter in charge of the Sisters of Charity of St. Augustine, a community founded by Bishop Rappe, with assistance of Mother M. Ursula, of sainted memory. She was known in the world as Miss C. Bissonette. In 1855 the Grey Nuns of Montreal established at Toledo an orphanage for boys and girls, which is known as St. Vincent's Asylum.

September, 1850, the Bishop bought a fine property on Lake street, near Dodge, known as "Spring Cottage." The frame building on the large plat of ground was fitted up as a seminary, which was opened in November of the same year, with Father Caron as superior. During the summer of 1853, the north wing of the present building was erected, and in 1859, owing to the rapidly increasing number of seminarists, the present main or central portion of the seminary was built.

To give young men an opportunity to receive a college education under Catholic auspices, Bishop Rappe purchased in 1854, an eligible property on the West Side, Cleveland, near St. Patrick's church. The incomplete frame buildings on the property were remodeled to serve the purpose of their purchase. September of the same year they were opened under the name of St. John's College. This institution had, however, a fitful existence, owing to lack of patronage, and was finally closed in 1859.

B.—1857-1867.

The second decade of Bishop Rappe's administration is remarkable for the large number of churches built, many of them handsome and spacious edifices. The following is a list of places in which churches were erected: 1857—Cleveland (St. Bridget's and St. Peter's); 1858—Fremont (St. Joseph's), Millersville, Norwalk (St. Mary's), Olmsted, Wellington; 1859—Bellevue, Big Springs, Crawfordsville, South Thompson; 1860—Alliance, Ashtabula, Cleveland, (St. Augustine's), Hudson, Junction, Port Clinton, Prout's, Rockport (St. Mary's);

1861—Crestline, Euclid, Kalida, Kelley's Island, North Ridge, Ottoville, Stryker, Toussaint; 1862—Akron (St. Bernard's), Bucyrus, Cleveland (Holy Rosary—since 1881 known as Holy Name, St. Joseph's), Clyde, Monroeville, Ravenna, Vermillion, Woodville; 1863—Ashland, Toledo (St. Patrick's); 1864—Conneaut, Convoy, Florence, French Settlement, Medina, Niles, Royalton, St. Patrick's Settlement, Strasburg, Upper Sandusky, Warren; 1865—Cleveland (St. Mary's of the Assumption), Grafton, Kirby, Marshallville, Milan; 1866—Mud Creek, Shelby—total, 56 churches.

In 1857 Bishop Rappe convoked the fourth diocesan synod, resulting in much wholesome legislation. One of the statutes promulgated made it obligatory on all congregations, financially and numerically able, to support parochial schools. This law gave new impulse to the parochial school system, encouraged in most earnest manner by Bishop Rappe almost immediately after he came to Cleveland.

In 1860 Bishop Rappe paid his first decennial visit to Rome. During his absence the Very Rev. James Conlan, V. G., was administrator of the diocese. Two years later he again went to Rome to assist at the canonization of the Japanese martyrs, to which ceremony many of the American bishops had been specially invited by Pius IX. Very Rev. A. Caron, V. G., administered the affairs of the diocese during the Bishop's absence.

In 1862 St. Joseph's Asylum for orphan girls was opened on Woodland avenue, Cleveland, to relieve the crowded condition of St. Mary's Asylum on Harmon street. In 1863 Bishop Rappe introduced into the diocese the Sisters of the Humility of Mary, and, by special agreement with Bishop O'Connor, of Pittsburg, located them on a large tract of land near New Bedford, Pa., where they founded a convent and an orphan asylum.

In 1863 the Ursulines of Cleveland established a mission at Tiffin, placing it in charge of Mother M. Joseph as superioress. In a few years it grew to a prosperous community, its academy meeting with public favor almost from the very opening.

In 1865, at the solicitation and with the generous aid of Cleveland's citizens, irrespective of creed, Bishop Rappe opened Charity Hospital—the first *public* hospital built in Cleveland.

The Bishop established St. Louis' College at Louisville Stark county, in 1866, to replace St. Mary's College and Preparatory Seminary, Cleveland, opened in September, 1860. It was placed in charge of secular priests. The following year its management was transferred to the Basilian Fathers of Sandwich, Canada, but the college was closed in 1873 for want of support.

C.—1867-1877.

For the fourth time Bishop Rappe went to Europe—in the fall of 1867—the Very Rev. Vicar General Caron administering the diocese during his three months' absence. Besides visiting his native country the Bishop also went to Rome to attend to some affairs in connection with his diocese.

During the first three years of the third decade of Bishop Rappe's administration, churches were erected in the following places: 1867—Cleveland (St. Wenceslas'), Hubbard, Landeck, Reed, Rootstown, Wellsville, West Brookfield; 1868—Edgerton, Kent, Leetonia, Marblehead, Mentor, Norwalk (St. Paul's), St. Mary's Corners, Toledo (Immaculate Conception); 1869—Cleveland (St. Malachy's, St. Stephen's), Galion (St. Patrick's), Jefferson, Madison, North Amherst, Willoughby, Youngstown (St. Joseph's)—in all twenty-three churches.

St. Francis' Orphan Asylum and Home for the Aged was established at Tiffin, in 1867, under the direction of the Rev. Joseph L. Bihn, who applied his patrimony and savings towards the purchase of the lands and the erection of buildings used for this excellent institution. He also established, in 1868, a sisterhood of the Third Order of St. Francis, which has charge of the domestic affairs of the asylum and home. Some of the sisters are also engaged as teachers in a number of parochial schools in the diocese.

In 1867 Bishop Rappe introduced the Franciscan Fathers, of Teutopolis, Ill., into the diocese, and gave them pastoral charge of St. Joseph's church, Cleveland. In the following year they erected their present monastery and chapel, corner of Chapel and Hazen streets.

St. Mary's church, Toledo, was given in charge of the Jesuit Fathers of the Provincial House of Buffalo, in 1869.

Bishop Rappe invited the Sisters of the Good Shepherd, of Cincinnati, to establish a house of their Order in Cleveland. The invitation was accepted in 1869. Their convent was a frame building on Lake street, situated on a large lot which had been secured for them by Bishop Rappe. Here they remained until the completion of their present large building, in 1875. Their silent, saving work in behalf of fallen, erring woman has resulted in untold good and has forced recognition even from an anti-Catholic public.

The paternal heart of good Bishop Rappe next prompted him to provide for a class of unfortunates, neglected and rejected by a cold, selfish world—the aged poor. To give them shelter and needed care he had the Little Sisters of the Poor establish a Home for them on Perry street, in 1870. This charitable work soon met with generous support on the part of the citizens of Cleveland, irrespective of creed. In a few years the old buildings first bought had to be enlarged and in part replaced by others more commodious and better adapted, so large was the number of applicants.

October, 1869, Bishop Rappe again went to Rome, this time to attend the Vatican Council which was opened December 8, of the same year.

Whilst in Rome he found that the years of opposition on the part of some, in regard to the administration of his diocese, had crystallized in charges preferred against him to the Holy See. Rather than further contend with his opponents and unwilling any longer to carry the burden of his episcopal labors, which he found so little appreciated on the part of a few, he concluded to resign the responsible and burdensome office of bishop he had borne for twenty-three years amid trials, difficulties and mental worry known to God alone. Where others would have met the enemy and contested position in the face of opposition and strife, he thought best to lay down crosier and mitre, thus to have peace in the evening of his life. This he believed himself the more constrained to do, as in his advanced age, sixty-eight years, he felt himself physically too weak to administer, with satisfaction to himself, his large and rapidly growing diocese. Added to this, he found his sight greatly impaired; in fact, he had lost the use of his right eye. He resigned August 22, 1870, and retired to the Diocese of Burlington, Vt., where he resumed the role of a missionary, so familiar to him.

For obvious reasons the details of this sad and painful chapter in the history of Bishop Rappe's saintly and self-sacrificing life are not yet for publication. This will be the task of the future historian of the Diocese of Cleveland, and the writer of Bishop Rappe's life and labors.

III.

VERY REV. EDWARD HANNIN, ADMINISTRATOR.

Sede Vacante—1870–1872.

Within a few days after Bishop Rappe's resignation, the Most Rev. Archbishop Purcell appointed the Very Rev. E. Hannin as administrator of the Diocese of Cleveland. During his term of office, which lasted till April, 1872, churches were erected in the following places: 1870—Antwerp, Briar Hill, Van Wert; 1871—Cleveland (Annunciation, St. Columbkill's—closed as a parish in 1872, Holy Family—St. Edward's since 1886), Loudonville, Mantua, Sandusky, (Sts. Peter and Paul's), Toledo (St. Louis')—total, ten congregations organized and churches built.

For ordinations, bishops of the neighboring dioceses were invited. Among them was the Rt. Rev. John H. Luers, Bishop of Fort Wayne. June 29, 1871, this worthy prelate conferred Holy Orders in the seminary chapel. After the ceremony he started for the Union depot, preferring to walk rather than to take the carriage which had been placed at his service. Reaching the corner of St. Clair and Bond streets, he fell to the pavement, stricken with apoplexy. He was carried to the Bishop's house, near by, where he expired in a few moments.

Beyond a suit of injunction, in connection with the building of a church, begun by the congregation of St. Bridget's, Cleveland, without proper authorization, nothing of special note occurred during Father Hannin's administration, except that he had not as peaceful a *regime* as he could have wished, or the good of religion demanded. No one was better pleased than he when he was relieved of his responsible post of duty, by the advent of Rt. Rev. Bishop Gilmour, in April, 1872.

IV.

BISHOP GILMOUR, 1872-1887.

The Rt. Rev. Richard Gilmour, present and second Bishop of the Diocese of Cleveland, was consecrated at Cincinnati, April 14, 1872. Within a few days after his consecration he took possession of his Episcopal See.

He soon found that the disturbance and opposition which had caused many a heart-ache to his predecessor, Bishop Rappe, and which had made the administration of Very Rev. Father Hannin anything but pleasant, had permeated the diocese to a large extent. Firmness and judgment were needed to put the disturbed elements to rights. Bishop Gilmour felt the difficulty of his position as well as the gravity of his impending work.

But he also found in the diocese at large a generous spirit among the laity, a willing, energetic clergy, and a readiness to second any effort for the advancement of diocesan interests. Often he had rather to repress than foster activity in matters pertaining to the material growth of the diocese.

November, 1872, he convoked a synod of his clergy—the first during his administration, and the fifth since the organization of the diocese. In this synod much of the legislation in force at present was enacted. It also embodied considerable of the legislation of the previous synods, notably that of 1868. Among the diocesan laws enacted, were those urging anew the necessity of parochial schools, regulating the financial affairs of congregations, assessing congregations for the support of seminary, etc., (Diocesan Fund), and for the support of sick and disabled priests, (Infirm Priests' Fund). The latter fund had been established some years previous, but it was now found necessary to modify and change many of the regulations governing it, so as to place it on a firm basis. This it has maintained ever since. With additional and needed changes made from time to time in its management, the Infirm Priests' Fund is now in excellent condition.

March, 1873, Bishop Gilmour published his first pastoral letter. It aroused the latent bigotry of the country, especially of Cleveland, the hot-bed of Puritanism and anti-Catholic hatred. Not that the Bishop published "doctrines strange and new," but that he dared to publish what he did. He took strong ground against the public school system, and urged upon his people the necessity of establishing and maintaining their own schools. He also insisted that Catholics assert their rights as citizens; that they are Catholic first, American next. For these and other utterances of like import he was denounced in unmeasured terms by pulpit and press.

To defend Catholic doctrine and the citizen rights of Catholics, the Bishop established the *Catholic Universe*, its first number appearing July 4, 1874. About this time also he organized in Cleveland the Catholic Central Association, composed of representatives from all the parishes and Catholic societies of the city.

Its influence for good was soon felt. Since the opening of the Workhouse in Cleveland, in 1870, the unfortunate Catholic inmates had been denied their rights as Catholics. No Catholic priest was permitted to visit or instruct them. After much opposition the Bishop finally succeeded in getting the consent of the Workhouse authorities to allow Catholic prisoners the consolation of their religion thus far denied them. To the Catholic Central Association, through some of its leading members, is due in large measure this concession. Since 1876 Mass has been regularly celebrated at the Workhouse on alternate Sundays, and on every Sunday morning the Catholic inmates of the refuge department receive catechetical instruction from a committee appointed for that purpose by the Catholic Central Association.

In 1875 the Catholic school property of Cleveland was placed on the tax duplicate, in spite of a decision of the supreme court of Ohio, rendered in 1874, to the effect that such property was not taxable. In 1876 suit of restraint was entered by the Bishop and finally carried to the supreme court of Ohio, the decision in each of the courts being in his favor.

The Bishop's house, on Bond street, was not diocesan property, but the personal property of Bishop Rappe, who, on his departure from Cleveland, leased it for a term of years. The lessee sublet it to the Very Rev. Administrator Hannin as a residence for himself and the cathedral clergy. Bishop Gilmour was informed of this fact within a few days after he came to Cleveland, and at the same time was curtly notified that the rent, considered high even then, would *at once* be raised. Unwilling to be a tenant any longer than he could help, the Bishop arranged for the erection of the present episcopal residence on Superior street, immediately east of the cathedral, the cost to be borne equally by the diocese and the cathedral parish. The building was begun in 1874 and completed early in 1876.

June 24, 1874, Bishop Gilmour fell seriously ill of nervous prostration, and for two years was unable to attend to the affairs of the diocese. On the advice of his physicians he went to Europe for the benefit of his shattered health, During his absence, the Very Rev. F. M. Boff, who had been made vicar-general in May, 1873, was appointed administrator of the diocese.

The Bishop returned from Europe, June, 1876, much improved, though by no means fully restored to health. Gradually he regained strength and by degrees resumed duty.

Between 1872 and 1877 the diocese showed a marked

degree of activity, as seen in the erection of a large number of churches, schools, and religious institutions. During this period churches were built in the following places: 1872—Carey, Green Spring, Mineral Ridge, New London, Oak Harbor, Ottawa, Plymouth, Roachton, Struthers, Sylvania, Vienna, Wakeman, Wauseon ; 1873—Defiance (Our Lady of Per. Help), Elmore, Parma, Salineville, Toledo (Good Shepherd's, St. Peter's); 1874—Berea (St. Adalbert's), Cleveland (St. Procop's), Genoa, Weston ; 1875--Brighton, Bryan, Deshler ; 1876--Bettsville, Leipsic, North Ridgeville, Spencerville, Toledo (St. Hedwig's)—in all thirty-one churches built, and as many new congregations established.

In 1872 the Sisters of St. Joseph, a teaching community, were welcomed to the diocese, as also, in 1874, the Sisters of Notre Dame, who had been exiled from Germany because of the "May Laws." Both these communities established themselves in Cleveland, the latter having a large and flourishing academy in connection with their convent.

In 1873 a foundling asylum was opened in Cleveland and placed in charge of the Sisters of Charity, for the reception of waifs. In connection with this asylum a lying-in hospital was also founded. Till the opening of these two institutions, wealthy Cleveland had no shelter to offer these helpless babes and their unfortunate mothers—the former, offsprings of sin, the latter, its victims.

On invitation of Bishop Gilmour, the Ladies of the Sacred Heart of Mary, connected with St. Mary's Orphan Asylum, Cleveland, established (1874) an academy at Louisville, Stark county, in the building known as St. Louis' College, but closed in 1873. With the academy was also an institute for deaf mutes. Both academy and institute were closed a few years later for want of support.

A convent of Ursuline Sisters was founded, in 1874, at Youngstown, to take charge of the parochial schools in that place, and eventually to establish an academy.

In 1875 the Grey Nuns of Montreal built a hospital in Toledo which was opened to the public in 1876. In the latter year the Franciscans established, near their monastery in Cleveland, St. Joseph's College for boys. Although this institution was fairly supported, the Franciscan Fathers found it impracticable to continue it longer than June, 1880.

D.—1877-1887.

September 8, 1877, the sad news of Bishop Rappe's death reached Cleveland from St. Albans, Vt. As eminently meet, as well as justly due to the memory of the deceased Bishop, arrangements were at once made to have his remains brought to Cleveland for burial. On their arrival an immense throng met them, and Cleveland's citizens, without creed or class distinction, vied with each other to pay their last tribute of respect to the remains of Bishop Rappe, whom in life they loved and respected, and whose memory, in death, they revered as that of a public benefactor, and noble hearted prelate. Silent and sad as was his departure from Cleveland seven years previous, grandly triumphant in death was his return to the city he loved so well, of which he spoke when in the throes of death, for which, during nearly a quarter of a century, he had given his best efforts. After the impressive obsequies his remains were placed in a crypt under the main altar of the cathedral, there to repose till the Last Call.

In 1877 Bishop Gilmour began to systematize the routine and business affairs of his diocese by establishing a chancery office. He had plats made of all the church property and the respective deeds indexed and labelled for ready reference. Parish, and "permit" records, records of priests and religious institutions were begun, and blank forms for annual reports, together with letter books and letter files, were introduced.

In 1878 the collecting of historical data in connection with every congregation and religious institution in the diocese was begun. So promptly and kindly did the clergy and heads of religious houses respond to the call for historical data that the future historian will have comparatively an easy task in writing the history of the Diocese of Cleveland. He will have but to sift and collate the adundance of historical matter in the diocesan archives.

March 13, 1879, Bishop Gilmour published a pastoral letter, which again, as in 1873, aroused the hatred of an anti-Catholic press and pulpit. For many months after its publication, the echo of bigotry resounded far and wide, simply because he enunciated doctrines, not new, but bold in their utterance. His expressions regarding human liberty, rights of Church and State, and Catholic schools, gave blatant bigotry food for many sensational sermons and "blood-curdling" editorials.

May, 1882, the sixth diocesan synod was held in St. Mary's Seminary, one hundred and thirty-nine priests of the secular and regular clergy being in attendance. As a result of this synod we have the present diocesan legislation, which, with the exception of about half a dozen of its two hundred and sixty-two statutes, is in perfect harmony with the laws of the Third Plenary Council of Baltimore, held in November, 1884.

In July, 1882, Bishop Gilmour went to Europe, to visit, among other countries, his native Scotland, which he had not seen since he left it in 1829.

Besides traveling extensively through Ireland, England, France and Germany, he also paid his *ad limina* visit to Rome, his first official visit to the Holy See, although he had been there for a few weeks in 1875, as an invalid.

During his absence, till February, 1883, Very Rev. Vicar General Boff administered the diocese.

In 1884 the diocesan seminary was enlarged by the addition of the present south wing, which contains suites of rooms for professors and separate rooms for students, neatly and comfortably furnished. During the following year, the main or centre building, was entirely remodeled by changing the upper two stories into a very handsome chapel, and locating a lecture hall and the library on the first floor. The wing and changes cost nearly $20,000.

March, 1887, Bishop Gilmour published the "Constitution and By-laws for the Government of the Parochial Schools of the Diocese of Cleveland," of which the principal features are: The examination of parish schools by district boards, and the annual examination of teachers by a diocesan board of examiners.

Between 1877 and 1887 the following institutions were established in the diocese: 1877—Convent of the Poor Clares, Cleveland, and the Ursuline Academy, at Villa Angela, near Nottingham; 1884—Cleveland—St. Alexis' Hospital, Protectory for Girls, in charge of the Sisters of Notre Dame; Louisville, St. Louis' Orphan Asylum for boys; 1885—Toledo, Little Sisters of the Poor. The Jesuit Fathers, to whom had been entrusted, in 1880, the pastorate of St. Mary's church, Cleveland, opened St. Ignatius' College, opposite their church, corner Carroll and Jersey streets, September, 1886. At this time, also, the Ursulines opened an institution at Nottingham for the education of boys under twelve years of age. It is known as St. Joseph's Seminary.

Since 1877 churches were erected in the following places: 1877—Put-in-Bay; 1878—Collinwood; 1879—Cecil, Chicago Junction, Honey Creek, Lorain; 1880—Cleveland (St. Colman's, Holy Trinity), East Palestine, Hicksville; 1881—Bowling Green, Cleveland (St. Stanislas'), Sterling; 1882—Attica, Peninsula, Toledo (St. Anthony's), Youngstown (Immaculate Conception); 1883—Cleveland (St. Adalbert's, St. Michael's, Our Lady of Lourdes'), Toledo (Sacred Heart), Tremblayville; 1884—Lowellville; 1886—Cuyahoga Falls, Holgate, Wadsworth; 1887—Akron (St. Mary's), Cleveland (St. Anthony's, St. Francis'), Hamler, Miller's City, New Lisbon, North Creek, Republic—total, thirty-five churches built and new congregations established.

Few dioceses in the country, if any, contain as many fine, large and costly churches as are in the Diocese of Cleveland. Many of these were built within the last fifteen years, replacing edifices of far less pretensions as to size and cost. Among the more noteworthy are the following: Cleveland, St. John's Cathedral (furnished in 1880 with the handsomest spire in the city, and renovated, 1884, in most artistic manner), St. Patrick's, St. Stephen's, Immaculate Conception and St. Edward's (large and beautiful stone churches), St. Bridget's, St. Joseph's, St. Peter's, (renovated in 1885); Canton, St.

John's and St. Peter's; Delphos, St. John's; Fremont, St. Joseph's; New Riegel, St. Boniface's; Sandusky, St. Mary's, Sts. Peter and Paul (both stone churches); Thompson, St. Michael's; Tiffin, St. Joseph's; Toledo, St. Francis', St. Mary's (enlarged and renovated in 1883), St. Patrick's, St. Peter's.

Within the last few years many fine schools have been built. Mention of a few of the larger and finer is here made: Cleveland, St. Bridget's, St. Malachy's, Holy Name, St. Joseph's; Toledo, St. Patrick's, St. Mary's; Defiance, Our Lady's. August, 1887, the cornerstone was laid for a $35,000 school house for St. Bernard's, Akron.

Wherever throughout the diocese churches or schools are built to replace similar edifices, they are of beautiful proportions, tasteful design, and commensurate with the means of congregations building them. There appears to be a healthy emulation to erect churches worthy their sacred use, and schools at least equal to those which Catholic parents help to build, but which in conscience they can not allow their children to attend.

The Diocese of Cleveland is provided with generously supported charitable institutions, covering nearly all wants of suffering and neglected humanity. But there is great need of a reformatory for wayward and homeless boys. A farm of nearly forty acres of excellent land, within a few miles of Cleveland, is already secured as a site for this most necessary institution. Lack of means, however, has thus far prevented the erection of suitable buildings to take from the streets and shelter, educate and train in virtue and future usefulness, boys who are now going to spiritual destruction.

The seminary, "the heart of the diocese," is also greatly in need of enlargement for the accommodation of a sufficient number of young levites, who are not only to take the place of the laborers in the Lord's vineyard, called to their reward, but also to meet the wants of a rapidly growing diocese, with missions and congregations springing into existence on every side—and no priests to serve them.

The enlargement of the seminary would also make it practicable to have spiritual retreats for the secular priests and frequent meetings of the clergy of the diocese—now impossible because there is no building in the diocese large enough and under its control, where such retreats or meetings could be held.

In 1817 Father Fenwick came for the first time to Northern Ohio to break the Bread of Life to the famishing children of God's Church, living in sparse numbers within the limits of the present flourishing Diocese of Cleveland. He was the first priest to visit at regular intervals this part of Ohio since the Jesuits were obliged to abandon their Indian missions on the southern shore of Lake Erie, and along the Vermillion, Sandusky and Portage rivers. Beyond a few Catholic settlers in Columbiana and Stark counties, Father Fenwick found no trace of Catholicity.

When the Diocese of Cleveland was erected in 1847, Bishop Rappe found but one church and one priest in Cleveland, and forty-two churches in the entire diocese, attended by twenty-one priests.

Were Father Fenwick, the apostle of Catholicity in Ohio, and Bishop Rappe, the *missionary bishop* of the Diocese of Cleveland, to return to the scene of their apostolic labors, their hearts would indeed be gladdened, as they are no doubt gladdened in heaven, to see the vigorous growth of the Tree of Life they planted. They would find more than two hundred churches, many of them cathedral-like in size and beauty, studding the territory formerly under their pastoral care and jurisdiction. Institutions of religion, education and charity would greet their eye; parochial schools, generously and willingly supported, would give them assurance that the children, the hope of the future, have every means placed within their reach to keep them in the Faith; they would find a zealous clergy, devoted religious, and a generous laity.

We have endeavored to outline the history of Catholicity in Northern Ohio, and in the Diocese of Cleveland. It is for the future historian to give in detail its foundation, growth and development, the struggles, trials and labors of the pioneers of religion in this part of our fair state. We close this sketch with the subjoined table, which gives, in a summarized form, and by decades of years, the growth of the Church in Northern Ohio and in the Diocese of Cleveland:

TABLE.

Year.		Churches	Resident Priests (Sec. and Reg.)	Female Rel. Com.	Charitable Institutions.	Educ'nl Institutions.	Paroc'l Schools
In Northern Ohio.	1817	.....	.....	....	... ..	......	
	1827	2	1	....	... ...	......	
	1837	14	7	.....			
In Diocese of Cleveland.	1847	42	21	3	...	1	....
	1857	78	54	7	3	4	7
	1867	150	90	9	5	5	70
	1877	190	158	17	10	7	110
	1887	225	187	18	10	8	126

BIOGRAPHICAL SKETCH

—OF THE—

RIGHT REV. EDWARD D. FENWICK, O. P., FIRST BISHOP OF CINCINNATI.

JANUARY, 1822—SEPTEMBER, 1832.

Edward D. Fenwick, a descendant of the ancient English family of Fenwick Tower, was born in St. Mary's county, Maryland, in 1768. After the death of his father, Edward was sent to Europe to complete his studies. When leaving home he was in his sixteenth year. He entered the Dominican college at Bornheim, Flanders.

Impressed with the spirit and virtues of his Dominican preceptors, he became attached to them and soon joined their Order. From his childhood he showed a tender and unaffected piety. This grew with his years, and impressed itself on his superiors, whose respect and confidence he easily won. During the French revolution he was engaged in the duties of a professor, and as procurator of the Dominican convent at Bornheim. When the French soldiery overran and pillaged the Netherlands, his convent was seized and he, with his brethren, imprisoned as Englishmen. Securing his release as an American citizen, he went to one of the Dominican convents in England. There he remained till 1804, when in compliance with his ardent wish he was sent by his Provincial to America, to labor there in behalf of the spiritual interests of his countrymen. His native state was his first field of priestly work in this country. Here he toiled in his Master's vineyard about one year. Then Bishop Carroll, of Baltimore, upon consultation, and with the advice and consent of the

RIGHT REVEREND EDWARD D. FENWICK, O. P.

Father General of the Dominicans, sent him to Kentucky to establish a colony of Friars Preachers. In compliance with instructions Father Fenwick, accompanied by three of his brethren, Fathers Wilson, Tuite and Anger, founded, in 1805, St. Rose's Convent, located in Washington county, Kentucky, on a farm he purchased with his patrimony. Here it was that the Dominican order had its first home in the United States, and from this place the light of the Gospel was carried far and wide. The Convent of St. Rose was soon crowned with benedictions. The children of St. Dominic, animated with the zeal of their pious founder, spread through the whole extent of Kentucky, and afforded to the inhabitants the benefits of the religion of Jesus Christ. A Bull was received from Rome constituting Father Fenwick Provincial of the Order in North America. He could not, however, resolve upon accepting that dignity, fearing it might prevent the conversion of souls to God. A remarkable circumstance, which has always been looked upon as the most certain evidence of the exalted virtue of Father Fenwick is, that, after having obtained from Rome the office of Provincial for Father Wilson, with the permission to annul the appointment should he himself choose to remain Provincial, or to abdicate it, he did not hesitate a moment, but asked Father Wilson to accept, as he himself preferred rather to obey than to command.

In 1814 Father Fenwick, the apostle and pioneer priest of this state, made his first missionary visit to Ohio, and went as far north as Perry county, in the present Diocese of Columbus, where he found three Catholic families, consisting in all of twenty members. These good people were so rejoiced to see him, that he could never recall his first pastoral visit to this part of his vast "parish" without experiencing the greatest consolation, because he considered it the first fruit of his mission in Ohio.

According to the most authentic information obtainable Father Fenwick's first visit to Northern Ohio—within the territory of the Diocese of Cleveland—was in 1817, when he came to Columbiana and Stark counties. There he found a number of Catholic families, some of whom had moved to Ohio from Pennsylvania and Maryland; others had emigrated from Ireland and Germany. None of them had seen a priest since they had settled in Ohio.

In 1818 Father Fenwick established, on a farm given for the purpose by Mr. P. Dittoe, a fervent and generous Catholic, the present flourishing Convent of St. Joseph's, near Somerset, Perry county, Ohio, and was its superior for nearly four years. From St. Joseph's he and his few brethren of the convent, among them his nephew, Rev. N. D. Young, regularly attended the missions in Perry and the neighboring counties, whilst those of Southern Ohio received pastoral care from St. Rose's, Kentucky, and occasionally, also, from St. Joseph's, Perry county.

Bishop Flaget, of Bardstown, had under his jurisdiction Kentucky, Indiana, Michigan and Ohio. He petitioned the Holy See to relieve him from the spiritual care of a part of his immense territory. In accordance with his wish the Diocese of Cincinnati was erected, in 1821, and Father Fenwick consecrated by Bishop Flaget as its first bishop in the church of St. Rose, Washington county, Kentucky, January 13, 1822. Soon after his consecration, Bishop Fenwick took possession of his Episcopal See. Arriving at Cincinnati he found neither church nor dwelling. He rented a small house, where he was obliged to sleep in the garret; the other part was destined for a chapel and a study. At times he was not able to pay the rent, and frequently had to seek his meals in the city. The cathedral, if we may call it by that name, was a barn-like plank building, about one mile from the town, and in rainy weather quite inaccessible. The attempt to move it to the town failed; it broke down on the road. A lot was wanting upon which to erect the cathedral again; but where were the means to pay for it?

Without money, without the hope of procuring it to pay the debts already contracted, everywhere even the most necessary things wanting, in 1823 the Bishop took the resolution to set out for Rome, with the intention of resigning his heavy charge. The Holy Father, Leo XII, however, encouraged him and presented him with 1,200 scudi for the expenses of his journey and those of the clergyman who traveled with him. A good God, in fact, loaded him with blessings, opening new sources to him, particularly in France, in the Association at Lyons, for the propagation of the faith. Belgium and Germany, in imitation of France, also contributed liberal sums to Bishop Fenwick in support of his poor diocese. On his return, in 1824, the debts were paid, and a brick cathedral erected on Sycamore street. Later he established the Athenæum College, near his cathedral church. He also introduced into his diocese the Dominican Sisters, and one or two other religious communities to instruct the children.

Full of courage, after his successful visit to Europe, he devoted all his energy and zeal to the development and visitation of his diocese. At or away from his episcopal city, he never had an idle moment. To reach all the missions of his immense diocese, covering Ohio and Michigan, he had to make long and tedious journeys by wagon, stage, or on horseback, often through forests, and more often over almost impassable roads.

His last visit to Northern Ohio was during the time of the cholera, in 1832. Before leaving Cincinnati, on a visit to Michigan, he had been ailing. Rallying somewhat, and prepared to die amidst his labors if God so willed, he proceeded on his long journey, visiting all the missions along the route, preaching, catechising, and giving confirmation.

In these missions difficulties of all kinds met him in constant succession; some persons imploring the aid of the Bishop, some to have churches erected, others to have the clergymen provided for. Much good was done in this last episcopal visit. Upon the lakes the Bishop assisted those dying of cholera. He himself fell so sick at Sault Sainte Marie, Mich., that it was feared he would not recover. But he rallied and soon resumed his return journey to Detroit, and thence through Northern Ohio to Canton, where he arrived, September 24, completely exhausted, with renewed symptoms of the dreadful scourge that visited the entire country and counted its victims by the thousand. He was attended with the greatest and most tender care. Next morning he said Mass and wrote several letters. The stage arriving at the door of the pastoral residence of Father Henni, he bade him good-bye and went on to Wooster, intending to go thence to Cincinnati. Arriving at Wooster about 8 P. M., he was taken from the stage with the fatal seal of cholera on him. He was brought to a hotel where he expired at noon, Wednesday, September 26, 1832. Before sunset of the same day a mound marked the resting place of his remains. It seemed he had a foreboding of his death, for wherever he passed he said: "This is my last visit." In one of his letters he wrote that he would visit two or three congregations in the neighborhood of St. Joseph's, Perry county, which would be the term of his mission, and that thence he would return to Cincinnati, because his strength failed him, but added, as was his custom, that he would do so: *Deo volente, quia homo proponit, sed Deus disponit.*

Father Henni was at once informed of the bishop's dying condition, but on arriving at Wooster a few hours later, he found him buried.

In February, 1833, Bishop Fenwick's remains were taken to Cincinnati and there entombed under the old cathedral. They now repose beneath the altar of the present St. Peter's cathedral, Cincinnati.

Bishop Fenwick was deservedly esteemed for his many noble qualities. He was a man of great simplicity of character. Delicate in health, he nevertheless devoted himself unsparingly as priest and bishop to the work within his sphere. The Catholics of Ohio owe him a debt of gratitude as the founder of the Church in this state.

"By his talents and amiable deportment he had gained himself many admirers and many personal friends. As a herald of the Cross he was always at his post, faithful, vigilant and indefatigable. In the ordinary walks of life he was dignified, affable and unostentatious. * * * He was truly the apostle of Ohio." 1.) "Though not gifted with great natural talents, he possessed a peculiar tact for winning souls to Christ. * * * Frank, open and sincere by nature, and an American himself, he possessed an instinctive talent for dealing with Americans, whether Catholic or Protestant. Multitudes of the latter were converted to Catholicity through his agency." 2.)

---

1) Catholic Almanac, 1848; 2) Spalding's "Sketches of Kentucky," p. 155.

BIOGRAPHICAL SKETCH

—OF THE—

MOST REV. JOHN B. PURCELL, D. D., SECOND BISHOP OF CINCINNATI, 1833-1850. FIRST ARCHBISHOP OF CINCINNATI,

1850-1883.

John Baptist Purcell, a native of Ireland, was born at Mallow, county Cork, February 26, 1800. After completing a collegiate course in his native country he set out for the United States, landing at Baltimore in his eighteenth year. For a short time he held a position as private tutor, but desirous of devoting himself to the priesthood, he entered Mt. St. Mary's College, at Emmittsburg, Maryland. Showing talent much above the ordinary, he was sent to the famous Sulpician Seminary, Paris, to complete his theological studies where he was ordained priest May 23, 1826. Shortly after his ordination he returned to the United States, and was appointed president and one of the professors of Mt. St. Mary's College, of which he was an alumnus. For seven years he held this important position when the Holy See appointed him successor to the lamented Bishop Fenwick, as second Bishop of Cincinnati. As such he was consecrated, in his thirty-fourth year, at Baltimore, by Archbishop Whitfield, October 13, 1833. After attending the Second Provincial Council of Baltimore, held a few days after his consecration, he set out for Cincinnati, arriving there November 14, 1833. In his episcopal city he found but one church, a college in embryo, (the Athenæum, on Sycamore street), and an orphan asylum. His diocese comprised the whole of Ohio and part of Kentucky. In Ohio there were at this time but sixteen churches, attended by fourteen priests, a Dominican convent in Perry county, and a Catholic population estimated at about six thousand souls.

Most Reverend John Baptist Purcell, D. D.

Within the limits of the present Diocese of Cleveland—with which this sketch will chiefly deal, so far as the labors of Bishop Purcell are concerned—there were but three churches, viz.: one near Dungannon, and one each in Canton and Tiffin. These churches were attended by two priests, Revs. J. M. Henni and Edmund Quinn, stationed respectively at Canton and Tiffin.

To visit his scattered flock Bishop Purcell could not avail himself of the convenience of travel now enjoyed, nor the hospitality now offered. On country wagons, by stage-coach, and on horseback he covered great distances over bad roads, through primeval forests and across unbridged streams, often partaking of primitive country hotel fare, and often taking shelter in log huts. But in spite of difficulties, hardships and frequent privations, he cheerfully and often made his diocesan visitations, instructing, consoling and encouraging the faithful committed to his charge. His episcopal visits were always red-letter days for clergy and laity. His cheerful disposition and buoyant spirit spread sunshine and joy wherever he went, and his sermons attracted by their brilliancy and eloquence.

His first visit to Northern Ohio was made during the months of June and July, 1834, viz.: Dungannon, Canton, Louisville, Canal Fulton, Chippewa (Doylestown), Wooster, Tiffin and McCutchenville. During the months of July, August and September, 1835, he visited, Dungannon, New Lisbon, Cleveland, Cuyahoga Falls, Randolph, Louisville and Canton, and in 1836, Tiffin and Fremont. June 7, 1840, he preached in Cleveland at the dedication of the Church of Our Lady of the Lake, known later and since as St. Mary's on the "Flats," Bishop de Forbin-Janson, on a visit from France, performing the dedicatory ceremony. During the same month Bishop Purcell also visited Liverpool, Chippewa, Canton and East Liverpool. November, 1840, he again came to Northern Ohio, visiting Findlay, Glandorf, and Ft. Jennings.

In 1841, during the months of June, July, August and November, he made an extensive tour through Northern Ohio, visiting the following places: Norwalk, Peru, Shelby, Shelby Settlement, Tiffin, McCutchenville, Wolf's Creek

(New Riegel), Sandusky, Fremont, LaPrairie, Perrysburg, Toledo, Canton, Louisville, Randolph, Akron, Chippewa, Wooster, Canal Fulton, Massillon and Bethlehem. In all these places he administered confirmation, and in many he dedicated churches or laid cornerstones for such. In June and July, 1846, he visited Sandusky, Cleveland, Peru, Norwalk, Tiffin, New Riegel, Toledo, Dungannon and Wooster, and in August, 1847, Wooster, Canal Fulton, Youngstown and Akron. At Akron he performed his last episcopal function in this part of his jurisdiction, ordaining to the priesthood, August 5, 1847, the Rev. J. Vincent Conlan.

In 1834 he sent a band of Redemptorist Fathers to Northern Ohio to take charge of missions in Huron, Erie and Seneca counties, with residence at Peru, near Norwalk. They were succeeded in 1844 by the Sanguinist Fathers, who had been invited by him in Europe, the year previous, to come and labor in the Ohio mission.

Finding his diocesan work far beyond his strength, he petitioned the Holy See for a division of his vast spiritual territory. In compliance with his wish the division was made in 1847, and all that part of Ohio, north of forty degrees and forty-one minutes, erected into a separate diocese, with the Episcopal See at Cleveland, and the Rt. Rev. Amadeus Rappe as its first bishop. When Bishop Rappe took possession of his See he found forty-two churches, fourteen secular priests and seven Sanguinists under his jurisdiction, an increase of thirty-nine churches and nineteen priests since 1833, when Bishop Purcell was appointed to the See of Cincinnati.

Although thus relieved of nearly one-third of his former jurisdiction, Bishop Purcell's zeal and labor did not diminish; on the contrary they grew and spread. Catholicity under his direction made wonderful strides in Central and Southern Ohio. With astonishing rapidity churches multiplied, congregations sprang into existence, religious, charitable and educational institutions were established, all demanding and receiving his watchful care and paternal guidance.

In 1850 Bishop Purcell was made Archbishop, with the

Bishops of Louisville, Vincennes, Detroit and Cleveland as his suffragans.

Under his direction Mt. St. Mary's Seminary of the West was opened near Cincinnati in 1852. Indefatigably he labored for the spread of religion, and everywhere throughout his diocese evidence of his zeal and of the steady growth of the Church could be seen.

In 1853 Archbishop Purcell was relieved of the charge of Eastern Kentucky, in the erection of the Diocese of Covington. In 1868 he asked for further relief from constantly increasing work. The result was the erection of the Diocese of Columbus, comprising the southeastern part of Ohio. The first bishop was the Rt. Rev. S. H. Rosecrans, who, as coadjutor since 1862, had lightened his labors.

In 1869 the Archbishop made the last of his many visits to Rome, this time to attend the Ecumenical Council of the Vatican, which opened in December of that year. He took a prominent part in its debates, notably in those connected with the definition of the infallibility of the Pope. He belonged to the *inopportunists*, but after the council defined papal infallibility to be of faith, he yielded assent.

Shortly after his advent to Cincinnati, in 1833, the rapid growth of Catholicity in that city, as in fact throughout the country, aroused bigotry and fanatical alarm. He was challenged by a Protestant preacher, named Alexander Campbell, to a public debate on Catholic doctrine. This was in 1837. For many days the disputants held sway over large and interested audiences. The brilliant young bishop vanquished his opponent and gained for himself the name of a profound theologian, accurate historian and keen debater.

He was a facile and pleasing writer, as his many learned pastorals will attest. He also contributed largely to the columns of the *Catholic Telegraph*, and had the habit of writing descriptions of his episcopal visitations, which will prove a storehouse of valuable material for the future historian of Catholicity in Ohio.*

---

*See Catholic Miscellanea, in the last section of this volume.

In connection with Archbishop Purcell's biography it becomes our duty to mention the clouded ending of an otherwise brilliant career, a singularly pure and unselfish life spent for God and His Church. We refer to his financial disaster, of which Dr. John Gilmary Shea, in his recent work, "*The Hierarchy of the Catholic Church in the United States*," pages 107 and 108, writes as follows :

"Early in 1879 financial affairs which had been managed by the Very Rev. Edward Purcell, ended in bankruptcy. How it all came about must ever remain a mystery. The venerable Archishop, as ignorant as a child of the system and its extent, at once came forward and assumed the whole responsibility of his brother's operations. This only complicated matters and raised a host of legal questions as to his ability, in character of trustee for the Catholic church in his diocese, to assume an individual indebtedness contracted by another ; and if he could, it became necessary to decide what property became liable for it—that owned by the diocese, or the property of every Catholic church and institution in the diocese. If the debt became a just charge on the whole diocese and all its churches and institutions, it was a debt on every Catholic, which he was bound in conscience to pay. This extreme view no theologian or canonist was found to take.

"The debts were at first supposed not to exceed a quarter of a million dollars, and attempts were made to meet or reduce it materially by subscriptions ; but when it was found that the indebtedness reached nearly four millions of dollars, the attempt was abandoned as hopeless. The Very Rev. Edward Purcell died broken-hearted. The Archbishop made an assignment of all property in his name, and long litigations began. The courts ultimately decided that the congregations were not liable except for moneys actually advanced to them."

In May, 1880, Archbishop Purcell retired to Brown county, Ohio, near the Ursuline Convent, where he lingered in illness brought on in the early part of 1881 by a paralytic stroke, till his death, July 4, 1883.

RIGHT REVEREND AMADEUS RAPPE, D. D.

BIOGRAPHICAL SKETCH

—OF THE—

RIGHT REV. AMADEUS RAPPE, D. D., FIRST BISHOP OF CLEVELAND.

OCTOBER, 1847—AUGUST, 1870.

Louis Amadeus Rappe, first Bishop of Cleveland, was born February 2, 1801, at Audrehem, a village near Ardres (district of St. Omer), Department of Pas-de-Calais, France. His parents, Eloi Rappe and Marie Antoinette Rappe, *nee* Noël, belonged to the peasantry and were highly esteemed for their probity, industry and Christian virtues. They had a family of ten children, five sons and five daughters. The subject of this sketch was the youngest of the sons. Of his four brothers, three were killed in the Napoleonic wars, the fourth died unmarried. Destined by his father to the life of a farmer, Louis Amadeus received but an elementary education, such as the village school afforded. Trained by his parents to habits of order and industry, he soon acquired a practical knowledge of husbandry and thus became very useful to his father in the management of the farm. He took delight in his avocation ; was passionately fond of horses, a liking which he retained all his life. He was also fond of youthful sports and athletic games. Sparkling with wit and cheerfulness, he was a general favorite with the young people of his native village. His career seemed well marked out and his family friends did not doubt his vocation—that of a farmer.

But God was there, with His secret and admirable designs ! One evening, toward the end of the year 1819, when Amadeus was in his 19th year, and the family were gathered around the domestic hearth, the father expressed a regret that not one of his sons had a vocation to the priesthood. He said he had always hoped to see one of them at the altar, this wish having been the dream of his life, but that now it was not to be realized. Amadeus, struck by this remark, answered: "Well, father, if you wish it I will become a priest." It need hardly be said that this answer was not taken by the family in a serious light. A general laughter ensued, so diametrically opposed to that sacred calling were his well-known tastes. On the following morning he went to his father, saying: "Father, the remark which I made to you last evening is serious. It occupied my thoughts all night; I have seriously reflected upon it, and wish to be a priest."

The sentiment thus made known to the father, and to the mother, consent was readily granted, but not without doubt and fear lest their son might not persevere. They were all the more apprehensive of his firmness and perseverance, as one of his older brothers began the course of studies for the sacred ministry, but failed to reach the altar.

Soon the necessary preparations for the departure of young Amadeus were made. He went to Furnes, a small village about six miles from Boulogne, to the pastoral residence of one of his relatives, the Rev. Mr. Noël, who was parish priest of the place. Our young aspirant to the sacred ministry took his first Latin lesson from this venerable priest, under whose wise direction he seriously reflected on his vocation, which as he acknowledged was put to a severe test for the first few months. October, 1820, he entered the college at Boulogne, then under the direction of the celebrated Abbe Haffreingue. As he was taller and older than his fellow students, he was given charge of one of the studyrooms, an office delicate, and at times difficult, but filled by him with kindness and prudence. Even at this epoch in his life he showed a keen sense of duty and a firm will. One of his relatives having seen him during a vacation full of mirth and glee, the life of the circles in which he moved, noticed that at college he was serious and sedate, and so told him. Amadeus replied, "When vacation is over I shut up all my mirth in a box, to be opened only the next vacation." As he was of a most cheerful disposition, it must have cost him no little effort to do so.

In 1821 he received tonsure at the hands of Cardinal de la Tour d' Auvergne Lauragais, Bishop of Arras. Having completed the collegiate course of studies in 1826, he went to the Diocesan seminary at Arras, receiving minor orders on December 22, of the following year. May 21, 1828, he was ordained subdeacon, and on December 20 of the same year, deacon. The same prelate who gave him tonsure also ordained him to the priesthood on March 14, 1829.* The parish of Wismes, a small village near Fauquembergues, district of St. Omer, was his first appointment. There he remained till 1834, meanwhile also attending a neighboring mission church. The chaplaincy of the Ursuline Convent at Boulogne-sur-Mer having become vacant and the sisters knowing the sterling worth, indomitable zeal, and great prudence of Father Rappe, were desirous of having him appointed their chaplain and spiritual director. Mother Ursula, the superioress of the community, petitioned his bishop to this effect, and her request was granted. Father Rappe remained chaplain to the Ursulines of Boulogne from January, 1834, till May, 1840. During this time he read with intense interest the "Annals of the Propagation of the Faith," which excited in him an ardent desire to devote himself to the American mission. In 1839 Bishop Purcell, of Cincinnati, passed through London on his way from America to Europe, and whilst in that city he was requested by the parents of three young English ladies to take them under his protection as far as the Ursuline Convent at Boulogne. There he met the zealous chaplain of the community, and future missionary, Father Rappe, to whom he made known the spiritual destitution of his large diocese. Rev. Amadeus Rappe then offered to go with him to America. This he did, however, with great diffidence, owing to his age, thirty-nine, which he felt would be no small hindrance in adapting himself to the life of a missionary in a strange land. Another great obstacle for him

*The facts in connection with Bishop Rappe's home, college and seminary life were furnished the writer July, 1888, by a gentleman intimately acquainted with the lamented prelate, his cousin—Dr. Dewulf, now residing in Paris.

was the fact that he was unacquainted with the English language. But he would allow none of these obstacles to hinder him from entering upon the toilsome and self-sacrificing life of a missionary. After receiving the necessary permission from his Ordinary to leave his diocese, and bidding farewell to his charge, which deeply regretted to lose him, who was to them a wise counselor and prudent director, he set sail for America, September, 1840, arriving at Cincinnati the following month. He was immediately sent by Bishop Purcell to Chillicothe in order to learn English. Mr. Marshall Anderson, a convert and most estimable gentleman, was his teacher. But Father Rappe found it very difficult to master even the rudiments of the language; in a few months, however, he was able to speak it sufficiently well to make himself understood, though his pronunciation always remained defective. About 1836 the present flourishing city of Toledo was founded. Catholics there were very few in number and had neither church nor priest; Tiffin was the nearest place whence sick calls were attended. The Miami and Erie canal was being built about that time, and there came quite a large influx of Catholic laborers who settled along the line of the canal and the Maumee river. There was much sickness then, the dread Maumee fever undermining the strongest constitution, and hurrying many of its victims to an early grave. There was also much intemperance among the laborers, who spent their hard earned money in drink and allowed their families to want. To this uncultivated and uninviting field of labor Father Rappe was sent about six months after his arrival at Cincinnati. His "parish limits" extended from Toledo to the Indiana state line and as far south as Allen county. From the summer of 1841 till the spring of 1846 his labors, privations and difficulties of all kinds were indeed trying; he never lost courage, but full of missionary zeal and self-sacrifice he labored faithfully among his people. It was here that he first saw the terrible effects of intemperance, which so filled him with a horror of this vice that he fought it then and during the remainder of his life by word and example. Thousands bless his memory for the energetic measures he took in rescuing them from a drunkard's grave. For five years, 1841-46, Father Rappe was alone in this section of the state, but his work grew beyond his strength. Hence Bishop Purcell sent him a co-laborer in the person of Father Louis de Goesbriand, present Bishop of Burlington, Vermont, who arrived at Toledo in January, 1846. At that time Toledo and the surrounding country, even as far west as the state line, were full of malaria of the most malignant type. Bishop de Goesbriand, in his reminiscences of Bishop Rappe's missionary life, says: "At certain seasons it was impossible to meet a healthy-looking person, and frequently entire families were sick and unable to help one another. Apart from the terrible malarial fever, we were occasionally visited by such epidemics as erysipelas, and towards the end of 1847 we saw ship-fever stricken emigrants landing on the docks, to die among strangers a few hours after arrival." After the Miami and Erie canal was finished many of the laborers left with their families to seek homes in a more healthy climate. As the majority of them were Catholics, Father Rappe's missions were greatly weakened. Very few Catholic families remained between Toledo and Defiance. Mass was said, however, each Sunday in Toledo and frequently at Maumee City, and on week days at Providence, Defiance, Poplar Ridge, and occasionally at Fremont and La Prairie. The roads were often almost impassable, but Father Rappe and his faithful companion found neither bad roads nor the inclemency of the weather a sufficient obstacle to prevent them from visiting each of their scattered missions at the time appointed. In his intercourse with his people, Father Rappe was most affable, and he knew well how to win their respect and confidence. He was acquainted with every family, and knew every member of each family. He had a special gift to teach catechism, and would spend weeks in a settlement preparing a few children for the reception of the sacraments. During this time of preparation he would instruct the children for hours each day, and always managed to rivet their attention. He was ever watchful of the spiritual welfare of the adult portion of his flock, urging them to frequent confession and a regular attendance at Mass.

To assist him in instructing the children at Toledo he secured several Sisters of Notre Dame from Cincinnati. They were of the band of *Religeuses* that had come with him from Namur, Belgium, in 1840, and established a branch of their community in Cincinnati. He secured a house, near the present site of St. Francis de Sales' church, Toledo, which was fitted up as a convent and select school for the little band of sisters that shared with him the trials and hardships of missionary life. They remained at Toledo from 1846 to 1848, when owing to lack of support they were recalled to Cincinnati.

Bishop Purcell finding the labor of properly attending to his vast diocese, comprising the state of Ohio, too much for him, petitioned the Holy See for a division of his jurisdiction. Cleveland was considered as the most fit city in the northern part of the state for an Episcopal See, and hence was so designated. Father Rappe, the zealous missionary of the Maumee, was chosen as the first bishop of this new diocese. Although the Papal Bulls to this effect were issued April 23, 1847, they did not reach Cincinnati till the following August. The fact of their arrival was published in the *Catholic Telegraph*, September 2, 1847, as follows:

"The Bulls for the consecration of Rt. Rev. Mr. Rappe for the new See of Cleveland have arrived. We very sincerely congratulate the clergy and congregations in the northern part of Ohio on this appointment; if zeal for the glory of God, and utter disregard of self, a blameless life, and fervent piety can qualify a man for the Episcopacy, we know no one more likely to see his hopes realized than the bishop-elect of Cleveland. This is his character amongst those who know him."

Father Rappe was consecrated at Cincinnati, October 10, 1847, by Bishop Purcell, assisted by Bishop Whelan, of Wheeling, Virginia. Two days after his consecration, and just before starting for Cleveland, he published his first pastoral letter, which is given here in full. It portrays clearly the apostolic zeal and devotedness to the cause of God on the part of Bishop Rappe.

AMADEUS.

BY THE GRACE OF GOD AND APPOINTMENT OF THE APOSTOLIC SEE BISHOP OF CLEVELAND.

To the Clergy and Laity of the Diocese of Cleveland:
Grace Unto You, and Peace from God our Father, and from the Lord Jesus Christ:

VENERABLE BRETHREN OF THE CLERGY AND BELOVED BRETHREN OF THE LAITY!

Overwhelmed by the labors and solicitude which his extensive diocese required, and full of zeal for the welfare of the flock which he has governed with unsurpassed wisdom and success, the Rt. Rev. John Baptist, Bishop of Cincinnati, humbly supplicated the late Provincial Council to establish another Episcopal See in the northern part of the state of Ohio. This request was granted, and the city of Cleveland has been chosen to be the See of the new diocese. The Roman Court has approved and sanctioned these proceedings, and His Holiness, Pius IX, at the request of the Council, has elevated me to the Episcopacy. Had I consulted my fears I would have immediately declined accepting a station so encompassed with difficulties, but yielding to the voice of authority, and thereby made strong by the favor of the Almighty, I consented to forego my weakness and inability, to rely solely on Him who can strengthen the weak, and prepare them for the labor. "Go, and teach all nations: behold I am with you all days until the consummation of the world." That divine mission given by Jesus Christ to His Apostles, has been confided to me by their successors and the Apostolic See. Invested with this sacred power, and comforted by the grace of the episcopal office, I feel encouraged to work for the glory of our common Master and the welfare of our immortal souls.

It is indeed consoling, venerable brethren of the clergy, that in discharging the functions of a ministry so sublime and perilous, I will be seconded by your devotion, your talents, your virtues, and your experience. For several years I have fought in your ranks, shared your toils, admired your zeal, and witnessed with joy the success that crowned your efforts. It was then one of my greatest pleasures, whilst associated with you in the ministry, to call you friends, and now, placed at your head, as the first sentinel of the camp of Israel, I desire more than ever to be regarded as your friend and father, rather than your superior. My happiness will be henceforth to have part in your labors, to direct your efforts, to alleviate your cares, and to console your sorrows. Our number is small, but let us pray to the Lord to send more laborers into His vineyard, and whilst waiting with patience His answer to our supplications, let our union, our piety, our prudence and zeal make amends for the deficiency. In the daily morning meditations we will find a divine fire which illumines and vivifies; the reading of the Holy Scriptures will furnish us with arms against our enemies, and be our comfort in tribulation. The works of the Fathers and the acts of the Councils, but particularly of the Councils of Baltimore, which are so appropriate to the circumstances and wants of our mission, will be a pure source from which we can draw sound doctrine and wisdom to direct us in the various exigencies of our ministry.

Your spiritual necessities, beloved brethren of the laity, are not unknown to us: we wish to be intimately acquainted with your desires for the advancement of religion, and although we may be unable to provide resident pastors for every congregation, we will endeavor to console you in their absence by frequent visits, and by sending you, from time to time, faithful missionaries who will speak your language, and animate your piety.

We sigh for the day when we will be able to appear amongst you, to bless you, to instruct you, and to be edified by your devotion. Many a time have we been moved by the constancy of your faith and the beauty of your example.

What a consolation for a pastor to be surrounded by a faithful flock, anxious to diffuse on all sides the sweetness of the doctrines of Jesus Christ. Those truly Catholic souls are His glory, and they give a powerful energy to His words. They are so many apostles before whose integrity and piety the demon of prejudice is passing away. The times are propitious! The eminent virtues of our prelates and clergy, their eloquence in the pulpit, their polemical works, so marked by ability and clearness, the numerous conversions, both at home and abroad, conversions in which the finger of God is so visible, since they can not with reason be attributed to any worldly motive—all these circumstances directed by Divine Providence for the triumph of truth seem to have mitigated the violence of our dissenting brethren, and prepared the minds of the more learned portion of the community to examine and appreciate the divine excellence of our holy religion. It is for you, beloved brethren of the laity, to encourage this disposition to a sounder system. If the eloquence of an upright life does not convert our opponents, at least it silences the hostility of the unwise and imprudent. It is thus that we can most efficaciously contribute to the propagation of that faith which has conquered the world. Console, beloved brethren of the laity, and help your pastors by the sanctity of your lives. Have but one mind, no matter what may be your nation, your language, your position in society. You are all the children of the same Father, the members of Jesus Christ, destined for the same inheritance. In order that you might preserve this sweet union of mind and heart, come often to the Sacred Table, to feed on the Bread of Life, to be strengthened by the God of charity. He will remind you that He loved you even to the shedding of His Blood, and therefore has the right to command that you love one another. Unite together every night in family worship, and the Lord will be amongst you. Observe punctually the Lord's day, and the laws of the Church and of the state, and educate your children in the fear and love of God. Do all in your power to provide for their instruction, orthodox and pious teachers. We beseech you also, beloved brethren, by the mercy of Jesus Christ, to live soberly. Drunkenness, and the debaucheries which attend it, degrade man, disgrace the faith, and precipitate many into endless misfortunes.

As for us, venerable fellow-laborers, we will all endeavor to be the models of the faithful in conversation, in charity, in faith, in chastity. Our mission is a glorious one, and our reward will be equally glorious if we live according to our sublime vocation.

†AMADEUS,
Bishop of Cleveland.

Given at Cincinnati, October 12, 1847.

Within a week after his consecration Bishop Rappe took possession of his diocese, comprising all that portion of Ohio lying north of the southern limits of Columbiana, Stark, Wayne, Ashland, Richland, Crawford, Wyandot, Hancock, Allen and Van Wert counties; and containing forty-two churches, attended by twenty-one priests. There was then but one church in Cleveland, St. Mary's on the "Flats," which served as his cathedral, and but one priest, the Rev. Maurice Howard. January, 1848, Father Howard was sent to Tiffin, and Father de Goesbriand was appointed his successor and vicar-general. St. Mary's congregation was composed of English and German speaking Catholics, who had far outgrown their church when Bishop Rappe came to Cleveland. He succeeded in getting a German priest, by whom separate services were given to the German portion of the congregation, thus tiding over the necessity of building another church at that time. For several months the Bishop resided in a rented house, south of the Public Square; but in 1848 he bought a house on Bond street, which he made his episcopal residence. To supply the wants of the growing Catholic population, a frame building, 30x60, was erected on Superior street, a short distance east of Erie, near the site of the present cathedral, and next to the lots which Rev. Peter McLaughlin had bought in 1845 for church purposes. This frame building served several years as a "chapel of ease" for St. Mary's church, and as a parochial school, the first in the city.

Folding doors cut off the sanctuary during school hours. This little church was commenced and finished in December, 1848. It was used for the first time on Christmas of same year, and hence was called the Church of the Nativity. Meanwhile Bishop Rappe had plans drawn and specifications made for a cathedral, to be erected on the northeast corner of Superior and Erie streets. Mr. Keily, of Brooklyn, N. Y., was the architect. The cornerstone was laid on Sunday, October 29, 1848, Bishop Timon, of Buffalo, preaching on the occasion. The cathedral was consecrated November 7, 1852.

In 1849 the Bishop went to Europe for the purpose of securing priests for his diocese, and members of religious communities for schools and charitable institutions. He returned in August, 1850, bringing four priests, *), five seminarists, †), two Sisters of Charity, and six Ursuline nuns. Two years previous he had opened a seminary back of the episcopal residence on Bond street, with Father de Goesbriand as its first superior. Thither the seminarists, just arrived from France, were sent, some to complete their studies and one or two to be ordained shortly.

During the Bishop's absence, Judge Cowles' mansion on Euclid avenue was bought for the Ursuline Sisters. It is the present Mother House of the Cleveland Ursulines. The sisters took possession of their new home on their arrival in Cleveland, and almost immediately opened a select school and an academy. In 1851 the Ladies of the Sacred Heart of Mary established St. Mary's Orphan Asylum for girls. The first building used for the purpose was located on St. Clair street, near Bond, Cleveland. Toward the end of 1853 the asylum was transferred to Harmon street, its present location. During the latter year Bishop Rappe opened St. Vincent's Orphan Asylum for boys on Monroe street, Cleveland, and placed it in charge of the Sisters of Charity of St. Augustine, a community he had established. Thus the most pressing wants of the diocese were supplied. The Bishop now directed his attention to details of diocesan work, visiting every church

* Revs. C. M. Coquerelle, C. Evrard, A. Gelaszewski, and J. B. Mareschal.

† Messrs. L. F. D'Arcy, Z. Druon, L. Filiere, L. Molon, and N. Ponchel,

and station at frequent intervals, giving missions, administering confirmation and preaching. Though constantly at work, either at home in his cathedral, or out in the diocese, he never showed signs of fatigue. Never satisfied with what he had already accomplished, he was always anxious to do still more for the glory of God and the good of religion. He was specially solicitous for Catholic schools, and where it was within the range of possibility priests were obliged to establish such in their respective parishes. He also established institutions in which charity in various forms might be dispensed, and to this end introduced the following female religious communities into the diocese, besides those already mentioned, viz.: the Grey Nuns *(Sœur-Grises)* of Montreal, 1855, the Sisters of the Good Shepherd, 1869, and the Little Sisters of the Poor, 1870. He also welcomed the Franciscans to the diocese in 1867, giving them charge of St. Joseph's congregation, Cleveland, and two years later the Jesuits, to whom he entrusted St. Mary's congregation, Toledo.

Previous to 1865 Cleveland had no public hospital. As early as 1850, two French Sisters of Charity attempted to establish one on the West Side—then known as Ohio City. Their noble purpose failed for want of means, and so they returned to their native France the following year.

In 1863, during the interstate war, then at its height of bloody carnage, many sick and wounded soldiers were sent to Cleveland for medical treatment, but no provision had been made to receive and care for them. It was then that Cleveland realized the necessity of a hospital, which Bishop Rappe would long before have built had he had the means. He now saw a near realization of his long-cherished plan. He offered to build a hospital and provide efficient nurses, on condition the public would come to his assistance. This offer was gladly accepted, and two years later (1865) Charity Hospital, costing about $75,000, was opened to the public, and placed in charge of the Sisters of Charity. In every good work Bishop Rappe was in the front ranks, never shirking his part, never refusing his aid or countenance. Though perhaps meeting with disappointment, or receiving insult for his pains, he never halted, but courageously went on in his work. He knew no such word as *fail.*

Time, incessant labor, and mental worry caused by opposition, began to tell on him. His sight also began to fail him. He lost the use of his right eye and was in danger of losing his sight entirely. In 1869 he attended the Vatican Council. Opposition and strife still growing, he felt it to be to the best interests of religion to resign the burden of the Episcopacy he had so long and patiently borne. His resignation as Bishop of Cleveland, tendered August 22, 1870, was accepted by the Holy See.

When Bishop Rappe came to Cleveland in 1847 he found a sparsely settled diocese awaiting organization at his hands. He left it flourishing, well provided with priests, churches, schools and religious institutions. The episcopal city in 1847 had but one small church; in 1870 there were eleven, with as many, and mostly large, congregations. His work as a missionary priest and as a missionary bishop, his burning zeal and noble self-sacrifice enshrine him in the history of the Church in the United States as an apostle of Catholicity in Ohio.

In this connection, and in justice to the memory of Bishop Rappe, we place the following on record :

Cardinal Simeoni, Prefect of the Propaganda, in a letter sent to the Rt. Rev. Bishop Gilmour, May 8, 1885, referring to Bishop Rappe, says :

"* * *in illa miserrima conspiratione contra episcopum Clevelandensem, praedecessorem Amplitudinis Tuae, in qua ille sanctus et apostolicus senex falso* * * *accusabatur.*"

Five years after Bishop Rappe resigned, the Holy See offered him another diocese, as appears from the subjoined letter addressed to Bishop Gilmour by the Rt. Rev. Bishop de Goesbriand :

"BURLINGTON, VT., 21st December, 1884.

Rt. Rev. R. Gilmour, Bishop of Cleveland:

RT. REV., DEAR SIR :

"After consulting my records I find that Mgr. Roncetti, Ablegate of the Holy Father, arrived at Burlington, from

Portland, in company of Father Ubaldo Ubaldi, Very Rev. Father Quinn and Rev. Father O'Farrell, of New York, on Saturday evening, July 24th, 1875. The object of his visit was to see Rt. Rev. A. Rappe, whom he thought to be living in Burlington, but who was living at St. Albans with Father Druon.

"The Ablegate expressed himself disappointed in not meeting him. I remember distinctly that after inquiring concerning Bishop Rappe, he opened in my presence, and read with much attention, a letter of Cardinal Franchi to himself, and said to me that he had been commanded to see Rt. Rev. A. Rappe, and authorized to offer him another diocese. The Ablegate left Burlington the next day and did not see Bishop Rappe. Whether or not he wrote to him I cannot tell, but it was certainly intended to speak to him of another See, for I remarked to Mgr. Roncetti, that the charge of a diocese would be too much for Bishop Rappe, who at that date must have been seventy-four years of age.

What I have here written I am ready to swear to.

†LOUIS,
Bishop of Burlington, Vt."

Dr. John Gilmary Shea in his recent work, *The Catholic Hierarchy in the United States*, (page 206,) referring to the resignation of Bishop Rappe, says :

"Bishop Rappe had built up the diocese and might have been expected in his declining years to enjoy a happy old age amid the clergy and people whom he had guided as a faithful pastor for twenty [twenty-three] years, but this was not to be. An ungrateful opposition sprung up, calumny assailed even the venerable bishop, who with a broken heart resigned his See on the 22d of August, 1870, and retired to the diocese of his good friend Bishop de Goesbriand, of Burlington."

In his *Lives of Deceased Bishops*, Dr. Richard H. Clarke says of Bishop Rappe: "While attending the [Vatican] council his reputation was assailed unjustly at Rome, by calumnies forwarded from the very diocese he had served so well. This movement was limited to a few. * * * Rome, misled by calumnies, which it afterwards discovered and pronounced to be the fruits of a conspiracy, counseled his retirement. But he was never removed from his office as Bishop of Cleveland. On his return to Cleveland from Rome, he resigned his bishopric August 22, 1870. He had been Bishop of Cleveland not only in name but in deed, and left that title unsullied before God."*) * * "Since his death I have seen the original letter, one from the Holy See, in which the means resorted to, to compel his retirement from his See, are spoken of as a 'miserable conspiracy,' the accusations against him are characterized as 'false' (falso accusabatur), and in which Bishop Rappe is himself spoken of as 'that holy and apostolic old man,' (ille sanctus et apostolicus senex)." †)

At the Pontifical Requiem High Mass for the deceased prelates of the Cincinnati province, celebrated in St. Peter's cathedral, Cincinnati, March 7, 1882, at the time the Fourth Provincial Council of Cincinnati was in session, Bishop Dwenger, of Fort Wayne, preached the sermon on the occasion. Referring to Bishop Rappe, he spoke as follows:

" * . * We remember today the first Bishop of Cleveland, Amadeus Rappe. Having known him from the days of my childhood, it is today a pleasant duty to do justice to his memory. He was elevated to the episcopal dignity, not so much on account of brilliant talent, as on account of piety and apostolic zeal. It was an edifying sight to see the hard working apostolic bishop visit every church of his wonderfully growing diocese every year, preaching, giving confirmation, hearing confessions; nothing was too hard for him; nothing could tire him. When I conducted missions and forty hours' devotions, I sometimes would feel a delicacy to urge the priests to go in the confessionals; but if the good bishop was present I never hesitated to ask him to hear confessions, if I knew there was a crowd. Witness the wonderful growth of the Diocese of Cleveland from the year 1847 to the time of his resignation. I do not deny that the saintly apostolic bishop, relying upon the advice and judgment of men whom he considered more learned than himself, did

* Vol. 3, pp. 244, 245; † Vol. 3, pp. 248, 249.

commit some error in the administration ; but the austere, hard-working, apostolic man was innocent of the cruel accusations that were concocted against him, and saddened the last days of his life. I know how these accusations were concocted. I have spoken with the principal witness. I know he [the Bishop] was innocent. Beautiful were the words the good bishop used, when in 1870 he tendered his resignation to the Holy See : That for the good of his diocese he not only resigned his dignity, but also his good name ; that for the sake of peace and harmony he desired no vindication."*

Immediately after his resignation he retired to St. Albans, Vermont, making his home with V. Rev. Father Druon, V. G., until his saintly death, at St. Albans, September 8, 1877. He was incessantly engaged in his former and favorite work of giving missions and catechising the young throughout the Diocese of Burlington. He conducted a very successful mission in the great parish church of Notre Dame, Montreal, preaching the entire course of sermons himself. Immense audiences heard his eloquent and impressive sermons, and thousands took from him on that occasion the pledge of total abstinence. He was the Father Mathew of Montreal. The last mission he gave was at Grand Isle, near St. Albans. Although seriously ailing of what proved to be his last illness, he closed the mission exercises, after one week of intense pain and suffering, September 7, 1877, the day before he died. On the same day he left for Milton, twelve miles from St. Albans.

The following particulars of Bishop Rappe's fatal illness and death were given to the writer by the Very Rev. Father Druon, in a letter dated September 20, 1888 : "He arrived at Milton in the morning (Friday, Sept. 7th,) when Father Cardinal telegraphed to me. I reached Milton at 12.30 P. M. and found Bishop Rappe a little delirious, though he had taken a good fish dinner. I brought him to St. Albans without any trouble, in the afternoon, when I telegraphed to Bishop de Goesbriand, who arrived in the evening. He heard his confession, for at that time he had entirely recovered his consci-

*Catholic Telegraph, March 9, 1882.

ousness. Dr. Fasset, who came to see him in the afternoon, found him pretty well, so that he then had hope of his recovery. After the Bishop's arrival at St. Albans, when he was still a little delirious, he wished to start for his missions, and it was then that he said: '*I have a grand mission to perform; I want to go to Cleveland by the way of Buffalo.*' On the following day he fell into a comatose state from which he never recovered; he died peacefully that night at 11:30 o'clock. The last words he breathed were: '*I have prayed for my friends; I have prayed for my enemies; now may God bless them all!*'" Words of apostolic benediction, of forgiving and loving charity; an echo of the Last Words on Calvary!

His remains were brought to Cleveland—to the city he loved so well. On arrival Thursday evening, September 13th, they were met by an immense concourse of people, Catholic and Protestant, all vieing to do honor to the dead Bishop whom in life they loved and venerated. By torchlight the immense funeral cortege passed from the Union Depot to the cathedral, where, on a magnificent catafalque, Bishop Rappe's mortal remains were placed in state for the night. Next day a Pontifical Requiem Mass was celebrated by Bishop Dwenger, of Ft. Wayne. Bishop Ryan, of Buffalo, preached the panegyric, pronouncing a beautiful tribute to the memory of the sainted dead. The remains of Bishop Rappe were then enclosed in a vault beneath the cathedral he had built, and beneath the alter at which for eighteen years he had offered up the divine sacrifice.

Tuesday, October 16, the Rt. Rev. Bishop Gilmour preached in the cathedral at the Month's Mind of Bishop Rappe. From his sermon on that occasion we quote the following passage: "Bishop Rappe came as a missionary, he abided as a missionary, he persevered as a missionary. The same brave old missionary bishop! Seeking his people far and wide; preaching incessantly to them from the pulpit, day after day and year after year; patiently awaiting them in the confessional; by the bed of the dying, consoling and exhorting, or by the side of youth, guiding and protecting, encouraging or chiding, he was ever the same—the indefatigable bishop, who knew no self, only God and the things of God. Preaching retreats, erecting temples, founding convents, giving instruction in his universal character of missionary, he died as he had lived—a true soldier of Christ, a man of God. It is the most beautiful episode, perhaps, in the Catholic annals of the United States. His last public act was to celebrate Mass and ask the prayers of the people for the grace of a happy death; his last words were an invocation of charity. It was meet that he should have been brought here to repose under the altar that he built; it was right that he should have come among his own for their prayers—those to whom he had given a life's earnest labors. It was fitting that his virtues and his memory should be placed before the people whom he so loved, for whom he had so labored."

In 1887, Bishop Gilmour authorized his vicar-general, Mgr. Boff, to raise a fund by collections in the churches of the diocese for a monument, to be erected to the memory of Bishop Rappe. The response of the diocese was most generous. Since then a fine marble bust of the deceased prelate has been executed and placed in the Bishop's residence, and in October, 1888, a life size statue in bronze of Bishop Rappe, in full pontifical robes, was cast in Rome. It will be permanently placed on a suitable pedestal, either in the vestibule of the cathedral* or on the cathedral grounds facing Superior street.

Few men on the missions of America ever excelled Bishop Rappe in the line of his work. Untiring in zeal, patient in hardships, generous, unselfish, no labor seemed to weary or exhaust him. Tall and wiry, quick and elastic in motion, good his aim, suffering and sorrow the objects of his charity, he lived for religion and his kind. Ill-versed in English, because learned late in life, defective in early education, yet by nature's gifts and his own energy of character, he ranked as an orator of more than ordinary powers. His wont was to preach thrice every Sunday—frequently four and five times—always to a different audience, and often in churches miles distant from each other. He was great as a missionary rather than as a bishop, and excelled as a pioneer who explored and out-lined,

* It is now (1889) temporarily placed in the cathedral vestibule.

leaving to others to shape and consolidate. A lover of his native land, he gave not only his allegiance but his most ardent support to his adopted country. A true patriot, a Christian man, tolerant of dissent, conceding to others what he asked for himself—religious and civil liberty—he died at the ripe old age of seventy-six, thirty years of which he had spent as priest and bishop on the missions of Ohio. He died amid the tears of his people, and the respect of his fellow citizens, with the well-merited reputation of a life spent for God and the good of his fellowmen.

BIOGRAPHICAL SKETCH

—OF THE—

RIGHT REV. RICHARD GILMOUR, SECOND AND PRESENT BISHOP OF CLEVELAND, SINCE APRIL, 1872.

Richard Gilmour was the only child of John and Marion (Callander) Gilmour. He was born in the city of Glasgow, Scotland, Sept. 28, 1824. His parents were in comfortable circumstances and strict Scotch covenanters. In 1829, when Richard was in his fifth year, they emigrated to Nova Scotia, but a few years later moved to Pennsylvania and settled on a farm near Latrobe, where their son attended the district schools. Not satisfied with the training there received, he made every effort to improve his mind by home reading. His love for books was fostered by his parents, who gave him every facility in this regard their means afforded. With his studious habits and retentive memory, he soon acquired a knowledge of general literature, history and mathematics much beyond that of boys of his age. He also gained considerable proficiency in music, which in later years came him in good stead, and was indirectly the means that brought him into the Catholic Church. After completing the branches taught in the common schools his parents sent him to Philadelphia, there to attend the more advanced schools. At this time he was in his eighteenth year. The Rev. Patrick Rafferty was then stationed at Philadelphia as pastor of St. Francis' Church, (Fairmount,) located near the school which young Richard attended. In this church was an organ on which Father Rafferty kindly allowed him to practice during the week. Father Rafferty's earnest and withal kindly ways won the heart of Richard so much that his inbred prejudice against

RIGHT REVEREND RICHARD GILMOUR, D. D.

the Catholic clergy yielded sufficiently to permit him to entertain a sincere esteem for this good priest. This esteem soon ripened into the closer relation of friendship. Occasionally he attended the Sunday services held by Father Rafferty, whose sermons struck him as clear, pointed and instructive. Richard, naturally of an inquiring mind, began of his own accord to direct his attention to the study of Catholic doctrine, which for him had been thus far a sealed book. All his reading was now turned in that direction. Finally, convinced in his own mind that he could no longer conscientiously profess and believe as he had been trained to in his childhood, he went to Father Rafferty for further instructions. Two years after he had made the acquaintance of this priest, and after calmly reflecting on the important step, he was received into the Church by his friend Father Rafferty. His parents were indeed much surprised at this, but they had the good sense not to interfere with what the son honestly believed in this important matter to be his duty. In fact, they followed his example ; first his mother and some years after her his father.

Richard was now in his twentieth year, and felt he must choose his role in the drama of life. After calm reflection, aided by the advice of his spiritual guide, Father Rafferty, he resolved to enter the priesthood. To fit himself for this important step, he entered Mount St. Mary's College and Seminary, Emmittsburg, Md., July, 1846, where by his ecclesiastical spirit, earnestness of purpose and diligence in study he soon won the esteem of his superiors and the respect of his fellow students. As an evidence of the confidence reposed in him he was appointed prefect of the collegians and professor of the higher mathematics within one year after entering Mount St. Mary's. These positions he held till the end of his seminary course. Owing to the fact that he was far advanced in his studies before entering college, he completed the collegiate course two years later (1848), when he received the degree of master of arts. At the completion of the theological course he was received by Archbishop Purcell for the Diocese of Cincinnati, and was ordained priest by him in the cathedral of that city, August 30, 1852. His first field of missionary labor, to which he was sent in September of the same year, embraced Portsmouth, as his place of residence, Ironton, Vinton and Gallipolis, besides a number of missions and stations in the neighborhood and in northeastern Kentucky and West Virginia. In all these places he labored with zeal, but not without encountering many hardships and difficulties of the most trying kind. His was the lot of the pioneer missionary, borne with patience, but crowned with success. In April, 1857, he was appointed successor to Rev. James F. Wood (the late Archbishop of Philadelphia), as pastor of St. Patrick's church, Cincinnati. Here his administrative qualities and pastoral zeal had full sway, and well did he come up to the expectations of Archbishop Purcell. During his pastorate St. Patrick's grew and flourished; under his direction a fine school building was erected, the parochial school system was brought to a high degree of perfection, and all else pertaining to the spiritual and temporal welfare of his charge was wrought with most gratifying results.

Feeling the need of some respite from the incessant strain in connection with pastoral work, done unremittingly since his ordination, and desirous of devoting some time to literary pursuits, so congenial to his taste, he asked for and obtained a professorship in Mt. St. Mary's Seminary, Cincinnati. But his valuable services as a pastor were not long to be dispensed with, as he remained at the seminary only a little more than a year—April, 1868, to July, 1869. He was called to fill a vacancy in the important and at the same time disturbed parish of St. Joseph's, Dayton. His prudent management and buiness tact soon brought things to rights in this new field of labor, so that in 1872, when he was called to the high and responsible position he now holds, St. Joseph's congregation, Dayton, was left by him in a most prosperous condition.

The Diocese of Cleveland was without a bishop since August, 1870. Factions had done disastrous work, and the diocese had become a by-word throughout the country. Whom to appoint under these difficult circumstances as successor to good Bishop Rappe, who had been made the victim of faction and discord —a man loved by his people and universally respected by those not of the Fold—was a question not so easily answered. Finally, after much deliberation, Rome decided to appoint from the several candidates presented by the Bishops of the province of Cincinnati, the Rev. Richard Gilmour as the one best fitted for this most difficult position. Father Gilmour well knew what was asked of him when made acquainted with his appointment. But trusting in God, and not shirking from duty where and when duty called, he obeyed the call and accepted the burden. He was consecrated Bishop of Cleveland by Archbishop Purcell in the cathedral at Cincinnati, April 14, 1872. A few days later he took possession of his cathedral church at Cleveland, thus relieving Very Rev. E. Hannin, who had filled the office of Administrator of the diocese since August, 1870. Cares, difficulties and trials were again his lot, but in a greater degree and of graver form than when first he became a priest. Within his sphere of office he had contentions to meet and opposition to encounter which came from the same sources that opposed the administrations of Bishop Rappe, and Very Rev. Father Hannin, and which taxed all his prudence and energy. From without he was held in disfavor by the non-Catholic friends of the revered Bishop Rappe. This disfavor was intensified when Bishop Gilmour published his first pastoral letter, March, 1873. In it he fearlessly discussed and defended the citizen rights of Catholics, who had till then been looked upon as "hewers of wood and drawers of water," and seemingly took that position rather than that of equals of their non-Catholic fellow citizens. In the same letter he also explained and defended the parochial school system and insisted on its acceptance by his people, many of whom had thus far opposed it. For these bold and fearless utterances of views he was fiercely attacked by the local press and pulpit, as well as by the press at large. But in spite of assault, calumny and misrepresentation he pursued the path of duty as he saw it and forced the public to acknowledge, at least, that he cared not for public opinion, if it ran counter to what he considered himself bound to do and say.

Meanwhile the strain of incessant work and care told on

his constitution. June 24, 1874, while attending the commencement exercises at St. Mary's Academy, Notre Dame, Indiana, he fell seriously ill of nervous prostration. For two years he was unable to attend to the affairs of his diocese, and for months was at the brink of death. His physicians ordered him to take absolute rest, and directed he should go to southern France for his health, which he did. June 1, 1876, he returned to Cleveland, to the great joy of his people, who received him with an ovation of welcome. Though not fully restored to health he resumed by degrees his episcopal duties and gradually regained his former strength and vigor. In 1877 he began to systematize the business affairs of his diocese; had all the deeds of church property indexed and plats made of every parcel of church land; blank forms and registers covering all the details of diocesan and parochial affairs were introduced, so that within a few years the Diocese of Cleveland took front rank with the best regulated dioceses of the country for its thorough system and order.

His jurisdiction embraces the whole of Northern Ohio, viz.: all the territory north of the southern limits of the counties of Columbiana, Stark, Wayne, Ashland, Richland, Crawford, Wyandot, Allen and Van Wert, thirty-six counties in all. There are at present (Sept. 1, 1887,) 225 churches in the diocese, 187 priests, secular and regular, 126 parochial schools, 7 orphan asylums, besides a number of other charitable and religious institutions, all requiring and receiving his careful supervision. The clergy is a most zealous, hard-working body of men, co-operating with the Bishop in all that pertains to the best interests of the diocese. The laity, numbering upwards of 200,000, is in harmony with Bishop and clergy, generously responding to every call made by faith or charity. All in all, Bishop Gilmour is at the head of a diocese second to none in the United States in point of organization and Catholic vigor and strength.

Above was remarked the disfavor in which Bishop Gilmour was held by the non-Catholic citizens of Cleveland for his public utterances. This has been thoroughly changed. Till 1881 he never had an opportunity offered him of addressing his fellow-citizens as such. His first appearance in public as a citizen was on the occasion of the Garfield meeting held in the Public Square, July 4, 1881, when the citizens of Cleveland assembled to give expression of sympathy with the assassinated president, then at the point of death. To most of that vast audience the Bishop was in person a stranger. After his speech, most eloquent and patriotic, Bishop Gilmour gained and ever since has held the esteem and respect of Cleveland's citizens. At the congress of churches, which held its sessions in Cleveland, Ohio, May, 1886, he was invited to speak. The subject assigned him, "Religion in the Public Schools," was treated in a thoughtful and masterly manner, and he held his immense and varied audience spell-bound. The address was copied fully or in part by the leading journals of the country. Since 1881 he has been called upon repeatedly to speak in public, always receiving a most respectful hearing, even on the part of those who dissent from his views.

In the Church he is esteemed a thoughtful and prudent prelate. In the Fourth Provincial Council of Cincinnati, and Third Plenary Council of Baltimore, he took a prominent part in the deliberations. In the summer of 1885 he was delegated by the Archbishops of this country to go to Rome in the interests of the decrees of the Baltimore council, sent there for review and approval. He had been there three years previous on his official visit in connection with his administration of the Diocese of Cleveland. He was, therefore, no stranger to the Roman authorities, who now, as then, received him most kindly. This mission, performed in connection with two other bishops who had preceded him to Rome, was most successful.

Bishop Gilmour has a national reputation as a defender and promoter of the Catholic parochial school system. Feeling the want of good readers for the schools under his jurisdiction, he compiled a series himself, known as the Catholic National Readers, six in all. They are in use throughout the United States, as is also the Bible History, published by him when a parish priest. He has made it incumbent on the parishes of his diocese to have parochial schools when at all possible. March, 1887, he also published a code of rules and regulations governing these schools, one feature being the annual examination, by a diocesan board of examiners, of the teachers engaged therein, and an annual examination, by district school boards composed of priests and laymen, of all pupils attending the parochial schools. It is his aim to make these schools at least equal to the public schools.

In 1876 he tested before the courts what he considered the unjust taxation of the parochial schools of Cleveland. Although the supreme court of Ohio had decided the question in the celebrated Purcell-Gerke suit, that Catholic schools were not taxable, one of the Cuyahoga county auditors (Mr. Benedict,) regardless of this decision, placed the Catholic schools of Cleveland on the tax duplicate. The Bishop entered suit of restraint, the common pleas, circuit and supreme courts deciding in his favor.

Recognizing the power and influence of the press, and desirous of giving the large and influential Catholic body of Northern Ohio a defender of Catholic thought and rights, to meet the almost daily assaults and insults heaped upon it by an antagonistic press, notably those of a certain paper, fittingly characterized by the Hon. B. F. Wade, the Bishop established the *Catholic Universe*, July 4, 1874. Rev. T. P. Thorpe was its first editor. Mr. Manly Tello, the present editor, succeeded him in September, 1877, and both these gentlemen did, and the latter is still doing, excellent work in Catholic journalism.

Bishop Gilmour is a man of strong individuality, firm, bold, fearless. As a preacher and public speaker he impresses with his eloquence, calm thought and earnestness. As a writer he is pointed and wields a strong pen, even trenchant at times. His style is the simplest, terse in expression, clear as his speech. Tall, commanding in appearance, with a markedly intellectual countenance, he would be singled out in any assembly as a man of force and strength of character. Not quick to express his views, he seldom, if ever, recedes from them when once expressed. Strictly just and fair-minded in his dealings, he resents keenly any injustice or deception.

Kind and forbearing with weakness, he is just as ready to measure swords with insult or assault, within the limits of his official position. At first sight he impresses one as stern and reserved, but those who know him, know his kindness of heart and generous impulses. As a conversationalist he has few superiors. With a fund of anecdote and quiet humor, and a retentive memory of his reading and travels, he is most entertaining in any circle. He is simple in his habits, methodical and painstaking in his work. Few men in like position spend more hours at "desk work" than Bishop Gilmour. He governs his diocese as much with his pen as with the crosier. Thoroughly American in sentiment, he has, nevertheless, an impartial respect and a kindly feeling for all nationalties composing his flock.

BIOGRAPHICAL NOTICES

—— OF ——

PRIESTS OF THE SECULAR AND REGULAR CLERGY, FORMERLY ON THE MISSION IN NORTHERN OHIO, OR IN THE DIOCESE OF CLEVELAND.

BETWEEN 1818 AND APRIL, 1890.

1. ABBREDERIS, Rev. Rudolf, (Sanguinist,) was born at Rankweil, near Feldkirch, Austria, September 18, 1850; came to the United States in 1869; was educated by the Sanguinists in their seminary at Carthagena, Mercer Co., O., where he was ordained for them by Archbishop Purcell, August 15, 1873. He had the following charges in this diocese: Ottawa, August, 1878, to August, 1882; Big Spring, August, 1882, to November, 1885, when he left the Sanguinists, and diocese.

2. ABEL, Rev. Anthony J., was born November 11, 1833, at Burgau, Bavaria; completed his studies for the priesthood at St. Mary's Seminary, Cleveland, where he was ordained by Bishop Rappe, June 28, 1863. Monroeville was his first appointment, which he retained till October, 1864, when he was sent to Ottoville as first resident pastor. July, 1865, he was sent to Shelby Settlement, where he remained till 1867, when he left the diocese and went to Colorado. In 1889 he was received into the Diocese of Concordia, Kansas, where he is pastor of Tipton.

3. ABOULIN, Rev. John J. M., (Basilian,) was born at St. Alban-en-Montagne, Diocese of Viviers, France, March 18, 1841; was ordained for the Basilians at Annonay, France, by

ST. MARY'S THEOLOGICAL SEMINARY, CLEVELAND, O.

Bishop de Charbonnel, September 21, 1867. Was in this diocese as professor at Louisville College, from February, 1868, till September, 1870. Returned to Sandwich, Canada, and since 1870 has been doing pastoral duty there, at Assumption Church.

4. AHERN, Rev. Joseph Loughlin, was born at Knuckancummer, county Cork, September 20, 1847. He made his studies for the ministry at All Hollows', Dublin, and St. Mary's Seminary, Cleveland. He was ordained for the Diocese of Cleveland by Bishop Fitzgerald, July 4, 1875, and appointed pastor of Alliance, August, 1875. This charge he held till August, 1877, when he met with a serious accident by breaking one of his legs. He was taken to the Charity Hospital, Cleveland, for treatment. In August, 1878, he resumed pastoral work as assistant to Rev. M. Healy, at St. Mary's, Tiffin, remaining till October of same year, when he was appointed assistant at St. Francis', Toledo. June, 1879, he resigned this position, and for the benefit of his shattered health, went on leave of indefinite absence to Ireland, and later (1881) to New Zealand, where he is now laboring on the mission.

5. ALBRECHT, Rev. J. M., (Sanguinist,) was born in Germany, January 6, 1800. He was ordained by Bishop Rappe, June 4, 1849. From Thompson he attended Peru, Huron county, in 1849; was assistant at Thompson till June, 1856, when he was sent to Liverpool. There he remained till May, 1859, when he left the Sanguinists and diocese and went to Minnesota, where he died in March, 1884.

6. ALĖMANY, Most Rev. Joseph Sadoc, (Dominican,) was born at Vich, in the province of Catalonia, 1814. He entered the Dominican Order in 1829, and was ordained at Viterbo, by Bishop Pianetto, in 1837. Soon after his ordination he was sent to Rome, where he was stationed at the church of Santa Maria Sopra Minerva till 1841, when he was sent to the American missions. He came to Ohio, and was stationed at Canton for a few months. He also attended Dungannon, and was the

first priest to visit the Catholics at Mansfield. His next field of labor was at Memphis, Tenn., as successor to Father McAleer, in 1846. In the following year he was elected Provincial of his Order in the United States. While at Rome in 1850, attending a General Chapter of the Dominican Order, he was consecrated Bishop of Monterey, Cal., June 13, 1850. Three years later he was appointed Archbishop of San Francisco, which office he resigned, November, 1884, and returned to Valencia, Spain, where he died a saintly death, April 14, 1888.

7. ALIG, Rev. L. M. (Redemptorist), was born at Pinen, Switzerland, November 1, 1805, and was ordained September 18, 1839. He attended St. Alphonse's congregation, Peru, Huron county, Ohio, with Father Tschenhens from June, 1841, till November, 1843. Later he left the Redemptorists and was for many years pastor of St. Mary's church, Washington city, where he died June 9, 1882.

8. ALLEMAN, Rev. John George (Dominican), a native of Alsace, was ordained at Zanesville, Ohio, by Bishop Purcell, June 1, 1834. In 1836 he was resident pastor of St. John's, Canton, whence he also attended Louisville, where he built the first church. About 1840 he left Ohio and went to Iowa, laboring with much zeal, there and in Illinois on the widespread and difficult missions. His health began to fail about 1860. Three years later, Nov. 26, 1863, he went to St. Vincent's Asylum, St. Louis, Mo., where he died July 14, 1865, aged 59 years. He was a faithful and hard working priest.

9. ALLWARD, Rev. John, was first resident pastor of Ashtabula, for fourteen months from May, 1862, till July, 1863, and attended South Thompson as a mission. This was the only appointment he had in the Diocese of Cleveland. No other record of him.

10. ANDERSON, Rev. Henry, came from Ireland on a visit to his cousin, the Rev. E. Hannin, of St. Patrick's, Toledo, whose assistant he was for some months in 1868, and as such

attended, for a while, the congregation of the Immaculate Conception, Toledo, just then organized.

11. ANDRESCHECK, Rev. Alardus, (Franciscan), born at Breslau, Silesia, May 29, 1839, was educated for the priesthood at Paderborn, and ordained at Teutopolis, Ill., by Bishop Juncker, February 7, 1868. He was sent to the Cleveland Monastery, as assistant at St. Joseph's church, January 23, 1877; was appointed pastor of the same church, July 16, 1885, retaining this position till August, 1888, when his superior transferred him to Teutopolis, Ill., where he now resides.

12. ANTL, Rev. Francis Joseph, was born at Jesenec, Moravia, Austria, March 30, 1843; ordained at Bruenn, Austria, July 11, 1869; came to America in same year; was in the Diocese of Cleveland as pastor of St. Procop's, Cleveland, from May, 1882, till July, 1883. Then he went to the Diocese of Chicago; is now stationed at Savanna, Ill.

13. AUGUSTINSKY, Rev. Cyril, (Franciscan), a Moravian, was born at Braunsburg, March 21, 1851. He studied for the ministry at Kremsier, Archdiocese of Olmuetz, and was ordained for the Franciscans, at St. Louis, Mo., by Bishop Ryan, July 25, 1877. He labored on the mission in Missouri and Nebraska till July, 1885, when he was sent by his superior to the Franciscan Monastery, at Cleveland, whence he attended Independence. He left the Franciscan Order May, 1887, and by dispensation was affiliated to the Diocese of Little Rock, Ark., where he is now stationed.

14. AUSTERMANN, V. Rev. Bernard, (Sanguinist), a native of Prussia, was born at Everswinkel, Westphalia, April 5, 1824; was educated for the priesthood at Thompson, O., and there ordained for the Sanguinists by Bishop Rappe, June 13, 1856. From New Riegel he attended Fostoria and Crawfordsville, July, 1856, to February, 1857. He was then appointed pastor of Thompson, remaining till September, 1857. Since then he had various posts of duty assigned him in other dioceses where

the Sanguinists have charge of congregations. He was also for some years their Provincial. He is now in the Diocese of Nashville.

15. BADIN, V. Rev. Stephen Theodore, the first priest ordained in the United States, was a native of Orleans, France, where he was born July 27, 1768. He came to Baltimore, March 28, 1792, and was there ordained by Archbishop Carroll, May 25, 1793. For many years he labored on the mission in Kentucky and Ohio. He did pastoral duty at Canton, Canal Fulton, Cleveland, Fremont and Tiffin, between 1835 and 1837. He was a man of fine, cultivated mind, of great energy and indomitable zeal. He was vicar-general of the Dioceses of Bardstown, Ky., and Cincinnati. Died in the latter city, April 19, 1853.

16. BALLY, Rev. William, was born in the city of Bonn, Prussia, May 4, 1831; educated at Bonn and Paris; came to Cleveland, December, 1856, and was ordained by Bishop Rappe, July 26, 1857. He was assistant at St. Peter's, Cleveland, till November of same year, when he received the pastorate of St. Nicholas' congregation, Berwick, Seneca county, remaining till July, 1861, when he left the diocese. October, 1861, he was appointed pastor of St. Mary's church, Galena, Ill., which charge he still holds.

17. BARBIER, Rev. Charles, was born of Protestant parents at Strassburg, Alsace, in 1829. He entered the French artillery, and whilst serving his term became a Catholic. He shortly after resolved to study for the priesthood. After leaving the army he made his preparatory studies at Strassburg. In 1862 Bishop Rappe adopted him for the Diocese of Cleveland, and ordained him toward the end of the same year. He was at the seminary for a few months as professor of philosophy, and had, besides, Independence as his first pastoral charge. From April to November, 1863, he had temporary charge of St. Louis' congregation, Louisville, during the absence, in Europe, of the pastor, Rev.

L. Hoffer. He then had, successively, the following pastoral charges in this diocese: Poplar Ridge (now New Bavaria), 1863-65, where he began the erection of a church destroyed by fire in 1887; first resident pastor of Six Mile Woods, 1865-67; Millersville, 1867-68; Avon, March, 1868, to September, 1871; Milan, 1871 to August, 1872; Youngstown, St. Joseph's, August, 1872 to April, 1873; first resident pastor of New Cleveland, April, 1873 to March, 1874. His last charge was St. Joseph's church, Fort Jennings, March, 1874, till death, August 23, 1876.

18. BEGEL, Rev. John Joseph, was born in France, April 5, 1817, where also he was ordained December 18, 1841. He established the community known as the Sisters of the Humility, B. V. M., August, 1854. He came to America July, 1864, and founded the present flourishing convent of same sisters at New Bedford, Pa., by special agreement under the jurisdiction of the Bishop of Cleveland. Father Begel was an exemplary priest, and a man of profound and varied learning. He wrote a historical description of "The Way of the Cross," published in 1880. It is an admirable and interesting book, containing personal observations of his journey made some years previous to Jerusalem and other places in Palestine. He died at New Bedford, after an illness of about four years, January 23, 1884.

19. BEHRENS, Rev. Henry, was born at Duesselldorf, Prussia; ordained by Bishop Rappe July 30, 1861; attended Avon, September, 1861 to March, 1862; was pastor of Findlay from 1862 to July, 1863, and during that time attended the missions of Fostoria and Liberty. He was transferred to Six Mile Woods, 1863, where he remained but a few months after having begun the erection of a church. His next charge was Maumee, December, 1863-65. During the latter year he also attended Perrysburg as a mission. In the fall of 1865 he received charge of French Creek. His next appointment was Millersville (Greensburg), November, 1866, to August, 1867. Then he was appointed pastor of Shelby Settlement, Septem-

ber, 1867. He remained here until 1869, when he left the diocese and returned to Europe, where he died a few years later.

20. BERANEK, Rev. George A. (Redemptorist), was born at Mistek, Olmuetz, Austria, April 23, 1806; ordained July 22, 1834; in the United States since June, 1843; had temporary charge of St. Wenceslas' congregation, Cleveland, from September, 1868, to February, 1869, as Bishop Rappe had no Bohemian priest during that time. Since 1869, Father Beranek has been stationed at Baltimore, Md., where he is still doing pastoral duty.

21. BERGER, Rev. August, was born in Germany in 1822; ordained by Bishop Rappe, November 19, 1848; was assistant to Rev. P. J. Machebeuf, at Sandusky, for one year; left the diocese in 1849; returned in 1851, and left again in 1852; died at Germantown, Ill., October 1, 1865.

22. BERTHELET, Rev. Francis A., was born in Detroit, Michigan, June 28, 1830. He was educated for the priesthood at the diocesan seminary of St. Hyacinthe, Province of Quebec, where he was ordained by Bishop Prince, November 14, 1853; Joined the Jesuits in 1854 at St. Acheul, France, and later, for several years, was professor in the Jesuit colleges at Fordham, New York and Montreal. In last mentioned place he had charge, for two years, of the erection of the present beautiful church of the Gesu. August, 1868, he was received into the Diocese of Cleveland, and was assistant at the cathedral for a few months, when he was sent to Canton, as pastor of St. John's congregation. There he remained till March, 1876. Whilst at Canton the present very handsome church of St. John's was built under his direction. After nearly three years' illness he died, October 31, 1878, at Detroit, where also his remains are buried.

23. BIRNBAUM, Rev. Irenaeus (Franciscan), a native of Germany, was ordained March 27, 1868. He was in the Diocese of Cleveland from July, 1877, to February, 1879, as

one of the professors at St. Mary's Seminary. Meanwhile he also attended Parma and Independence, from August, 1877, to January, 1878, and from March, 1878, to February, 1879. Returned to Europe in 1879.

24. BIRNBAUM, Rev. John Baptist (Sanguinist), born in Wuerttemberg, May 8, 1823; came to United States in 1864; was ordained July 10, 1867; had pastoral charge of Big Spring; was assistant at Glandorf, Thompson, New Riegel; was pastor of Reed, Seneca county, which mission he attended from Thompson, where he died May 28, 1882.

25. BODEN, Rev. Gregory (Franciscan), was born at Goldscheid, Prussia, in 1838; ordained April 3, 1868; in Franciscan Monastery, Cleveland, from September, 1874, to February, 1876, with charge of asylum and convent chapels, and of Independence, from 1875 to 1876.

26. BOE, Rev. ——, was stationed at Louisville, as assistant to Rev. L. F. D'Arcy, from September, 1859, to January, 1860, when he returned to New Orleans, whence he came.

27. BOEHNE, Rev. George, born 1799 in Neuenkirchen Osnabrueck, Germany, was ordained in 1831. He came to America in the fall of 1841, when he was received by Bishop Purcell and sent to Glandorf as assistant to Rev. William J. Horstmann, whom he succeeded as pastor, February, 1843. In the summer of 1848 he was appointed pastor of Fort Jennings, where he remained till his death, September 20, 1860. His remains are buried at Fort Jennings. Though an invalid (epileptic) for many years of his priesthood, he did much for religion. Under his direction churches were built in Glandorf and Fort Jennings, the second in each place.

28. BORGESS, Rev. Otto H., was born in Westphalia, Germany, January 12, 1805; ordained in Muenster, 1830; came to this country in 1832; was in the Diocese of Cleveland from 1862 to February, 1863, as pastor of St. Clement's,

Navarre. Returned to Europe and died at Steinerberg, Switzerland, January 11, 1876.

29. BOURJADE, Rev. Julian, a native of the Diocese of St. Flour, France, came to Cleveland in September, 1853, and was ordained by Bishop Rappe a few months later. From Fremont he attended the stations of La Prairie and Toussaint (1853-56). His next charge was Providence, where he resided from 1856 to February, 1857, meanwhile attending St. Mary's Corners for a few months. He had been ailing of consumption for some time and was ordered to Cleveland, where he died in the Bishop's house, March 8th, 1857, aged about thirty. His remains are entombed in the cathedral basement. He was a very worthy priest.

30. BOWLES, Rev. Joseph D., was a native of the city of Limerick, Ireland, where he was born April 12, 1829. After finishing the collegiate course of studies in his native city he entered All Hallows', Dublin, where he studied philosophy and theology. March 26, 1853, he was ordained priest by Archbishop Cullen, in the cathedral of Dublin, for the Diocese of Glasgow. He remained, however, but a few months in the diocese for which he was ordained. December, 1853, he was received by Bishop Bayley into the Diocese of Newark, N. J., where he did pastoral work till January, 1868, when he became affiliated with the Diocese of Chicago. His first appointment there was as assistant, then as pastor *pro tem.* at Immaculate Conception church, Chicago. Later he was pastor at Hyde Park and Monmouth, May, 1869 to July, 1872. He was then received into the Diocese of Cleveland, and appointed pastor of Clyde, with charge of Green Spring as a mission, July, 1872 to January, 1875. Bellevue was his next appointment, to May, 1876. He was then transferred to Ravenna, where he remained till April, 1883, when he was assigned the pastorate of St. Ann's, Fremont. This charge he held till his death, July 4, 1887. He was identified with the Catholic Total Abstinence Union of Ohio as its president, and was for a number of years the treasurer of the National

Total Abstinence Union. His remains are buried at Washington, D. C.

31. BRAUN, Rev. Julian von, born and ordained in Germany, was received into the Diocese of Cleveland, September, 1851; had charge of St. Mary's congregation, Massillon, till 1852, meanwhile attending Bethlehem (Navarre). He died of cholera, August 2, 1852, at Massillon, where his remains repose.

32. BREDEICK, Rev. John Otto, a native of Westphalia, was born at Verl, January 23, 1789. After the usual collegiate and theological course of studies he was ordained at Osnabrueck, Hanover, in 1822. For twenty-two years he held various ecclesiastical positions in his native country, notably that of a member of the Cathedral Chapter at Osnabrueck. After some deliberation he resolved to devote himself to the American mission. For this purpose he came to the United States in 1844, and chose Northern Ohio as his future field of labor. He brought with him a few sturdy Westphalians and some means. With the latter he purchased large tracts of government land in "Section Ten," on a portion of which he established the present flourishing town of Delphos. There also he formed the nucleus of St. John's congregation, building its first church and pastoral residence at his own expense. Much of the prosperity of the town and congregation must be credited to his zeal, prudence and generosity. He shared privations and hardships with the "settlers," and at his death, August 19, 1858, had the satisfaction to see his long, laborious work crowned with success. He also organized and attended the congregation of Ottoville (1848-58). During the time of his pastorate at Delphos and Ottoville he not only refused to accept the salary to which he was entitled, but gave largely of his purse to support the churches and the schools built and established by him. He also gave to each of these places valuable real estate for the same purpose. St. John's congregation, Delphos, is indebted to Father Bredeick for the finest and largest church property

in the Diocese of Cleveland. Though long dead, he lives in the memory of a grateful people for whom, to this day, the name of "Father Bredeick" is a household word.

33. BREHM, Rev. Fidelis, a Swiss, was born at Butekon, Canton Aargau. He was received into the Diocese of Cleveland in 1870, and appointed pastor of Landeck, which charge he held till 1878. From Landeck he also attended Spencerville (1871-77.) During his absence in Europe on a vacation, (1876,) the pastoral residence at Landeck was destroyed by fire, entailing a loss of his library and personal effects. In 1878 he left the diocese with a Catholic colony, for Arkansas. His project there failed of success, but Bishop Gilmour declining to receive him back he returned to Europe, in 1879, where in his native country he is pastor of Stetten.

34. BREYMANN, Rev. Francis (Jesuit), was born at Ascheberg, Diocese of Muenster, Westphalia, September 16, 1836; made his studies at the Gymnasium of Muenster and with the Jesuits; was ordained for them by Cardinal Melchers, Archbishop of Cologne, September 13, 1868. He came to this country in 1869, and was stationed at St. Michael's, Buffalo, till 1871. He was then sent to St. Mary's Seminary, Cleveland, as professor of moral theology, remaining till 1872; was recalled to Buffalo, remaining there till 1875. He was next on the mission in the Diocese of St. Paul, till 1880. His next appointment was as assistant at St. Mary's, Toledo, till July, 1885, when he was transferred to Buffalo. In 1889 he was sent to Prairie du Chien, Wis., where he now resides.

35. BRENNAN, Rev. George H., was born in county Roscommon, Ireland. He was ordained by Bishop Rappe in April, 1852. His first charge was Doylestown and Wooster, May, 1852, to January, 1854. He was then appointed resident pastor of Wooster, remaining till 1856. From Wooster he attended Ashland, Crestline and Mansfield as missions. In 1856 he left the diocese and was successively connected with the Dioceses of Milwaukee, Dubuque and Boston. He was

next affiliated with the Diocese of Springfield, Mass., from 1870 till 1874, when he returned to Ireland. He now resides in Dublin.

36. BROWN, Rev. Michael Bernard, was born May 20, 1840, at Beckmantown, Clinton county, New York; made his ecclesiastical studies at the seminary in Cleveland, and in Notre Dame University, Indiana. He was ordained by Bishop Luers for the Society of the Holy Cross, Notre Dame, Indiana, June 10, 1867. He remained with the society till August, 1876. From that time till August, 1883, he was on the mission in the Diocese of Cleveland, viz.: assistant at St. Columba's, Youngstown, till July, 1877; pastor of Crestline to March, 1881; again assistant at St. Columba's, Youngstown, till December, 1881. He then had temporary charge of St. Joseph's, Youngstown, till March, 1882. His next appointment was Wellsville, where he remained till August, 1883. Between 1883 and 1888 he was on the mission in the Dioceses of Mobile and Cincinnati, in the former, however, but a short time. His last appointment was as pastor of St. Paris, Champaign county, Ohio, where he died suddenly, September 19, 1888. He was a facile writer, a good pulpit orator, and a man of scholarly attainments.

37. BROWN, Rev. Patrick Henry, was born at Sherrington, Canada, December 21, 1834; ordained by Bishop Rappe, June 30, 1861; appointed pastor of Hudson the following month, attending as missions Ravenna and Kent. In the latter place he built the present church. In 1862 he was stationed at Ravenna, where he remained till August, 1872, meanwhile (1862-67) attending Kent. His next and last charge was St. Columba's, Youngstown. He resigned this pastorate July, 1877, owing to protracted illness; was brought to Charity Hospital, Cleveland, where, after nearly a year of suffering, he died September 26, 1878.

38. BRUEGGEMANN, Rev. Eustace (Franciscan), was born at Werl, Westphalia, April 2, 1830; ordained March 17, 1866;

in the United States since October, 1869; was in the Diocese of Cleveland as superior of Franciscan Monastery, Cleveland, from 1879 to 1882, attending Independence and Parma as missions from January to July, 1881. Is at present in the Diocese of St. Louis, Mo.

39. BRUNNER, Very Rev. Francis Salesius (Sanguinist), was born in Switzerland, January 19, 1795, and ordained in March, 1819. He was the founder and Provincial of the Sanguinist Society in America, and with a band of faithful co-laborers took charge of Peru and surrounding missions, January, 1844. He established a Sanguinist Convent at Thompson (1844), one at New Riegel (1845), and in 1848 a third one of the same society at Glandorf. He and his faithful followers deserve well of the Catholics of the Diocese of Cleveland. Their work has been unostentatious, but none the less successful and lasting. He was in Northern Ohio till 1858, when he went to Europe. He died at Schellenberg, in the Principality of Lichtenstein, Austria, December 29, 1859. Father Brunner was a saintly priest and a wise and prudent superior.

40. BUCHHOLZ, Rev. Lucius (Franciscan), was born at Dorsten, Prussia, Diocese of Muenster, April 3, 1838; ordained August 16, 1868; in Cleveland Monastery from 1869 to 1871

41. BYRNE, Rev. Michael Ambrose, was born, 1821, near Stranorlar, county Donegal, Ireland; came to the United States at the age of 17. A few years later he entered Mt. St. Mary's College, Emmittsburg, Md., and finished his studies at Cincinnati where he was ordained by Bishop Purcell, November 1, 1845. January, 1846, he was sent to Cleveland as assistant to Rev. P. McLaughlin. From Cleveland he also attended Avon, Painesville and South Thompson. In 1847 he returned to Cincinnati and was appointed first resident pastor of All Saints' church, Fulton, then a suburb of Cincinnati, where he died of cholera August 22, 1850.

42. BYRNE, Rev. Robert Alexis, brother to Rev. Michael A. Byrne, was born near Stranorlar, county Donegal, Ireland,

in 1828; made part of his studies for the ministry in Londonderry (Ireland), Emmittsburg and Fordham. He was ordained by Archbishop Hughes in 1856. Remained in the Diocese of New York till 1873, when he was received by Bishop Gilmour and sent to Toledo. There he organized the present Good Shepherd congregation, whose church was built under his direction. His health failing, he resigned this charge March 20, 1875, and returned to his home in Ireland, where he died August 23d, of the same year.

43. CAMPION, V. Rev. Augustine S., was born at Henin-Lietard, pas-de-Calais, France, February 18, 1811. After completing his studies for the ministry at the seminary of Arras, France, he was ordained by Bishop d'Auvergne, December 18, 1834. He did pastoral duty in his native country till 1848, when he came to Cleveland, November of same year. On his arrival Bishop Rappe sent him to Fremont as assistant to Rev. L. Nightingale, pastor of St. Ann's. From Fremont he attended a number of smaller missions in the vicinity, viz.: Toussaint, LaPrairie, etc. In 1849 he was sent to Wooster, whence he also attended French Settlement and Doylestown. In the last mentioned place he built the church, since replaced by the present handsome structure. In 1851 he was given the pastoral charge of St. John's, Canton, and attended Canal Fulton and Massillon as missions. November, 1853, he was called to the cathedral and made vicar-general. His next and last appointment in this diocese was the pastorate of St. Francis de Sales', Toledo, November, 1854, to May, 1856. He then left the diocese to join the Sulpitians at Montreal, where he remained till his death, June 10, 1886. He had been ill for nearly two years previous to his demise and was unable to do duty. He bore his sufferings with Christian patience till his Master's summons came. While pastor of St. Francis de Sales', Toledo, he arranged for the opening of an orphan asylum in that city. At his earnest request the Mother Superioress of the Grey Nuns at Montreal sent four of these sisters, October, 1855, to open and take charge of the asylum. Before Father Campion left, in 1856, he saw the good work of

these sisters fully and practically appreciated by the citizens of Toledo. Father Campion was a most devoted priest, charitable, kind-hearted and full of zeal for religion.

44. CAPEDER, Rev. Peter Anthony (Sanguinist), was born at Lumbrein, Canton Graubuendten, Switzerland, January 1, 1817. After completing his studies at Loewenburg, Switzerland, he was ordained at Feldkirch, Austria, by Bishop George Pruenster, May 11, 1843. He came to this country in 1844, with the first band of Sanguinist Fathers. From 1844 to 1888 he was stationed in and outside the Diocese of Cleveland, in places committed to the Sanguinists; he shared the hardships of the pioneer priest. He was in the Diocese of Cleveland from 1844–57; 1865–70; 1872–80; 1884, to May, 1886, with Peru, Thompson, New Riegel, Tiffin, Liverpool and Glandorf as the several fields of his pastoral work. In November, 1887, he was again sent by his superior to Thompson, where he remained till his sudden death, October 2, 1888. During the last few years of his life he did no pastoral work, owing to physical inability, his hearing and memory having been seriously impaired. "Father Peter Anthony," as he was familiarly called, was truly a priest—a man without guile. Although neither a brilliant scholar nor an eloquent preacher his daily life was an edifying sermon and a practical illustration of humility and simplicity. Full of sunshine in his character he won all who had any intercourse with him, by his kindly words, genial humor and sparkling wit.

45. CARABIN, Rev. A., was born in France, 1807, and there educated; ordained by Bishop Fenwick in 1831; received into the Diocese of Cleveland, 1847, after having been on the missions of Upper Michigan for a number of years. Bishop Rappe sent him to Peru, where he remained from December, 1847, to September, 1850. His next charge was St. Ann's, Fremont, till 1852, when he was stricken with paralysis. He rallied for a short time sufficiently to do pastoral duty at St. Peter's, Canton, February to July, 1853; was then obliged to give up all work, and for twenty years was a patient sufferer.

Ursuline Convent and Academy, Cleveland, O.

The Sisters of Charity of St. Vincent's Asylum, Cleveland, had charge of him for many years, and he died there August 1, 1873. His remains are interred in St. John's cemetery, Cleveland.

46. CARAHER, Rev. Bernard, born, educated and ordained in Ireland, was received by Bishop Rappe, November, 1853. Till August, 1854, he was connected with the cathedral. He was next appointed pastor of St. John's, Canton, residing there from December, 1854, till his death, on Good Friday, (April 10,) 1857. From Canton he also attended, monthly, St. Joseph's, Massillon.

47. CARON, Very Rev. Alexis, was born at Bilquem, near St. Omer, Diocese of Arras, France, December 8, 1802. After finishing the collegiate course at the "*petite seminaire*" of St. Omer, he began to study theology under the direction of a venerable priest, Rev. M. Delahage, who, on his return from exile, held a professor's chair in this preparatory seminary. On leaving St. Omer, Father Caron entered the society of the "*Missionnaires de France*," (known now as that of the "Fathers of Mercy,") the superior of which was the celebrated Abbe Ranyan. In this society Father Caron was raised to the dignity of the priesthood in the year 1827. Meanwhile the revolution of 1840 broke out, and the house of these good fathers, like many other religious institutions, was pillaged and plundered. The inmates were constrained to abandon their dwelling in order to avoid death. Father Caron made his escape in the disguise of a peasant. Shortly after this event the Bishop of Arras, Mgr. de la Tour d'Auvergne, appointed him assistant priest at Flechin, a small parish in the Canton of Fauquemberg. Here, as elsewhere, his pastoral zeal, and his charity toward the poor endeared him to all his parishioners. From Flechin Father Caron was sent to Wimille as second assistant to Rev. Father Elin. In the fall of 1848 an ever all-ruling Providence brought about for him the possibility of realizing a desire which he had long formed—that of devoting himself to the American missions.

In company with Father Campion he offered his priestly services to Bishop Rappe and was gladly welcomed and received by him. He arrived in Cleveland November, 1848, and soon after was appointed successor to Father de Goesbriand, as superior of the diocesan seminary. This position he held till June, 1856, when Bishop Rappe granted him a six months' leave of absence to visit his native France. He returned in January, 1857, when he was appointed pastor of Holy Angels' church, Sandusky, where he remained till May, 1861. He then went to Painesville to reside with Father Coquerelle, and, although assigned no regular duty from the time he left Sandusky, because of his impaired health, yet he volunteered to attend Ashtabula (1861-62.) Repeatedly, during Bishop Rappe's visits to Europe, 1862–1867, and from November, 1869 to August, 1870, Father Caron held the responsible position of Administrator of the diocese. He was also one of Bishop Rappe's vicars-general for about twenty years. From 1869 till his death, December 21, 1873, he resided at Charity Hospital, where, as long as his illness (cancer) permitted, he acted as chaplain. His remains are buried in St. John's cemetery, Cleveland, a very handsome monument, erected by his clerical friends, marking his grave, as well as that of Very Rev. James Conlan and Rev. John Dillon, both of whose remains are inclosed in the same coffin.

48. CARROLL, Rev. Thomas, was born at Ardagh, Ireland, August 17, 1833; educated at Notre Dame, Ind., and ordained by Bishop Luers for the Holy Cross Society in 1858. He left the society, 1863, on account of ill health. January, 1864, he was received into the Diocese of Cleveland and appointed assistant at the cathedral. He remained till October, 1867, when he was received into the Diocese of Erie where he has been since. He is now stationed at Oil City, Penn.

49. CEBULLA, Rev. Sebastian (Franciscan), was born March 10, 1838, in Silesia; ordained March 12, 1869; in the Franciscan Monastery of Cleveland from 1883 to 1884. He is now stationed in the Diocese of Belleville, Ill.

50. CHERRIER, Rev. Leo (Basilian), was born at Dundas, Ont., Canada, October 28, 1834; educated at St. Michael's College, Toronto, and there ordained by Bishop Lynch, March 25, 1864; was in the Diocese of Cleveland from 1872 to 1873 as professor at St. Louis' College, Louisville, Ohio; is now in the Diocese of Hamilton, Ont.

51. CHRISTOPHORY, Rev. Jacob, a native of Luxemburg, was born at Merl, April 26, 1848; was trained for the priesthood in the city of Luxemburg, and for five years in the diocesan seminary at Cleveland, where he was ordained by Bishop Gilmour, June 15, 1878. North Ridge, with the mission of Mud Creek, was his first appointment, July, 1878, to June, 1881. From latter date till September, 1887, he was resident pastor of St. Patrick's Settlement, with charge of Liberty as a mission. From this position he was removed to Medina, with charge of the missions of French Settlement, Sterling and Wadsworth, but remained only four months. His last appointment in this diocese was as assistant at St. Peter's, Cleveland, till July, 1888, when he was received into the Diocese of Leavenworth, where he now is.

52. CLEMENT, Rev. Julius, a native of France, was ordained there about 1850. He was received by Bishop Rappe July, 1864, and appointed one of the professors at St. Mary's Seminary, Cleveland, and in 1866, superior at the college at Louisville, O., where he remained till July, 1867. He was then received into the Diocese of Vincennes, where he died, as pastor of Green Castle, Ind., in October, 1871.

53. COADY, Rev. Peter, was born in Bally-Callan, county Kilkenny, Ireland; came to the Diocese of Cleveland from Canada, December, 1870; was at St. Mary's Seminary for a few months, when he was appointed pastor of South Thompson, with charge of Jefferson as a mission. He remained there from March, 1871, till some time in 1872, when he left the diocese.

54. COLLINS, Very Rev. Edward Timothy, a native of Philadelphia, Pa., was born February 26, 1802; studied for the

ministry at Mt. St. Mary's Seminary, Emmittsburg, Md.; was ordained by Bishop Kenrick, July 1, 1832, for the Diocese of Cincinnati, where he was stationed at the cathedral. May, 1838, Bishop Purcell appointed him as one of his vicars-general. Between 1837 and 1839 he visited the missions along the Miami canal, from Cincinnati as far up as Toledo, making the entire journey on horseback. He also attended missions in Columbiana county (Dungannon, etc.,) about 1834. Father Collins was a scholarly man and a keen judge of books, of which he had a very fine and large collection, covering every branch of ecclesiastical lore. He gave his library to Mt. St. Mary's Seminary. He was a most worthy priest, genial and companionable, without ever forgetting what he owed his priestly dignity. He died at Cincinnati, August 26, 1865.

55. CONLAN, Very Rev. James, was born at Mohill, county Leitrim, Ireland, August 22, 1801; made his course of studies in Ireland, and at Cincinnati, where he was ordained by Bishop Purcell, September 20, 1834. His first appointment was as assistant to the Rev. James Reid, pastor of St. Martin's, Brown county, Ohio. There he remained for a few months, when he was appointed pastor of Steubenville, whence he attended the stations and missions located in the counties of Columbiana, Mahoning, Carroll, Jefferson and the eastern portion of Stark. He resided at Steubenville from 1834 to 1842, and then removed to St. Paul's, near the present village of Dungannon, Columbiana county. A journey of fifty or a hundred miles to say Mass or attend a sick-call was among the ordinary occurrences of his missionary life. Neither distance nor hardship prevented him from cheerfully responding to any demand made on him for priestly aid. October, 1849, he was called to Cleveland, and for four years lived with the Bishop, attending the cathedral. November, 1853, he was appointed first resident pastor of St. Patrick's, Cleveland, his last charge. For many years he also held the position of vicar-general under Bishop Rappe, till the latter's resignation. In 1860, during the Bishop's absence in Europe, he was administrator of the diocese. Under his direction old St.

Patrick's was enlarged and completed, two schools were built, and the present handsome church begun and brought under roof. He died at Charity Hospital, March 5, 1875, full of years and merits. He was one of God's noblemen, a true priest, loved and respected by all who knew him. His remains rest in St. John's cemetery, Cleveland, with those of the Rev. John Dillon, with whom he had been ordained.

56. CONLAN, Rev. James V., was born at Mohill, county Leitrim, Ireland, September 27, 1820; made his ecclesiastical studies at Cincinnati; was ordained in (old) St. Vincent's church, Akron, Ohio, by Bishop Purcell, September 5, 1847, five weeks before the consecration of Father Rappe as first Bishop of Cleveland, and was appointed assistant to Rev. James Conlan at Dungannon. "Father Vincent" as he was called, to distinguish him from his cousin, Very Rev. James Conlan, was next placed in charge of St. John's church, Canton, August 1848; remained there till January, 1851, when he was appointed pastor of Holy Angels', Sandusky. December, 1855, he was assigned as assistant to Rev. James Conlan, at St. Patrick's, Cleveland, where they zealously and successfully labored together till March 5, 1875, when the latter died. Father Vincent succeeded as pastor of St. Patrick's. August, 1877, he resigned this charge and took the pastorate of St. Ann's, Fremont. There he remained till January 15, 1883. Owing to protracted illness, which prevented him from doing pastoral duty he resigned and went to Charity Hospital, Cleveland, where he died March 15, 1883. His remains are buried in St. John's cemetery, Cleveland. He was a genial, kind-hearted priest.

57. CONLAN, Rev. Thomas J., was born in Summitville, Columbiana county, Ohio, February 6, 1846; commenced his ecclesiastical studies in St. John's College, formerly existing in Cleveland; finished them in St. Mary's Seminary, Lake street; was ordained by Bishop Rappe, March 7, 1869. For a while he was a professor in the diocesan seminary; then (1870) he was transferred to the cathedral as assistant. In

1873 he accepted the position of secretary to Bishop Gilmour, but from 1874, owing to ill health, was unable to render much service either in this capacity, or while having charge at the cathedral. He made every effort to recuperate his fast waning strength, traveling extensively for his health, but all to no purpose. For five years he was a patient sufferer from consumption, till finally death relieved him August 20, 1879. He died at his father's residence in Cleveland. His remains are buried in St. John's cemetery, Cleveland, near those of his uncle, the Very Rev. James Conlan. He was of a kind, gentle nature, gifted, and thoroughly a priest. "Father Tom," though no more among the living, lives in the memory of those with whom and for whom he labored, as one of God's chosen ministers, and as a model ecclesiastic.

58. COPPINGER, Rev. Thomas J. J., was born and educated in Ireland (no record of date or place of birth). As a young man he was in the British army; then came to the United States, and was ordained by Bishop Purcell at Cincinnati, October 21, 1854, and appointed assistant at the cathedral. Left the Diocese of Cincinnati and came to Cleveland, September, 1862, and was an assistant at cathedral till July, 1863. He then enlisted in the army, was wounded in the battle of Winchester, and then discharged. Returned to Ireland, where he remained but a short time; then went to England, and there entered a Cistercian Monastery. A few months later he again returned to his native diocese, Cloyne, where, after doing pastoral duty for a short time, he died about 1874.

59. COQUERELLE, Rev. Charles M., born at Etaples, Diocese of Arras, France, May 31, 1804, was ordained in 1833; came to Cleveland August, 1850; was appointed resident pastor of Port Clinton and thence attended Marblehead, Toussaint and La Prairie. After nearly two years of laborious mission work there, he was appointed pastor of Painesville in the latter part of 1852. There he remained till 1869, when he resigned his pastorate on account of deafness and old age.

Shortly after his resignation he returned to France where he died September 5th, 1880.

60. COUILLARD, Rev. J. B., born and ordained in Canada; was received into the diocese by Bishop Rappe in 1869; assistant to Rev. F. M. Boff at St. Francis' church, Toledo, October, 1869, till February, 1871, when he left the Diocese of Cleveland. He was then received into the Diocese of Springfield, where he died in 1874.

61. CULLEN, Rev. James, was born in Wexford, Ireland, June 29, 1814. Made his collegiate studies in Ireland; entered Mt. St. Mary's Seminary, Emmittsburg, Md., and there studied philosophy and theology, meanwhile, (for three years), teaching the collegians the higher mathematics, in which branch he was quite proficient. He was ordained for the Diocese of Philadelphia by Bishop Kenrick, July 19, 1847. He remained in that diocese, holding various positions, till 1870, when he went to Albany. Two years later he was received by Bishop Gilmour, who appointed him resident pastor of East Liverpool, with charge of Wellsville as a mission. In 1875 he was transferred to Vermillion, and in 1878 to Olmsted. July, 1882, he was appointed assistant at Sts. Philip and James' church, Canal Fulton. Six months later he was obliged to give up all pastoral work owing to ill health and failing memory, the latter often a blank at times. Since January, 1883, he has been on the retired list. September, 1888, he went to Chicago to reside with his relatives, and has remained there since.

62. CZAKERT, Rev. Peter (Redemptorist), was born December 12, 1808, in Bohemia. In his twenty-fourth year he joined the Redemptorists; was ordained January 12, 1834, and soon after came to the United States. He was sent to Northern Ohio, (Peru, Huron county), in 1835, and remained till 1839, when he returned to Baltimore. In 1844 he was appointed Provincial of the Redemptorists in this country, retaining this position till 1847, when he was sent to Lafayette city, near New Orleans, where he died September 2, 1848. He was a model priest and full of missionary zeal.

63. DALEY, Rev. Cornelius, born in county Cork, Ireland, was ordained by Bishop Purcell, March 2, 1844. For nearly a year he labored on the mission in Southern Ohio. He was then appointed first resident pastor of St. Vincent's, Akron, (1845-46). Meanwhile he also attended Doylestown, whither he was transferred, February, 1846. He also attended Youngstown (1845). When the Diocese of Cleveland was organized (October, 1847), he affiliated with the Diocese of Cincinnati, where he remained till his death, at Fayetteville, Brown county, January 24, 1876.

64. D'ARCY, Rev. Louis Florence, was born and educated in France (Diocese of Arras) ; came to Cleveland in August, 1850; was ordained by Bishop Rappe, April 2, 1851; was assistant at the cathedral till September, 1851, when he was appointed pastor of Louisville, remaining till May, 1854. He then went to France for the benefit of his health, returning in 1856. He again had charge of Louisville congregation, till 1861, when he left the Diocese of Cleveland. Whilst at Louisville he also attended Strasburg and there built the present (second) church. Between 1861 and 1866 he labored in the Dioceses of Mobile and Cincinnati, and for a short time he was also at Notre Dame, Ind. In 1866 he was again received by Bishop Rappe and appointed pastor of St. Ann's, Fremont, but remained in charge only till July, 1867, when he returned to France, where he died a few years later.

65. DAVY, Rev. —, for a few months pastor of Elmore (1872); meanwhile attended the missions of Genoa and Woodville. No other record of him.

66. DEGOESBRIAND, Rt. Rev. Louis M. J., the present Bishop of Burlington, was born at St. Urbain, Finistere, France, August 4, 1816; made his ecclesiastical studies at Point-Croix, Guimper, in his native diocese, and at St. Sulpice, Paris. He was ordained at Paris, July 13, 1840, by Bishop Rosati, of St. Louis, Mo., then in Europe on a visit. He came to Ohio in 1840 and was appointed successor to Rev.

M. Wuerz, as the second resident pastor of Louisville, where he remained from October, 1840 to January, 1846. He was then sent as assistant to Father Rappe, who had charge of Toledo and the "Maumee" section of northwestern Ohio, and with whom he shared the hardships and privations of that extensive and uninviting mission. There he remained till January, 1848, when Bishop Rappe appointed him vicar-general, with residence at Cleveland. This office he held till he was consecrated first Bishop of Burlington, October 30, 1853, which responsible and important dignity he still holds, and with eminent success.

67. DELBAERE, Rev. Polydore Henry, born at Ingoyghem, West Flanders, Belgium, December 21, 1838; made his studies for the ministry in Flanders and at the University of Louvain; was ordained by Cardinal Stercks, Archbishop of Mechlin, May 21, 1864; was in the Diocese of Detroit for some years; received by Bishop Gilmour, *ad interim*, February, 1875, and appointed pastor of Archbold and missions. April, 1877, he was sent to Antwerp with charge of a number of missions. April, 1879, he left the diocese, and was received into the Diocese of Peoria, where he now is.

68. DELHEZ, Rev. Francis X. (Jesuit), was born at Aix-la-Chapelle, Diocese of Cologne, October 6, 1837; ordained August 24, 1869; in this country since September, 1869; was assistant at St. Mary's, Toledo, from 1870 to 1871, and again from 1873 to 1874. He is now in the Diocese of Buffalo.

69. DENENY, Rev. Thomas, was born at Maghera, county Cavan, Ireland, January 9, 1849; ordained by Bishop Hogan at St. Joseph, Mo., September 9, 1874; was received into the Diocese of Cleveland, *pro tempore*, September, 1887, and had charge of Wellington, with the mission of New London, till June, 1889, when through illness he was obliged to give up pastoral duty and go to St. Joseph's Retreat, near Detroit where he has been since, for treatment.

70. DE RAYMACHER, Rev. Vincent (Dominican), a native of Belgium, was ordained by Bishop Fenwick in 1822. He was stationed at Cincinnati for a short time and then sent to the Dominican Convent near Somerset, Perry county, whence he attended the stations and missions in Stark and Columbiana counties between 1823 and 1835. He was resident pastor of St. John's, Canton, in 1835. Returned to Belgium where he died in 1870, aged 72 years.

71. DICKMANN, Rev. Bernard (Sanguinist), was born at Minster, Auglaize county, O., in 1839; educated at Carthagena, Mercer county, Ohio; ordained at Minster, Ohio, by Bishop Rosecrans, for the Sanguinists, August 17, 1862; was pastor at Glandorf from April, 1874, to May, 1881, where he also directed the building of the present beautiful church. In 1881 he was sent by his superior to California; is now pastor of Sacred Heart Church, Sedalia, Mo.

72. DICKNEITE, Rev. Raynerius (Franciscan), was born at Bokel, near Rietberg, Westphalia, November 11, 1832; in this country since November, 1859; ordained July 2, 1860; member of Franciscan Monastery, Cleveland, from 1870 to 1874; had charge of Independence from 1871 to 1873. At present he is stationed in the Diocese of Monterey, Cal.

73. DILLON, Rev. John, was born in Drumcunny, county Leitrim, Ireland, in 1807. He was ordained in Cincinnati with Very Rev. James Conlan, by Bishop Purcell, September 20, 1834. He was sent to Cleveland in 1835 as the first resident priest, where also he organized the first congregation, the members of which had as their first place of worship Judge Underhill's office, a small room on Spring street; next on Main street hill, opposite Union Lane; then on Prospect street, in "Farmer's Hall," in the Mechanics' block, which is now the Prospect house. He raised a collection for the erection of a church on the Flats, but had not the happiness to begin the work. He died of bilious fever, October 16, 1836. Rev. Father Badin, the pioneer priest of Kentucky, attended

him in his last illness. His remains, at first interred in the Erie Street cemetery, were transferred to the cathedral shortly after its completion in 1852, and entombed in one of the vaults beneath the main altar. In compliance with the dying request of Very Rev. James Conlan, whose intimate friend and class-mate he had been, they were then (March, 1875) taken to St. John's cemetery, Cleveland—what little remained of them—and enclosed in the same coffin with his, the same monument marking their joint grave. But a little more than two years a priest, Father Dillon labored with much success, and endeared himself to all who knew him. He was talented, energetic, pious, and a pulpit orator of far more than ordinary force and ability. His zeal for God's cause was bounded only by his physical strength. He was held in the highest esteem by the citizens of Cleveland, irrespective of creed.

74. DOEBBING, Rev. Bernard (Franciscan), was born at Muenster, Westphalia, in 1855; was ordained June 1, 1879; professor of philosophy at St. Mary's Seminary, Cleveland, and member of Franciscan Monastery, same city, from February, 1880 to July 1881. He is now in Rome, Italy, engaged as professor.

75. DOHERTY, Rev. John J., was born at Glen of Aherlow, county Tipperary, Ireland, November 20, 1817; studied for the priesthood at Mt. St. Mary's Seminary, Emmittsburg, Md.; was ordained by Bishop Purcell, at Cincinnati, April 23, 1843. His first appointment was as assistant at the cathedral, Cincinnati, till February, 1844; was then transferred to Massillon, where he built the first (stone) church, used by St. Mary's congregation. He remained till August of same year, attending during this time, and alternately with Rev. M. Wuerz, the mission of Bethlehem (Navarre). His next appointment was to the pastorate of St. John's, Canton, which he retained till he left the diocese, August, 1848. From Canton he attended several missions, among which were Canal Fulton, and Canal Dover. He is at present pastor of St. John's, Honesdale, Pa., Diocese of Scranton, where he has been for many years.

76. DOLWECK, Rev. John Peter, was born at Benning, Diocese of Metz, Lorraine, August 26, 1828. He studied for the priesthood at Metz and in St. Mary's Seminary, Cleveland, and was ordained by Bishop Rappe, December 11, 1853. He was pastor of St. Mary's, Sandusky, from December, 1853, till April, 1855; St. Alphonse's, Peru, Huron county, till August, 1861, with charge of St. Peter's, Norwalk, from September, 1860; Berwick, from September, 1861, till April, 1862. Then he was transferred to Liverpool, Medina county, where he remained till January, 1864. He then left the diocese to join the Benedictines, of whose Order he has been a member ever since. He was Prior at Chicago for some years. Is now in the Diocese of Monterey, Cal.

77. DREES, Very Rev. Henry Joseph (Sanguinist), was born at Garell, Oldenburg, Germany, March 5, 1830; in America since 1833; ordained November 7, 1861; was in this diocese as pastor of New Riegel, from September, 1864, to August, 1866. At present he is the Provincial of the Sanguinists in the United States, with residence at Carthagena, Mercer county, Ohio.

78. DROESSLER, Rev. Dominic (Franciscan), was born in the Diocese of Paderborn, Prussia, August 2, 1843; came to the United States, June, 1862; ordained January 13, 1867; belonged to the Franciscan Monastery, Cleveland, from 1868 to 1871; and again from January, 1873, to April, 1875; had charge of Independence from 1868 to 1869. Now lives in Germany.

79. DROLSHAGEN, Rev. Gustave, was received by Bishop Rappe, in 1868; after a short stay at Antwerp, Paulding county, he was appointed pastor of Shelby Settlement, January, 1870, to September, 1872; then of St. Peter's, Norwalk, till 1874, during which year he left the diocese and went to Tennessee. No other record of him.

80. DRUON, Very Rev. Zephyrin, was born at Ven-din-

le-Viel, Pas-de-Calais, France, March 14, 1830; made his studies for the ministry at Arras, France, in St. Mary's Seminary, Cleveland, and St. Sulpice, Paris; was ordained in France by Bishop Beauvais, July 3, 1853; returned to Cleveland and was assistant at the cathedral from September to December, 1853, when he affiliated with the Diocese of Burlington, Vt., where he has been since. For many years he has been one of Bishop de Goesbriand's vicars-general; also pastor of Immaculate Conception church, St. Albans, Vt., where he is at present stationed.

81. EBERSCHWEILER, Rev. Fridolin (Jesuit), was born at Maxweiler, Diocese of Treves, Rhenish-Prussia, July 19, 1839; ordained July 15, 1870; came to this country in 1870; was professor at St. Mary's Seminary, Cleveland, from 1871 to 1873; assistant at St. Mary's church, Toledo, from 1873 to 1881, and at St. Mary's, Cleveland, from 1881 to 1882. He was then sent to Montana, where he has been since on the mission.

82. EISENRING, Rev. Joseph Thomas (Sanguinist), was born at Mosnang, Canton St. Gallen, Switzerland, November 1, 1844; was educated at St. Gallen, Switzerland, and at Carthagena, Mercer county, Ohio. He was ordained for the Sanguinists by Archbishop Purcell, August 15, 1873; was in the Diocese of Cleveland, from January, 1876 to August, 1878, as pastor of St. Boniface's church, and local superior of convent, New Riegel. During the time he was pastor there the present beautiful church (third) was built. In 1878 he was sent to Europe; returned October, 1882. He is now stationed in the Diocese of Ft. Wayne, Ind.

83. EISENRING, Rev. Sebastian (Sanguinist), was born at Waldkirchen, Switzerland, May 10, 1852. He was ordained for the Sanguinists by Archbishop Purcell, March 17, 1878; appointed assistant at St. John's, Glandorf, where he died of consumption, July 30, 1880, aged 28 years.

84. ENGELHARD, Rev. Zephyrin (Franciscan), was born at Bilshausen, Westphalia, November 13, 1851; came to the United States in 1852; ordained June 18, 1878; in Franciscan Monastery, Cleveland, from 1879 to 1880. He is now in the Diocese of San Francisco, Cal.

85. EVRARD, Rev. Charles, was born in the city of Metz, Lorraine, June 13, 1822. He was educated for the ministry at Versailles, where also he was ordained by Mgr. Gross, Bishop of Versailles. June 22, 1845. After five years' service as chaplain and parish priest in France, he came to Cleveland, August, 1850. September 15, the same year, he was sent to Peru, Huron county, where under his direction the present church and pastoral residence were built. January 6, 1854, he was assigned to St. Mary's, Toledo. There he built the present church, since enlarged. He held this charge till September 29, 1867, when Bishop Rappe appointed him pastor of Fort Jennings. This position he declined and remained without pastoral charge till August 1, 1868, when he again accepted the pastorate of Peru. He held this charge till November 30, 1873, when Bishop Gilmour appointed him pastor of St. Joseph's, Tiffin, where he remained till his death, May 11, 1885. He was for many years a very active member of the Board of Infirm Priest's Fund, and was also a member of the Bishop's Council for some time. Father Evrard was a man of strong will, decided and clear views, and a ceaseless worker who knew not self. Wherever he labored his memory is cherished as that of a priest full of zeal for God's work and the good of souls.

86. FAHEY, Rev. Anthony (Dominican), a native of Ireland, was educated in Rome for the priesthood; came to the United States in December, 1834. He had pastoral charge of St. Paul's near Dungannon, between 1834 and 1835, and of St. John's, Canton, between 1836 and 1837. No other record of him.

87. FAHLE, Rev. Arsenius (Franciscan), was born at

Paderborn, Westphalia, September 23, 1843; ordained March 12, 1869; member of Franciscan Monastery, Cleveland, from 1880 to 1881. At present he is stationed in the Diocese of Kansas City, Mo.

88. FAHLE, Rev. Ewaldus (Franciscan), was born at Paderborn, Westphalia, August 20, 1848; studied for the ministry at Duesseldorf; was ordained at Paderborn by Bishop Martin in 1873; came to Franciscan Monastery, Cleveland, March, 1879, remaining till February, 1880. During this time he was professor of philosophy at St. Mary's Seminary, Cleveland. In 1880 he was sent by his superiors to Holland, where he is at present.

89. FAULHABER, Rev. Bonaventure (Franciscan), a native of Baden, was born March 28, 1842; made his ecclesiastical studies at Constance and Freiburg, Baden, and Teutopolis, Ill. He was ordained at St. Louis, Mo., for the Franciscans, by Rt. Rev. P. Ryan, January 6, 1873; was in the Franciscan Monastery, Cleveland, from July, 1873, to July, 1875, and from July, 1881, to January, 1887. While here he attended the mission of Independence, 1873-75; Parma from July, 1881, to January, 1887, when he was sent by his superiors to Nebraska, where he now is.

90. FERGUSON, Rev. Michael Joseph (Basilian), was born at Ontario, Canada, March 23, 1839; educated at St. Michael's College, Toronto; ordained by Bishop Lynch, October 23, 1861; in the Diocese of Cleveland from 1872 to 1873, as one of the professors at Louisville College. Returned to Canada, where he is now engaged as professor at Assumption College, Sandwich, Ontario.

91. FILIERE, Rev. Louis J., was born at Dohen, Pas-de-Calais, France, March 31, 1822. Studied for the priesthood at Arras, France, where he received part of Holy orders. He was ordained by Bishop Rappe, September 8, 1850; was pastor of St. John's, Defiance, November, 1850, to March, 1854; had charge of Providence till 1852, also of eighteen other mis-

sions and stations in Lucas, Henry, Wood, Paulding and Fulton counties, between 1850 and 1856. He was resident pastor of Providence from April, 1854, till December, 1856, with Archbold, Napoleon, Bryan, Stryker and Wauseon as missions. He next had charge of Berea, as resident pastor, from December, 1856, to February, 1876. From Berea he attended Rockport till 1866, and Olmsted till 1876. February, 1876, he resigned all pastoral charge and retired to Milton Centre, Wood county, Ohio, where he has been since.

92. FINUCAN, Rev. William J., a native of Toledo, Ohio, was born November 30, 1853. He began his ecclesiastical studies at St. Louis' College, Louisville, Stark county, and completed them in St. Mary's Seminary, Cleveland, where he was ordained by Bishop Gilmour June 15, 1878. Shortly after his ordination he was sent to Massillon to take temporary charge of St. Joseph's congregation during the absence of the pastor. November, 1878, he received the pastorate of St. Michael's, Kelley's Island and the mission of Put-in-Bay. July, 1880, he was transferred to Jefferson, whence he also attended Conneaut. This charge he held till March, 1881, when he was appointed pastor of Crestline, remaining till June, 1887. Owing to failing health he then asked to be removed to another place. Salem was his choice and there he was sent, with charge of East Palestine as a mission. But he was soon obliged to give up pastoral work because of protracted and serious illness. Resigning December, 1887, he received a leave of absence to spend the winter in a southern climate. A few months later he returned, but not improved. He retired to Toledo, remaining till his death, October 18, 1888. He was a man of more than ordinary ability, an excellent pulpit orator, and had the confidence of the people among whom he labored. His remains rest in Calvary cemetery, Toledo.

93. FITZGERALD, Rev. William J., was born in New York city August 7, 1853; educated at Toronto, Cincinnati, Montreal; finished his studies at St. Mary's Seminary, Cleve-

land. He was ordained by Bishop Gilmour, December 26, 1876; was appointed assistant at St. Malachy's, Cleveland, remaining till July, 1880. Then he received charge of St. Patrick's, Leetonia, where he began the erection of the present church, but did not live to see its completion. It pleased God to call this noble-hearted young priest after a brief illness, at a time when all, to human eye, was fair and promising to him. He died at his father's residence, Columbus, Ohio, March 22, 1882. His remains are buried in Cathedral cemetery, same city.

94. FLAMMANG, Rev. Nicholas, was born at Consdorf, Luxemburg, May 9, 1844. He came to Cleveland Seminary, March, 1866, and, after completing his theological studies, was ordained by Bishop Rappe, March 7, 1869. He had the following pastoral charges in the Diocese of Cleveland: Findlay, March, 1869, to August, 1870; Doylestown, to September, 1871; Avon, to August, 1872; New Bavaria, from February to July, 1873, when he left the diocese. He was for several years on the mission in Minnesota and Dakota, and from 1885 to the time of his death, was a member of the Benedictine Order. He died at Yankton, Dakota, February 10, 1887.

95. FLEISCH, Rev. George (Sanguinist), a native of Austria, was born at Goetzis, Tyrol, November 1, 1846; made his ecclesiastical studies at Feldkirch, Austria, and St. Charles' Seminary, Carthagena, Mercer county, Ohio; ordained at Cincinnati for the Sanguinists, by Archbishop Purcell, June 30, 1874; was in the Diocese of Cleveland as pastor of Big Spring, from December, 1876, to August, 1877. Since then he has had charge of missions in various dioceses, under direction of the Sanguinists. He is now chaplain of St. Johns' Hospital, New York city.

96. FLUM, Rev. Philip, born at Constance, Baden, in 1829; was ordained by Bishop Rappe, July, 1852. The pastorate of Maumee was his first appointment, 1852-54. There

he enlarged the church, bought in 1842 by Rev. A. Rappe; during this time also attended Providence. Between 1854 and 1855 he was superior of St. John's College, Cleveland. August, 1855, he was appointed pastor of Dungannon, remaining till May, 1856, when ill health obliged him to resign. He then left the diocese and went to Texas, where he died. Date of death not recorded. He was a fine linguist and a man of varied learning.

97. FOCHENKRESS, Rev. P. (Dominican), was stationed at Canton about 1836. No other record of him.

98. FOLEY, Rev. Philip, was born near Mallow, Ireland, about 1820, and was ordained by Bishop Purcell, March 2, 1844. His first charge in Northern Ohio and Diocese of Cleveland was at Massillon, 1846 to 1848, whence he attended Canal Fulton, also Wooster, where he built the first church. He was then transferred, February, 1848, to St. Francis', Toledo, where he remained till November, 1854, meanwhile attending New Bavaria (Poplar Ridge), 1849, St. John's, Defiance, till 1849; Six Mile Woods, 1848; St. Mary's Corners, 1853. He was then affiliated to the Diocese of Cincinnati, where he remained till 1857. Then he went to St. Louis, Mo., owing to ill health. He died there May 1, 1857. His remains rest in St. Francis de Sales' cemetery, Toledo.

99. FRAUENHOFER, Rev. Thomas, was born at Pfeffenhausen, Bavaria, December 6, 1817; ordained July 1, 1844; came to this country May, 1852; was in the Diocese of Chicago for some time (at McHenry, Ill.); was in the Diocese of Cleveland as pastor of French Creek from July 24, 1864, till January 20, 1868; also attended Avon as a mission. He then returned to Illinois, where he died August 21, 1881.

100. FREIGANG, Rev. Joseph, a native of Baden, came to this country in 1837; was first stationed at Boston, then at Detroit. From the latter place he came to the Diocese of Cincinnati in 1840, and was appointed pastor of Peru, Huron

county, whence he also occasionally attended New Washington and Tiffin. Contrary to the wish of Bishop Purcell he organized St. Peter's congregation, Norwalk, and in so doing caused his bishop much trouble. He was dismissed February, 1841. No other record of him.

101. FRENSCH, Rev. Christian (Sanguinist), was born at Hahn, near Nassau, Diocese of Limburg, Prussia, August 27, 1827. He came to America, October, 1855; was ordained for the Sanguinists October 24, 1863; in the Diocese of Cleveland from January, 1864, to August, 1866, as assistant at New Riegel, and pastor of Big Spring; from April, 1865, to August, 1866, he also attended Crawfordsville, Wyandot county. He left the Sanguinists March, 1869, and has since been affiliated with the Diocese of Cincinnati.

102. FRERE, Rev. Julius Alfred, was born at St. Germain-en-Laye, France, June 23, 1821; studied at Versailles, France, where he was ordained in June, 1853; did pastoral duty in his native country till 1858, when he was received by Bishop Rappe and appointed pastor of Harrisburg, Stark county, where he remained till 1863. He then left the diocese and went to Detroit. In 1865 he joined the Society of the Holy Cross, Notre Dame, Ind., and has since continued a member thereof.

103. FRITZ, Rev. Ehrhard (Sanguinist), was born at Buechlerthal, Baden, January 4, 1848; made his ecclesiastical studies at St. Charles' Seminary, Carthagena, Mercer county, O., and was ordained at Cincinnati by Archbishop Elder, May 30, 1885. He was in this diocese as pastor *pro tem.* of Assumption church, Reed, from September till December, 1885. He is now stationed in the Diocese of Cincinnati.

104. FRUZZINI, Rev. Joseph (Jesuit), was born at Brig, Canton Wallis, Switzerland, April 13, 1816; joined the Society of Jesus November 4, 1833; was ordained in 1847; came to America the following year, after the expulsion of the Jesuits

from Switzerland. He was stationed for some time at Williamsville, N. Y., in the present Diocese of Buffalo. In 1853 he returned to Europe where he was employed in several colleges and houses of the society in Germany, France and Switzerland. In 1869 he returned to America; was assistant priest at St. Mary's Toledo, O., in 1870 and again in 1877. After an illness of several months, which he bore with exemplary patience, he died in Canisius College, Buffalo, N. Y., May 21, 1880.

105. GAECHTER, Rev. Joseph (Jesuit), was born at Koblach, Austria, November 6, 1847; educated by and for the Jesuits in Maria Laach, and for them ordained in Liverpool, England, by Bishop O'Reilly, February 25, 1878. For two years he was professor in Europe. In 1880 he was sent to Canisius College, Buffalo, N. Y., where he was engaged in like position till August, 1886, when he was appointed one of the professors in St. Ignatius' College, Cleveland. August, 1889, he was again transferred to Canisius College, Buffalo, where he now is.

106. GALES, Rev. Nicholas (Sanguinist), was born in Wellenstein (Kleinmacher), Luxemburg, September 2, 1814; came to the United States in August, 1846; joined the Sanguinists and was ordained by Bishop Rappe, January 27, 1851. His field of labor was chiefly in this diocese—Glandorf, New Riegel, Thompson and St. Stephen's. For twenty-five years he abstained from the use of meat and led a most mortified life. He died at Himmelgarten, Mercer county, Ohio, January 1, 1882.

107. GALLAGHER, Rev. Joseph F., was born at Newport, county Mayo, Ireland, May 22, 836, and 1arrived in Cleveland July 9, 1847. Made his studies for the ministry in St. John's College, Cleveland, at Loretto, Pa., and St. Mary's Seminary, Cleveland. Bishop Rappe ordained him June 30, 1861. Mansfield was his first appointment, July, 1861, till May, 1862. He was then sent to Wooster where he remained till Septem-

ber, 1865. From Mansfield he attended Crestline, till May, 1862, where he built the present frame church. While stationed at Wooster he attended Mansfield, till December, 1863, Loudonville, Orrville, and Lakeville, from May, 1862, till September, 1865. His next appointment was as one of the assistants at the cathedral, October, 1865, to September, 1870, when he was sent to Toledo to take temporary charge of St. Patrick's congregation. December, 1870, he was appointed pastor of Holy Rosary congregation, Cleveland, which charge he held till his death, January 30, 1886. During last mentioned period he built St. Columba's Academy, and nearly brought to completion the present (Holy Name) church, begun by same congregation, under his direction, in 1881. Father Gallagher was a zealous worker for Catholic education and total abstinence.

108. GANTHER, Rev. Sebastian (Sanguinist), a native of Germany, was born in Unter-Muensterthal, Baden, August 20, 1821; in the United States since May, 1847; ordained for the Sanguinists, by Bishop Rappe, at Peru, Huron county, June 5, 1849. Between 1849 and 1852, he attended from Thompson (where he was assistant) the missions of Bismarck (Sherman), New Washington, and St. Stephen's, Seneca county. From 1852 to 1853, he attended Fostoria, Liberty, Crawfordsville, Big Springs and Upper Sandusky, from New Riegel. For a few months in 1853 he was assistant at Glandorf. From 1863 to 1868 he had charge of the mission of New Cleveland, attending it from Glandorf; and between 1870 and 1872 he attended Reed from Thompson. During the interims and since 1872, he did pastoral duty in the Dioceses of Fort Wayne and Cincinnati. He is now stationed in the former diocese.

109. GAUTHIER, Rev. F., D. D., was born in Quebec, Canada, January 22, 1836; studied in Quebec and Rome; was ordained at Rome by Cardinal Patrizzi, October 7, 1860; was twice in the Diocese of Cleveland, first, as pastor of St. Louis' church, East Toledo, from September, 1872, to March, 1876;

then as first resident pastor of St. Mary's Corners, Fulton county, from February, 1877, to October, 1880, when he left and was received into the Diocese of Detroit, to which he at present belongs.

110. GAYER, Rev. Adolph (Jesuit), was stationed at St. Mary's, Toledo, from March to June, 1875. He then left the Jesuits, became a secular priest, and returned to Europe. He is now chaplain to a family of nobility in Sigmaringen.

111. GEHLING, Rev. W., attended Dungannon from February to May, 1858, which was the only charge he held in the Diocese of Cleveland.

112. GELASZEWSKI, Rev. Alexander, a native of Poland, was in this diocese as first resident pastor of French Creek congregation, of which he had charge from August till December, 1850. During this time he also attended Sheffield and Avon as missions. No other record of him.

113. GEZOWSKI, Rev. Joseph, was born in Koeniggraetz, Bohemia, February 13, 1811; ordained January 29, 1838; came to the United States July, 1850; was in the Diocese of Cleveland from 1854 to 1855, first as assistant to Rev. J. H. Luhr, at St. Peter's, Cleveland, then assistant at St. Mary's, same city. In 1855 he left the diocese and joined the Carmelite Order. Was for a time in Covington diocese. Then went to New York city, where he died July 25, 1881, as chaplain of St. Joseph's Asylum, of which he was the founder.

114. GIBBONS, Rev. Walter John, was born in Cleveland, Ohio, March 5, 1844, where he was also educated for the ministry. He was ordained by Bishop Rappe, May 18, 1867. His charges were: Maumee, June 9, 1867 to September 1, 1870; professor at St. Mary's Seminary, September, 1870 to July, 1871; Youngstown, St. Columba's, August, 1871 to July, 1872; Ravenna and Kent, July, 1872 to May, 1874. After a few months' leave of absence on account of sickness he was

pastor of St. Augustine's, Cleveland, from September, 1874 to July, 1875. He was again compelled to give up pastoral work because of ill health, remaining off duty till November, 1876. Next he was assistant at St. Francis', Toledo, till February, 1877, when he again assumed charge of St. Augustine's, Cleveland. May 30, 1878, he was appointed pastor of Bellevue, where he died April 1, 1885, soon after completing the present beautiful church. His remains are buried in St. John's cemetery, Cleveland. Father Gibbons was an eloquent preacher and an earnest worker in the cause of Catholic schools.

115. GILLIBERTI, Rev. A. R., a native of Italy, was stationed at the cathedral as assistant from March to September, 1862. No other record of him.

116. GOCKE, Rev. Joseph J., was born at Howesville, Preston county, W. Va., October 18, 1854. With much success he made his collegiate studies at St. Vincent's, Wheeling, 1871-72, and St. Vincent's, Westmoreland county, Pa., 1872-76. In September, 1876, supplied with excellent testimonial letters, he was received into St. Mary's Seminary, Cleveland, where he studied philosophy and theology. He was elevated to the priesthood by Bishop Gilmour, July 2, 1881. Shortly after his ordination he was assigned the pastorate of South Thompson, Geauga county, from which place he also attended Madison as a mission. Four years later, June 2, 1885, he was transferred to St. Anthony's church, Milan, Erie county, with charge of the mission at Prout's Station. There, as in South Thompson, he discharged his priestly duties faithfully and with success. He died at Milan, after a brief illness of but five days, from the effects of *la grippe*, on January 31, 1890. His remains were taken to Howesville, W. Va.

117. GOEBBELS, Rev. Joseph J., was born at Duesseldorf, Prussia, August 30, 1816; came to the United States February, 1857; was ordained February 24, 1859; in the Diocese of Cleveland from 1861 to 1864, during which time he was pastor

of Fort Jennings. Whilst there he built the present pastoral residence. From Fort Jennings he also attended Kalida (1861) and Ottoville (1861-63). He died at Covington, Ky., October 11, 1885.

118. GONTHYN, Rev. Edward, a Belgian, was in this diocese from 1869 to 1870, and during that time had charge of the Catholic French in Cleveland, who then attended Mass in St. Mary's church on the Flats. He left Cleveland for Wisconsin, and died suddenly at Preble, Diocese of Green Bay, March 9, 1879.

119. GOODWIN, Rev. Jacob, was pastor of St. Vincent's, Akron, from 1849 to 1850, when he left the diocese. From Akron he also attended Doylestown. No other record of him.

120. GRANDMOUGIN, Rev. C. A., was born at Bezange-la-Petite, France, in 1842; finished his studies for the ministry in St. Mary's Seminary, Cleveland, and was ordained by Bishop Rappe, February 14, 1867; was appointed pastor of St. Augustine's, Cleveland, where he died, November 25, 1871, of small-pox, contracted whilst attending a sick call.

121. GREISCH, Rev. Nicholas (Jesuit), was born at Esch-an-der-Sauer, Luxemburg, February 9, 1831; ordained August 30, 1855; was at St. Mary's, Toledo, from March, 1869, till February, 1875, first as assistant, then as pastor, from March, 1872. He is now stationed in the Diocese of La Crosse.

122. GREVIN, Rev. Louis, was born and ordained in France; came to this diocese November, 1855, when he was appointed pastor of Harrisburg. There he remained till 1857, when he was transferred to the cathedral, remaining, however, but a few months, when he left the diocese. He was then received into the Diocese of Ft. Wayne where he remained till 1865. Then he returned to France and died about 1870.

123. HACKSPIEL, Rev. John, was born at Riefensberg, Tyrol, Austria, August 15, 1825; ordained July, 1849; came

to the United States November 18, 1857; was at once received into the diocese (November, 1857) when he was made pastor of Randolph, which charge he held till July, 1861; His next appointment was the pastorate of St. Mary's, Sandusky, where he remained till October, 1862, meanwhile beginning the erection of the present parochial school. November, 1862, he was transferred to French Creek, from which place he also attended Avon and Sheffield. March, 1864, he was sent to St. Peter's, Canton, of which congregation he had charge till August, 1865, when he left the diocese to join the Jesuits. He remained in this society till his death in New York city, as pastor of St. Joseph's church, March 31, 1885. He was a learned and saintly priest.

124. HAEMERS, Rev. H. E., was pastor of Fort Jennings from 1864 till September, 1866; had temporary charge of St. Joseph's, Toledo, and Sylvania, during the fall of 1866, when, about November of the same year, he was sent to Peru. There he remained only till January, 1867, when he was dismissed from the diocese.

125. HAETSCHER, Rev. Francis Xavier (Redemptorist), was born in Vienna, Austria, December 1, 1784; ordained there January 23, 1816; was stationed at Peru, Huron county, between 1832 and 1833; during the summer of 1832 he attended Tiffin from Peru; returned to Europe in the autumn of 1837; died at Loeben, Austria, January 3, 1863.

126. HAHN, Rev. Florian (Sanguinist), was born at Ravensburg, Wuerttemberg, September 4, 1850; was educated for the ministry in St. Charles' Seminary, Carthagena, O., and there ordained by Archbishop Elder, June 8, 1882. He was stationed in the Diocese of Cleveland, from August, 1882, to March, 1889, as pastor of Assumption church, Reed, Seneca county. He was then transferred by his superior to the Diocese of Ft. Wayne, where he is at present.

127. HALLEY, Rev. Thomas F., was born at Tramore, county Waterford, Ireland, January 14, 1833; made his course of studies for the ministry in Waterford, Mt. Melleray and All

Hallows', Ireland, and Cincinnati, Ohio, completing them at St. Mary's Seminary, Cleveland, where he was ordained by Bishop Rappe, December 2, 1860. Immediately after his ordination he was sent as assistant to St. Francis', Toledo, whence after a short time he was tranferred as professor to St. Mary's Seminary. August, 1862, he was appointed pastor of Grafton, where he began and brought under roof the present church. April, 1868, he was assigned the pastorate of St. Mary's, Norwalk, where he remained till his death, January 4, 1885. He was for years a patient sufferer from a hurt received when a youth, which caused him more or less pain through life, especially in his latter years.

128. HAMENE, Rev. James, was born, 1825, in the village of Chemery, Diocese of Metz, Lorraine, France; made his collegiate studies at Sierk. and philosophy and part of theology in the diocesan seminary of Metz. He was received as a student for the Diocese of Cleveland in the beginning of 1852, and was ordained by Bishop Rappe, December 11, 1853. Peru, Huron county, was his first charge, January, 1854, to April, 1855. At Peru he established a parochial school; also attended St. Peter's, Norwalk, from Peru. He next had charge of St. Mary's, Sandusky, June, 1855, to July, 1861, where, under his direction, the congregation built their first church, the present pastoral residence, and a school. From Sandusky he was transferred to St. Mary's, Cleveland, where he remained till September, 1862, when he was appointed pastor of Maumee with charge of Perrysburg as a mission, remaining till 1863. His next appointment was St. Mary's, Massillon, till 1867. There also he built the present pastoral residence. In 1867 he returned to France, where he did duty till his death, April 14, 1886. His remains are buried in his native village, Chemery.

129. HANSEN, Rev. H. Beda (Franciscan), was born at Bedburg, Rhenish Prussia, November 26, 1847; ordained March 21, 1874; in the United States since July, 1875; at Franciscan Monastery, Cleveland, from 1881 to 1882. He is now a secular priest, and stationed in the Diocese of Columbus.

130. HARTMANN, Rev. Hubert (Jesuit), born in Muenster, Westphalia, was ordained in the same city by Bishop Brinkmann, August 10, 1873. Was sent by his superiors to the United States, in September, 1888. He was assistant at St. Mary's, Toledo, and pastor of Sylvania from September, 1888, till September, 1889. Since that he has been at Canisius' College, Buffalo, as professor.

131. HAUSSNER, Rev. Victor, was born at Erlinsbach, Switzerland, December 7, 1833; came to the United States, April, 1856, when he joined the Sanguinists and was ordained by Bishop Rappe, August 28, 1857. No record of his pastoral charges till 1861 (the year he left the Sanguinists), when he was pastor of Avon, from June to August, 1861. He was then assigned the pastorate of Randolph, remaining till July 12, 1868; there also, he built the present church. His next charge was St. Mary's, Sandusky, till September, 1872. Bismarck (Sherman), Huron county, was his next field of labor. There he remained till March, 1879, when because of ill health he did no pastoral duty for four months. In June of same year he was sent to St. Peter's, North Ridgeville, where he labored till December, 1880, when a relapse disabled him permanently. January, 1881, he went to Charity Hospital, Cleveland, and after many weeks of suffering, died April 28, 1881.

132. HECHT, Rev. Edward, D. D., a native of Alsace, was born at Rufach, October 1, 1836. He made his ecclesiastical studies at Strassburg and Rome; obtained in the latter city the doctorate in philosophy, theology and canon law. He was ordained at Strassburg by Bishop Raess, December 17, 1859. From 1860 to 1864, he was chaplain at St. Louis-des-Francais', Rome; then preceptor in Hungary from 1865 to 1869. September, 1869, he came to the United States and was appointed professor of philosophy and dogmatic theology at Mt. St. Mary's Seminary, Cincinnati, which position he held till the closing of the seminary in 1880. In September of same year he was received into St. Mary's Seminary, Cleveland, and appointed professor of the same branches he taught at Cincin-

nati. In August, 1887, he was recalled to Mt. St. Mary's Seminary, Cincinnati, where he died after a few days' illness, January 9, 1888. He was a true Nathanael—a man without guile, learned, unostentatious, devoted to his work as a professor, and a man of solid piety. His remains repose in St. Joseph's Cemetery, Cincinnati.

133. HEIMO, Rev. Joseph Anthony, was born in Freiburg, Switzerland; ordained in his native country, from which he and the inmates of his convent (Black Friars) were expelled by the Swiss government in 1848; came to Cleveland July, 1860, and was given charge of the missions of Strasburg and Harrisburg, which he attended from Calmoutier, Holmes county, from 1849 to 1868 under the jurisdiction of the Bishop of Cleveland. He died at Calmoutier, April 12, 1859, aged fifty years.

134. HEITZ, Rev. Joseph (Sanguinist), was born at Sherman (Bismarck) Huron county, Ohio, June 9, 1856; educated at Carthagena, Ohio, and Teutopolis, Ill.; ordained for the Sanguinists by Bishop Elder, June 11, 1881; was in the Diocese of Cleveland as assistant at Glandorf from January to August, 1882; and as pastor of Big Spring from August, 1882 to October 20, 1883. He is now in the Diocese of Cincinnati.

135. HENNEBERRY, Rev. Patrick (Sanguinist), a native of Ireland, was born January 30, 1830; ordained by Bishop Rappe, at New Riegel, for the Sanguinists, November 21, 1853; was pastor of St. John's, Defiance, in 1855; of Lima between 1856 and 1860, with charge of the missions of Convoy (1859), and Spencerville (1858). He was also superior of the Sanguinist Convent at New Riegel, from February, 1860, to August, 1864, meanwhile attending, at irregular intervals, the missions of Kenton, Hardin county (Diocese of Cincinnati), McCutchenville, Crawfordsville and Upper Sandusky. In 1864 he went to California to establish a college under the direction of the Sanguinist Society. This project

failing, he went to preach missions and total abstinence in Australia, South Africa and East India. He is now engaged giving missions in the western part of the United States. He preaches equally well in the English and German languages.

136. HENNI, Most Rev. John Martin, was born in Switzerland, June 15, 1805; ordained by Bishop Fenwick, February 2, 1829; pastor of Canton, Stark county, from 1830 to 1834, attending meanwhile Dungannon and the scattered missions of Columbiana and Wayne counties. From Canton he also attended Doylestown (1830), Canal Fulton (1830) and occasionally Peru, Huron county. In 1834 he was transferred to Cincinnati, where he organized Holy Trinity congregation. A few years later he also established the *Wahrheits Freund*, the oldest Catholic German paper in the United States. May, 1838, he was appointed vicar-general of the Cincinnati diocese. March 19, 1844, he was consecrated first Bishop of Milwaukee. Died as Archbishop of same See, September 7, 1881, full of years and merit. He was a true man of God.

137. HENRIOT, Rev. Stephen, was stationed at cathedral, Cleveland, from March to May, 1854; came from and returned to the Diocese of New Orleans. No other record of him.

138. HENRY, Rev. Francis J., was born near Dreenan, county Derry, Ireland, April 14, 1848; made part of his ecclesiastical studies in Ireland, St. Vincent's, Westmoreland county, Pa., and finished them in St. Mary's Seminary, Cleveland. May 7, 1871, he was ordained at Toledo for the Diocese of Cleveland by Bishop Luers, of Ft. Wayne. Had temporary charge of St. Patrick's, Toledo, till May 1, 1872, when he was appointed pastor of Briar Hill, with charge of Mineral Ridge, Girard and Canfield as missions. June, 1876, he was sent to St. Rose's, Lima, whose successful pastor he was till his death, February 22, 1886. Father Henry was an earnest, hard-working priest.

139. HENSELER, Rev. Augustine (Franciscan), a Westphalian, was born at Guetersloh, August 8, 1836; ordained

June 14, 1862; in the United States since October, 1876; member of the Franciscan Monastery and assistant at St. Joseph's, Cleveland, from 1876 to 1879; then pastor of St. Peter's, Chicago, till 1884. He is now stationed at Indianapolis, Ind.

140. HENZLER, Rev. Eusebius, was born at Muelheim, Wuerttemberg, August 14, 1823; ordained September, 1853; received into the Diocese of Cleveland June, 1859, when he was appointed assistant to Rev. A. Dambach, at French Creek, acting as such till June, 1860, and meanwhile attending Avon, of which place he had charge till June, 1861. He then left the diocese and went to Wisconsin, where he died about 1870, as pastor of French Creek, Kossuth county.

141. HERBSTRITT, Rev. Andrew (Sanguinist), was born at Fuehrenthal, Baden, September 15, 1823; came to the United States July, 1844; was ordained February 23, 1848, for the Sanguinist Society; did pastoral work at Avon, New Riegel and Glandorf in the Diocese of Cleveland, and at Wapakoneta, Auglaize county, Ohio, whilst a Sanguinist. He left the Sanguinist Society in 1865 and became a secular priest. Then, for nearly three years, he was pastor of St. Mary's, Sandusky, where he bought the lots on which the present beautiful church is built. July, 1868, he was transferred to Randolph, remaining till February, 1869, when he left the diocese and was received by the Bishop of Detroit. He died at Wyandotte, Mich., September 3, 1880.

142. HERZOG, Rev. Henry, was first resident pastor of Ft. Jennings, Putnam county, between 1840 and 1848. In 1850 he was stationed at St. Henry's, Mercer county, O. Died at Minster, Auglaize county, O., in 1851.

143. HETET, Rev. Joseph, was born at Auray, France, January 24, 1838; ordained at Laval, France, by Mgr. Vicard, March 8, 1873. After filling various positions in his native country he came to the United States in 1886, and to the Diocese of Cleveland in 1888. December, 1888, he was

assigned the pastorate of Harrisburg, with the mission of Strasburg. He left the diocese January, 1890, and went to live with the Fathers of Mercy, in New York city.

144. HIEBER, Rev. John George (Jesuit), was born at Kleinkuchen, Wuerttemberg, July 22, 1837; educated for the ministry at Augsburg and Munich; ordained by Mgr. von Dinkel, Bishop of Augsburg, August 9, 1863; held various positions in Europe and United States, first as a secular priest, then as a member of the Society of Jesus. Was in the Diocese of Cleveland as assistant at St. Mary's, Toledo, from 1869 to July, 1870; again from 1877 to 1883; then assistant at St. Mary's, Cleveland, from 1883 to July, 1886. He is now stationed at Davenport, Iowa.

145. HILL, Very Rev. John Austin (Dominican), a native of England, was born in 1777. His parents were Anglicans, and persons of distinction and wealth. They sent him to the college of St. Omer, France, where he made his classical studies. After completing them he entered the English army, but soon asked and obtained his release from military service, which had become distasteful to him. Shortly after this he married an estimable lady and entered the Catholic church. Soon he felt that he was called to serve God in the priesthood. His wife, seconding his holy ambition, voluntarily embraced the life of a nun in a Belgian convent, whilst Mr. Hill entered a seminary in France to prosecute his studies for the sacred ministry. Before he entered he was arrested by the French authorities, who held him for two years a prisoner of state. Upon his release he returned to England and was received into the college of Old Hall Green. Two years later he went to Rome and entered the Dominican Convent of the Minerva. In 1821 he received the Dominican habit and Holy Orders. Ardently desirous of devoting himself to the American missions his wish was gratified by his superiors, who sent him to St. Rose's, Kentucky, in 1822. The Rt. Rev. E. Fenwick had been consecrated bishop of the newly erected See of Cincinnati during that year and was much in

need of priests for the missions of his vast diocese. Father Hill was sent to him, remaining for some time at Cincinnati. Six months after his arrival he was appointed vicar-general. In 1824 he was sent to Northern Ohio to take charge of the missions and stations in Columbiana and Stark counties, attending them for a few months from the Dominican convent in Perry county. November, 1824, he was appointed resident pastor of St. John's, Canton, where he remained till his death, September 3, 1828. In compliance with his wish his remains were interred beneath the eaves of the south side of the church which had been built under his direction. Some years later, however, they were reinterred in the center of St. John's Cemetery, Canton, and a plain white marble slab placed over them, containing, in classical latin, an epitaph composed by Father Henni, descriptive, in brief, of his virtues and worth. Father Hill was a man of commanding, soldierly appearance, due no doubt to his early military training. He was an eloquent preacher, a keen controversialist, a thorough scholar, and as a priest a living example of sacerdotal virtues.

146. HILLS, Rev. E. M. W., a convert from Anglicanism, studied for the priesthood for some time at Mt. St. Mary's Seminary, Cincinnati; was ordained for the Diocese of Covington by Bishop Toebbe, in 1871, and stationed at Immaculate Conception church, Newport, Ky., till 1873, when he came to the Diocese of Cleveland. Bishop Gilmour sent him to South Thompson, where he remained till 1875. His next appointment, after a few months' illness, was Kelley's Island, November, 1876, which charge he held till July, 1878, when he left the diocese and the ministry, and again joined the Anglican sect, of which he is at present a minister.

147. HIPELIUS, Rev. Edward, was born at Stadtlauringen, Bavaria, February 7, 1836; studied at the Royal College of Muennerstadt, Bavaria, St. Vincent's College, Westmoreland county, Pa., and at Rome. In the last mentioned place he received the doctorate in canon law. He was ordained for the Benedictines by Bishop Young, of Erie, August 8, 1858.

Ursuline Convent and Academy, Toledo, O.

Became a secular priest, and was in the Diocese of Cleveland as pastor of Holy Family church, New Cleveland, from May, 1878, to June 20, 1880, when he left. He is now in the Diocese of Albany.

148. HOFFMANN, Rev. ——, D.D., a native of Strassburg, France, was pastor of St. John's, Canton, from 1836 to 1837, whence he also attended Louisville, Stark county, and Doylestown, Wayne county. Returned to Europe in 1838, where he died.

149. HOMBURGER, Rev. Maximilian (Sanguinist), was born at Gruenkraut, Wuerttemberg, Germany, in 1817. Came to the United States in 1844, and after completing his studies under direction of Very Rev. Father Brunner, was ordained by Bishop Rappe, February 28, 1848. He did pastoral duty at Thompson (1848-53) and Glandorf, 1853, till June, 1854, when he returned to Europe, where he did pastoral duty in various dioceses as a Sanguinist, till his death, at Wolpertswende, Wuerttemberg, May 28, 1875. He was a model religious and a zealous priest.

150. HORSTMANN, Rev. William John, was born, 1778, in Germany; ordained in Osnabrueck, by Bishop von Gruben, May 31, 1806; was professor for many years in Westphalia. He came to the United States in 1833, with a band of emigrants, and with them settled in Putnam county, O., founding the village and congregation of Glandorf, where in the midst of hardships and privations he labored among his flock till his death, February 21, 1843. He attended Fort Jennings from Glandorf, first from 1834 to 1840, and then as successor to Rev. Father Herzog in 1841. His remains are buried at Glandorf, where the congregation, in grateful remembrance of his labors among them, erected (1883) a beautiful and costly monument over his grave.

151. HOURS, Rev. Francis (Basilian), born 1834, at Ardeche, France, was educated at Annonay; ordained at

Viviers, France, in 1856. Was in the Diocese of Cleveland as superior of Louisville College, from 1867 to 1873. Is now a professor at St. Michael's College, Toronto, Can.

152. HOWARD, Rev. Maurice, was born in the parish of Effin, county Limerick, Ireland, January 4, 1813. He began his ecclesiastical studies in Ireland and finished them in this country. He was ordained in the old cathedral at Cincinnati by Bishop Purcell, October, 23, 1842. Doylestown was his first charge, December 25, 1842, to February 25, 1846, whence he also attended Mansfield, Wooster and Cuyahoga Falls. He was then sent to take charge of St. Mary's, on the Flats, Cleveland, where he remained till January 22, 1848, when he received the pastorate of St. Mary's, Tiffin. There he remained till he left the diocese, May 1, 1850. From Doylestown he attended missions in Richland, Crawford, Medina, Summit, Portage and Mahoning counties, and occasionally in Huron county. From Cleveland he also attended missions in Geauga and Lake counties. After leaving this diocese he was appointed pastor of St. Raphael's church, Springfield, Ohio, remaining till November, 1863, when he was received into the Diocese of Chicago and appointed pastor of Galesburg —February, 1864, to August, 1877; and of St. Augustine's, Knox county, (now in the Diocese of Peoria), August, 1877, to May, 1878. He then affiliated with the Diocese of Dubuque, and was appointed pastor of St. Francis de Sales' church, Keokuk, Iowa. This charge he held from May, 1878, till his death, February 25, 1887.

153. HUNT, Rev. James, was born at Gurteen, county Sligo, Ireland, in 1849; began his studies for the ministry in Ireland, and completed them in St. Mary's Seminary, Cleveland; was ordained at Notre Dame, Ind., by Bishop Gilmour, August 8, 1874. Some years previous to his ordination he failed in health and never recovered. He was sent as assistant to St. Columba's, Youngstown, but was soon obliged to give up work owing to sickness. He was taken to Charity Hospital, Cleveland, for medical treatment, but he was beyond

the reach of medicine and the physician's skill. He died at Charity Hospital, October 31, 1875. He was a talented young priest and a thorough ecclesiastic. His remains rest in St. John's Cemetery, Cleveland.

154. IVERS, Rev. Michael, was born, educated and ordained in Ireland; was in the Diocese of Cleveland from 1869 till 1873, first as *locum tenens* at St. Francis', Toledo, for several months, then as assistant at the cathedral, whence he also attended Niles during 1871. He left the diocese in 1873. No record of him till his death at sea, when, October 14, 1881, he was lost from the steamer *Havana*, on its way from Europe to Baltimore.

155. JACOMET, Rev. John B. (Sanguinist), was born in Switzerland, June 17, 1811; ordained for the Sanguinists at Feldkirch, Austria, by Bishop Fuender, May 11, 1843. He remained with the Sanguinists till 1845, when he was appointed assistant to Rev. J. H. Luhr, at St. Peter's, Canton, where he remained till 1851. During this time he also attended St. Mary's, Massillon, Navarre, and occasionally St. John's, Canton. He also attended Tiffin about 1845. In 1852 he left the diocese. In March, 1886, he returned to the Sanguinists, and now resides with them at Thompson, Seneca county, Ohio.

156. JANIETZ, Rev. Wolfgang (Franciscan), was born at Belmsdorf, Silesia, November 27, 1832; ordained April 15, 1860; was engaged on the mission in Europe till July, 1875, when his superior sent him to the United States, his first appointment here being the pastorate of the Catholic Poles of Cleveland, whom he organized into a congregation, now known as St. Stanislas'. Under his direction was bought their splendid property, located at the corner of Forman and Tod streets. He also had charge of the erection of their first church, which he attended from the Franciscan Monastery from July, 1875, till August, 1883, when he was transferred to St. Louis, Mo. In July, 1886, he again returned to the Cleveland

Monastery, where he did chaplain's duty till he returned to Europe in July, 1889.

157. JECKER, Rev. Modestus, was born, educated and ordained in France; was received into the Diocese of Cleveland in 1868, and appointed pastor of St. Joseph's, Toledo, where he remained till January, 1878. Whilst at St. Joseph's, he also established and, for six months in 1871, had charge of St. Louis' congregation, East Toledo, and again for a few months in 1872. He left the diocese in 1878 and returned to France, where he died in December, 1885.

158. JUNCKER, Rt. Rev. Henry Damian, was born August 22, 1809 at Fenetrange, Lorraine, France; came to America in 1831. He was elevated to the priesthood by Bishop Purcell, March 16, 1834. He was the first priest ordained by that prelate. He did pastoral duty at Holy Trinity church, Cincinnati, till 1836, when he was sent to St. John's, Canton, whence he attended Circleville, Portsmouth, Zanesville and occasionally Louisville, Stark county, and Peru, Huron county. In 1837 he was appointed pastor of Chillicothe, remaining till 1844, when he was sent to Emmanuel church, Dayton. This charge he retained till his elevation to the episcopate, as first Bishop of Alton, April 26, 1857. While stationed at Dayton he attended Springfield, Urbana, and during April and May, 1847, he did missionary work among the Catholic Germans of Cleveland. He was a saintly priest and bishop. Died October 2, 1868.

159. JUNG, Rev. August, was born in France, Diocese of Strassburg, in 1842; ordained by Bishop Rappe, December 21, 1867; had charge of Randolph from July, 1868, till February, 1869, when he left the Diocese of Cleveland and went to Grand Rapids, Mich., where he was appointed pastor of St. Mary's church. No other record of him.

160. KAERCHER, Rev. Fidelis (Franciscan), was born at Ersingen, Baden, October 21, 1847; came to the United States

in 1852; ordained November 1, 1873; was in Franciscan Monastery, Cleveland, from 1875 to 1881; had pastoral charge of Parma from July, 1879, to January, 1881; and of Independence from February, 1879, to September, 1880. During this time he was also a professor at St. Joseph's College, Cleveland, closed since 1880. He is now in the Diocese of Kansas City, Mo.

161. KANZLEITER, Rev. John B. (Jesuit), was born February 28, 1828, at Bierlingen, Wuerttemberg; ordained January 6, 1860; came to the United States, September, 1869; was stationed at St. Mary's, Toledo, as assistant, October, 1869–70, and then as pastor, to March, 1872. He then left the Diocese of Cleveland and Jesuits in 1872 and became a secular priest. He was in the Diocese of Chicago for a number of years. Went to Europe in 1888 for medical treatment. Died there, March 29, 1889. He was an eloquent preacher and a facile writer, contributing largely to many of the Catholic German papers.

162. KEARNEY, Rev. James F., was born in Frederick county, Md., in 1820; educated for the ministry at Cincinnati; was ordained by Bishop Purcell December 28, 1844, and sent to Steubenville as assistant to Rev. James Conlan. In 1845 and 1846 he attended East Liverpool and Wellsville from Steubenville, where he was pastor at the time. Later he exercised the ministry at Springfield and Hamilton, O.; and for many years at Urbana, O., where he died January 10, 1878.

163. KELLEY, Rev. Bernard B., was born at Cavan, Ireland, October 28, 1845; was educated at Fordham, St. Xavier College, New York, and St. Mary's Seminary, Cleveland; ordained by Bishop Rappe January 20, 1868. He had the following charges in this diocese: Cleveland, St. Patrick's, as assistant, February to May, 1868; Niles, to May, 1871: Cleveland, St. Bridget's, to August, 1874; Summitville, December, 1874, to February, 1876; Warren, May, 1876, to February, 1877; Toledo, St. Patrick's, as assistant, to October, 1877;

St. Mary's Corners, Fulton county, December, 1880, to February, 1881. Since last mentioned date he has had no pastoral charge. During the intervals between his appointments, he was in Cleveland, Kentucky, Illinois, Dakota, Texas, Oregon and Mexico.

164. KENDELER, Rev. ——, was in the Diocese of Cleveland with the Sanguinists at Glandorf, Putnam county, for a few months during 1856, as assistant. No other record of him.

165. KENNEDY, Rev. Edward (Basilian), was born in Toronto, Canada, in 1846; educated at St. Michael's College, Toronto; ordained at London, Ont., by Bishop Walsh, May 1, 1872. Was at Louisville, Stark county, as one of the professors of St. Louis' College, September, 1872, to June, 1873, and then returned to Canada. Died at Toronto, June 24, 1876.

166. KENNEDY, Rev. Michael, a native of Ireland, was ordained by Bishop Rappe July, 1852. His first appointment, till December, 1852, was as assistant to Rev. James Monahan, pastor at Dungannon. He also attended Summitville in 1853. He was pastor of St. John's, Canton, from July, 1853, till November, 1854, when he was sent to St. Patrick's, Cleveland, to take charge of that congregation during the absence of Very Rev. James Conlan, till September, 1855. Meanwhile he continued the erection of St. Patrick's church, on Whitman street, begun by Father Conlan. During this time he also attended St. Patrick's, Rockport, and Berea, 1854. Left the Diocese of Cleveland and was received into that of Cincinnati. His last charge there was as pastor at Chillicothe. He died at St. John's Hospital, Cincinnati, January 13, 1864. His remains repose in Sts. Peter and Paul's Cemetery, Sandusky.

167. KENNY, Rev. John C., was born at Roebuck, county Meath, Ireland, February 6, 1847; made his ecclesiastical

studies at All Hallow's and Carlow, Ireland ; was ordained at Allegany, N. Y., for the Diocese of Rochester, by Bishop Ryan, of Buffalo, June 20, 1872. March, 1888, he came to the Diocese of Cleveland and was appointed assistant at Sts. Peter and Paul's church, Sandusky. October, 1889, he was appointed to the pastorate of Vermillion, which he resigned the following December, when he left the diocese.

168. KERCKHOFF, Rev. Hermann (Jesuit), a native of Hanover, was born at Haren-Ems, June 26, 1836. He was educated for the priesthood at Muenster and Maria-Laach ; ordained at Osnabrueck for the Jesuits, by Mgr. Melchers, July 16, 1861. Till 1872 he exercised the ministry in Europe. Then he came to the United States and was assigned various positions by his superiors. August, 1886, he was sent to Cleveland as one of the professors at St. Ignatius' College. Left Cleveland, September, 1887. Is now at Canisius College, Buffalo, N. Y.

169. KLEEKAM, Rev. Sebastian (Franciscan), was born at Elbroch, Diocese of Paderborn, Germany, April 25, 1844 ; ordained August 12, 1869 ; belonged to Franciscan Monastery, Cleveland, from 1869 to 1871, meanwhile (1870) attending Independence and Parma. Died at Sherman, Missouri, September 13, 1875.

170. KOCKEROLS, Rev. William (Jesuit), was born at Wuerm, Diocese of Cologne, August 3, 1824 ; entered the Society of Jesus, October 30, 1855, and made the regular course of studies for the ministry under direction of the Jesuits ; was ordained priest at Maria-Laach by Archbishop Melchers, of Cologne, September 14, 1868 ; came to this country in 1869, and was engaged in giving missions in the Diocese of Buffalo and elsewhere. February 15, 1875, he was sent to Toledo as pastor of St. Mary's church. This charge he held till June, 1886. During this time, and under his direction, the large brick residence of the Jesuit Fathers near the church was built; also the splendid parochial schoolhouse,

which is an ornament to Toledo and the just pride of St. Mary's congregation. His next appointment was at Prairie-du-Chien, Wis., where he remained nearly three years. In 1889 he was sent to St. Ann's, Buffalo, where he took seriously ill. In the hope of obtaining relief, or a possible cure, his superior sent him to the celebrated springs at Mt. Clement, Mich., near Detroit. But he was not to be cured. Feeling that his end was rapidly approaching, he asked to be taken to St. Vincent's Hospital, Toledo, there to prepare for death, which five weeks later, December 11, 1889, ended his sufferings. His obsequies took place at St. Mary's church, Toledo, where for over eleven years he had done faithful pastoral work. A large funeral cortege accompanied his remains to their last resting place, in St. Mary's Cemetery.

171. KOEHN, Rev. John, was born in Niederlahnstein, Nassau-Limburg, September 10, 1831, ordained by Bishop Rappe, June 24, 1866; had charge of the missions of Marblehead, La Prairie and Toussaint, also of Port Clinton, where he resided from July, 1866, to March, 1868. From December, 1868, to February, 1869, he was pastor of Kelley's Island; then received the pastorate of Randolph, where he remained till March, 1875. His next charge was St. Mary's, Massillon, March 20, 1875, to March 1, 1879, during which time he began the present magnificent church. His health failing he was unequal to the labor of attending so large a congregation as St. Mary's, hence he resigned on last mentioned date (March, 1879,) and went to Charity Hospital, Cleveland. There he rallied sufficiently, he thought, to resume pastoral work. Bishop Gilmour then appointed him pastor of Bismarck (Sherman), April, 1879, but in October of same year he was again obliged to resign because of his shattered health. After a lingering illness and much suffering he died at Bismarck, January 24, 1880. There also his remains repose. Father Koehn was a hard-working, self-sacrificing priest.

172. KOENEN, Rev. N., was assistant to Rev. F. Westerholt at Defiance for some months, between 1856 and 1857.

He also attended Providence during this time. He left the Diocese of Cleveland in 1857.

173. KOERLING, Rev. Ignatius (Jesuit), a native of Westphalia, was born at Altenbueren, February 11, 1838. He was educated in Europe, by and for the Jesuits, and for them ordained at Maria-Laach, by Mgr. Melchers, September 13, 1868. Two years later he was sent to the United States, doing pastoral duty in New York city and Buffalo. In September, 1871, he was appointed assistant at St. Mary's, Toledo, remaining there till 1881, when he was given a like position at St. Mary's, Cleveland. August, 1883, he was transferred to Wisconsin, as professor in the Jesuit College at Prairie-du-Chien, remaining till July, 1886; then to Mankato, July to September, 1886. On last mentioned date he was again sent to Toledo, as assistant at St. Mary's, where he remained till July, 1887. St. Mary's, Cleveland, as assistant, was his next appointment, July, 1887, to August, 1888; then again St. Mary's, Toledo, as assistant, with pastoral charge of Sylvania. One month later he was transferred to Buffalo, where he now resides.

174. KOHLER, Rev. Peter, a Swiss, studied for a time with the Sanguinists at Thompson, and was there ordained deacon by Bishop Purcell, in 1844. Shortly after this he returned to Switzerland, but came back within a year. Nearly eleven years after his ordination as deacon, Bishop Rappe received him, and ordained him a priest, December 31, 1854. He was sent to Shelby Settlement as assistant; was next stationed at Navarre, from which place he attended Canal Fulton and Doylestown. In the summer of 1855 he left the Diocese of Cleveland. No other record of him.

175. KOLOPP, Rev. Hyacinthe N. M., was born at Abreschwiller, Diocese of Nancy, Lorraine, May 7, 1850. He made part of his ecclesiastical studies at Fenetrange and Pont-a-Mousson, France, and completed them at St. Mary's Seminary, Cleveland, having been received in 1870 on the

recommendation of his uncle, Rev. Peter Kolopp, as a student for this diocese. August 8, 1874, he was ordained by Bishop Gilmour. His first appointment was Elmore, whence he attended the missions of Genoa, Oak Harbor and Woodville. December, 1875, he was appointed to take charge of Antwerp, with the missions of Cecil, Delaware Bend and Junction, besides a number of stations, some of which have since developed into missions. Providence, Lucas county, was his next pastoral charge, from April 10, 1877, to August, 1883. From Providence he attended Bowling Green, where he secured several lots on which, under his direction, the present church was built. August 19, 1883, he assumed charge of his last appointment, Holy Trinity congregation, Bucyrus, where the beautiful church, completed in the fall of 1886, was erected during his pastorate. He died at Bucyrus, March 22, 1887.

176. KOLOPP, Rev. Peter, was born at Heinrichsdorf, Lorraine, July 4, 1834; made his ecclesiastical studies in Phalsburg, Lorraine; was received into the Diocese of Alton by Bishop Juncker, and by him ordained July 14, 1858; was received into the Diocese of Cleveland, October, 1864, and sent as assistant to Rev. L. Hoffer, Louisville, Ohio, where he remained till June, 1866. He was then, successively, pastor of Doylestown, June, 1866, to August, 1870; Six Mile Woods, till October, 1875; St. Peter's, Norwalk, till June, 1881, and Avon, till May, 1883. After an illness of nearly eight months he died at St. Vincent's Hospital, Toledo, November 20, 1883.

177. KRAMER, Rev. J. J., was born, educated and ordained in Alsace; was received into the Diocese of Cleveland in 1853, and sent as assistant to Rev. J. H. Luhr, at St. Peter's, Cleveland. November, 1854, he was appointed pastor of St. Mary's, Cleveland, and remained till May, 1856, when he was sent to Dungannon. This charge he held till he left the diocese, July of same year. He was then received into the Diocese of Alton. Later he returned to Europe, where he died in 1882.

178. KRAMER, Rev. Maria Anton (Sanguinist), was born at Hirschbach, Wuerttemberg, February 3, 1817; came to the United States October, 1852, and was ordained at New Riegel for the Sanguinists by Bishop Rappe, November 21, 1853; did pastoral work in the Diocese of Cleveland, off and on, between 1855 and 1877, at Avon, French Creek, Thompson, New Riegel and Glandorf. At other times he was on missions in the Dioceses of Cincinnati and Ft. Wayne. His last charge in the Diocese of Cleveland was at Thompson, from December, 1874, till his death, February 17, 1877.

179. KRASNEY, Rev. Anthony, was born, educated and ordained in Bohemia; came to this country in 1857, and was stationed for a while in New York city; was received into the Diocese of Cleveland in May, 1858, and from St. Peter's, Cleveland, attended Independence till 1862, when he was appointed first pastor of St. Joseph's, on Woodland avenue. There he remained in charge till October, 1867, when he was appointed the first pastor of St. Wenceslas' (Bohemian) congregation, Cleveland, then organized by Bishop Rappe. Because of ill health he resigned this charge, October, 1869, and died at Charity Hospital, Cleveland, March 3, 1870. He was a fine German and Bohemian scholar. He had been in bad health for some years previous to his death, and much of his sickness could be traced to the unkind treatment he received from his countrymen of St. Wenceslas' congregation, who embittered his life by their un-Catholic spirit; also to the severity of prison life he endured in Austria, from 1849 to 1857, as a prisoner of war, because of the part he took in the "Czech movement" in 1848.

180. KREIDLER, Rev. John B. (Jesuit), a native of Wuerttemberg, was born at Horb, June 8, 1848. He was educated by and for the Jesuits, and for them ordained by Bishop Brown, at Salpoint, England, September 21, 1873. For three years he was on the mission in England; came to the United States in August, 1876, and was sent to Burlington, Iowa, where he remained till September, 1881. His next appoint-

ment was as assistant at St. Mary's, Toledo, till August, 1888. During this time he also had pastoral charge of the mission of Sylvania. He now resides at Mankato, Minn., as pastor of Sts. Peter and Paul's church.

181. KREUSCH, Rev. Matthias (Sanguinist), was born at Longwich, near Schweich, Diocese of Treves, Prussia, October 7, 1820; came to the United States, December, 1843; was ordained for the Sanguinists by Bishop Purcell, June 10, 1845; had pastoral charge of the Catholic Germans of Cleveland, about 1848; attended Avon from July, 1849, to July, 1850, and again from July to December, 1856; was also at New Riegel, Thompson and Glandorf, 1856-65. Then, till his death, he was on duty in other dioceses where the Sanguinists had charge of congregations. In 1859 he attended Lima, where he built the first church. He died near Minster, O., of cholera morbus, July 21, 1874. "Father Matthias," as he was called, did much good for religion. He was a saintly priest, a man without guile.

182. KREUSCH, Rev. John Peter, brother to Rev. M. Kreusch, was born at Longwich, Diocese of Treves, Prussia, December 2, 1818. He received a common school education in his native city, but feeling himself called to the priesthood he made his preparatory studies at Castle Loewenburg, and in Switzerland. About 1844 he came to the United States. Bishop Purcell sent him to the Sanguinist Fathers, at Thompson, where he continued his ecclesiastical studies for a time. When the Diocese of Cleveland was erected in 1847 he sought and received adoption from Bishop Rappe as a seminarist. He was ordained November 19, 1848, after finishing his theological course in the first diocesan seminary, then in the rear of the Bishop's residence on Bond street. He had the following pastoral charges in the Diocese of Cleveland between the time of his ordination and 1854: Cleveland, St. Mary's on the Flats, 1848-51; French Creek, as resident pastor, with Sheffield as a mission, 1851-52; Shelby Settlement, with charge of the missions of Crestline, Bucyrus, Galion, Loudonville, New

Washington and Mansfield, 1852-54. In 1854 he was received into the Diocese of Vincennes where he remained about four years. He then was again received by Bishop Rappe, who gave him pastoral charge of Dungannon, where he remained till 1859, when he was received into the Diocese of Wheeling by Bishop Whelan. He was engaged in parochial work in the city of Wheeling from the time of his entry into the diocese until about 1886, when owing to age and illness he retired from the ministry to seek rest and medical care. For over twenty-five years he had charge of St. Alphonsus' church, Wheeling. May 11, 1888, he died full of years and merit. In order to aid his fellow-priests in obtaining pure altar wine he devoted his savings and spare time to an extensive vineyard he had established near Wheeling. Though he succeeded in supplying pure altar wine, the project had ended in financial failure, a short time before he died.

183. KUEHR, Rev. Ferdinand, D. D., was born at Eslohe, Prussia, August 25, 1806; made his studies for the priesthood at the Propaganda, Rome, and was there ordained by Cardinal Reisach, August 10, 1830. He was stationed at St. John's, Canton, as temporary pastor, November, 1837, to January, 1838. He was pastor of St. Mary's church, Covington, from 1841 to November 20, 1870, the date of his death.

184. KUEMIN, Rev. Charles, a Swiss, was born in 1802. He was in the Diocese of Cleveland from May, 1865, till February 27, 1867, as pastor of Kelley's Island, with charge of Put-in-Bay as a mission. Before coming here he served seven years in the Diocese of Buffalo, and six years in that of Chicago. In 1867 he returned to his native country, Switzerland, and died the following year in the hospital at Chur, aged 66.

185. KUHNMUENCH, Rev. Peter (Sanguinist), was born at Nerbach, Baden, October 31, 1843; educated for the ministry at Bischofsheim, Baden, and at Carthagena, Mercer county, O.; ordained at Cincinnati for the Sanguinists by Archbishop

Purcell, June 24, 1876; was in the Diocese of Cleveland from July, 1881, to September 8, 1884, as assistant at New Riegel. He is now stationed in the Diocese of Cincinnati.

186. KUNKLER, Very Rev. Andrew (Sanguinist), was born at Glotterthal, Baden, November 25, 1825; in the United States since 1843; ordained at New Riegel for the Sanguinists by Bishop Rappe, February 23, 1848. The only appointment he held in the Diocese of Cleveland was St. John's, Glandorf, from 1848 to 1849, and assistant at St. Michael's, Thompson, from April to September, 1857. From 1858 to 1874 he was Provincial of the Sanguinists in this country. He died suddenly at Weston, Mo., December 6, 1889. He was a thorough ecclesiastic and a model religious.

187. LAIS, Rev. Joseph, was born at Griessheim, Baden, September 29, 1829. After devoting several years to studies under the Benedictines in Switzerland he came to America, March, 1852, and entered the Cleveland Diocesan Seminary. He was ordained by Bishop Rappe, July 8, 1855. His first mission was St. Mary's, Massillon, of which he had charge from 1855 to 1858. Then he was pastor of Navarre (Bethlehem), 1859-60; of Doylestown with charge of Canal Fulton and French Settlement as missions, 1860-62. In 1862 he was appointed resident pastor of Canal Fulton, attending several missions from that place. There he remained till 1867, when he again received the pastorate of St. Mary's, Massillon, retaining this appointment till he died, February 5, 1875. His remains are buried in St. Mary's Cemetery, Massillon. Father Lais took special interest in Catholic schools. Whilst at Massillon he erected the present handsome and commodious school. He was ever faithful to his sacerdotal duties, and left the record of a devoted and true priest.

188. LANGEVIN, Rev. Alfred, a Canadian, was born at St. Pie, P. Q., April 1, 1861; educated for the priesthood at St. Hyacinth and Montreal, Canada; ordained at St. Albans, Vt., by Bishop de Goesbriand for the Diocese of Burlington, June

22, 1884. Was on the mission in Vermont till January, 1888, when he came to the Diocese of Cleveland. Bishop Gilmour sent him to Dungannon, where he remained but four weeks, when he returned to Vermont. He is now engaged in pastoral work at Chicopee, Mass., Diocese of Springfield.

189. LAUX, Rev. Alphonse (Sanguinist), was born September 11, 1835, in the town of Stolzenberg, Grand-Duchy of Luxemburg. He came to this country in 1859, and was ordained at Cincinnati for the Sanguinists by Archbishop Purcell, November 7, 1861. From 1862 to 1863 he was stationed at New Riegel, whence he attended Berwick, St. Patrick's Settlement, McCutchenville and Crawfordsville. In 1864 he attended Bismarck (Sherman) from Thompson. In 1869 he was appointed pastor of New Riegel. July, 1875, whilst directing the building of the present beautiful church at New Riegel, (begun during his pastorate) he fell and broke one of his legs, and has since been more or less unable to do pastoral duty. From 1877, to February, 1880, he assisted the pastor of Glandorf. Since then he has held the position of chaplain in various hospitals and asylums. He is now stationed at Jersey City, N. J., charged with a similar position.

190. LEDDY, Rev. James H., was born at Newark, N. J., May 14, 1837; made his ecclesiastical studies at St. Mary's College, Wilmington, Del., and Seton Hall, N. J. He was ordained for the Diocese of Buffalo by Bishop Timon, March 18, 1863. He was in the Diocese of Cleveland between 1876 and 1877—at the cathedral for two months as assistant, then pastor for four months at Van Wert, when he returned to the Diocese of Buffalo, where he has been since.

191. LEWANDOWSKI, Rev. Vincent, a native of Gralewo-Posen, Austria, was born May 31, 1841. He made his collegiate studies in the Gymnasium of the city of Posen, and his theological course with the Franciscans, in the same city, for whose Order he was ordained, October 30, 1864. He became a secular priest, and was in the Diocese of Cleveland as pastor

of St. Hedwig's (Polish) congregation, Toledo, from October, 1875, till July, 1885, when he left the diocese. From St. Hedwig's he attended St. Anthony's congregation (Toledo), which he organized, and whose church was built under his direction. This latter charge he held from November, 1882, till August, 1884. He is now stationed in the Diocese of Milwaukee.

192. LINDESMITH, Rev. Edward W. J., a native of Ohio, was born in Center township, Columbiana county, September 7, 1827. He made his studies for the ministry at St. Mary's Seminary, Cleveland, and was ordained by Bishop Rappe, July 8, 1855. Doylestown was his first pastoral charge, together with the missions of Canal Fulton, French Settlement and Marshallville, July, 1855, to February, 1858. St. John's, Canton, was his next appointment, with New Berlin as a mission, February, 1858, to October, 1868. From this date to May, 1872, he was resident pastor of Alliance, meanwhile attending Leetonia. May, 1872, he was appointed first resident pastor of Leetonia. There he resided till July, 1880, when he accepted a chaplaincy in the U. S. army, Bishop Gilmour having granted him temporary leave of absence from the diocese for the purpose. His residence is at Fort Keogh, Montana.

193. LOCHERT, Rev. Gabriel M., was born, 1810, at Niederlauterbach, Alsace; educated and ordained in Alsace, France. He came to the Diocese of Cleveland in the spring of 1859, and was appointed first resident pastor of Navarre (Bethlehem), where after a brief illness he died July 13, of the same year.

194. LUDWIG, Rev. Frederick C., a native of the Duchy of Braunschweig, Germany, was born of Protestant parents in the town of Wolfenbuettel, January 13, 1823. After his entry into the Church he made his studies for the priesthood at the Seminaries of St. Mary's, Cleveland, and St. Sulpice, Paris. He was ordained by Bishop Rappe, July 3, 1864. Louisville was his first appointment, August to October, 1864. He then, successively, had pastoral charge of the following places:

Dungannon, October, 1864, to February, 1867; Peru, to March, 1868; Rockport and Independence, to May, 1869; Shelby Settlement, to December, 1869. He then became mentally deranged and was made a pensioner of the Infirm Priest's Fund from January, 1870, to October, 1882, residing in retirement at East Liverpool, O. On the supposition that he had recovered from his mental illness, Very Rev. Administrator Boff, in absence of the Bishop in Rome, then assigned him the pastorate of St. Peter's, Norwalk, where he remained only till January, 1883. Then he was appointed assistant at St. Stephen's, Cleveland, February to July, 1883, when he was again on the sick list till December, 1886. At last mentioned date he left the Diocese of Cleveland, and went about as caprice dictated. Finally death put an end to his blighted existence, June 25, 1889. His remains rest in St. Philip's Cemetery, Dungannon, O.

195. LUHR, Very Rev. John Henry, was born at Steinfeld, Oldenburg, Diocese of Muenster, April 21, 1808, and was ordained September 21, 1831. In 1844 he was received into the Diocese of Cincinnati, at that time comprising the state of Ohio. After a short stay in Cincinnati, the pastorate of St. John's, Canton, was assigned him. This position he held from October, 1844, till the organization, by him, of St. Peter's congregation, Canton, June, 1845. During 1848 he also attended Randolph for a few months. February, 1853, he was transferred from Canton to Cleveland, where he organized St. Peter's congregation, whose first school and present church were built under his direction. He was pastor of the last mentioned congregation till January, 1868, when he left the diocese and returned to Cincinnati, where he was appointed pastor of St. Augustine's. This position he held till his death, August 2, 1872. Whilst at Canton he also had charge of Massillon (where he built the first church), Navarre and New Berlin. He was one of Bishop Rappe's vicars-general from 1854 to 1868. Father Luhr was a faithful priest, full of zeal, and an earnest worker in the cause of religion.

196. McALEER, Rev. Michael, born in county Tyrone, Ireland, March 4, 1811, was ordained by Bishop Purcell, November 23, 1837; did pastoral work at Canton, Navarre and Dungannon, between 1837 and 1840. He then left Ohio and went to the Diocese of Nashville with Bishop Miles, and was stationed at Memphis, Tenn., where he remained some years. Later he was received into the Diocese of New York; was appointed pastor of St. Columba's, New York city, where he died February 22, 1881.

197. McCAFFREY, Rev. Patrick, was born in New York state, October, 1841; made his preparatory course of studies in Cleveland, Louisville, Ohio, and finished same in St. Mary's Seminary, Cleveland, where, July 17, 1870, he was ordained for the Diocese of Cleveland by Bishop Mullen, of Erie. His first appointment was St. Ann's, Briar Hill, from which place he attended as missions Girard and Struthers. In the latter place, as also at Briar Hill, he built the present churches. Being of delicate health, he was obliged, with great reluctance, to resign his charge, April, 1872. He then went to live with his parents at Toledo, to receive the care and attention he so much needed. Every effort was made to restore health but without avail. Though he said Mass, and occasionally preached in St. Patrick's and St. Francis de Sales' churches, Toledo, he was unable to do any continued pastoral duty. For two years after leaving Briar Hill he suffered greatly, but patiently, till death's summons came, April 7, 1874. His remains are buried at Toledo.

198. McDONALD, Rev. Patrick, a native of Ireland, was born at Castlemagner, county Cork, September 24, 1855. He made his higher ecclesiastical studies in the Louvain University, and at Rome, where he received the divinity doctorate. He was ordained at Liege, Belgium, for the Diocese of Cloyne, by Bishop Doutreloup, April 14, 1879. After filling a number of positions in Ireland and elsewhere he came to the Diocese of Cleveland in November, 1888. Shelby and its four missions were assigned to his pastoral care. He left the diocese June 5, 1889.

199. McGANN, Rev. Francis, was born, 1823, in county Roscommon, Ireland; came to America in 1837; was received as a student by Bishop Rappe in 1848, and ordained by him September 8, 1850. He was at once appointed pastor of St. Vincent's, Akron, where he remained till August, 1855, meanwhile attending Youngstown and Ravenna (1854-55). He established a parochial school at Akron. Bishop Rappe then recalled him to Cleveland, directing him to attend Rockport, Berea and Olmsted. Unwilling to accept this appointment he left the Diocese of Cleveland and was received by Bishop O'Regan, of Chicago, under whose jurisdiction he remained about two years. Next he was in the Diocese of Milwaukee, where, as pastor of Mineral Point, Wis., he died September 18, 1870.

200. McGLONE, Rev. J. B., was born in the parish of Glenfarn, Diocese of Kilmore, Ireland, December 23, 1853; came with his relatives some years later to America, and for a time lived in the Diocese of Providence. He made his ecclesiastical studies at St. Michael's College, Toronto, and Holy Angels' Seminary, near Niagara Falls; was received by Bishop Gilmour as a student for the Diocese of Cleveland, January, 1881, and by him ordained April 1, 1882. His first appointment was as assistant at Holy Rosary church, Cleveland, where he remained till February, 1883. In the following month he was sent to St. Columba's, Youngstown, as assistant. March, 1884, he became seriously ill, and till his death, at Providence, R. I., August 12, 1884, was unable to do duty.

201. McGOVERN, Rev. Francis, a native of parish Kinawley, county Cavan, Ireland, was born March 18, 1843. He commenced his studies for the priesthood in his native Diocese of Kilmore. In 1868 he came to the United States and entered the Augustinian College at Villanova, Delaware county, Pa., where he remained about one year, when he was admitted to the diocesan seminary of Philadelphia. In 1873 he was received for the Diocese of Cleveland by Bishop Gilmour, who ordained him June 7th of the same year, and

then stationed him at the cathedral as one of the assistants. This position he held for three years, when he was appointed pastor of St. Ann's, Briar Hill. Such he was from June, 1876, till his death (after five weeks' illness), August 28, 1887. While stationed at Briar Hill, he also attended Mineral Ridge and Lowellville as missions till 1881.

202. McGRADY, Rev. John H. M. (Dominican), born in 1799, of Irish parentage, was ordained at Cincinnati by Bishop Fenwick in 1822. He had pastoral charge of Dungannon from November, 1830, to February, 1834, residing there as first resident priest from January, 1831, to November, 1833. From Dungannon he also attended, occasionally, Canal Fulton, Canton and Youngstown. He died at St. Rose's, Kentucky, December 27, 1838.

203. McGRATH, Rev. John P., a native of Pennsylvania, was born at Pottsville, April 6, 1853. He studied mental philosophy at St. Charles' Seminary, Philadelphia, theology at Mt. St. Mary's, Emmittsburg, and St. Mary's, Cleveland. Bishop Gilmour ordained him July 1, 1882, and sent him to Defiance, to take temporary charge of the church of Our Lady. October, 1882, he was assigned the pastorate of Salineville, where he remained till August, 1884. February, 1885, he was sent to Providence, with charge of Bowling Green. He left this charge and the diocese, December, 1888.

204. McGRATH, Rev. Patrick C., born near Malleray Abbey, Ireland, was ordained for the Diocese of Erie by Bishop Mullen in 1869; was received into the Diocese of Rochester in 1870, where he remained till 1878, when Bishop Gilmour received him. He was sent to St. Mary's, Tiffin, as assistant to Rev. M. Healy; remained but a few months when he left the Diocese of Cleveland and was received by the Bishop of Peoria, whose subject he was till death, July 21, 1882. He died at St. Mary's Hospital, Milwaukee, where he had gone for medical treatment.

205. McLAUGHLIN, Rev. Peter, a native of Ireland, was born in 1805. He was ordained at Cincinnati, in 1840, by Bishop Purcell, and sent to Cleveland as its third resident pastor. There he finished St. Mary's church on the Flats, begun by his predecessor, Father O'Dwyer. From Cleveland he attended Avon, 1840-42 ; South Thompson, Akron, Cuyahoga Falls, Ravenna and Painesville, 1840-45 ; and Randolph, occasionally, 1841-42. He left Cleveland in February, 1846, and went to the Diocese of Milwaukee, where he remained a short time. He was then received into the Diocese of Brooklyn (1854) and later into that of Portland, Me.; died as pastor of Bath, same diocese, March 12, 1861, aged 56 years. His remains are buried in Calvary Cemetery, Portland, Me. "Father Peter," as he was familiarly called, was a man of medium height, stoutly built, and of a strong constitution. Every feature of his countenance indicated force of character. He was to a great extent a "self-made man," having had to undergo almost insurmountable difficulties to acquire an education. A part of his college course he made while watching and attending to his father's flocks, using his spare time in studying latin and the higher mathematics. His eloquenee attracted great audiences of Catholics and Protestants. Many times on Sundays and on Holydays the church on the Flats was filled to overflowing by people who had come from all parts of the city to hear his learned and impressive sermons. During his pastorate in Cleveland he fought hard among his people against the vice of intemperance. He established the first total abstinence society in Cleveland, and thus succeeded in reclaiming many from a drunkard's grave. In his zeal for the elevation of his people he went even so far as to go to their homes and teach them how to work, and to be clean and comfortable. On occasion of public or civic celebrations Father McLaughlin was invariably invited as one of the speakers. He was universally respected by the non-Catholic citizens of Cleveland for his zeal, earnestness and blunt honesty. He was also a pungent and forcible writer, as evidenced by a series of controversial articles he contributed to the *Catholic Telegraph*, of Cincinnati, in 1843. For a further

account of his pastoral labors the reader is referred to the "Historical Sketch of Early Catholicity in Cleveland, etc.," in this work.

206. McLoy, Rev. John B., a native of Ireland, was educated in France and in Rome. For fourteen years he was on the mission in Scotland and in the Diocese of Newark, N. J.; was in the Diocese of Cleveland as assistant to Rev. Joseph F. Gallagher, pastor of Holy Name church, Cleveland, from February to May, 1883. Since November, 1888, he has been a "disciple" of the apostate priest, in New York city, Rev. J. O'Connor.

207. McNamee, Rev. Joseph, came to this country from Ireland about 1836. He was ordained at Cincinnati, in the absence of Bishop Purcell, by the Rt. Rev. Bishop Chabrat of Bardstown, Ky., April 8, 1839. After a few months of pastoral duty at Cincinnati, he was sent to St. Mary's, Tiffin, October, 1839. There he remained till July, 1847, meanwhile, though in poor health, attending Maumee, Toledo, Providence and in fact all the missions in Northwestern Ohio, 1839-41; Findlay, New Riegel, McCutchenville and Fremont, between 1839-43. In July, 1847, he left the Diocese of Cincinnati. He died at Pawtucket, R. I., (Diocese of Providence), March 28, 1853. He was a faithful and zealous priest.

208 McShane, Rev. Patrick A., was born at Poynt's Pass, county Armagh, Ireland, April 8, 1854. Made the latter part of his ecclesiastical studies in Rome, where he also received his "degree" as a doctor of divinity. He was ordained for the Peoria diocese by Bishop Spalding, May 15, 1878. About ten years later he was received, *pro tempore*, into the Diocese of Cleveland (April, 1888), and given pastoral charge of Salineville and Summitville. He left the diocese January, 1889.

209. Machebeuf, Rt. Rev. Joseph Projectus, was born at Riom, Preu-de-Dome, Diocese of Clermont, France, August

11, 1812; made his studies at Riom, at St. Sulpice and Mont-Ferrand, France. He was ordained at Clermont by Bishop Feron, December 21, 1836. After nearly three years of priestly labor in his native country he came to the Diocese of Cincinnati, August, 1839, and in the following month was sent to Tiffin, as assistant to Rev. Joseph McNamee, pastor of St. Mary's, attending Fremont, (Lower Sandusky), Napoleon, Sandusky, Maumee and Toledo as missions. He remained at Tiffin till the end of December of the same year, when he was transferred to Sandusky where he organized Holy Angels' congregation and built their first (and present) church. From Sandusky he continued to attend Fremont, where he established St. Ann's congregation and directed the building of their first church. He also made pastoral visits to Peru for a few months. He was stationed at Sandusky till January, 1851, when on invitation of his life-long friend, Bishop Lamy, he went to New Mexico. He labored there and in Colorado on the hard and scattered missions of these territories, till his consecration as Vicar Apostolic of Colorado, August 15, 1868, with residence at Denver. In 1887 he was appointed first Bishop of Denver. October 18, 1888, he contributed a very interesting article to the *Catholic Universe*, in which he described his eleven years' labor on the mission in Northern Ohio. He died at Denver, Col., July 10, 1889, full of years and merit. He was a man full of zeal, not sparing self, but always busy with the things of God. His memory will be revered as of "the Apostle of Colorado."

210. MACHUI, Rev. Bonaventure (Franciscan), a native of Silesia, was born at Gramschuetz, July 8, 1825. After completing his ecclesiastical studies at Breslau he was ordained priest by Cardinal Diepenbrock for the Diocese of Breslau, June 22, 1850. After serving as a secular priest till December, 1853, he entered the Franciscan Order at Breslau on the 21st of same month. Later and successively he was transferred to Paderborn, Muenster, and Cologne. When the "May Laws" were executed against the Franciscan Order in Germany, he came to the United States in July, 1875. On

arrival in this country he was sent to the Cleveland Monastery where he resided till his death. Father Bonaventure was a learned and pious priest—a true religious. For nearly ten years he was a member of the diocesan board of examiners of seminarists and junior clergy and as such did good and appreciated service. He was also repeatedly appointed vicar or assistant superior of the Franciscan Monastery. For the last five or six years of his life he was in poor health and hence unable to do active duty in the ministry. He died of apoplexy, April 2, 1889.

211. MAESFRANCX, Rev. Elias, was born in Belgium October 5, 1819; ordained in 1846; came to the United States in 1866; was received into the Diocese of Cleveland by Bishop Rappe in 1867, and sent to Delphos as assistant to Rev. F. Westerholt, when after a short stay he was transferred to St. John's, Landeck, Allen county, as first resident pastor. This charge he left in April of the following year, when he was received into the Diocese of Detroit by Bishop Lefevre. He remained there a few years and then returned to his native country, where he now resides.

212. MAHONY, Rev. Timothy M., was born in Tipperary, county Tipperary, Ireland, August 16, 1836. He came to the United States with his parents in 1849. For some years his home was in Sandusky. In his 18th year he began his ecclesiastical studies with the Dominicans, at St. Joseph's, Perry county, O. He continued his collegiate course at Bardstown, Ky. He began to study mental philosophy at Mt. St. Mary's, Emmittsburg. In 1861 he entered St. Mary's Seminary, Cleveland. June 29, 1863, he was elevated to the priesthood in the cathedral by Bishop Rappe, who appointed him as one of the assistants in the church where he received Holy Orders. Whilst holding this position he aided largely in raising means for the erection of Father Mathew hall and the building used as a school for the girls, since replaced by the present splendid school edifice. Bellevue was his next field of labor, August, 1866, to August, 1871. He was then appointed pas-

NOTRE DAME CONVENT AND ACADEMY, CLEVELAND, O.

tor of Niles, where he remained till November, 1873, when he was assigned to the pastorate of St. Vincent's, Akron. Here he had a large parish to attend and a heavy debt to face, and here he was the same zealous and successful pastor as in his former and more limited sphere of labor. During his seven years' pastorate at Akron he won the hearts of his people by his disinterestedness and strict attention to duty. He also succeeded in largely reducing the burdensome debt. August 1, 1880, he entered upon the discharge of the onerous duties of pastor of St. Patrick's, Cleveland. He found the shell of the present beautiful structure, and a debt of over $25,000. During his nine years of pastorate of St. Patrick's he paid the entire debt, finished the church and furnished it with every needed comfort and convenience. In 1888 he purchased a lot on which he intended building a pastoral residence and at the hour of his death (September 29, 1889, after but one days' illness) was actively engaged in creating the the needed means for his work. Father Mahony was a man of kindly disposition, and untiring zeal. Wherever he was his memory is held in merited benediction. Single in purpose, honest of intent, untiring in zeal, he was always ready at the call of duty and the bidding of charity.

213. MARECHAL, Rev. John B., born in Normandy, France, May 17, 1812, was ordained for the Diocese of Arras, in 1835; was received by Bishop Rappe in August, 1850, and appointed pastor of Louisville, which charge he held from September, 1850, till September, 1851, when he was appointed one of the professors in St. Mary's Seminary, Cleveland. He was connected with the seminary and assisted in the parochial work at the cathedral till June, 1855. He then returned to France to assist the celebrated Abbe Migne, in publishing the voluminous edition of the Fathers of the Church, a work for which by his scholarly attainments he was eminently fitted. He was a "book-worm," a learned man and a pious priest. By too close application to study in his latter years his sight became greatly impaired, so that he could no longer pursue the work he had undertaken in France. He then

retired to a convent as chaplain, which position he held till he died, December, 1882.

214. MARSCHAL, Rev. John A., a native of East Prussia, and for a time a Dominican, was born at Allenstein, in 1819; ordained in 1844; was in the Diocese of Cleveland from 1866 to April, 1867, as pastor of Maumee. Bishop Rappe then dismissed him, and for a number of years he was on the mission elsewhere, viz.: in the Dioceses of Chicago and Milwaukee. October, 1877, he was again received into the diocese by Bishop Gilmour, to whom he was a stranger. He was appointed pastor of the Poles, in Cleveland, then worshiping in St. Mary's, on the Flats. He also attended Parma as a mission from January till March, 1878; Brighton, from October, 1877, to January, 1879, at which last date he left the diocese and returned to Europe.

215. MARSHALL, Rev. Francis, was born in Adams county, Pa.; attended Chippewa, near Doylestown, in 1827. No other record of him.

216. MARTE, Rev. Jacob (Sanguinist), was born at Rankweil, Diocese of Brixen, Austria, in the year 1843; came to the United States in 1860; was ordained for the Sanguinists, June 6, 1866; was in the Diocese of Cleveland as pastor of New Cleveland from August, 1872, to April, 1873; assistant at Glandorf till July, 1877, and as pastor of Big Spring (where he built the present church) till August, 1882, when he returned to Europe. There he remained till 1889, when he was recalled to this country. He is now in the Archdiocese of Cincinnati (Ft. Recovery).

217. MARTIN, Rev. Edward, was born at Grenoble, France, about 1827. After following the profession of a lawyer for a few years he became a Franciscan, went to Rome and was there ordained priest. Later he left the Franciscan Order, and in 1863 came to America, when he was received into the Diocese of Cleveland and appointed one of the pro-

fessors at St. Mary's Seminary, Cleveland. In 1864 he was appointed pastor of Harrisburg, remaining till 1865, when he left the diocese.

218. MARTIN, Rev. Thomas H. (Dominican), was ordained by Bishop Fenwick in 1822; attended Dunganno and several missions in Stark and Wayne counties between 1825 and 1827, and was the first priest to visit (1826) the Catholics of Cleveland. He was assistant pastor of St. John's, Canton, in 1830, and again from July to December, 1835. He died in New York city, May 10, 1859.

219. MASZOTAS, Rev. Joseph, a native of Russia, was born at Wladislawow, January 8, 1861. He made his ecclesiastical studies in St. Mary's Seminary, Cleveland, and was there ordained by Bishop Gilmour, December 17, 1887. He was appointed assistant at St. Stanislas' church, Cleveland, but left that position and the diocese in August, 1889, and was received into the Diocese of Scranton, where he is at present.

220. MAUCLERC, Rev. A. L., was born about 1820, and ordained in France; received into the Diocese of Cleveland in 1859, and appointed pastor of St. Louis' congregation, Louisville, Ohio, remaining till the beginning of the year 1861, when for a few months he had charge of St. Peter's, Norwalk. He then left the diocese to join the Society of Mary, near Dayton, where he remained till 1876, when he returned to France (St. Remy), and died there May 6, 1876.

221. MAZURET, Rev. Peter Patrick, was born at Rouse's Point, N. Y., in 1834; made his studies for the priesthood at the Sulpician Seminary, Montreal, and was ordained at Sandwich, Ont., by Bishop Pinsouneault, March 15, 1863. He was on the mission in Canada till August, 1864, and in the Diocese of Buffalo till 1874, when he was received into the Diocese of Cleveland, and appointed one of the cathedral assistants. March, 1875, he was sent to Defiance to organize the present congregation of Our Lady of Perpetual Help. Under his

direction their beautiful church was also begun and partly finished. He left the diocese January 4, 1877, and was received into the Diocese of Cincinnati, where he is at present.

222. MEILI, Rev. Aloysius Maria, was born of Protestant parents at Zurich, Switzerland, March 8, 1840; entered the Church when about twenty-eight years of age; made his studies at Zurich, Basle, Spring Hills (near Mobile), St. Mary's Seminary, Cincinnati, and St. Meinrad's, Ind.; was ordained for the Diocese of Ft. Wayne by Bishop Luers, February 27, 1870. Came to the Diocese of Cleveland, September, 1872, and was sent as assistant to St. Joseph's, Tiffin, remaining till July, 1873, when he was appointed pastor of Crestline. There he remained till March 20, 1874, when he left his charge and the diocese. July, 1883, he assumed pastoral duty in the Diocese of Leavenworth, Kansas, where he has since been engaged on the mission.

223. MERTES, Rev. Anthony, was born at Wagenhausen, Diocese of Treves, Prussia, January 8, 1826; ordained at Treves by Bishop Arnoldi, March 23, 1853. Did pastoral duty in his native diocese till expelled, in 1876, by the Prussian government, under the May laws. April, 1876, he came to the Diocese of Cleveland, and was appointed pastor of New Bavaria. March, 1879, he was transferred to Edgerton, with charge of Florence as a mission, August, 1883, he returned to Europe, where he is now doing pastoral duty.

224. MEYER, Rev. Charles W. (Sanguinist), was born in Cincinnati, O., June 25, 1856. He was educated for the priesthood in St. Charles' Seminary, Carthagena, O., and ordained in Cincinnati, by Archbishop Elder, for the Sanguinists, May 30, 1885. After doing pastoral work in Missouri, and for eleven months in Mercer county, O., he was sent to the Diocese of Cleveland as assistant at St. John's church, Glandorf, (May-August, 1889); then as assistant at Thompson, where he remained till April, 1890, when he was transferred to the Diocese of Cincinnati.

225. MEYER, Rev. Maria Anton (Sanguinist), born at Aesch, Canton Basel, Switzerland, February 21, 1817; studied for the ministry at Graubuendten, Switzerland; was ordained at Feldkirch, Austria, September 8, 1843; came to Ohio in 1844, and till 1846 had pastoral charge of the following places: Peru, Thompson, Tiffin, New Riegel; also attended the Catholic settlers in Huron, Richland, Crawford, Hancock, Stark, Wayne, Ashland, Summit, Lorain, Lucas and Ottawa counties, making the entire journey on horseback. In 1846 he went with Bishop Henni to the Diocese of Milwaukee, but was recalled in 1848, when he was stationed at Cleveland for a short time, with charge of Avon and French Creek as missions. Bishop Rappe then gave him pastoral charge of the following places in the Diocese of Cleveland: Glandorf and Fort Jennings, 1849-51; Thompson, 1855, to July, 1856; Avon, July to December, 1856. He was also at New Riegel for a while, but no record of time given. In 1858 he left the Sanguinists and became a secular priest, and as such he has continued ever since, in the Dioceses of Cincinnati and Covington.

226. MILES, Rt. Rev. Richard P. (Dominican), a native of Maryland, was born May 17, 1791, and ordained in September, 1816. He had pastoral charge of St. John's, Canton, between 1828 and 1830; was consecrated first Bishop of Nashville, September 16, 1838. He died February 21, 1860.

227. MOENNING, Rev. Francis (Franciscan), was born at Bakum, Diocese of Osnabrueck, Prussia, December 28, 1837; ordained at Teutopolis, Ill., by Bishop Juncker, January 13, 1867. He was attached to the Franciscan Monastery, Cleveland, from July, 1883, till January, 1887. While there he assisted the secular clergy, and attended to the spiritual wants of a number of religious communities. He is now in the Diocese of Nashville.

228. MOES, Rev. Nicholas. a native of Luxemburg, was born at Bous, February 8, 1826. He was educated for the

ministry in the Athenæum in the city of Luxemburg (seven years), in Belgium, under direction of Jesuits (two years), and for two years in the Diocesan Seminary at Cleveland. Bishop Rappe ordained him April 16, 1859, and assigned him the pastorate of St. Phillip's, Dungannon, where he remained till July, 1861, when he was made pastor of St. Joseph's, Fremont. September of the following year he was transferred to St. Mary's, Sandusky, remaining till 1864, when he was sent to St. Nicholas', Berwick. September, 1865, he was called to the Diocesan Seminary as professor of mental philosophy, and attended Louisville, for a short time from Cleveland. In 1867 he went to Europe for a few months. On his return Bishop Rappe sent him to St. Francis de Sales', Toledo, as assistant, and eight months later to New Bavaria, (Poplar Ridge), as pastor. In 1873 he was again appointed pastor of St. Mary's, Sandusky, where under his direction the present very beautiful church was built at a cost of over $80,000, with but a comparatively small debt remaining. Since 1878 his health has been poor. Twice during this time he was obliged to give up pastoral work. Although his two trips to his native country, in 1878 and 1885, benefited his health to some extent, he never fully rallied, chronic rheumatism being one of his afflictions. He resigned his pastorate in October, 1888, and returned to Luxemburg on an indefinite leave of absence. Father Moes is noted for his eloquence and scholarly attainments.

229. MOITRIER, Rev. Francis, born at Saizerais, France, February 19, 1839, was educated for the priesthood at Nancy, and St. Mary's Seminary, Cleveland. He was ordained by Bishop Rappe, January 6, 1865, when he was sent as assistant to Rev. V. Arnould, of Shelby Settlement. August, 1865, he was appointed pastor of Harrisburg, remaining till May, 1866, when he was sent to Alliance, whence he attended Leetonia. This charge he held till 1867, when he was received into the Diocese of Vincennes. Since 1871 he has been affiliated with the Diocese of Columbus.

230. MOLLOY, Rev. James, was born at Tullamore, Kings county, Ireland, October 13, 1844; made his ecclesiastical studies at St. Bridget's Seminary, Tullamore, and All Hallow's, Dublin; was ordained at Nashville, Tenn., by Bishop Feehan, November 30, 1867. He was on the mission in the Diocese of Nashville till received into the Diocese of Cleveland in 1872; was assistant at Sts. Peter and Paul's, Sandusky, till 1875; then assistant at St. Columba's, Youngstown, till July, 1876. He was next appointed pastor of Bellevue, remaining till May, 1879. Then he left the diocese, but returned July, 1880, when he received the pastorate of Kent. There he remained till August, 1881, when he again left. He is now in the Diocese of Cincinnati.

231. MOLON, Rev. Louis, was born in the Diocese of Arras, France, 1826; came to Cleveland as a Seminarist, August, 1850, and was ordained by Bishop Rappe, the following month, September 8. Soon after his ordination he was sent to Tiffin, as pastor of St. Mary's, remaining till September, 1852. Meanwhile (January to September, 1852) he also attended St. Joseph's congregation, same place. His next appointment was the pastorate of St. Mary's, Massillon, September, 1852, to July, 1855. During this time (1854) he also organized St. Joseph's congregation, Massillon. He was next appointed superior and professor of St. John's College, then (1855) in existence in Ohio City, now West Side, Cleveland. He retained this charge but a few months, as he preferred the active life of a pastor to that of a professor. Bishop Rappe accordingly assigned him the pastorate of St. Vincent's, Akron, January, 1856. In the fall of the same year he was appointed pastor of Berwick, remaining till November, 1857. His next charge was St. Ann's, Fremont, December, 1857, to July, 1861. From December, 1857, till 1860, he also attended St. Joseph's, Fremont, organized by Rev. John Roos, in 1857. He also had charge of Port Clinton, La Prairie, Marblehead and Toussaint, from June, 1860, to July, 1861. From July, 1861, till September, 1863, he was pastor of Holy Angels', Sandusky, and attended Kelley's Island and Put-in-Bay. In

the fall of 1863 he visited his native France on a six months' leave of absence, and on his return succeeded Rev. D. Tighe in the pastorate of St. Joseph's, Massillon, the congregation he had organized in 1854. There he remained till September, 1865, when he was appointed pastor of St. Mary's, Elyria, and attended for a while as missions, Norwalk, North Amherst, Vermillion, Lorain (Black River), and several small stations. He remained in Elyria till his death, November 16, 1880, although he had resigned his charge in March of same year, owing to an apoplectic stroke, which disabled him from doing any pastoral work. His remains are buried at Elyria, and near those of a former pastor of same place, the Rev. Francis Sullivan.

232. MONAHAN, Rev. James, was born in parish Tubbercurry, county Sligo, Ireland, December 8, 1822. He was ordained in St. Mary's church, on the Flats, Cleveland, November 19, 1848—the first priest ordained by Bishop Rappe. From December, 1848, to July, 1849, he was stationed at the cathedral (St. Mary's church, on the Flats), Cleveland, and was then sent to Holy Angels', Sandusky. His next charge was Dungannon, December, 1849, to October, 1852, with Summitville, Wellsville and East Liverpool as missions. In 1853 he was sent to Maumee, and in 1854 to Toledo as assistant to Father Foley at St. Francis' church, where he remained till 1855. His next appointment was as assistant to Very Rev. James Conlan, at St. Patrick's, Cleveland, where he remained but a short time when he left the Diocese of Cleveland. He was received by Archbishop Purcell and sent on the mission in Perry county. He was also for a time in the Diocese of Philadelphia. In 1863, after a visit to Ireland, he was again received by Bishop Rappe and sent to Bellevue, 1863-65; then to St. Bridget's, Cleveland, 1866-70. His next appointments were South Thompson, 1870-72; Alliance, 1872-75; assistant at St. Francis', Toledo, 1876-77; and assistant at Holy Rosary church, Cleveland, 1877 to July, 1880. Bishop Gilmour then gave him charge of St. Stephen's congregation, Niles, where he remained from July, 1880, till

his death, September 6, 1884. His remains are buried in St. John's Cemetery, Cleveland.

233. MONTGOMERY, Rev. Charles P. (Dominican), was ordained in 1830; had charge of missions in Columbiana and Stark counties between 1837 and 1840. For many years he was pastor of Zanesville, where, on Easter Monday, 1860, he was found dead in bed at the pastoral residence. He was an excellent priest and much beloved by his people.

234. MORAN, Rev. James, was assistant to Rev. Philip Foley, at St. Francis' church, Toledo, 1848; attended Dungannon from autumn of 1848 to 1849. No other record of him.

235. MOURET, Rev. Casimir, was stationed at Doylestown in 1847 and 1848. October, 1848, he was appointed pastor of St. Vincent's, Akron, where he resided till June, 1850, meanwhile attending Harrisburg and New Berlin as missions. No other record of him.

236. MUEHE, Rev. Michael (Sanguinist), born at Biesenhofen, Bavaria, July 5, 1865, was educated for the priesthood at Carthagena, Mercer county, O., and there ordained for the Sanguinists by Archbishop Elder, March 17, 1889. From March to November of same year he was engaged in pastoral work in the Diocese of Cincinnati; from November till December, 1889, as temporary pastor of St. Mary's, Tiffin, O. Since then he has been in the Diocese of Kansas City.

237. MULCAHY, Rev. Michael (Basilian), was born in Cork, Ireland, December 28, 1840; educated at St. Michael's College, Toronto; ordained at Lyons, France, by Bishop Charbonnel, May 21, 1864; was in the Diocese of Cleveland for one year (1867-68) as one of the professors of St. Louis' College, Louisville, Stark county; also attended Leetonia as a mission from 1867 to July, 1868. At present he is at St. Michael's College, Toronto.

238. MULLON, Rev. James Ignatius, a native of Ireland, studied for the ministry at Mt. St. Mary's Seminary, Emmittsburg, Md., and was ordained by Bishop Fenwick in 1824. Shortly after his ordination he attended the Catholic settlers in Columbiana county, and repeatedly make pastoral visits to Canton, Tiffin and Fremont. He was stationed at the cathedral in Cincinnati for nearly ten years, and while there he published the *Catholic Telegraph* (1831-34), of which he was the first editor. He was a brilliant writer and an eloquent preacher. He left Ohio in 1834 and went to the Diocese of New Orleans, where he died in September, 1866, aged seventy-two years.

239. MYLER, Rev. James P., was born in Cleveland, O., July 27, 1856. In his seventeenth year he entered Mount St. Mary's Seminary, Cincinnati, where he made his collegiate studies. After completing them he was received into St. Mary's Seminary, Cleveland, where he made the usual course of philosophy and theology. He was ordained in the Seminary chapel by Bishop Gilmour, July 6, 1884. A few weeks after his ordination he was sent to St. Augustine's, Cleveland, to supply, for a short time, the place of the pastor, then off on a leave of absence because of ill health. He was next sent to Niles to take temporary charge of St. Stephen's congregation. He filled a like position at St. Mary's, Norwalk, for a few weeks. January 20, 1885, he was sent to Holy Name church, Cleveland, as assistant. This last position he held till July, 1887, when he was relieved from all duty owing to consumption, to which he had fallen a victim. He then retired to his home at Painesville, Ohio, where he died August 31, 1887. He was a model priest, and a man of much promise. Gentle in manner, of quiet and retiring disposition, he impressed all within his circle as an earnest and sincere worker in the ministry.

240. NEUMANN, Rt. Rev. John Nepomucene (Redemptorist), was born on Good Friday, March 28, 1811, at Prachatitz, Bohemia. His parents were from Bavaria, but in 1802

had settled in Bohemia. He made his studies at the Seminaries of Budweis and Prague, where he distinguished himself by his talent and piety. He came to the United States in 1836, and was ordained in New York city by Bishop Dubois, June 25, of same year. Remaining a secular priest until October, 1840, he sought admission from the Redemptorists and was received at Pittsburg as a novice. During the summer of the following year he was sent to Peru, Huron county, O., as assistant to Rev. F. X. Tschenhens, also a Redemptorist. November, 1841, he was sent to Baltimore to finish his novitiate. On his way thither he met Bishop Purcell at Canton, who asked him to go to Randolph for a few weeks and there reorganize the congregation that had been without spiritual attendance since the destruction of their church, by a bigoted incendiary, in 1838. Father Neumann did as asked, and then resumed his journey to Baltimore. March 28, 1852, he was consecrated Bishop of Philadelphia. He died suddenly in that city, January 5, 1860. He was distinguished for his great humility, piety, learning and zeal, and was known as a saintly priest and bishop. May, 1886, a commission was appointed to inquire into the life, character and works of Bishop Neumann, and to send to Rome the testimony procured, with a view to having him eventually canonized. It is the belief of all who came in contact with Bishop Neumann during his life that he possessed the virtues and attributes of a saint. This belief has been strengthened since his death by the many miraculous cures which are said to have taken place at the tomb where his remains lie, in St. Peter's church, Philadelphia.

241. NEUMANN, Rev. Maximilian (Franciscan), was born in Neustadt, Silesia, July 7, 1846. He was educated for the Franciscans at Neisse (Silesia), Duesseldorf and Paderborn (Germany), and was also ordained for their Order by Archbishop Melchers, at Cologne, March 13, 1875. He was sent to this country by his superiors in September, 1875, and stationed as assistant at St. Francis' church, Quincy, Ill., where he remained till July, 1885. His next appointment was as supe-

rior of the Franciscan Monastery, Cleveland, from July, 1885, to August 6, 1888. He was then made pastor of St. Peter's church, Chicago, where he now resides.

242. NEUMANN, Rev. Nicholas Lawrence, was a native of Boulogne, Diocese of Metz, France, where he was also educated for the ministry. He was ordained at Metz by Bishop Besson, and was engaged on the mission in his native diocese till 1850, when he came to America, and was received into the Diocese of St. Louis. January, 1852, he was received into the Diocese of Cleveland by Bishop Rappe, who directed him to attend the Catholic Germans of Cleveland. Left the diocese about April, 1852, and went to Toronto; later he returned to Europe, where he died.

243. NIEMOELLER, Rev. Eustace (Franciscan), was born at Visbeck, Westphalia, April 9, 1837; in the United States since August, 1860; ordained at Teutopolis, Ill., for the Franciscans by Bishop Juncker, December 4, 1868; attached to Franciscan Monastery, Cleveland, from September, 1871, to August, 1880. He was chaplain and spiritual director to several religious communities. He also assisted the secular clergy in pastoral work. He is now stationed at Chicago.

244. NIGHTINGALE, Rev. William L., of English birth, was received into the Diocese of Cleveland July, 1848, and for a few weeks assisted at the cathedral, then on the "Flats," Cleveland. He was then appointed first resident pastor of St. Ann's, Fremont, where he remained till he left the diocese, some time during the early part of 1850. He was a zealous priest and an eloquent preacher. No other record of him.

245. NOLTE, Rev. Jacob (Franciscan), was born August 8, 1851, at Gesecke, Diocese of Paderborn, Westphalia; came to the United States July, 1875; ordained July 25, 1877; in Franciscan Monastery, Cleveland, from 1878 to 1879. At present he is in the Diocese of Omaha.

246. NOLTE, Rev. Paschalis (Franciscan), was born at Germete, Westphalia, Germany, June 12, 1845; educated at Franciscan Monastery, Quincy, Ill.; was ordained at St. Louis for the Franciscans by Bishop Ryan, June 5, 1881; a member of Franciscan Monastery, Cleveland, from July, 1882, to July, 1885. He is now in the Diocese of Chicago.

247. NUNAN, Rev. F. X., was born in county Limerick, Ireland, May 10, 1845; made his studies at St. Mary's Seminary, Baltimore, and St. Sulpice, Paris; was ordained by Archbishop Alemany for the Diocese of San Francisco, September, 1869. Till 1875 he was engaged on the mission in California and Kansas, when he came to the Diocese of Cleveland, where he had charge of the following places: Wakeman, with Medina as mission, October, 1875, to May, 1878; Vermillion and several missions, till March, 1879; Clyde and the mission of Green Spring, to June, 1881; Archbold and missions, till April, 1882; St. Mary's Corners, till August, 1883; Wellsville, till September 15, 1884, when he went to the Diocese of Peoria. Present residence not known.

248. O'BAIRNE, Rev. — (Dominican); stationed at St. John's, Canton, in 1835. No other record of him.

249. O'BRIEN, Rev. Denis P., born in the parish of Knockainy, county Limerick, Ireland, July 8, 1859, was educated for the priesthood at Mt. Melleray, and St. John's, Waterford, Ireland. Bishop Powers ordained him at Waterford, June 17, 1883. Shortly after his ordination he came to the United States and was received into the Diocese of Kansas City, where he was stationed at St. Patrick's church, in the city of St. Joseph, Mo., November, 1883, to January 23, 1884. Bishop Gilmour received him in February, 1884, and appointed him resident pastor of Warren with charge of Mantua and a number of stations. From Warren he also attended Niles for several months. He was transferred to Niles, September, 1884, and remained till April 4, 1888, when he left the diocese of his own accord and went to Chicago, where he is now engaged in pastoral work.

250. O'CALLAGHAN, Rev. Cornelius J., was born at Kanturk, county Cork, Ireland, March 10, 1832; made his ecclesiastical studies at Cork, Ireland, and Fordham, N. Y.; was ordained by Archbishop Hughes for the Diocese of Portland, October 20, 1860. Bishop Rappe received him into the Diocese of Cleveland in 1869 and sent him as assistant to St. Francis', Toledo, where he remained till 1871, when he was appointed assistant at the cathedral, Cleveland. There he remained till 1874, when he returned to the Diocese of Portland, where he now is.

251. O'CONNOR, Rev. John B., born and educated in Ireland, was ordained at Pittsburgh by Bishop O'Connor about 1854. Bishop Rappe received him into the Diocese of Cleveland and appointed him assistant at the cathedral, May, 1857, where he remained till June, 1860, when he left the diocese. No other record of him.

252. O'CONNOR, Rev. William, was born in Ballyorgan, county Limerick, Ireland, March 30, 1827; made his theological studies at St. Mary's Seminary, Cleveland, and was ordained by Bishop Rappe, November 21, 1851. He had charge of Elyria, Grafton, Rockport, Liverpool and Medina till 1853, attending these places from Cleveland. Between 1853 and 1855 he attended Youngstown, Wellsville and East Liverpool from Dungannon. From July, 1855, to July, 1858, he was stationed at St. Francis', Toledo, first as assistant to Rev. A. Campion, and from May, 1856, as pastor. During this time he also attended Sylvania and several stations. Youngstown was his next appointment as first resident pastor of St. Columba's, with Briar Hill, Warren, Niles and New Bedford as missions, besides a number of stations—1858 to 1862, when he left the Diocese of Cleveland and joined the Redemptorists, with whom he has since remained. At present he resides at Boston.

253. O'DWYER, Rev. Patrick, a native of Cashel, county Tipperary, Ireland, was ordained at Quebec in 1829. Sep-

tember, 1837, he came to Cleveland as successor to Rev. John Dillon, where he did pastoral duty till June, 1840, besides attending a number of missions and stations in Lorain, Summit and Portage counties. He commenced the frame church on the Flats, for which his predecessor had collected about $1,100. He left in 1840 and went to London, Canada, and later he was received into the Diocese of Chicago. He died at St. Charles, Ill., August 30, 1871.

254. O'HIGGINS, Rev. William, of Irish birth, was educated at Maynooth; ordained in British Guinea about 1853. He was nephew to Bishop O'Higgins of Ardagh. Came to Cincinnati in 1857, and was appointed successor to Rev. R. Gilmour, at Ironton. Remained there about one year, when he was appointed pastor of St. Thomas', Cincinnati, (1858-60); then assistant to Father Gilmour, at St. Patrick's, same city. From 1862 to 1864 he was chaplain of the Tenth Regiment, O. V. I. Next he had charge of Sedamsville mission, near Cincinnati, for nearly a year, when he was received into the Diocese of Little Rock, where he remained till about 1870. He then came to Cleveland in 1871, and was appointed professor at St. Mary's Seminary, where he remained till his appointment as pastor of St. Augustine's, Cleveland, December, 1871, to June, 1872. Was a few months at Charity Hospital as a patient, in 1872, and then left the Diocese of Cleveland. Returned to Ireland, where he died in 1875.

255. O'KEEFE, Rev. Daniel, was born at Middleton, county Cork, Ireland, in 1835; began his studies in Cork, continued at St. Vincent's College, Westmoreland county, Pa., and finished them in St. Mary's Seminary, Cleveland, where he was ordained by Bishop Rappe, June 25, 1865. He was appointed first resident pastor of South Thompson, 1865-66, attending Jefferson as a mission. He was then sent to Defiance as assistant to Rev. A. I. Hoeffel, with charge of Antwerp (where he began the present church), Mud Creek, Delaware Bend, and several smaller missions. October, 1869, he was appointed pastor of Providence, where he remained

till January, 1871, when he was obliged to resign, owing to ill health. He was lying sick in the pastoral residence at Perrysburg for ten weeks, when he was removed to St. Vincent's Hospital, Toledo, where he died June 16, 1871. His remains are buried in St. Francis' Cemetery, Toledo. Father O'Keefe was a zealous, earnest priest, and won the esteem of his parishioners wherever he was engaged in the ministry.

256. O'LEARY, Rev. D. J., (Dominican), a native of Ireland, made his ecclesiastical studies at the Minerva, Rome; came to the United States in 1821, and was ordained by Bishop Flaget, at St. Rose's, Kentucky, in 1823. He attended Dungannon, Columbiana county, in 1834. Died at the Dominican Convent, near Somerset, Perry county, February 8, 1845, aged fifty-one.

257. O'MARA, Rev. Patrick H., was born in Chicago, Ill., February 22, 1852. He was educated for the priesthood at Louisville College, and St. Mary's Seminary, Cleveland. Bishop Gilmour ordained him July 5, 1877, and a few days later appointed him resident pastor of Hudson, with charge of the missions of Cuyahoga Falls and Peninsula. He remained there till July, 1881. In the following month he was appointed assistant to Rev. M. Healy, pastor of St. Mary's, Tiffin. December of same year he received a like appointment to St. Columba's, Youngstown, where he remained one year. His last mission was as assistant to Rev. A. I. Hoeffel, pastor of St. John's church, Delphos, from August, 1886, to September, 1888, when owing to sickness he went to St. Elizabeth's Hospital, Fort Wayne. There, after four weeks' illness, he died October 22, 1888. His remains are interred in St. John's Cemetery, Cleveland.

258. O'MEALY, Rev. Joseph, was born in Ireland, 1815. He was stationed at St. John's, Canton, for a few months in 1840. Later he was superior of the Diocesan Seminary, in Brown county, Ohio (at present the well-known Ursuline Convent); he was also, for a number of years, at Portsmouth

and Dayton. He died in 1856. His grave is in Calvary Cemetery, Dayton, Ohio.

259. O'MEARA, Rev. J., (Dominican), was stationed at St. John's, Canton, 1835-36, and attended Canal Fulton. Left Ohio about 1840 and went to Illinois, where he died. No other record of him.

260. O'NEILL, Rev. Michael, was born in the parish of Bruff, county Limerick, Ireland, June 24, 1830; made his ecclesiastical studies at Cork and Castle Knock, Ireland, and in the Diocesan Seminary of Cleveland. He was ordained by Bishop Rappe, January 1, 1855, and remained at the cathedral as assistant, with charge of Berea, Hudson and Mantua as missions, till July, 1856. Then he was appointed pastor of Wooster, remaining till July, 1861. He also attended Mansfield, Crestline and Bucyrus as missions, besides several small stations, while pastor of Wooster. July, 1861, he was transferred to St. Ann's, Fremont, which charge he held till May, 1865, when he left the Diocese of Cleveland and went to Cincinnati. There he was appointed pastor of Holy Angels' church. This charge he held till his death, April 24, 1885.

261. O'REILLY, Rev. James, was born in Rossduff, county Longford, Ireland, February 14, 1841, and made his studies at New Orleans, Niagara Falls, and in St. Mary's Seminary, Cleveland. He was ordained by Bishop Rappe, June 24, 1866, and appointed assistant at the cathedral, where he remained till October 1, 1869. He was then appointed pastor of St. Rose's, Lima. January 6, 1871, he was recalled to Cleveland to take charge of St. Columbkill's congregation, just then organized. He remained there till October 1, 1872, when he was sent to Toledo as pastor of St. Francis de Sales' church, where he continued till his death, September 30, 1885.

262. O'SULLIVAN, Rev. Michael, was born in Ireland (no record of date or place); finished his studies for the ministry at St. Mary's Seminary, Cleveland, and was ordained by Bishop

Rappe, August —, 1852. His first appointment was at St. Mary's, Tiffin, September, 1852, to February, 1859, where under great difficulties, he built the present church. There he also established a parochial school. From Tiffin he attended Findlay till 1854. February, 1859, he was received by Archbishop Purcell, who sent him to Urbana. Five months later he was appointed pastor of Holy Angels' church, Cincinnati. In 1860 he went to the Diocese of Chicago, and remained there till his death, as pastor of Amara, Ill., July —, 1865. His remains were interred in Calvary Cemetery, Chicago, July 28, 1865. Father O'Sullivan was a man of sterling qualities, firm but kind in his dealings with those committed to his care. He was also an excellent preacher. The writer will ever treasure most pleasant recollections of this warm-hearted priest, whose parochial school he attended, and one of whose altar boys he was for several years. Father O'Sullivan's greatest delight was to be with the children of his parish. His genial ways spread sunshine and joy on those whom he honored with his presence. To the children as well as to the adults committed to his care, he was indeed a spiritual father, a wise counselor and true friend.

263. OBERLE, Rev. Francis Joseph, born in Schweinheim, Bavaria, May 7, 1842, was ordained for the Redemptorists, April 1, 1865. In 1874 he became a secular priest. He was in the Diocese of Cleveland from February, 1877, till March, 1881, and had charge of Shelby as resident pastor, and attended Chicago Junction (where he organized a congregation and built the present church), also Plymouth and Republic. After leaving the Diocese of Cleveland he was admitted, some time after, by Bishop Gross, to the Vicariate of North Carolina, where he was on the mission till 1883, when he became an invalid of consumption. He was received by his friend, Rev. A. J. Sauer, pastor of St. Andrew's, Ellenville, Ulster county, New York, with whom he made his home till death, March 16, 1885.

264. OBERMUELLER, Rev. Francis Xavier, a native of Austria, was born at Schwarzenberg, Tyrol, October 6, 1810.

He came to this country in July, 1844, and was ordained by Bishop Henni for the Diocese of Milwaukee, June 11, 1846. Shortly after his ordination he expressed a desire to join the Sanguinist Fathers, whose community in Tyrol he had learned to esteem. His wish was granted by his Ordinary. He was therefore received at New Riegel, Ohio, by the Very Rev. Provincial Brunner, under whose direction he did pastoral duty in various places in the Diocese of Cleveland, viz.: New Riegel, as assistant pastor, from 1847 to 1848; also attended as missions, St. Joseph's, Tiffin, 1850; Fostoria and Liberty, 1848. Next he was assistant at Thompson, from 1848 to 1850, when he left the Sanguinists and returned to the Diocese of Milwaukee, where he had pastoral charges till 1852. He then went back to his native Tyrol, where he was pastor till October, 1856. In the following month he returned to America with Very Rev. Father Brunner, having been received again as a member of the Sanguinist society. February, 1857, he was given charge of a congregation in Mercer county, O., and later a professorship in the Sanguinist college, then existing at Gruenewald, same county. September 12, 1857, he was sent to Cleveland as pastor of St. Mary of the Assumption congregation, then occupying the old frame church on the Flats. This charge he retained till August, 1861. Meanwhile, December, 1860, he again left the Sanguinists and became a secular priest, and so continued till death. During his pastorate of St. Mary's, Cleveland, a portion of the present church property was bought. The parochial school was enlarged and placed in charge of Brothers of Mary and Ursuline Sisters. August, 1861, he was sent by Bishop Rappe to Norwalk as pastor of St. Peter's, where he remained till he again left the diocese, October, 1865. From Norwalk he attended Peru, September, 1861, to September, 1862; Milan, 1863-65; Monroeville, where he organized the present congregation, September, 1861, to July, 1863. In October, 1865, he returned to the Diocese of Milwaukee, having been reclaimed by Bishop Henni. He was sent to Jefferson, Wis., as pastor of St. Lawrence's church and chaplain of the Franciscan Sisters, remaining till 1871, when he became affiliated with the Diocese of

La Crosse, on invitation of its first bishop, the Rt. Rev. M. Heiss, whose intimate friend he was for many years. As he was of advanced years and delicate health he was unable to do pastoral duty. Bishop Heiss therefore assigned him the chaplaincy of St. Rose's Convent, at La Crosse, where he resided till his death, June 12, 1886. Whilst connected with the Diocese of La Crosse he was a member of the Bishop's Council. He was always held in high esteem by his superiors, and by his co-laborers on the missions, for his priestly virtues and worth. He was a fine scholar, a saintly and self-sacrificing priest.

265. ORZECHOWSKI, Rev. M. F., a native of Poland, was born at Stopnica, May 30, 1838, and educated for the priesthood in Poland and in the seminary at Sans, France. He was ordained for the Diocese of Galveston, Texas, by Bishop Dubuis, November 1, 1866. He was on the mission in Texas till 1882; then in the Diocese of Milwaukee till August, 1884, when he was received by Bishop Gilmour and appointed pastor of St. Anthony's (Polish) congregation, Toledo. This position he held till November, 1887, when he went to Europe. He returned in May, 1888, and went to the Diocese of Buffalo; then to Davenport, Iowa, where he is now engaged in the ministry.

266. PAGANINI, Rev. Angelo, was born, educated and ordained in Italy. After being on the mission in several dioceses in the east, in New Jersey and Maryland, he was received by Bishop Gilmour in 1873, and appointed resident pastor of Warren. There he remained till 1875, when after a few months' absence, he was sent to Hudson, February, 1876, remaining till May, 1877, when he left the Diocese of Cleveland, and later returned to Italy. He died there of cholera, near Assisi, August —, 1884.

267. PAGANINI, Rev. Joseph, was received into the Diocese of Cleveland, in 1875 and appointed pastor of Warren. Remained but a short time. No other record of him.

268. PETER, Rev. George, was born in Somborn, Chur-Hessen, Europe, May 19, 1835; made his studies at St. Mary's Seminary, Cleveland; was ordained by Bishop Rappe, June 26, 1859. He had the following pastoral charges in the Diocese of Cleveland: Fremont, St. Joseph's, as assistant, with charge of the missions of Millersville (Greensburg), Clyde, Elmore, Woodville, Port Clinton and Toussaint, July, 1859, to June, 1861; Dungannon, with Leetonia as a mission, and the stations of New Lisbon and Salem, June, 1861, to June, 1864; Liverpool, June, 1864, to January, 1866; Milan to October, 1868; Upper Sandusky to March, 1873, from which place he also attended Kirby, January, 1869, to March, 1873. After three months' illness he was sent to Avon in the fall of 1873, and attended Sheffield as a mission. In the following year he was appointed pastor of St. Peter's, Norwalk. He remained there till October, 1875. Edgerton and Florence were his next charges, October, 1875, to May, 1879, when he was sent to Fort Jennings, remaining there till June, 1881. Since last mentioned date he has not done pastoral duty. For the last few years he has been residing at Put-in-Bay.

269. PEUDEPRAT, Rev. Peter, was born, educated and ordained in the Diocese of Clermont, France; came to Northern Ohio in 1845, and was sent to Sandusky as assistant to Rev. P. J. Machebeuf, pastor of Holy Angels' church, whence he also attended the mission of Fremont. January, 1846, he was sent to Louisville, Stark county, as successor to Rev. L. de Goesbriand. From this place he attended Harrisburg, and occasionally, also, Wellsville. He remained at Louisville till April, 1850, when he went to reside at St. Mary's Seminary, Cleveland, for a few months. In the latter part of 1850 he assumed charge of Painesville, as first resident pastor. At once he secured the present church lot and had moved on it an old carpenter shop, which he bought and changed it into a temporary church. From Painesville he attended as missions, South Thompson, Willoughby and Conneaut. He left Painesville and the Diocese of Cleveland, in the summer of 1852, to join his life-long friend, Bishop Lamy, in the hard missionary

life of New Mexico. On his way thither he fell a victim to cholera, at St. Louis, Mo., where he died, July —, 1852.

270. PONCHEL, Rev. Narcissus, was born at Hermelinghen, France, September 19, 1825; completed his studies for the priesthood in the Diocesan Seminary, Cleveland, where he was ordained by Bishop Rappe, January 1, 1851. Till March, 1851, he attended Avon from Cleveland, and was then sent as assistant to Rev. Philip Foley, pastor of St. Francis de Sales', Toledo, remaining until 1854. During his stay at Toledo, he also had charge of the missions of Six Mile Woods (1851-52), Providence (1851-54), Toussaint (1852-53), and Maumee (1852-53). February, 1854, he was appointed pastor of Doylestown and attended Canal Fulton as a mission till January, 1855, when he accepted a professorship at St. John's College, then in existence in Cleveland. He retained this position till 1856, when Bishop Rappe sent him to Norwalk to take charge of St. Peter's congregation, and to organize the English-speaking Catholics of the same town as a congregation (St. Mary's), whose first church was commenced and nearly completed under his direction. He was pastor of St. Peter's till 1858, and of St. Mary's till his death, September 15, 1860. His remains repose beneath the church he built, and in it a memorial tablet is erected to his memory. Father Ponchel was a man of large acquirements, a priestly character and a thorough gentleman. By his refined manners and gentle ways he made friends of all who had dealings with him. To this day his memory is cherished by Protestants and Catholics of Norwalk, and wherever he labored in the diocese.

271. PRAESSAR, Rev. Hugo (Jesuit), was born January 11, 1838, at Ahrlweiler, Diocese of Treves; ordained August 27, 1863; in this country since September, 1868; was assistant at St. Mary's, Toledo, from 1871 to 1873. No record of his present residence.

272. PRENDERGAST, Rev. Michael, was born, educated and ordained in Ireland. He was received into the Diocese

of Cleveland in 1855, and stationed at the cathedral for a few months. His next appointment was Summitville, with Leetonia, Niles, Youngstown and Warren as missions, April, 1856, to 1858. He then left the Diocese of Cleveland, and resided with the Sanguinists at Wapakoneta, (Diocese of Cincinnati,) from which place he attended Lima for a short time in 1861. During this last mentioned year he affiliated with the Diocese of St. Paul, Minn., where he was pastor at Winona. He died about 1862.

273. PRIMEAU, Rev. John B., a French Canadian, was born at Chateauguay, P. Q., April 29, 1836; ordained at Montreal, by Bishop Bourget, October 21, 1860; was engaged as pastor and professor in the Diocese of Montreal from 1860 till 1869, when he went to the Diocese of Springfield, Mass He remained there till July, 1882, when Bishop Gilmour assigned him pastoral work at Archbold, Fulton county, with charge of several missions. November 15, 1883, he left the Diocese of Cleveland. Asking Bishop Gilmour, in September, 1884, to again give him pastoral work he was sent to St. Louis' church, East Toledo. December, 1888, he was removed from this charge and dismissed from the diocese, but refused to vacate the pastoral residence, which he has continued to occupy since, and up to present time, (April, 1890).

274. PROST, Very Rev. Joseph (Redemptorist), was born in Austria, January, 1804; ordained July 16, 1832; came to the United States in 1834; attended Peru, Huron county, between 1835 and 1839; was Provincial of the Redemptorists in the United States between 1840 and 1843; returned to Europe; died at Tuchheim, Austria, March 19, 1885.

275. PUETZ, Rev. Anselm (Franciscan), was born at Dueren, Diocese of Cologne, Prussia, September 1, 1834; ordained September 1, 1862; in the United States since July, 1875; belonged to Franciscan Monastery, Cleveland, from 1884 to July, 1885. He is now in the Diocese of Chicago, Ill.

276. QUINN, Rev. Bernard, was born in Ireland in 1840. He made his studies for the ministry, in part, at St. Mary's Seminary, Cleveland, and was ordained by Bishop Rappe, July 3, 1864. Was sent to Louisville, Stark county, in 1865, as professor in the college then and there in existence, where he remained till June, 1867. He was appointed first resident pastor of Upper Sandusky, but retained this position only two months. His next and last appointment in the Diocese of Cleveland was St. Joseph's, Maumee, where he remained till September, 1867, when he left the diocese.

277. QUINN, Rev. Edmund, a native of Ireland, made his ecclesiastical studies at Bardstown, Ky., and was ordained at Cincinnati by Bishop Fenwick, January 1, 1831. He was the first resident pastor of St. Mary's, Tiffin, receiving his appointment in May, 1831, after having done pastoral duty in Cincinnati. He organized St. Mary's congregation, Tiffin, and had its first (brick) church built on a lot near the present Ursuline Convent. From Tiffin he attended the Catholic families along and near the Miami canal, from Providence, Lucas county, O., to Peru, Indiana, at which latter place he died, September 5, 1835, a victim of the dreaded Maumee fever. He was a most zealous, self-sacrificing priest.

278. QUINN, Rev. John, was born at Kanturk, county Cork, Ireland, December 1, 1824. He came to this country in 1852, and two years later entered St. Mary's Seminary, Cleveland, where he made his theological studies. June 13, 1858, he was elevated to the priesthood by Bishop Rappe, who sent him, the following month to Toledo, as assistant at St. Francis de Sales' church. There he remained till December, 1860, when he was appointed pastor of St. Mary's, Norwalk. He held this charge till April, 1864, besides attending the mission of Wakeman about one year, 1863-64. At Norwalk the church, commenced by his predecessor, Rev. N. Ponchel, was completed under his direction. April, 1864, he was appointed superior of the Diocesan Seminary, and one of its professors. This post of honor he filled quite satisfactorily

till July, 1866, when his impaired health, never robust, obliged him to retire for a while for much needed rest and medical treatment. In 1867 he felt himself again able to take charge of a congregation. He was accordingly appointed pastor of St. Ann's, Fremont. This charge he held till August, 1868, when he was transferred to the pastorate of the Immaculate Conception congregation, Toledo. The present frame church, school and brick pastoral residence were built under his direction. In May, 1878, he was removed to St. Mary's, Wakeman, where he remained till obliged by sickness to cease all pastoral work, January, 1885. He lingered in patiently borne sickness at St. Vincent's Hospital, Toledo, until death released him, March 26, 1887. His remains are buried at Sandusky.

279. QUINN, Rev. William, D. D., a native of Ireland, was born in Limerick, October 14, 1839. For nine years he was a student at the Propaganda, Rome, and was there ordained for the Diocese of Dublin. He came from Cincinnati to Cleveland in September, 1873, and was appointed one of the professors at the seminary, but remained only till the following March. He died at Valetta, Isle of Malta, November 25, 1885. He was an able professor, a fine classical scholar and an eloquent preacher.

280. REICHERT, Rev. Augustine (Sanguinist), was born at Nussloch, Baden, February 20, 1831; came to America in 1834; ordained at New Riegel for the Sanguinists, by Bishop Rappe, November 21, 1853; was in the Diocese of Cleveland, at Thompson, as assistant, with charge of neighboring missions, from June, 1854, to November, 1855; from 1856 to 1859 as assistant at Glandorf; from 1859 to 1862 as pastor of New Riegel; and as pastor of Glandorf, from 1862 to May, 1874, when he was sent by his superior to Kansas, where for fifteen years he did pastoral duty, amid hardships and privations such as few would care to endure. He died at St. Joseph's Hospital, Kansas City, Mo., February 13, 1889. A priest in the true sense of the word he realized the dignity and respon-

sibility of pastor of souls; he was one of his Master's faithful servants.

281. REINHARDT, Rev. Joseph, born in Bavaria, about 1842, was ordained for the Diocese of Cleveland by Bishop Rappe, January 22, 1865. New Bavaria (Poplar Ridge) was his first appointment, May, 1865, to May, 1867. For a few months he also attended Perrysburg as a mission. His next charge was Upper Sandusky, with Bucyrus and Kirby as missions. On the morning of February 22, 1868, he intended to go to Bucyrus to meet Bishop Rappe, who was to give confirmation there on that day. Having missed the passenger train he attempted to board a freight train and so reach Bucyrus in time for the ceremony, although told by the trainmen that they could not take him. Shortly after the freight train left Upper Sandusky his mangled remains were found near the railway station. The coroner's jury found that the railway employes were not to blame for his death. His untimely and sad ending cast a gloom over the entire community of Upper Sandusky, where he was highly esteemed by all classes for his amiable qualities. His remains are buried at Upper Sandusky.

282. REVIS, Rev. Wenceslas, was born, 1822, at Wodnau, Bohemia; ordained in the year 1846; came to America in 1852, and was on the mission in the Dioceses of Philadelphia, Alton and Nashville. He left Nashville during the civil war and returned to his native country. At the close of the war, in 1865, he went back to Nashville, remaining till 1870, when he accepted an invitation from Very Rev. Administrator Hannin to take charge of St. Wenceslas' (Bohemian) congregation, Cleveland. He came in January, 1870, and remained till March, 1873. While pastor of St. Wenceslas' he shared the fate of his predecessor, Father Krasney, by being vilified and persecuted by his infidel countrymen, and some of his parishioners, who did all they could to obstruct his pastoral work and embitter his stay among them. Disheartened he left his difficult charge and went to the Diocese of Chicago,

ST. IGNATIUS' COLLEGE, CLEVELAND, O.

where he remained till death, at Feehanville, June 19, 1886. Father Revis was a zealous priest and an eloquent preacher.

283. RICHARD, Rev. Charles Hermann (Jesuit), was born at Osnabrueck, Hanover, May 8, 1834; ordained August 25, 1867; came to America, October, 1867; was stationed at St. Mary's, Toledo, as assistant, from 1869 to 1872.

284. RINGELE, Rev. Jacob (Sanguinist), was born 1806, at Doettingen, Canton Solothurn, Switzerland; ordained December 21, 1842; came to the United States December 31, 1843. He was engaged on the mission in Northern Ohio and Diocese of Cleveland between 1845 and 1865, and from 1870 till his death, December 15, 1871. Among his charges were Peru (1845); Cleveland (1848-49); Dungannon (1850); Defiance (about 1855); Shelby Settlement (1855-56); Thompson (1865-66) and New Riegel (1867), in all of which places he was full of zeal for religion, and did faithful missionary work.

285. ROEDIGER, Rev. Edmund (Franciscan), was born at Kalmerode, Eichfeld, Prussia, in 1857 (?); ordained at Teutopolis, Ill., May 28, 1882; in Cleveland Monastery from July, 1883, to April, 1884. Is at present on the mission in China.

286. ROESSNER, Rev. Clement (Sanguinist), was born at St. Peter's, Mercer county, Ohio, September 20, 1849; educated by and for the Sanguinists at Carthagena, Ohio; ordained January 20, 1876; was in the Diocese of Cleveland as pastor of Ottawa, 1876-77; then of New Riegel from July, 1878, to August, 1880. He died in the Diocese of Nashville, October 1, 1887.

287. ROETZER, Rev. J. M., was born in Bavaria about 1834. He came to Cleveland in 1856; was received by Bishop Rappe as a student for the Diocese of Cleveland and by him ordained June 26, 1859. Was professor at the seminary for a short time after his ordination; then pastor of Findlay, 1860, till March, 1862, meanwhile attending Fostoria as a mission. He was next in charge of French Creek, as resident

pastor, from March to September, 1862, during that time also attending Avon and Sheffield. He then left the diocese. Died a few years after in Michigan. Date and place of death not recorded.

288. ROHAN, Rev. Edmund, was born at Goulane, county Kerry, Ireland, January 8, 1854. He made his college course of studies at Mt. Melleray, Ireland; philosophy and theology at St. Mary's Seminary, Cleveland, where he was received in September, 1880. Five years later, July 9, 1885, he was ordained for the Diocese of Cleveland by the Rt. Rev. Bishop de Goesbriand, during the absence of Bishop Gilmour, then in Rome. August, 1885, he was appointed pastor of South Thompson, with charge of Madison. April 11, 1886, he was transferred to Van Wert, from which place he attended Convoy and Spencerville. January, 1888, Bishop Gilmour appointed him assistant at Holy Name church, Cleveland, where he remained about one month. Owing to ill health he performed no priestly duties till March 25, of same year, when he was sent to Dungannon, with charge of New Lisbon as a mission. This position he held till his death, February 19, 1889. He was an earnest worker and had the good will of those intrusted to his pastoral care.

289. ROLLINET, Rev. August Joseph, was born, 1796, at Long-Sancey, Diocese of Besancon, France; studied for the ministry at Aix, in Provence; was ordained about 1820, and after doing pastoral work in his native diocese came to America in 1848. Remaining a few months in Canada, he came to Ohio and was appointed first resident pastor of Calmoutier, Holmes county, then under the jurisdiction of the Bishop of Cleveland. This charge he held till 1858. He then joined the Society of Mary at Dayton. He also had temporary charge of the congregation at Louisville, Stark county, June, 1857, till June, 1858. He left the Society of Mary after a short time, and again received the pastorate of Calmoutier, where he died suddenly, January 1, 1859. Father Rollinet was a most zealous priest, and enjoyed the esteem of all who knew him.

290. ROOS, Rev. John, a Bavarian, was born in 1832, at Dirmstein, Diocese of Speyer; came to the United States in 1850. After finishing his studies at St. Mary's Seminary, Cleveland, he was ordained by Bishop Rappe, June 1, 1856. He was sent to St. Ann's, Fremont, shortly after his ordination, remaining till December, 1857. During his pastorate the German members of St. Ann's left, and organized a separate congregation, known as St. Joseph's. From Fremont he attended Clyde and several other missions in Sandusky county. December, 1857, he was sent to St. John's, Canton, remaining till August, 1858, when he apostatized and became a member and minister of the Episcopal sect. Is now and has been for many years a resident minister of an Episcopal congregation in Baltimore, and is known as Rev. *Rose*.

291. ROSENBAUM, Rev. Balthasar, (Jesuit), was born at Enskirchen, Rhenish Prussia, October 5, 1847; was ordained in Liverpool, England, by the bishop of that diocese, the Right Rev. Bernard O'Reilly, August 31, 1877; was on the mission in England till September, 1885, when he was sent by his superior to St. Mary's, Toledo, as assistant, remaining till August, 1886.

292. ROTH, Rev. Francis Xavier, a native of Alsace, France, attended Avon, Lorain county, between 1845 and 1847. He was next stationed at the cathedral from November, 1847, to February, 1848, when he left the Diocese of Cleveland. In 1854 he was in the Diocese of Detroit, where he died.

293. ROUPP, Rev. Nicholas, was born at Puttelange, Lorraine, France, April 25, 1825; studied in the Diocesan Seminaries of Metz and Cleveland. Was ordained by Bishop Rappe, August 15, 1849. Shelby Settlement was his first appointment, August, 1849, to February, 1851, with Galion as a mission. He was then called to the cathedral, Cleveland, to attend the Catholic Germans, remaining till June, 1853, when he received the pastorate of St. Peter's, Norwalk. This charge he held till September, 1854, when he was sent to

Maumee, where he remained till June, 1858. He was appointed pastor of St. Mary's, Massillon, December, 1858, after a six months' visit to his native country. From Massillon he was transferred to St. Mary's, Sandusky, November, 1863, and remained till he left the diocese, June, 1864; returned to the Diocese of Metz, where he is still engaged in the ministry.

294. RUDOLF, Rev. George P., was born at Ems, Canton Chur, Switzerland, September 13, 1843. After completing his studies in the Diocean Seminary, Cleveland, he was ordained by Bishop Rappe, May 16, 1868. He had the following pastoral appointments in the Diocese of Cleveland: Defiance, St. John's, May, 1868, to August, 1869; Port Clinton, with La Prairie, Marblehead and Toussaint as missions, from November, 1869, to March, 1871; Liverpool to September, 1872; Milan, to January, 1875; Clyde, to March, 1879; Findlay, to March, 1881, when he was relieved of all pastoral duty. He then left the ministry.

295. RUFF, Rev. Engelbert (Sanguinist), was born at St. Maergen, Baden, October 5, 1817; came to this country in 1845; was ordained at Thompson, Seneca county, for the Sanguinists, by Bishop Rappe, February 23, 1848. He labored on the mission in the Diocese of Cleveland in the following places: New Riegel, 1848 to 1854; Thompson and neighboring missions till 1867, when he was sent by his superior to missions in other dioceses. He is now stationed in the Diocese of Nashville, Tenn.

296. RUSS, Rev. Bernard (Sanguinist), was born at Minster, Auglaize county, Ohio, December 25, 1851; made his studies at St. Charles' Seminary, Carthagena, Ohio; was ordained at Cincinnati by Archbishop Purcell, May 17, 1879; was assistant at Glandorf, Putnam county, Ohio, from May 31, 1879, to November 15, 1880. He was then sent on the mission in Kansas, remaining till January 1883. Since then he has had various positions in the Diocese of Cincinnati. Is at present stationed in Mercer county, Ohio.

297. RYAN, Rev. Edmund F., a native of Ireland, was born at Knockany, county Limerick, August 24, 1856; was educated for the priesthood at Thurles, Ireland, and Versailles, France. Bishop Dorrian ordained him at Belfast, October 28, 1875. After doing pastoral work in his native country till 1884, he came to the United States. Four years later he was received *pro tempore* into the Diocese of Cleveland, and appointed assistant to the pastor of St. Malachy's church, Cleveland, July, 1888. He left the diocese in August, 1889.

298. SAENDERL, Rev. Simon (Redemptorist), was born at Malgersdorf, Bavaria, September 30, 1800; ordained June 2, 1825; came to the United States, March, 1832; was stationed at Peru, Huron county, between 1835–36, and occasionally attended Wolf's Creek (New Riegel), during this time; was pastor of St. John's, Canton, 1836–37; left the Redemptorists in 1847, and joined the Trappists at Gethsemani, Ky., where he received the Habit, March 15, 1852. Died at Gethsemani, February 22, 1879.

299. SALAUN, Rev. John F., was born at Landevenneque, Finistere, France, November 18, 1818; was educated in France, and ordained at Point Croix, Diocese of Quimper, by Bishop Graverond, June 10, 1843. Came to the Diocese of Cleveland December, 1855, and shortly after his arrival he was appointed superior of St. Mary's Seminary. This position he held with distinction till August, 1864, when he left the diocese. For many years he has been doing pastoral duty at South Orange, Diocese of Newark, N. J., where he is now stationed. Whilst superior of Cleveland Seminary he had charge of the following missions: Hudson, Euclid and Newburgh (Cleveland).

300. SANNER, Rev. Sebastian, was born, educated and ordained in Germany. He was received into the Diocese of Cincinnati by Bishop Purcell, in 1846, and sent to Calmoutier, Holmes county. In 1848 Bishop Rappe appointed him assistant at St. Francis de Sales' church, Toledo, to attend the Catholic Germans residing there. In 1850 he was given the

pastorate of St. Joseph's, Maumee, from which place he attended New Bavaria, Six Mile Woods, Defiance and Providence. December, 1853, he was transferred to Shelby Settlement, where he remained till he left the Diocese of Cleveland, September, 1854.

301. SCHALK, Rev. Frederick (Sanguinist), was born in New Riegel, Seneca county, Ohio, March 2, 1850; educated by the Sanguinists at Carthagena, Mercer county, Ohio, and for them ordained by Archbishop Purcell, January 17, 1873; was pastor of Ottawa, Putnam county, from February, 1873, to February, 1876. Is at present stationed at Wapakoneta, Diocese of Cincinnati.

302. SCHEDLER, Rev. Caspar (Sanguinist), was born at Schwabeck, Bavaria, May 6, 1842; came to the United States in 1866, and was ordained for the Sanguinists by Archbishop Purcell, Nov. 21, 1868. Was in the Diocese of Cleveland as assistant at New Riegel from August, 1869, to September, 1870, and during that time also attended Big Spring. He has since been in the Diocese of Cincinnati.

303. SCHELBERT, Rev. Aloysius (Sanguinist), was born at Monthenthal, Canton Schwyz, Switzerland, October 12, 1813; ordained July 28, 1850, and came to this country October of the same year. He was in the Diocese of Cleveland between October, 1853, and November, 1864, viz.: at Glandorf till November, 1858, and at New Riegel till 1864. His superior then appointed him pastor of Himmelgarten, Mercer county, Ohio. In 1865 he was sent to St. Joseph's, same county, where he remained till July, 1876, when he returned to Europe, (Schellenberg, Austria), remaining there as pastor and local superior of the Sanguinist Convent till his death, April 10, 1878.

304. SCHERER, Rev. Peter D., a Swiss, was born at Liesberg, June 29, 1840; made his studies for the ministry in his native town and at Mt. Calvary, Wis., with the Capuchins

for whose Order he was ordained by Bishop Henni, July 25, 1863. As a Capuchin he held various positions from 1863 to 1886, eight in all. December, 1887, the Holy See permitted him to become a secular priest. As such he was received *pro tempore* by Bishop Gilmour, who appointed him resident pastor of Independence, with charge of Brighton as a mission. He remained till June, 1888, when he was recalled to the Diocese of Solothurn, Switzerland, to which he had been assigned when secularized by the Holy See.

305. SCHILL, Rev. Kilian (Sanguinist), was born at Henweiler, Baden, July 8, 1854; educated at St. Charles' Seminary, Carthagena, Ohio, and there ordained by Archbishop Elder, June 8, 1882; was assistant at Glandorf, from September, 1882, to July, 1885. Is now stationed in Mercer county, Diocese of Cincinnati.

306. SCHLOESSER, Rev. Kilian (Franciscan), was born at Cologne, Rhenish Prussia, May 9, 1826; ordained March 11, 1857; in the United States since 1860. Was superior of Franciscan Monastery, Cleveland, from 1871 to 1879, and pastor of St. Joseph's, same city, from 1871 to July, 1885. During his pastorate in Cleveland, the Franciscan Monastery and the present church of St. Joseph's congregation were built. He is at present pastor at Santa Barbara, in the Diocese of Monterey, Cal.

307. SCHMIDT, Rev. —, (Sanguinist?); at Thompson from 1856 to 1857. No other record of him.

308. SCHMITZ, Rev. Meinolph (Franciscan), was born in the city of Cologne, Germany, February 16, 1840; came to America, December, 1867; ordained February 7, 1868; was a member of the Franciscan Monastery, Cleveland, from 1875 to 1879; he was also superior of Franciscan College, same city. Is now a secular priest in the Diocese of Jamestown, N. D.

309. SCHNEIDER, Rev. Thomas (Franciscan), was born December 31, 1850, at Neustadt, Silesia; in the United States

since October, 1869; ordained June 18, 1878; was attached to the Franciscan Monastery, Cleveland, from July, 1881, to July, 1885, during which time he was also pastor of Parma and Independence. He is now a secular priest and stationed in the Diocese of Grand Rapids.

310. SCHOCH, Rev. Theobald (Sanguinist), was born at St. Peter's, Mercer county, Ohio, July 24, 1848; educated for and by the Sanguinists at Carthagena, Ohio; ordained by Bishop Dwenger, January 18, 1873. He was in the Diocese of Cleveland from February, 1873, to September, 1875, as pastor of St. Peter's, Big Spring, and of St. Joseph's, Crawfordsville, till June, 1875. Next he had charge of one of the Sanguinist missions in Mercer county, Ohio. He then went to Europe (Schellenberg, Austria,) where he died, November 19, 1889.

311. SCHORB, Rev. Basil, was born, 1810, in Adams county, Pa.; ordained by Bishop Purcell at Cincinnati, May 20, 1837. Shortly after his ordination he was sent to Chippewa, near Doylestown, Wayne county, from which place he attended the missions of Canal Fulton, St. John's, Canton (1837), Massillon (1843), Peru (1840), Liverpool, Randolph and Wooster (1842). In 1843 he left Ohio and returned to Pennsylvania, where he died as pastor of York, April 4, 1871.

312. SCHWEIGER, Rev. Andrew J. M., was stationed in Cleveland from October, 1852, till some time in 1853, to minister to the spiritual wants of the Catholic Germans. No other record of him.

313. SCHWEITZER, Rev. Clement (Sanguinist), was born in Baden, Germany, 1810; ordained by Bishop Rappe for the Sanguinists in 1849; was stationed at Thompson, Seneca county, from 1849 till his death, April 23, 1850.

314. SCHWICK, Rev. Joseph (Jesuit), was assistant at St. Mary's church, Toledo, from November, 1877, to October 12,

1878. On latter date he left the Jesuits and became a secular priest. He is now stationed in the Diocese of Grand Rapids.

315. SEEBERGER, Rev. Cosmas (Sanguinist), was born at Frastanz, near Feldkirch, Austria, March 4, 1840; in the United States since January, 1866; ordained for the Sanguinists June 30, 1874; was assistant at New Riegel and pastor of Big Spring from October, 1875, to December, 1876. He is now in Diocese of Fort Wayne, Ind.

316. SIGG, Rev. Aloysius (Jesuit), a native of Wuerttemberg, Germany, was born at Eberhardzell, December 4, 1839. After completing his ecclesiastical studies at St. Francis' Seminary, Milwaukee, he was ordained by Bishop Henni, November 5, 1865. Till 1874 he was engaged in various positions, the last two years as secretary to Bishop Heiss, at La Crosse, Wis. He then went to Holland and became a Jesuit. In 1880 he was sent back to this country, (Mankato, Minn.) In 1885 he was appointed pastor of St. Mary's, Toledo, which position he held till January, 1890, when his superiors sent him to St. Ann's, Buffalo, N. Y., where he is now stationed. At Toledo he was superior of the Jesuit Fathers for four years.

317. SIMEON, Rev. Nicholas, (Jesuit), a Swiss, was born at Lenz, November 28, 1834. Bishop Baudri ordained him at Maria-Laach, for the Jesuits, August 29, 1865. He was stationed at St. Ignatius' College, Cleveland, from September, 1889, to February, 1890, and during that time was engaged giving missions and retreats. He is now in Prairie-du-Chien, Wis.

318. SOMMER, Rev. Severin, was received by Bishop Rappe, October, 1854, and appointed resident pastor of Shelby Settlement, where he remained about a year, when he left the Diocese of Cleveland. No other record of him.

319. SPICHER, Rev. Peter (Jesuit), was born in Switzerland, Canton Freiburg, December 22, 1811. He joined the

Society of Jesus, October 1, 1832, and was ordained in 1842. After the expulsion of the Jesuits from Switzerland he came to America in 1848, and was appointed professor of theology for the members of the Society of Jesus at St. Louis, Mo. So highly were his learning, his virtues, and his zeal in the care of souls appreciated, that he was put first on the list of candidates for the Episcopal See to be erected in Quincy, later transferred to Alton, Ill. Aware of this he returned to Europe. For many years he was superior of several houses of the society in Germany, and was also for a time Master of Novices. In 1868 he returned to this country to found a mission of the German Jesuits, of which he was appointed first superior the following year. He took up his residence at Toledo, O., where Bishop Rappe had given the Jesuit Fathers of the Buffalo Province charge of St. Mary's church. Relieved at his request in 1870 of the office of superior, he went to Buffalo, N. Y., where he died at St. Ann's church on March 29, 1874. Father Spicher was a man of rare charity, meekness and humility—qualities which endeared him everywhere to clergy and laity.

320. SPIERINGS, Rev. Gerard Augustine, a native of Holland, was born at Uden, August 24, 1828, where also he was educated for the ministry. He was ordained by Mgr. Caroli, Bishop of Cambray, France, November 17, 1855. October, 1865, he was received into the Diocese of Cleveland, and appointed pastor of Upper Sandusky. There he remained till April, 1867, when he was sent to Dungannon. This charge he retained till 1869, when he left the diocese. While pastor of Upper Sandusky he also attended Kirby (1865-66), and Bucyrus (November, 1865, April, 1867). Since 1869 he has been on the mission in New Jersey, and is at present pastor of Keyport, Diocese of Trenton.

321. STEIN, Rev. George, a native of Baden, was in the Diocese of Cleveland from 1852 to 1858, first as pastor of Randolph, till 1857, then for a few months in 1858, pastor of St. Mary's, Massillon, when he left the Diocese. No other record of him.

322. STIEFVATER, Rev. Andrew, (Sanguinist), was born at Kirchhofen, Baden, November 28, 1830; ordained at Thompson, Seneca county, O., by Bishop Rappe, August 27, 1857. He had the following charges in the Diocese of Cleveland, viz.: Glandorf, assistant, 1857-60; Reed, as pastor, and Thompson, as assistant, 1877-83; chaplain of Ursuline Convent, Tiffin, 1883, June, 1886; Thompson, assistant, June, 1886—September, 1887; same place, chaplain, October, 1888—September, 1889. He is now in the Diocese of Nashville.

323. STREMLER, Rev. James, D. D., was born, educated and ordained in Lorraine, France. About 1859 he received the doctorate at Rome, where he was chaplain for three years of the collegiate church of St. Louis of France. Came to the Diocese of Cleveland from Laval University, Quebec, and was superior of St. Mary's Seminary, Cleveland, from September, 1866, to August, 1870, when he left; then affiliated with the Diocese of Alton, and later with Vincennes, (1873), where he now is as pastor of Floyd Knobs, Ind. In 1860 he published the well known and frequently quoted work, "Traite des Peines Ecclesiastiques."

324. STROKER, Rev. Francis, was born at Strokestown, county Roscommon, Ireland, in 1829. He made his theological studies at the seminary in Cleveland, and was ordained by Bishop Rappe, December 11, 1853. Dungannon was his first appointment, December, 1853, to June, 1855. He was then transferred to Summitville, where he remained till April, 1856. While resident pastor of Dungannon and Summitville, he also had charge of several missions: Niles (1853-56), Warren, (1853-56), and St. Columba's, Youngstown, (1853-54). April, 1856, he left the Diocese of Cleveland and was received by Bishop Henni, of Milwaukee, in whose diocese he remained as pastor of Milford, Wis., till death, some time in 1864. He was killed by railway cars.

325. STUECKER, Rev. Quirinus (Franciscan), a native of Germany, was born at Bidefeld, August 6, 1851; educated for

the sacred ministry at Teutopolis and St. Louis; ordained in latter city for the Franciscans by Bishop Ryan, June 21, 1879. Owing to illness shortly after his ordination he was unable to do duty till August, 1880, when he attended pastoral work at Teutopolis till October, 1887. He was then sent to the Franciscan Monastery, Cleveland, where he remained from October 13, 1887, to August 7, 1888. His superiors then sent him on the mission to Hermann, Mo.

326. SULLIVAN, Rev. Francis Augustine, was born in Ireland, August 2, 1837. He was received by Bishop Rappe, and after a few years' stay in the Diocesan Seminary, was sent to the Sulpitian Seminary at Paris to complete his studies. There he remained about three years. On his return he was ordained by Bishop Rappe, December 2, 1860. January after his ordination he was appointed one of the professors at St. Mary's Seminary, Cleveland, and for a few months attended Ravenna and Newburgh (Cleveland). In the latter place he commenced the erection of the old church (Holy Rosary) on North Park street. Owing to failing health he resigned his position as professor and accepted the pastorate of St. Mary's, Elyria, August, 1863, with charge of Vermillion as a mission. He died of consumption at Elyria, February 4, 1864.

327. SUTER, Rev. Aloysius (Jesuit), was born at Mutathal, Canton Schwyz, Switzerland, February 16, 1835; ordained September 10, 1867; in this country since September, 1868; was assistant at St. Mary's, Toledo, from 1876 to 1880, and from August to September, 1889. He is now stationed in the Diocese of Dubuque, Iowa.

328. THIELE, Rev. Henry L., was born in the Diocese of Muenster, Germany, 1819; ordained by Bishop Baraga for the Diocese of Marquette, in 1854; received into the Diocese of Cleveland in 1861 and sent to Akron, where he organized St. Bernard's congregation, remaining till May, 1863. His next appointment was St. Joseph's congregation, Massillon, whose first resident pastor he was, July, 1863, to December, 1864.

During this time he also attended Navarre (Bethlehem). From January to June, 1865, he had charge of St. Martin's, Liverpool. He then returned to the Diocese of Marquette, where he did pastoral duty till 1873, when he went to Notre Dame, Ind. There he died August 17, of same year. He was a man of fine literary taste and wrote much for magazines and other periodicals.

329. THIENPONT, Rev. Emanuel, a native of Belgium, was ordained in Cincinnati, January 20, 1833, by Bishop Rosati, of St. Louis. In 1835 he was sent to attend the missions along the Miami Canal as far north as Toledo. In 1835 he was also at St. Mary's, Tiffin, for six months as successor to Rev. E. Quinn. From 1836 to 1842 he was pastor of the Catholic Germans of Dayton. Then he had charge of Portsmouth, Steubenville and other places. Died October 19, 1873, aged about 70 years.

330. THOMA, Rev. John M., (Sanguinist), was born at Werbach, Baden, August 13, 1833; educated at Rome, and there ordained for the Sanguinists, August 19, 1857. After doing pastoral duty in Europe till 1868, he came to the Diocese of Cleveland during the same year, and from Thompson, under direction of the Provincial of the Sanguinists, attended St. Sebastian's congregation, Sherman (Bismarck), from July, 1868, to July, 1869. He then returned to Europe, but came back to this country, February, 1886, as a secular priest, and was received into the Diocese of St. Joseph, Mo., where, as pastor of New Hirrlingen, he died April 18, 1887.

331. TIGHE, Rev. Denis, was born in Ireland; received into the Diocesan Seminary, Cleveland, about 1855. Before completing his studies for the ministry he was ordained by Bishop Rappe, in 1857, and sent to Holy Angels', Sandusky, as assistant to Father Caron. In 1859 he was appointed pastor of Summitville, remaining till September, 1864, meanwhile attending East Liverpool and Wellsville as missions. He was then appointed first resident pastor of St. Bridget's,

Cleveland, which position he held till his death, June 19, 1866. His simplicity of character and earnest piety made him a noble example for those committed to his spiritual guidance.

332. TREACY, Rev. James, was born at Ballymagill, county Kilkenny, Ireland, May 12, 1857. He made his collegiate studies at Knocktopher, and mental philosophy and one year of theology in St. John's College, Waterford. September, 1883, he was received by Bishop Gilmour as a student for the Diocese of Cleveland and sent to St. Mary's Seminary, Cleveland. January 8, 1885, he was elevated to the priesthood, and on the 20th of the same month entered on the discharge of his duties as one of the assistants at the cathedral. Not of strong frame, and never of robust health, he soon showed signs of failing strength. His condition growing worse, in spite of prompt medical care, he obtained from his bishop, in May, 1887, an indefinite leave of absence to return to his native Ireland, where he hoped to find relief. He came back to Cleveland in October, 1888, very little improved in health. One month later, on the advice of his physicians, he went to Santa Fe, New Mexico, where, in the well known sanitarium, under the efficient charge of the Sisters of Charity, he gained steadily in strength for many months, and his hopes for recovery brightened. But grim death only dallied with its victim. Consumption had gone too far in its destructive course to leave hope for recovery. When he finally realized that his end was near, he cheerfully awaited the final summons. Fortified with all the Rites of Holy Church, he yielded his soul to God on Friday morning, March 21, 1890. Father Treacy was a priest of gentle piety and prudent zeal. He had also a sweetness of soul, which constantly won men to God, and made him a favorite with all who knew him. Charity, modesty, and a spirit of priestly obedience richly blended in his character.

333. TRUEMPER, Rev. William (Jesuit), a Prussian, was born at Lutter, in November, 1840, and ordained for the Jesuits at Maria-Laach, by Bishop Eberhardt, of Treves, May

31, 1871. He was stationed at St. Mary's, Cleveland, as assistant, from July, 1887, till September, 1889, and during this time also attended Willoughby for some months. He is now at St. Ann's, Buffalo.

334. TSCHENHENS, Rev. F. X. (Redemptorist), was born in Holland, July 24, 1801; ordained August 15, 1827. He was among the first Redemptorists that came to the United States, landing June 20, 1832. He went directly to Cincinnati, where he resided for some time. In 1834 Bishop Purcell sent him to Peru, Huron county, whence he attended Tiffin, New Riegel, McCutchenville, Norwalk, Sandusky and Fremont. He had charge of Peru till 1839, but returned in 1841 from Pittsburgh, where he had been appointed superior of a Redemptorist convent he established there. He remained for nearly one year, when he was recalled to Pittsburgh. Wherever he labored on the mission in Northern Ohio his memory is revered by the old Catholic settlers yet living, as that of a saintly, self-sacrificing minister of God. His last visit to Ohio was in December, 1858, when he preached the funeral sermon of a dear friend and former parishioner of his, who died in Tiffin. He was a priest devoted to his work with apostolic zeal. He died at Baltimore, May 10, 1877.

335. UHLMANN, Rev. John Baptist, was born at Constance, Baden, February 19, 1804; ordained at Freiburg, Baden, by Archbishop Bernard Boll, September 17, 1828. Till 1850 he did pastoral duty in the Diocese of Freiburg, when he concluded to come to America, owing to the continued disturbed condition of his native Baden, caused by the Revolution in 1848. In 1852 he was received by Bishop Rappe and appointed pastor of St. Joseph's, Tiffin, where he built the first pastoral residence. From Tiffin he also attended Liberty, 1853–56. He remained at Tiffin from September, 1852, till May, 1856, when he was transferred to St. Peter's, Canton. He remained there from June, 1856, till June, 1864, when he was appointed pastor of St. Mary's, Sandusky, where he resided till he left the Diocese of Cleveland to return to

his native country, July, 1865. He died at Bonndorf, Baden, February 18, 1882. Father Uhlmann was a man of varied and deep learning and an eloquent preacher.

336. VAN DEN BROEK, Rev. John (Sanguinist), was born at Oss, Province of Nord Braband, Holland, December 3, 1819; was ordained at Feldkirch, June 19, 1843, and came to the United States in December of same year. He had pastoral charge of the following places in the Diocese of Cleveland: Randolph, about 1845; assistant at Louisville, with charge of New Berlin, 1848 to 1849; Tiffin, St. Joseph's, 1850; French Creek and Avon, 1851 to 1853; New Riegel, 1854 to 1856; Liverpool, 1859 to 1861. Since then he has been in the Diocese of Cincinnati.

337. VAN DE WEYER, Rev. A. F. (Dominican), a native of Holland, attended Dungannon between November, 1833, and April, 1835, and Louisville, Stark county, from Canton, between 1835 and 1838. No other record of him.

338. VERLET, Rev. George, was born at Phalsburg, Lorraine, March 27, 1839; began his studies for the priesthood in his native city, and coming to this country in 1858, completed them in St. Mary's Seminary, Cleveland, where he was ordained by Bishop Rappe, September 30, 1861. His first appointment was as assistant at St. Mary's Sandusky, whence he also attended Kelley's Island, Oak Harbor, Port Clinton, Marblehead, Toussaint, and a number of stations, October, 1861—January, 1862. He was then sent to Port Clinton as first resident pastor. From this place he continued attending the above named missions till June, 1865, when he was transferred to St. Joseph's, Massillon. There he remained till his removal to New Bavaria, May, 1888, where he remained till his death, August 3, 1889. He was a genial and kind hearted priest.

339. VERNIMONT, Rev. Raymund (Sanguinist), a native of Ohio, was born at Berwick, Seneca county, October 13, 1856; was educated for the Sanguinists at Carthagena, O., and

for them ordained at Cincinnati, by Archbishop Elder, May 30, 1885. He had charge of St. Mary's, Tiffin, during the absence of the pastor, Rev. M. Healy, from December, 1889, till February, 1890. He is now stationed in the Diocese of Cincinnati.

340. VIERE, Rev. Christian, was born at Osnabrueck, Prussia, October 9, 1831; ordained March 14, 1856; came to America in 1865. He was received into the Diocese of Cleveland in 1866, and appointed pastor of Fort Jennings, remaining till September, 1867, when he was made pastor of St. Mary's, Toledo. In August, 1869, he was transferred to St. John's, Defiance, of which charge he was relieved by Bishop Gilmour, October, 1878. He then left the ministry, and now resides at Fort Jennings, Putnam county, O.

341. VIGEAUT, Rev. Alfred, a Canadian, was born at St. Mary de Monnoir, Province of Quebec, May 10, 1844; ordained at Rimouski by Bishop Langevin, October 12, 1873; was in the Diocese of Cleveland as pastor of Toussaint and La Prairie, from June, 1881, to February, 1883. He then left the diocese and was received into the Vicariate of Dakota.

342. VOISARD, Rev. Joseph A., was born at Indevilliers, (Doubs) France, June 29, 1828; ordained at Besancon, France, September 18, 1858. Came to the Diocese of Toronto, November of same year. Was received into the Diocese of Cleveland, September, 1865, and appointed pastor of St. Ann's, Fremont, which he found in a disturbed and rebellious condition. He soon became dissatisfied with his charge and returned to Canada in April, 1866, and has been there ever since, doing pastoral duty. Now at Fort Erie, Ontario.

343. VOLM, Rev. Frederick A., a native of Baden, was ordained at Cincinnati by Bishop Purcell, December, 1860. He was in the Diocese of Cleveland from July, 1866, to March, 1867, as pastor of Millersville. He was next at Goshen, Ind., Diocese of Fort Wayne, for a short time, and then disappeared. No other record of him.

344. VUILLEMOT, Rev. F., was born in the Diocese of Nancy, Lorraine, about 1834; was ordained at Nancy in 1859, came to the Diocese of Cleveland, April, 1864; was assistant to Rev. L. Hoffer, at Louisville, from May to July of same year. Then he was sent to St. Mary's Seminary, Cleveland, where he taught philosophy for a few months. Returned to France in 1865, where he is at present.

345. WALSH, Rev. Francis (Basilian), was born at Kingston, Ontario, in 1843; was ordained at Louisville. Stark county, for the Basilians, by Bishop Rappe; was at Louisville College, as professor, about four years, 1868-72. He is now stationed in Colorado.

346. WALSH, Rev. John, a native of Ireland, was born at Tullardon, county Kilkenny, December 13, 1844; completed his ecclesiastical studies at Maynooth, and was there ordained by Bishop Quinn, for the Diocese of Ossory, on June 15, 1870. June, 1888, he was received, *pro tempore*, into the Diocese of Cleveland, and sent to St. Columba's, Youngstown, as assistant, where he remained till his transfer to the cathedral, Cleveland, as first assistant, September, 1888. In January, 1890, he was appointed pastor of St. Mary's Corners, Fulton county, where remained two months, when he left the diocese and went to that of Duluth, Minn., where he now is.

347. WALSH, Rev. Thomas, born in county Cork, Ireland, about 1830, was ordained by Bishop Rappe, January, 1854, and appointed assistant at the cathedral, whence he also attended Berea for a few months in 1854. He remained at the cathedral till December, 1856, when he went to the Diocese of Alton, Ill. He was pastor of St. Joseph's church, Cairo, Ill. Whilst preaching he suddenly took seriously ill and shortly after died, March 5, 1863. He was a fine preacher and of amiable disposition. Whilst at the cathedral, Cleveland, he was the ordinary confessor of the students at the seminary, by whom he was loved and highly esteemed as a wise spiritual director.

348. WALSH, Rev. Thomas J., was born near Wexford, county Wexford, Ireland, in 1828; was educated for the ministry in Wexford College, and St. Mary's Seminary, Cleveland; ordained by Bishop Rappe, July —, 1852, and appointed pastor of St. Ann's, Fremont, remaining till 1856, when he was sent to St. Vincent's, Akron. From Akron he attended Ravenna. In 1858 he was appointed pastor of Summitville, where he remained till 1859, when he was received into the Diocese of Wheeling. Some time later he affiliated with the Diocese of Alton, and lastly with that of St. Joseph, Mo. In these three dioceses he labored on the missions about twenty-two years, the last two years as pastor of St. Patrick's, in the city of St. Joseph, Mo., where he died November 27, 1881, after ailing about sixteen months of heart disease.

349. WARDY, Rev. Charles Thaddeus, was born, educated and ordained in France. He came to the Diocese of Cleveland from St. Catharine's, Diocese of Toronto, July, 1865, and was sent to Port Clinton, with charge of La Prairie and Toussaint as missions. He remained till July, 1866. October of same year he was appointed pastor of St. Joseph's, Toledo, which charge he held till 1868, meanwhile attending Sylvania; also the asylum and Ursuline Convent, Toledo, as chaplain. In 1870 he was sent to Kelley's Island, remaining there till 1874. During his pastorate of this place he also attended Put-in-Bay. New Bavaria (Poplar Ridge), was his next appointment, where he remained till he left the diocese, October, 1875. He was received into the Diocese of Fort Wayne, where he remained till 1879, when he joined the Benedictines. Died at Monte Casino Priory, near Covington, Ky., October 29, 1880. He was a zealous priest. Although he learned the English language late in life he had perfect command of it, speaking and writing it with greatest ease.

350. WEBER, Rev. Peter (Sanguinist), was born in Germany. Date and place of birth or ordination not recorded. Had charge of St. Joseph's congregation, Randolph, from 1851 to 1853; Harrisburg from 1853 to 1854, with New Ber-

lin as a mission. He attended the Catholic Germans of Cleveland, between October, 1850, and March, 1851; Avon and French Creek in 1851-54. In 1854 he left the Diocese of Cleveland and the Sanguinists; was received into the Diocese of Vincennes, where he was appointed pastor of New Alsace, Ind. No other record of him.

351. WEIKMANN, Rev. John Baptist, a native of Wuerttemberg, was born at Gmuend, June 24, 1811; studied at Ellwangen, Rottweil and Tuebingen; was ordained September 12, 1838; came to the United States, December, 1855, and was appointed by Bishop Rappe as pastor of St. Peter's, Canton. This position he held for about six weeks, till February 26, 1856, when he was dismissed. He then went to the Benedictine Convent, in Westmoreland county, Pa. April, 1856, he was received into the Diocese of Milwaukee, where he held several charges, till November, 1861. He then affiliated with the Diocese of Vincennes, and in 1863 with that of Dubuque. In last mentioned diocese he remained till his death, as pastor of New Vienna, Iowa, October 11, 1870.

352. WEIS, Rev. Bernardine (Franciscan), was born at Mursbach, Bavaria, October 14, 1851; came with his parents to the United States in 1852; was ordained December 27, 1874; in Cleveland Monastery from 1880 to 1882. At present he is in the Diocese of St. Louis, Mo.

353. WEISS, Rev. Paulinus (Franciscan), born at Lindau, Diocese of Augsburg, March 21, 1831; in the United States since 1862; ordained November 9, 1865; was in the Franciscan Monastery, Cleveland, from 1882 to July, 1885. He is now in the Diocese of Chicago, Ill.

354. WILHELMI, Rev. Peter (Sanguinist), a native of Luxemberg, was born at Wellenstein, March 18, 1817; made his ecclesiastical studies at Thompson and New Riegel. He was ordained at Tiffin by Bishop Rappe, January 27, 1851. He was stationed in the Diocese of Cleveland from 1853 to 1856, 1884 to 1886, September, 1887, to September, 1888,—

ST. VINCENT'S ORPHAN ASYLUM
ST. VINCENT'S HOSPITAL TOLEDO, O.

first at Thompson for three years, then at Glandorf for one year, and again at Thompson for nearly three years, in each of which places he was assistant pastor. He is now in the Diocese of Cincinnati.

355. WILLI, Rev. Willibald (Sanguinist), was born at Ems, Switzerland, in 1820. He came to America, August, 1850, and was ordained for the Sanguinists by Bishop Rappe, January, 1851. Owing to ill health, even at his ordination, he was never able to do much of pastoral work. He was stationed at Glandorf till the autumn of 1853. He died at Maria Heim, Jay county, Indiana, December 15, 1854.

356. WIRTZ, Rev. Hermann (Franciscan), was born at Cologne-on-the-Rhine, January 6, 1842; in America since April, 1861; ordained September 7, 1872. Was in the Cleveland Monastery and professor in St. Joseph's College, December, 1878, to July, 1879.

357. WITTMER, Rev. John (Sanguinist), was born at Ober-Erlinsbach, Canton Solothurn, Switzerland, November 4, 1818; ordained at Feldkirch, Austria, by Bishop Bruenster, November 21, 1841; came to this country with the first Sanguinist Fathers in 1844. He had the following pastoral charges in the Diocese of Cleveland: assistant at Peru, 1844–46; first resident pastor of Randolph, 1846; assistant at Thompson, whence he also attended St. Joseph's, Tiffin, 1847–48; pastor of Thompson, March, 1849, to 1853. He was then for many years on the mission in the Diocese of Cincinnati, especially in Mercer, Auglaize and Shelby counties. In 1885 he was sent by his superior to the Diocese of Nashville, where he is at present.

358. WOCHNER, Rev. Henry (Jesuit), was born, 1839, in Haslach, Wuerttemberg; ordained September 8, 1868; in the United States since 1876; was assistant at St. Mary's, Cleveland, from 1881 to August, 1885. He is now in the Diocese of Winona.

359. WUERZ, Rev. Matthias, was born, 1807, in Schoenbach, Diocese of Metz, France. He came to America in 1833 and made his theological studies at Cincinnati, where he was ordained by Bishop Purcell, June 13, 1835. He was appointed first resident pastor of Louisville, Stark county, February, 1838, having been transferred from Cincinnati. From Louisville he also attended Randolph. He was pastor of St. John's, Canton, from October, 1840 to 1843, and had charge of Massillon and Navarre; also occasionally visited the mission of Peru. He returned to France in 1845, where he died of apoplexy, April 2, 1858.

360. YOUNG, Very Rev. Nicholas D. (Dominican), nephew of Bishop Fenwick, first Bishop of Cincinnati, was born in Maryland, 1783; studied at St. Rose's, Ky., and Rome; was ordained by Bishop Flaget, December 10, 1817; came to Northern Ohio from Kentucky, November, 1818; attended Dungannon, Columbiana county, from Somerset, Perry county, about 1820, and again between 1833 and 1835. January, 1833, he was elected Provincial of the Dominicans in the United States. He was stationed for many years at Somerset, O., St. Rose's, Ky., and Washington, D. C. Died at Giesboro, Md., October 28, 1878, aged 95. He was one of the pioneer priests of Northern Ohio, and a man full of apostolic zeal.

361. ZAHNER, Rev. —; at Shelby Settlement from 1852 to 1853. During his pastorate he completed the present church, begun by Rev. P. Kreusch. No other record of him.

362. ZANDERS, Rev. Raymundus (Franciscan), was born at Friemersdorf, Rhenish Prussia, August 8, 1846; educated at Duesseldorf and Paderborn for the ministry; ordained at Paderborn by Bishop Conrad Martin, in 1873; came to the United States in 1884 and was appointed, October of the same year, as assistant at St. Anthony's church, St. Louis, Mo. July, 1885, he was sent to the Franciscan Monastery, Cleveland, remaining till February, 1886, when he was appointed chaplain of St. Francis' Hospital, Jersey City, N. J.

363. ZARECZNY, Rev. Victor, was born at Lemberg, Galicia-Austria, December 3, 1841. He was educated in Bohemia, Italy, and in the city of Vienna, Austria; ordained at Tarnow, Galicia, July 21, 1868, by Bishop Putkalski; was received into the Diocese of Cleveland, December, 1873, and appointed pastor of the Poles in Berea, where he organized St. Adalbert's congregation, and built their present church and school. He also attended Royalton, 1877–82, and the Poles living in Cleveland, 1879. He left Berea, and the diocese, February, 1884. He is at present in the Diocese of Detroit.

364. ZUMBUEHL, Rev. Leonz, was born in Luzern, Switzerland, May 1, 1846; studied for the ministry at Luzern, Schwytz, Freiburg and Chur; was ordained at Feldkirch, Austria, for the Diocese of Cleveland, by Bishop Amberg, April 19, 1870. Came to Cleveland, September, 1870, and was made pastor of Fort Jennings, where he remained till January, 1872, when he was appointed professor of philosophy in St. Mary's Seminary, Cleveland. This position he held till July of same year, when he was again sent to take pastoral charge of Fort Jennings. In September, 1873, he was recalled to his former position at the seminary, remaining till August, 1877, when he left the diocese. From April, 1876, to July, 1877, he also had pastoral charge of Independence. Since August, 1877, he has been in the Diocese of Peoria.

365. ZWINGE, Rev. Capistran (Franciscan), was born in Grosender, Diocese of Paderborn, Prussia, March 30, 1823; ordained September 4, 1849; came to the United States, September, 1858; was first superior of Franciscan Monastery, and pastor of St. Joseph's church, Cleveland, from 1867 to 1871. Died at Teutopolis, Ill., July 24, 1874.

TABLE I.

List of Priests in the Diocese of Cleveland,

April, 1890.

I. SECULARS.

No.	Name.	Native of:	Date of Birth.	Date of Ordination.	In the Diocese since:	Residence.	Present Appointment.	Date of Appointment.
	Reverends:							
1	Ankly, Fridolin	Switzerland	Mar. 29, 1840	June 28, 1863	Ordination	Wooster	Pastor, Im. Conception Church	Oct., 1865
2	Arnoldi, Matthias	Prussia	July 16, 1851	July 1, 1875	"	Berwick	Pastor, St. Nicholas' Church	May, 1886
3	Arnould, Victor	Lorraine	May 24, 1837	June 30, 1861	"	Canton	Pastor, St. Peter's Church	Aug., 1865
4	Barry, John P.	Massachusetts	Oct. 7, 1861	July 9, 1885	"	Briar Hill	Pastor, St. Ann's Church	Dec., 1887
5	Barry, Patrick	Ireland	Feb. 5, 1841	July 5, 1876	"	Toledo	Pastor, Good Shepherd's Church	Aug., 1887
6	Bauer, Seraph	France	Oct. 17, 1835	June 13, 1858	"	Fremont	Rector, St. Joseph's Church	Sept., 1862
7	Becker, Michael	Lorraine	Nov. 1, 1832	June 25, 1865	"	Shelby Settlm't.	Pastor, Sacred Heart of Jesus' Church	Aug., 1883
8	Becker, Peter	Lorraine	Nov. 25, 1834	Nov. 16, 1867	"	Cleveland	Pastor, Holy Trinity Church	July, 1880
9	Bertemes, John	Luxemburg	Dec. 24, 1861	Dec. 19, 1888	"	New Cleveland	Pastor, Holy Family Church*	Jan., 1889
10	Best, Henry D.	Nassau	Feb. 5, 1833	June 25, 1865	"	West Brookfield	Pastor, St. Barbara's Church	Jan., 1888
11	Bihn, Joseph L.	Bavaria	Jan. 2, 1822	June 1, 1856	"	Tiffin	Superior, St. Francis' Orphan Asylum	Oct., 1873
12	Blaser, Joseph	Wuerttemberg	Nov. 8, 1846	July 31, 1870	March, 1873	Peru	Pastor, St. Alphonsus' Church	Jan., 1888
13	Boff, Felix M.	Alsace	Jan. 25, 1831	May 26, 1853	Ordination	Nottingham	(1) Vicar Gen., (2) Chaplain Urs. Acad.	(1) May, 1873 (2) Dec., 1878
14	Braire, Louis	France	Mar. 17, 1835	Dec. 18, 1858	Sept., 1881	Toledo	Pastor, St. Joseph's Church	Feb., 1884
15	Braschler, Charles	Switzerland	Nov. 2, 1843	July 17, 1870	Ordination	Fort Jennings	Pastor, St. Joseph's Church	Nov., 1888
16	Brennan, Michael J.	Ireland	Oct. 2, 1850	May 23, 1875	August, 1888	Akron	Assistant, St. Vincent's Church	Aug., 1888
17	Broun, John B.	Lorraine	Mar. 2, 1834	Aug. 30, 1863	July, 1866	Akron	Pastor, St. Bernard's Church	July, 1866
18	Buerkel, John B.	Lorraine	June 7, 1842	May 18, 1867	Ordination	Canton	(1) Asst. St. Peter's, (2) Pastor, New Berlin	July, 1882
19	Cahill, John T.	New York	Dec. 5, 1853	June 15, 1878	"	Massillon	Pastor, St. Joseph's Church	Sept., 1889

20	Capitani, Pacifico N	Italy	Aug. 5, 1848	Sept. 27, 1870	July, 1886	Cleveland	Pastor, St. Anthony's Church	July, 1886
21	Carroll, John P.	New York	Nov. 8, 1839	May 4, 1862	Ordination	East Liverpool	Pastor, St. Aloysius' Church	Nov., 1879
22	Carroll, John T.	New York	Aug. 17, 1852	July 5, 1876	"	Cleveland	Pastor, Holy Name Church	Feb., 1886
23	Chevraux, Charles V.	France	Jan. 22, 1848	Aug. 8, 1874	"	Norwalk	Pastor, St. Mary's Church	Jan., 1885
24	Clarke, Joseph J.	Ireland	Dec. 22, 1853	Nov. 11, 1883	"		(Sick).	
25	Clear, Maurice J.	Ireland	Dec. 13, 1863	Dec. 17, 1887	"	Van Wert	Pastor, St. Mary's Church*	Jan., 1888
26	Conway, Edward J.	New York	Nov. 23, 1844	Dec. 16, 1867	"	Painesville	Pastor, St. Mary's Church*	Aug., 1887
27	Dambach, Amadeus	Baden	Nov. 16, 1827	Nov. 21, 1853	Jan. 1857	Norwalk	Pastor, St. Peter's Church	Aug., 1886
28	Danenhoffer, Peter	Lorraine	Feb. 21, 1834	June 28, 1863	Ordination	Toledo	Pastor, St. Peter's Church	July, 1866
29	Daudet, John	France	Aug. 15, 1810	Oct. 26, 1834	June, 1865	Grafton	Pastor, Immaculate Conception Church	Dec., 1871
30	Dechant, Michael	Bavaria	June 23, 1832	June 28, 1863	Ordination	Millersville	Pastor, St. Mary's Church*	Jan., 1888
31	Desmond, John C.	Ireland	Sept. 19, 1849	July 5, 1879	"	Wellsville	Pastor, Immaculate Conception Church	July, 1889
32	Doerner, Henry	Prussia	Aug. 8, 1835	Aug. 8, 1874	"	Findlay	Pastor, St. Michael's Church*	Mar., 1881
33	Doherty, Francis J	New York	April 4, 1861	May 26, 1888	"	Hudson	Pastor, St. Mary's Church*	Jan., 1890
34	Drohan, Nicholas J.	Massachusetts	Sept. 27, 1858	May 26, 1888	"	Hubbard	Pastor, St. Patrick's Church*	July, 1889
35	Eilert, Anthony H. G.	Westphalia	July 5, 1844	May 14, 1871	Oct. 1871	Toledo	Pastor, Sacred Heart Church	May, 1888
36	Eyler, Joseph	Lorraine	Oct. 21, 1845	Mar. 7, 1869	Ordination	Summitville	Pastor, St. John's Church	Jan., 1889
37	Falk, Stephen	Baden	Dec. 17, 1825	Nov. 21, 1853	Sept., 1857	French Creek	Pastor, Immaculate Conception Church	Sept., 1890
38	Farrell, James J.	Ireland	Oct. 18, 1860	Jan. 8, 1885	Ordination	Ravenna	Pastor, Immaculate Conception Church	Sept., 1889
39	Franche, Nicholas J.	France	June 2, 1851	July 4, 1875	"	New Bedford, Pa	Chaplain, "Villa Maria" Convent*	June, 1881
40	Furdek, Stephen	Hungary	Sept. 2, 1855	July 1, 1882	"	Cleveland	Pastor, O. L. of Lourdes' Church*	Feb., 1884
41	Galvin, John L.	New York	Aug. 10, 1854	June 15, 1878	"		(On sick list since January, 1880)	
42	Gerardin, Augustine	France	May 4, 1844	Dec. 21, 1867	"	Cleveland	Pastor, Annunciation Church	April, 1878
43	Gloden, Joseph Peter	Luxemburg	Jan. 12, 1842	Sept. 30, 1869	"	Fostoria	Pastor, St. Wendelin's Church	May, 1886
44	Graham, Ambrose	Ireland	Jan. 1, 1852	Feb. 2, 1876	Sept., 1888	Kent	Pastor, St. Patrick's Church	Sept., 1888
45	Griss, Charles	Alsace	Sept. 5, 1837	June 28, 1863	Ordination	Oak Harbor	Pastor, St. Boniface's Church*	Oct., 1885
46	Hamelin, Armand	France	April 18, 1841	June 15, 1867	Feb., 1883	Toussaint	Pastor, St. Joseph's Church*	Aug., 1886
47	Hannan, John	Ireland	May 4, 1842	June 25, 1865	Ordination			

*Mission attached.

I. SECULARS.—CONTINUED.

No.	Name.	Native of	Date of Birth.	Date of Ordination.	In the Diocese since:	Residence.	Present Appointment.	Date of Appointment.
	Reverends:							
48	Hannin, Edward	Ireland	Dec. 22, 1826	June 1, 1856	Ordination	Toledo	Rector, St. Patrick's Church	April, 1872
49	Harks, William A.	Ohio	Aug. 7, 1854	July 4, 1880	"	New Bavaria	Pastor, Sacred Heart Church	Aug., 1889
50	Healy, Michael	Ireland	Sept. 26, 1823	April 2, 1851	"	Tiffin	Pastor, St. Mary's Church	Feb., 1859
51	Heidegger, Jacob	Austria	Mar. 18, 1846	July 5, 1871	"	Sandusky	Pastor, St. Mary's Church	Nov., 1888
52	Heiland, John B.	Bavaria	Aug. 31, 1839	July 17, 1870	"	Landeck	Pastor, St. John Ev. Church	April, 1878
53	Heiland, Lawrence	Bavaria	Dec. 21, 1841	July 17, 1870	"	Delaware Bend	Pastor, St. Stephen's Church*	Aug., 1888
54	Hennessy, Edward M.	New York	Nov. 3, 1851	Feb. 25, 1876	April, 1888	Dungannon	Pastor, St. Philip's Church*	Mar., 1889
55	Hennessy, James J.	Massachusetts	Nov. 1, 1859	Dec. 19, 1888	Ordination	Cleveland	Assistant, Immaculate Conception Church	Mar., 1890
56	Hoeffel, Aloysius I.	Lorraine	May 14, 1832	June 13, 1858	"	Delphos	Rector, St. John Ev. Church	Jan., 1868
57	Hoerstmann, Joseph	Ohio	Dec. 23, 1858	Nov. 11, 1683	"	Port Clinton	Pastor, Immaculate Conception Church*	Dec., 1885
58	Hoffer, Louis	Lorraine	Nov. 18, 1824	June 3, 1849	April, 1859	Louisville	Pastor, St. Louis' Church	July, 1861
59	Hofstetter, Nicholas	Switzerland	June 5, 1835	June 26, 1864	June, 1888	Independence	Pastor, St. Michael's Church*	June, 1888
60	Horst, Nicholas N.	Luxemburg	Oct. 17, 1865	Dec. 21, 1889	Ordination	Wellington	Pastor, St. Patrick's Church*	Jan., 1890
61	Houck, George F.	Ohio	July 9, 1847	July 4, 1875	"	Cleveland	Bishop's Sec'y and Diocesan Chancellor	July, 1877
62	Hroch, Francis J.	Bohemia	Sept. 13, 1864	Dec. 21, 1889	"	So. Thompson	Pastor, St. Patrick's Church*	Jan., 1890
63	Hultgen, Francis L.	Lorraine	April 4, 1864	Dec. 21, 1889	"	Kirby	Pastor, St. Mary's Church	Jan., 1890
64	Huthmacher, Aloysius	Westphalia	Sept. 17, 1856	June 3, 1882	"	Upper Sandusky	Pastor, St. Peter's Church	Nov., 1888
65	Hynek, Anthony	Bohemia	Mar. 14, 1839	July 27, 1865	Sept., 1872	Cleveland	Pastor, St. Wenceslas' Church*	April, 1873
66	Jennings, Gilbert P.	Ohio	Oct. 25, 1856	July 6, 1884	Ordination	Conneaut	Pastor, St. Mary's Church*	July, 1884
67	Jung, John B.	Switzerland	Nov. 16, 1844	April 19, 1870	Aug., 1870†	Defiance	Pastor, St. John's Ev. Church	Oct., 1878
68	Kaempker, Henry	Westphalia	Dec. 5, 1848	May 30, 1870	Oct., 1874†	Galion	Pastor, St. Joseph's Church*	April, 1878
69	Kikuem, Henry	Westphalia	Mar. 22, 1835	June 22, 1859	June, 1879	Cleveland	Chapl., Sisters of Notre Dame, Cleveland	June, 1879
70	Kinkead, Michael	Ireland	Sept. 28, 1851	Oct. 8, 1875	Ordination	Defiance	Pastor, Our Lady of P. H. Church	Jan., 1876
71	Kirch, Nicholas	Luxemburg	Oct. 8, 1831	June 25, 1865	"	Cleveland	Pastor, St. Francis' Church	March, 1888
72	Kleekamp, John H.	Hanover	Feb. 20, 1856	July 2, 1881	"	Bucyrus	Pastor, Holy Trinity Church	April, 1887
73	Klute, John W.	Westphalia	Oct. 17, 1847	Aug. 8, 1874	"	Youngstown	Pastor, St. Joseph's Church	Aug., 1883

74	Kolasinski, Nicodemus	Galicia	Sept. 14, 1846	Sept. 18, 1875	July, 1884	Toledo	Pastor, St. Anthony's Church	March, 1889
75	Kolaszewski, A Francis	Poland	Sept. 5, 1851	July 1, 1883	Ordination	Cleveland	Pastor, St. Stanislas' Church	Aug., 1883
76	Koudelka, Joseph M.	Bohemia	Dec. 8, 1852	Oct. 8, 1875	"	Cleveland	Pastor, St. Michael's Church	July, 1884
77	Kress, William S.	Ohio	Feb. 15, 1863	May 26, 1888	"	Washington	Student, Catholic University	Nov., 1889
78	Kuebler, Jacob F.	Ohio	June 21, 1849	July 4, 1875	"	Rockport	Pastor, St. Mary's Church*	July, 1875
79	Kuhn, Jacob A.	Rhenish Prussia	April 20, 1836	June 28, 1863	"	Massillon	Pastor, St. Mary's Church	April, 1879
80	Kunnert, John P.	Luxemburg	Oct. 27, 1856	July 3, 1886	"	Harrisburg	Pastor, Sacred Heart Church*	April, 1890
81	Leeming, George	England	May 12, 1844	April 4, 1869	Oct., 1883	Haselton	Pastor, Sacred Heart Church*	Sept., 1888
82	Litterst, Theodore	Baden	April 2, 1835	Mar. 4, 1871	Ordination	Bismarck	Pastor, St. Sebastian's Church	Nov., 1879
83	McCarthy, Timothy P.	Ireland	Nov. 6, 1843	July 5, 1877	"	Toledo	Pastor, Immaculation Conception Church	March, 1890
84	McGuire, Patrick J.	Ireland	Mar. 12, 1841	Oct. 21, 1863	"	Canton	Pastor, St. John's Ev. Church	July, 1879
85	McGuire, Thomas F.	Ireland	Nov. 6, 1847	July 1, 1883	"	St. Mary's Corners	Pastor, St. Mary's Church	April, 1890
86	McHale, John	England	Nov. 23, 1852	Oct. 28, 1876	Oct., 1889	Cleveland	Assistant, St. Malachy's Church	Oct., 1889
87	McMahon, John	Ohio	Oct. 6, 1860	Nov. 11, 1883	Ordination	Alliance	Pastor, St. Joseph's Church	Mar., 1886
88	McMahon, William	Ireland	Feb. 9, 1847	July 21, 1872	"	Cleveland	Pastor, St. Bridget's Church	Feb., 1876
89	Magenhann, Andrew	Alsace	Feb. 28, 1839	July 30, 1861	"	Mansfield	Pastor, St. Peter's Church	Oct., 1869
90	Mahar, Thomas F.	Pennsylvania	Sept. 28, 1851	May 30, 1874	Aug., 1875†	Akron	Pastor, St. Vincent de Paul's Church*	Aug., 1880
91	Mahon, Thomas F.	Ireland	Nov. 26, 1862	Dec. 19, 1888	Ordination	Cleveland	Assistant, St. John's Cathedral	Jan., 1890
92	Major, Thomas S.	Kentucky	July 13, 1844	Nov. 14, 1875	April, 1887	Edgerton	Pastor, St. Mary's Church*	April, 1887
93	Malecha, John W.	Bohemia	June 23, 1861	July 3, 1886	Ordination	Cleveland	*Locum tenens*, St. Adalbert's Church	Sept., 1888
94	Manning, Alfred E.	Ohio	Sept. 1, 1856	July 2, 1881	"	Fremont	Pastor, St. Ann's Church	Mar., 1890
95	Manning, William J.	Massachusetts	Dec. 24, 1847	July 5, 1879	"	Youngstown	Pastor, Immaculate Conception Church	Dec., 1882
96	Martin, Anthony T.	France	Nov. 28, 1831	July 26, 1857	"	Euclid	Pastor, St. Paul's Church*	June, 1864
97	Mears, Edward	Ireland	July 18, 1844	Mar. 7, 1869	"	Youngstown	Rector, St. Columba's Church	July, 1877
98	Mertes, John B.	Luxemburg	April 15, 1851	July 4, 1880	Ordination	Maumee	Pastor, St. Joseph's Church	May, 1885
99	Metternich, Francis	Rhenish Prussia	May 18, 1851	May 31, 1874	"	Navarre	Pastor, St. Clement's Church	Oct., 1876
100	Michenfelder, John A.	Baden	May 1, 1850	June 7, 1873	"	Norwalk	Pastor, St. Paul's Church	May, 1888
101	Mizer, John G.	Ohio	Dec. 24, 1854	July 4, 1880	"	Carey	Pastor, O. L. of Consolation Church*	Jan., 1890
102	Moes, Nicholas A.	Luxemburg	April 10, 1844	May 18, 1867	"	Cleveland	Rector, St. Mary's Seminary	Sept., 1870
103	Molony, James P.	Ireland	June 19, 1830	June 26, 1859	"	Cleveland	Rector, St. Malachy's Church	Nov., 1865
104	Moran, Thomas F.	Indiana	Feb. 16, 1865	Dec. 19, 1888	"	Clyde	Pastor, St. Mary's Church*	Mar., 1890
105	Möhlenbeck, John A.	Westphalia	Sept. 27, 1857	July 2, 1881	"	Archbold	Pastor, St. Peter's Church*	Mar., 1886

† Ordained for Diocese of Cleveland. * Mission attached.

I. SECULARS.—CONTINUED.

No.	Name.	Native of:	Date of Birth.	Date of Ordination.	In the Diocese Since:	Residence.	Present Appointment.	Date of Appointment.
	Reverends:							
106	Müller, Michael	Bavaria	Feb. 21, 1833	June 27, 1865	Ordination	Ottoville	Pastor, Immaculate Conception Church	Mar., 1868
107	Müller, Wimar	Rhenish Prussia	Nov. 30, 1846	July 21, 1872	"	Lorain	Pastor, St. Mary's Church	April, 1888
108	Murphy, Edward J.	Ireland	Aug. 15, 1836	Sept. 30, 1861	"	Leetonia	Pastor, St. Patrick's Church	Oct., 1884
109	Murphy, Michael	New York	Aug. 29, 1851	July 5, 1876	"	Cleveland	Professor, St. Mary's Seminary	Sept., 1888
110	Murphy, William F.	Ohio	Nov. 5, 1857	July 6, 1884	"		(On sick list since May, 1888)	
111	O'Brien, Cornelius L.	Ireland	Nov. 17, 1837	June 29, 1865	Aug., 1888	Salineville	Pastor, St. Patrick's Church	Jan., 1890
112	O'Brien, Patrick	Ireland	Feb. 20, 1844	July 21, 1872	Ordination	Cleveland	Pastor, St. Patrick's Church	Dec., 1889
113	O'Callaghan, Eugene M	Ireland	May 4, 1831	June 26, 1859	"	Cleveland	Pastor, St. Colman's Church	Aug., 1880
114	O'Connell, John T.	Ireland	Jan. 15, 1860	July 9, 1885	"	Cleveland	Professor, St. Mary's Seminary	Jan., 1887
115	O'Connor, Jer. P.	Massachusetts	Nov. 9, 1860	Dec. 19, 1888	"	Genoa	Pastor, O. L. of Lourdes' Church*	Jan., 1889
116	O'Connor, John	Ohio	Feb. 28, 1853	July 4, 1880	"	Cleveland	Pastor, St. Augustine's Church	Aug., 1888
117	O'Leary, James	Ireland	May 21, 1851	July 5, 1877	"	Lima	Pastor, St. Rose's Church	Mar., 1886
118	O'Neill, Francis J.	Ireland	Oct. 9, 1852	June 15, 1878	"	Berea	Pastor, St. Mary's Church*	Mar., 1886
119	Panuska, Wenceslas	Bohemia	Nov. 2, 1861	June 15, 1889	"	Holgate	Pastor, St. Mary's Church*	June, 1889
120	Pfeil, Nicholas	Ohio	Nov. 4, 1859	July 1, 1883	"	Avon	Pastor, Holy Trinity Church*	Feb., 1884
121	Philippart, Michael	Luxemburg	Mar. 21, 1854	July 3, 1886	"	Toledo	Assistant, St. Peter's Church	Nov., 1889
122	Powers, John J.	Ohio	April 24, 1862	Dec. 21, 1889	"	Cleveland	Assistant, Holy Name Church	Jan., 1890
123	Pütz, John Martin	Rhenish Prussia	Sept. 11, 1836	June 28, 1863	"	Tiffin	Rector, St. Joseph's Church	May, 1885
124	Pütz, John Peter	Rhenish Prussia	Dec. 20, 1833	June 25, 1865	"	Tiffin	Assistant, St. Joseph's Church	June, 1885
125	Pütz, Michael	Luxemburg	Dec. 29, 1845	Mar. 7, 1869	"	Napoleon	Pastor, St. Augustine's Church	Oct., 1880
126	Quigley, P. F.	Ireland	Feb. 26, 1846	June 19, 1869	"	Toledo	Pastor, St. Francis de Sales' Church	Nov., 1885
127	Quinn, James J.	Ireland	Jan. 10, 1860	Aug. 22, 1882	July, 1888	Youngstown	Assistant, St. Columba's Church	Sept., 1888
128	Rebholz, Sylvan	Baden	May 18, 1844	Feb. 12, 1870	June, 1870 †	Randolph	Pastor, St. Joseph's Church*	Mar., 1885
129	Reichlin, Casimir	Switzerland	Dec. 16, 1843	April 19, 1870	Ordination	Cleveland	Rector, St. Stephen's Church	May, 1870

130	**Reichlin, Charles**	Switzerland	Dec. 10, 1863	Dec. 18, 1886	Ordination	Kelley's Island	Pastor, St. Michael's Church*	Jan.,	1887
131	**Rieken, Gustave H**	Illinois	Dec. 23, 1855	July 4, 1880	"	Perrysburg	Pastor, St. Rose's Church*	Feb.,	1886
132	**Romer, Joseph**	Switzerland	Aug. 27, 1841	July 4, 1875	"	North Amherst	Pastor, St. Joseph's Church	July,	1875
133	**Rosenberg, Joseph**	Switzerland	April 8, 1844	July 4, 1875	"	Six Mile Wood	Pastor, Immaculate Conception Church	April,	1888
134	**Rosinski, Benedict**	Poland	Mar. 20, 1860	Dec. 17, 1887	"	Sandusky	Assistant, St. Mary's Church	Jan.,	1888
135	**Rouchy, James**	France	Sept. 22, 1828	May 21, 1853	Nov., 1862		(Resides at Canal Fulton)		
136	**Rupert, Frederick**	Ohio	Nov. 21, 1846	July 5, 1879	Ordination	Bellevue	Pastor, Immaculate Conception Church	April,	1885
137	Sauvadet, Andrew	France	Mar. 1, 1833	June 18, 1859	June, 1865	Wakeman	Pastor, St. Mary's Church	Feb.,	1880
138	Scanlon, Matthew A.	Pennsylvania	Jan. 13, 1830	June 26, 1859	Ordination	Cleveland	Pastor, St. Edward's (H. Fam.) Church	July,	1880
139	Schaffeld, John T.	Rhenish Prussia	Oct. 16, 1837	July 17, 1870	"	Elyria	Pastor, St. Mary's Church*	May,	1880
140	Schmitz, Nicholas	Rhenish Prussia	May 21, 1833	June 28, 1863	"	Monroeville	Pastor, St. Joseph's Church	May,	1885
141	Shoenemann, G. C.	Ohio	April 21, 1861	July 6, 1884	"	Milan	Pastor, St. Anthony's Church*	Feb.,	1890
142	Schreiber, Ferd. A.	New York	July 3, 1861	July 3, 1886	"	Antwerp	Pastor, St. Mary's Church*	Aug.,	1886
143	Schreiner, August H.	New York	Aug. 31, 1866	April 12, 1890	"	Cleveland	Assistant, St. Peter's Church	April,	1890
144	Scullin, Felix M.	Ireland	Jan. 29, 1856	July 4, 1880	"	Niles	Pastor, St. Stephen's Church*	May,	1890
145	Seltzer, Charles	Lorraine	July 15, 1845	May 16, 1868	"	Doylestown	Pastor, St. Peter's Church*.	Dec.,	1882
146	Sheridan, John	Ireland	Aug. 15, 1818	Aug. 15, 1844	Aug., 1873	Cleveland	Chaplain, St. Vincent's Asylum	Feb.,	1890
147	Sidley, Alexander R.	Ohio	Aug. 19, 1842	June 25, 1865	Ordination	Cleveland	Pastor, Immaculate Conception Church	June,	1876
148	Sidley, Robert A	Ireland	Nov. 1, 1828	June 1, 1856	"	Sandusky	Rector, Sts. Peter and Paul's Church	April,	1871
149	Sinner, Francis	Luxemburg	Sept. 15, 1855	July 21, 1878	"	Salem	Pastor, St. Paul's Church*	Jan.,	1888
150	Slowikowski, E. J.	Poland	May 6, 1823	Dec. 20, 1849	Oct., 1887	Berea	Pastor, St. Adalbert's Church	Mar.,	1889
151	Smith, Joseph F.	Ohio	Feb. 7, 1865	June 15, 1889	"	Shelby	Pastor, Sacred Heart Church*	June,	1889
152	Smith, Matthew S.	Pennsylvania	Aug. 28, 1859	July 1, 1882	"		(Sick)		
153	Smith, William J.	Canada	May 6, 1859	Sept. 23, 1883	July, 1888	Toledo	Pastor, St. Louis' Church	Dec.,	1888
154	Smyth, Thomas M.	New Jersey	May 27, 1847	July 5, 1871	Ordination	Ashtabula	Pastor, St. Joseph's Church*	Aug.,	1887
155	Sproll, Joseph	Wuerttemberg	Jan. 11, 1845	July 21, 1872	"	Loudonville	Pastor, St. Peter's Church*	July,	1885
156	Stafford, Denis J.	Dist. of Columbia	Nov. 3, 1860	Dec. 19, 1885	"	Cleveland	Assistant, St. John's Cathedral	Jan.,	1886
156	Te Pas, Anthony J.	Ohio	Dec. 3, 1852	May 22, 1880	Oct., 1882†	Cleveland	**Prof. St. Mary's Seminary***	Oct.,	1882
157	Thein, John	Luxemburg	Sept. 8, 1848	July 4, 1875	Ordination	Liverpool	Pastor, St. Martin's Church	Nov.	1885
158	Thorpe, Thomas P.	Ireland	Feb. 26, 1838	June 30, 1861	"	Cleveland	Pastor, St. John's Cathedral*	June,	1876
159	Tracy, John	Ireland	Nov. 20, 1837	June 28, 1863	"	Sandusky	Pastor, Holy Angels' Church	Aug.,	1887
160	Treiber, Clement	Ohio	July 20, 1856	July 4, 1880	"	Crestline	Pastor, St. Joseph's Church	June,	1887

† Ordained for Diocese of Cleveland.   * Mission attached.

I. SECULARS.—CONCLUDED.

No.	Name.	Native of:	Date of Birth.	Date of Ordination.	In the Diocese since.	Residence.	Present Appointment.	Date of Appointment.
	Reverends:							
161	Valley, George	Massachusetts	June 24, 1861	Dec. 17, 1887	Ordination	Cleveland	Assistant, St. John's Cathedral	Sept., 1888
162	Vattmann, Edward J.	Westphalia	Sept. 11, 1840	April 1, 1865	May, 1867	Canal Fulton	Pastor, Sts. Philip and James' Church*	Oct., 1877
163	Vleck, Anthony	Moravia	June 5, 1862	Aug. 7, 1885	Ordination	Cleveland	Pastor, St. Procop's Church	Aug., 1885
164	Vogt, John George	Baden	June 22, 1847	June 7, 1873	"	New Washington,	Pastor, St. Bernard's Church*	Jan., 1888
165	Vollmayer, Michael	Ohio	Mar. 19, 1856	July 9, 1885	"	Custar	Pastor, St. Louis' Church*	July, 1885
166	Weber, Ambrose A.	Baden	Mar. 25, 1854	July 3, 1886	"	Warren	Pastor, O. L. of Mt. Carmel Church*	Aug., 1886
167	Westerholt, Francis	Westphalia	May 31, 1827	July 8, 1855	"	Cleveland	Rector, St. Peter's Church	Jan., 1868
168	Wieczorek, Simon J.	Russian Poland	July 18, 1838	June 29, 1868	July, 1886.	Toledo	Pastor, St. Hedwig's Church	July, 1886
169	Wonderly, Ignatius J.	Ohio	June 7, 1860	Dec. 21, 1889	Ordination	Vermillion	Pastor, St. Mary's Church*	Jan., 1890
170	Zinsmayer, Dominic	Baden	July 29, 1844	Nov. 30, 1869	April, 1870†	Sheffield	Pastor, St. Teresa's Church	Aug., 1883

† Ordained for Diocese of Cleveland.   * Mission attached.

SUPPLEMENT TO LIST OF PRIESTS.

August, 1890.

ADDITIONS.

Reverends:	Native of	Born.	Ordained.	Residence.	Present Appointment.	Date of Appointment.
Graham, Edward P.	Ireland	July 1, 1862	July 6, 1890	Antwerp	Pastor, St. Mary's Church *	Aug., 1890
Hartmann, Hubert (S.J.)	Westphalia	August 9, 1849	August 10, 1873	Cleveland	Professor, St. Ignatius College	July, 1890
Kreusch, Joseph (S.J.)	Prussia	March 22, 1829	Sept. 4, 1854	Cleveland	Missionary, etc., St. Ignatius College	May, 1890
Lamb, Thomas P.	Ohio	April 28, 1863	July 6, 1890	Cleveland	Assistant, (pro tem.) St. Patrick's Church	Aug., 1890
Mahar, William G.	Ohio	March 14, 1864	July 6, 1890	Akron	Assistant, St. Vincent's Church	July, 1890

CHANGES.

Reverends:	Transferred from	Transferred to	Date of Transfer.
Becker, Michael	Sacred Heart Church, (Pastor), Shelby Settlement	(Off duty for a three months' leave of absence.)	July, 1890
Brennan, Michael J.	Left the diocese July, 1890.		
Hannan, John		St. Colman's Church, (Assistant), Cleveland	May, 1890
Philippart, Michael	St. Peter's Church, (Assistant), Toledo	St. Aloysius' Church, * (Pastor), Bowling Green	June, 1890
Rosinski, Benedict	St. Mary's Church, (Assistant), Sandusky	St. Adalbert's Church, (Pastor), Berea	May, 1890
Shreiber, Ferd. A.	St. Mary's Church, (Pastor), Antwerp	S. Heart Church, (Pastor), Shelby Settlement	Aug., 1890
Slowikowski, E. J.	St. Mary's Church, (Pastor), Berea	St. Stanislas' Church, (Assistant pro tem.), Cleveland	May, 1890
Smith, Matthew S.	(Left the diocese May, 1890.)		

* Mission attached.

CORRECTIONS.

Reverends: Mueller, Michael............for June 27, 1865............read June 25, 1865.
Puetz, Michael............ " October, 1880............ " October, 1870.
Scullin, Felix M. .... " May, 1890............ " May, 1889.

II. REGULARS.

A. Sanguinists.

No.	Name.	Native of:	Date of Birth.	Date of Ordination.	In the Diocese since:	Residence.	Present Appointment.	Date of Appointment.
	Reverends:							
1	Boehmer, J. Benedict	Ohio	Jan. 14, 1860	July 29, 1883	Oct., 1883	Glandorf	Pastor, Sts. Peter and Paul's Ch., Ottawa	Oct., 1883
2	Buechel, Francis	Austria	Sept. 2, 1825	June 13, 1871	June, 1885	Glandorf	Assistant, St. John's Church	June, 1885
3	Glueck, Ehrhard	Baden	Nov. 24, 1824	June 13, 1856	June, 1862	New Riegel	Pastor, Liberty and St. Patrick's	Oct., 1887
4	Griessmayer, F. Xavier,	Wuerttemberg	Dec. 29, 1829	Oct. 24, 1853	Mar., 1878	Thompson	Pastor, St. Michael's Church	Mar., 1878
5	Hengarten, Isidore	Switzerland	July 7, 1857	Mar. 9, 1884	April, 1890	Thompson	Assistant, St. Michael's Church	April, 1890
6	Kenk, Matthias	Baden	Jan. 18, 1846	Nov. 21, 1868	Dec., 1885	New Riegel	Pastor, St. Peter's Church, Big Spring	Dec., 1885
7	Mielinger, Francis X	Bavaria	Mar. 26, 1865	Mar. 17, 1889	Mar., 1889	Reedtown	Pastor, Assumption Church	Mar., 1889
8	Nigsch, Francis	Tyrol	May 24, 1846	Jan. 25, 1872	Oct., 1881	Glandorf	Pastor, St. John's Church	Oct., 1881
9	Rist, Philip	Wuerttemberg	May 9, 1842	June 7, 1866	July, 1866	St. Stephen's	Pastor, St. Stephen's Church	Feb., 1874
10	Russ, Boniface	Ohio	Nov. 12, 1855	Sept. 19, 1878	Aug., 1880	New Riegel	Pastor, St. Boniface's Church	Aug., 1880
11	Shirack, Peter W	Indiana	Feb. 22, 1859	Sept. 8, 1887	Mar., 1890	Akron	*Loc. tenens*, St. Bernard's Church	Mar., 1890
12	Schuele, Rochus	Baden	Aug. 14, 1829	Nov. 21, 1853	Dec., 1887	Glandorf	Pastor, St. Michael's Church, Kalida	Dec., 1887

B. Franciscans.

No.	Name.	Native of:	Date of Birth.	Date of Ordination.	In the Diocese since:	Residence.	Present Appointment.	Date of Appointment.
	Reverends.							
1	Arentz, Theodore	Germany	Jan. 7, 1849	June 4, 1876	Aug., 1888	Cleve'd Monast'y	Sup'r of Monast'y & Pastor, St. Joseph's Ch.	Aug., 1888
2	Bernard, Alexius	Westphalia	Jan. 16, 1836	Mar. 15, 1872	July, 1889	Cleve'd Monast'y	Chaplain, &c.	July, 1889
3	Depmann, Boniface	Westphalia	July 29, 1841	Feb. 2, 1864	Aug., 1888	Cleve'd Monast'y	Assistant, St. Joseph's Church	Aug., 1888
4	Freimuth, Firmatus	Germany	April 11, 1838	May 27, 1877	Aug., 1888	Cleve'd Monast'y	Chaplain, &c.	Aug., 1888
5	Girschewski, Cletus	W. Prussia	Mar. 11, 1846	May 22, 1884	July, 1887	Cleve'd Monast'y	Chaplain, &c.	July, 1887
6	McClory, Augustine	Pennsylvania	Nov. 15, 1847	June 29, 1875	Jan., 1887	Cleve'd Monast'y	Chaplain, &c.	Jan., 1887
7	Rheindorff, Romual	Germany	July 22, 1856	May 12, 1883	July, 1889	Cleve'd Monast'y	Chaplain, &c.	July, 1889
8	Wenzel, Camillus	Silesia	Mar. 28, 1850	Sept. 8, 1874	Aug., 1884	Clevel'd Monasty	Chaplain, &c.	Aug., 1884

II. REGULARS.—CONCLUDED.

C. JESUITS.

No.	Name.	Native of:	Date of Birth.	Date of Ordination.	In the Diocese since:	Residence.	Present Appointment.	Date of Appointment.
	Reverends:							
1	Becker, William	Westphalia	April 15, 1830	April 16, 1859	June, 1885	Cleveland	Assistant, St. Mary's Church	June, 1885
2	Bochmer, Henry	Germany	Mar. 10, 1834	Sept. 22, 1866	Sept., 1889	Toledo	Pastor of Sylvania, &c.	Sept., 1889
3	Gunneiner, Barth.	Austria	Mar. 24, 1851	Aug. 21, 1887	Aug., 1889	Cleveland	Professor, St. Ignatius' College	Aug., 1889
4	Groenings, Jacob	Germany	Feb. 15, 1833	July 2, 1868	Jan., 1890	Toledo	Assistant, St. Mary's Church	Jan., 1890
5	Haefely, Basil	Switzerland	Feb. 4, 1822	Aug. 1, 1854	Sept., 1885	Cleveland	Assistant, &c., St. Mary's Church	Sept., 1885
6	Hauser, Theodore	Baden	Sept. 18, 1836	Sept. 10, 1867	Aug., 1888	Cleveland	Assistant, St. Mary's Church	Aug., 1888
7	Knappmeyer, Henry	Westphalia	June 9, 1835	Aug. 24, 1869	Nov., 1888	Cleveland	Rector, St. Ignatius' College, and Superior	Nov., 1888
8	Kramer, Louis M.	Rhenish Prussia	Aug. 7, 1839	July 15, 1870	Nov., 1879	Toledo	Assistant, St. Mary's Church	Nov., 1879
9	Leiter, Anselm	Switzerland	Jan. 20, 1826	Sept. 15, 1855	Sept., 1889	Toledo	Superior of Jesuits	Sept., 1889
10	Ming, John	Switzerland	Sept. 20, 1838	Sept. 13, 1868	Sept., 1889	Toledo	Assistant, St. Mary's Church	Sept., 1889
11	Neubrand, Francis X.	Wuerttemberg	Dec. 7, 1832	Aug. 10, 1857	Feb., 1890	Cleveland	Missionary, res. St. Ignatius' College	Feb., 1890
12	Neumueller, Matthias	Bavaria	Feb. 8, 1843	Sept. 7, 1874	Aug., 1888	Toledo	Assistant, &c., St. Mary's Church	Aug., 1888
13	Neustich, John B.	Westphalia	May 19, 1840	Mar. 30, 1865	June, 1886	Cleveland	Pastor, St. Mary's Church	June, 1886
14	Packisch, William von	Prussia	April 14, 1849	Aug. 28, 1878	Sept., 1888	Cleveland	Professor, St. Ignatius' College	Sept., 1888
15	Ruebsaat, Gustave	Germany	July 29, 1845	Sept. —, 1876	Aug., 1888	Cleveland	Professor, St. Ignatius' College	Sept., 1888
16	Schulte, Godfrey	Germany	May 25, 1850	Mar. 28, 1886	Aug., 1889	Cleveland	Professor, St. Ignatius' College	Aug., 1889
17	Steffen, Augustin	Germany	April 10, 1853	Sept. 8, 1883	Aug., 1889	Cleveland	Professor, St. Ignatius' College	Aug., 1889
18	Zoeller, Michael	Bavaria	April 16, 1836	Aug. 12, 1859	Aug., 1881	Toledo	Pastor, St. Mary's Church	June, 1886

TABLE II.

A List of Churches, with Resident Pastors.

October, 1847.

Number.	Congregation Organized.	Place, (Present Name.)	Former Name of Place.	County.	Church Dedicated to	Church Built in	Church Built of	Resident Pastor.
1	1823	Canton		Stark	St. John Baptist	1823	Brick	J. J. Doherty
2	1845	Canton		Stark	St. Peter	1845	Brick	J. H. Luhr, J. B. Jacomet
3	1835	Cleveland		Cuyahoga	St. Mary's (on "Flats")	1840	Frame	M. Howard
4	1844	Delphos		Allen	St. John Ev	1844	Log	O. J. Bredeick
5	1827	Doylestown	Chippewa	Wayne	St. Peter	1829	Log	C. Mouret
6	1817	Dungannon	St. Paul's Settlement	Columbiana	St. Paul	1820	Brick	J. Conlan and J. V. Conlan
7	1834	Glandorf		Putnam	St. John Bapt. (2d ch.)	1837	Log	George Boehne
8	1823	Louisville	Beechland	Stark	St. Louis	1835	Brick	Peter Peudeprat
9	1829	Massillon		Stark	St. Mary	1844	Stone	Ph. Foley
10	1833	New Riegel	Wolf's Creek	Seneca	St. Boniface	1833	Log	John Wittmer, J. Van den Broek, P. A. Capoder
11	1834	Sandusky		Erie	Holy Angels	1842	Stone	P. J. Machebeuf
12	1834	Thompson		Seneca	St. Michael	1839	Log	F. S. Brunner, M. A. Meyer, M. Kreusch, J. Ringele
13	1841	Toledo		Lucas	St. Francis de Sales	1842*	Frame	L. de Goesbriand, A. Rappe

* Bought.

B. MISSION CHURCHES.

October, 1847.

Number.	Congregation Organized.	Place. (Present Name.)	Former Name of Place.	County.	Church Dedicated to	Church Built in	Church Built of	Church Attended From
14	1840	Abbeyville		Medina	St. Mary	1842	Log	Thompson
15	1835	Akron	Cascade	Summit	St. Vincent de Paul	1844	Frame	Doylestown
16	1823	Avon		Lorain	Holy Trinity	1844	Frame	Cleveland and Thompson
17	1846	Bismarck	Sherman	Huron	St. Sebastian	1846	Log	Thompson
18	1825	Canal Fulton	Lawrence	Stark	Sts. Philip and James	1831	Log	Massillon
19	1841	Defiance		Defiance	St. John Ev	1844	Frame	Toledo
20	1834	East Liverpool		Columbiana	St. Aloysius	1840	Brick	Dungannon
21	1841	Fremont	Lower Sandusky	Sandusky	St. Ann	1844	Frame	Toledo
22	1842	French Creek		Lorain	St. Mary	1844*	Frame	Thompson
23	1845	Harrisburg		Stark	Sacred Heart of Jesus	1845	Frame	Louisville
24	1835	La Porte	Rawsonville	Lorain	St. John of the Cross	1835	Frame	Cleveland
25	1841	La Prairie		Sandusky	St. Philomena	1841	Log	Sandusky and Toledo
26	1834	Liberty		Seneca	St. Andrew	1842	Log	New Riegel
27	1842	Liverpool		Medina	St. Martin	1842	Log	Thompson
28	1830	McCutchenville		Wyandot	Visitation B. V. M	1837	Frame	New Riegel
29	1838	Maumee	Maumee City, S. Toledo	Lucas	St. Joseph	1841*	Frame	Toledo
30	1832	Navarro	Bethlehem	Stark	St. Clement	1833	Log	Canton and Massillon
31	1843	New Bavaria	Poplar Ridge	Henry	Sacred Heart of Jesus	1847	Log	Toledo
32	1845	New Berlin		Stark	St. Paul	1845	Brick	Canton
33	1841	New Washington		Crawford	St. Bernard	1841	Log	Thompson
34	1840	Norwalk		Huron	St. Peter	1840	Frame	Sandusky
35	1829	Peru		Huron	St. Alphonse	1834	Frame	Thompson

* Bought.

B. Mission Churches.—Concluded.

October, 1847.

Number.	Congregation Organized.	Place. (Present Name.)	Former Name of Place.	County.	Church Dedicated to	Church Built in	Church Built of	Church Attended From
36	1838	Providence		Lucas	St. Patrick	1845	Brick	Toledo
37	1832	Randolph		Portage	St. Joseph (2d ch.)	1845	Frame	Thompson and Canton
38	1842	St. Stephen's Settlement	St. Maurice	Seneca	St. Stephen	1842	Frame	Thompson
39	1842	Sheffield		Lorain	St. Teresa	1842	Log	Thompson
40	1833	Shelby Settlement		Crawford	Sacred Heart of Jesus	1836	Frame	Thompson
41	1845	Tiffin		Seneca	St. Joseph	1845	Brick	New Riegel
42	1832	Tiffin		Seneca	St. Mary	1832	Br. & Fr.	Vacant

C. STATIONS.

October, 1847.

Places.	Attended From	Places.	Attended From
1. Archbold	Toledo.	15. Oak Harbor	Toledo.
2. Bucyrus	Thompson.	16. Ottoville	Glandorf.
3. Cuyahoga Falls	Doylestown.	17. Painesville	Cleveland.
4. Delaware Bend	Toledo.	18. Port Clinton	Sandusky.
5. Elyria	Cleveland.	19. Ravenna	Cleveland and Doylestown.
6. Findlay	New Riegel.	20. Six-Mile Woods	Toledo.
7. Fostoria (Rome)	New Riegel.	21. South Thompson	Cleveland.
8. Hicksville	Toledo.	22. Summitville	Dungannon.
9. Junction	Toledo.	23. Toussaint	Sandusky.
10. Lima	Delphos and Glandorf.	24. Vermillion	Cleveland.
11. Mansfield	Thompson.	25. Wellsville	Dungannon.
12. Marblehead	Sandusky.	26. Woodville	Toledo.
13. Marshallville(Bristol)	Doylestown.	27. Wooster	Massillon.
14. Napoleon	Toledo.	28. Youngstown	Doylestown.

D. CONVENTS.

October, 1847.

1. New Riegel .... Sanguinist.
2. Thompson .... Sanguinist.
3. Toledo .... Notre Dame Convent and Academy.

SUMMARY.

Churches (with Resident Pastors)	13	
Churches (Mission)	29	
Total		42
Stations		28
Priests (Secular)	14	
Priests (Regular)	7	
Total		21
Convents		3
Academy		1

TABLE III.

LIST OF CHURCHES, RESIDENT PASTORS, ETC.

April, 1890.

Number.	Congregation Organized in:	Place.	County.	Church Dedicated to:	Present Church is the:	Present Church Built or First Used.	Size. Exterior Length, Ft.	Size. Exterior Width, Ft.	Church Built of:	Pastoral Residence Built of:	Language of Congregation.	Resident Pastor: Mission Attended From: (*In Italic.*)	Parochial Schools?
1	1861	Akron	Summit	St. Bernard	First[1]	1862	140	60	Brick	Wood	German	Rev. J. B. Broun	Yes.
2	1887	"	"	St. Mary of Holy Rosary	First	1887	62	40	Brick		English	*St. Vincent's, Akron*	Yes.
3	1835	"	"	St. Vincent de Paul	Second	1866	100	50	Stone	Brick	English	Rev. T. F. Mahar	Yes.
4	1852	Alliance	Stark	St. Joseph	Second	1880	110	60	Brick	Wood	English	Rev. J. McMahon	Yes.
5	1864	Antwerp	Paulding	St. Mary	First	1867?	46	26	Wood	Wood	Eng., Ger. & Fr.	Rev. F. A. Schreiber	No.
6	1846	Archbold	Fulton	St. Peter	Second	1869	60	36	Wood	Wood	Eng., Ger. & Fr.	Rev. J. H. Mühlenbeck	No.
7	1853	Ashland	Ashland	St. Edward	Second	1871?	52	36	Brick		Eng. and Ger.	*Loudonville*	No.
8	1858	Ashtabula	Ashtabula	St. Joseph	First[1]	1860	95	30	Wood	Wood	English	Rev. T. M. Smyth	Yes.
9	1889	Ashtabula Har.	Ashtabula	Mater Dolorosa	First	1890	64	38	Wood		English	*Ashtabula*	Yes.
10	1882	Attica	Seneca	Sts. Peter and Paul	First	1882	50	33	Wood		Ger. and Eng.	*Shelby*	No.
11	1833	Avon	Lorain	Holy Trinity	Sec'nd[1]	1862	100	40	Wood	Wood	German	Rev. N. Pfeil	Yes.
12	1859	Bellevue	Huron	Immaculate Conception	Second	1884	106	44	Brick	Wood	Eng. and Ger.	Rev. F. Rupert	Yes.
13	1873	Berea	Cuyahoga	St. Adalbert	First[1]	1874	118	48	Brick	Wood	Polish and Ger.	Rev. E. J. Slowikowski	Yes.
14	1856	"	"	St. Mary	Second	1867?	100	44	Stone	(Rented)	English	Rev. F. J. O'Neil	Yes.
15	1856	Berwick	Seneca	St. Nicholas	Second	1889	123	56	Brick	Brick	Fr. and Ger.	Rev. M. Arnoldi	Yes.
16	1875	Bettsville	"	Immaculate Conception	First	1875	45	33	Wood		Ger. and Eng.	*Millersville*	No.
17	1883	Big Ditch	Lucas	St. Ignatius	First	1884	45	30	Wood		Fr. and Eng.	*Toussaint*	No.
18	1858	Big Spring	Seneca	St. Peter	Second	1881	110	45	Brick		German	*N. Riegel, Rev. M. Kenk*	Yes.
19	1846	Bismarck	Huron	St. Sebastian	Second	1857	72	40	Brick	Brick	German	Rev. T. Litterst	Yes.
20	1856	Bluffton	Allen	St. Mary	First	1865	45	27	Wood		Eng. and Ger.	*Findlay*	No.

[1] Enlarged since first built.

TABLE III.—CONTINUED.

Number.	Congregation Organized in:	Place.	County.	Church Dedicated to:	Present Church is the:	Present Church Built and First Used:	Size, Exterior: Length, Ft.	Size, Exterior: Width, Ft.	Church Built of:	Pastoral Residence Built of:	Language of Congregation.	Resident Pastor: Mission Attended From: (In Italic.)	Parochial School?
21	1869	Bowling Green	Wood	St. Aloysius	First	1881	50	35	Brick		Eng. and Ger.	(*Vacant.*)	No.
22	1869	Briar Hill	Mahoning	St. Ann	First	1870	65	45	Wood	Wood	English	Rev. J. P. Barry	Yes.
23	1873	Brighton	Cuyahoga	Sacred Heart of Jesus	First	1875	70	31	Brick		Eng. and Ger.	*Independence*	No.
24	1865	Bryan	Williams	St. Patrick	First [1]	1876	36	21	Wood		English	*Archbold*	No.
25	1835	Bucyrus	Crawford	Holy Trinity	Second	1886	100	45	Brick	Wood	Eng. and Ger.	Rev. J. H. Kleekamp	Yes.
26	1825	Canal Fulton	Stark	Sts. Philip and James	Third	1868	100	45	Brick	Brick	Eng. and Ger.	Rev. E. J. Vattmann	Yes.
27	1824	Canton	"	St. John Baptist	Second	1870	140	64	Brick	Wood	English	Rev. P. J. McGuire	Yes.
28	1845	"	"	St. Peter	Second	1879	164	74	Brick	Brick	German	Rev. V. Arnould	Yes.
29	1868	Carey	Wyandot	Our Lady of Consolation	First	1872	60	38	Wood	(Rented)	Ger. and Eng.	Rev. J. G. Mizer	Yes.
30	1875	Cecil	Paulding	Immaculate Conception	First	1879	80	28	Wood		Eng. & French	*Antwerp*	No.
31	1876	Chicago Jct.	Huron	St. Francis Xavier	First	1879	40	18	Wood		Eng. and Ger.	*Shelby*	No.
32	1835	Cleveland	Cuyahoga	St. John Ev. (Cathedral)	Sec'nd [2]	1852	170	75	Brick	Brick	English	Rev. T. P. Thorpe	Yes.
33	1883	"	"	St. Adalbert	First	1883	87	31	Wood	Wood	Bohemian	Rev. J. W. Malecha, Lt.	Yes.
34	1887	"	"	St. Anthony	First [3]	1887	124	44	Wood	(Res. r. of ch.)	Italian	Rev. P. Capitani	No.
35	1860	"	"	St. Augustine	First [4]	1860	110	40	Wood	Brick	English	Rev. J. O'Connor	Yes.
36	1857	"	"	St. Bridget	Second	1877	150	50	Brick	(Res. in sch.)	English	Rev. W. McMahon	Yes.
37	1880	"	"	St. Colman	First [4]	1880	124	59	Wood	Brick	English	Rev. E. M. O'Callaghan	Yes.
38	1871	"	"	St. Columbkill. [5]	First [4]	1871	110	35	Wood		English	*Cathedral*	Yes.
39	1871	"	"	St. Edward (Holy Family)	Second	1886	120	65	Stone	(Res. r. of sch)	English	Rev. M. A. Scanlon	Yes.
40	1887	"	"	St. Francis	First [4]	1887	143	36	Wood	Wood	German	Rev. N. Kirch	Yes.
41	1889	"	"	Sacred Heart	First	1889	115	36	Wood		Polish	*St. Stanislas, Cleveland*	Yes.
42	1862	"	"	Holy Name (Holy Rosary)	Second	1887	160	65	Brick	(Rented)	English	Rev. J. T. Carroll	Yes.
43	1860	"	"	Holy Trinity	First	1861	108	40	Wood	Wood	German	Rev. P. Becker	Yes.
44	1856	"	"	Immaculate Conception	Second	1885	176	76	Stone	Brick	English	Rev. A. R. Sidley	Yes.
45	1856	"	"	St. Joseph	Second	1873	145	66	Brick	(Conv. Res.)	German	Rev. T. Arentz, O. S. F.	Yes.

46	1888	"	"	St. Ladislas	First	1888	70	40	Wood		Hungarian	*O. L. of Lourdes, Clev'd*	Yes.
47	1866	"	"	St. Malachy	First	1869	131	67	Brick	Brick	English	Rev. J. P. Molony	Yes.
48	1870	"	"	St. Mary (Annunciation)	First	1870	90	38	Wood	Wood	French & Eng.	Rev. A. Gerardin	Yes.
49	1854	"	"	St. Mary (Assumption)	First	1863?	128	66	Brick	Brick	German	Rev. J. B. Neustich, S.J	Yes.
50	1893	"	"	St. Michael	First [1]	1893	130	32	Wood	Wood	German	Rev. J. M. Koudelka	Yes.
51	1893	"	"	Our Lady of Lourdes	First	1893	100	40	Wood	Wood	Bohemian	Rev. S. Furlek	Yes.
52	1854	"	"	St. Patrick	Second	1877	132	80	Stone	Wood	English	Rev. P. O'Brien	Yes.
53	1853	"	"	St. Peter	First	1859	142	66	Brick	Brick	German	Rev. F. Westerholt	Yes.
54	1874	"	"	St. Procop	First	1874	92	40	Wood	Wood	Bohemian	Rev. A. Vlcek	Yes.
55	1873	"	"	St. Stanislas	Second	1887	200	86	Brick	Wood	Polish	Rev. A. F. Kolaszewski	Yes.
56	1869	"	"	St. Stephen	Second	1876	165	75	Stone	Brick	German	Rev. Casimir Reichlin	Yes.
57	1867	"	"	St. Wenceslas	First	1867	90	40	Brick	Wood	Bohemian	Rev. A. Hynek	Yes.
58	1853	Clyde	Sandusky	St. Mary	First [1]	1862	50	35	Wood	Wood	English	Rev. T. F. Moran	No.
59	1877	Collinwood	Cuyahoga	St. Joseph	First [4]	1879	70	24	Wood		English	*Euclid*	Yes.
60	1857	Conneaut	Ashtabula	St. Mary	Second	1888	80	40	Brick	(Rented)	English	Rev. G. P. Jennings	No.
61	1860	Convoy	Van Wert	St. Mary	First	1870?	30	20	Wood		English	*Van Wert*	No.
62	1854	Crawfordsville	Wyandot	St. Joseph	Second	1883	80	40	Wood		German	*Carey*	Yes.
63	1861	Crestline	Crawford	St. Joseph	First [3]	1861	50	30	Wood	Brick	Eng. and Ger.	Rev. C. Treiber	Yes.
64	1858	Custar	Wood	St. Louis	First [3]	1866	50	29	Wood	Wood	Eng. and Ger.	Rev. M. Vollmayer	Yes.
65	1841	Cuyahoga Falls	Summit	St. Joseph	First	1884?	50	25	Brick		English	*Hudson*	No.
66	1841	Defiance	Defiance	St. John Evangelist	Sec'nd [4]	1855	100	36	Brick	Brick	German	Rev. J. B. Jung	Yes.
67	1873	"	"	Our Lady of Per. Help	First	1870	130	55	Brick	Wood	English	Rev. M. P. Kinkead	Yes.
68	1846	Delaware Bend	"	St. Stephen	Second	1881	67	38	Wood	Wood	Eng. and Fr.	Rev. L. Heiland	No.
69	1844	Delphos	Allen	St. John Evangelist	Third	1884	192	77	Brick	Brick	Ger. and Eng.	Rev. A. I. Hoeffel	Yes.
70	1875	Deshler	Henry	Immaculate Conception	First	1876?	25	18	Wood		Eng. and Ger.	*Custar*	No.
71	1827	Doylestown	Wayne	St. Peter	Second	1877	112	56	Brick	Brick	Eng. and Ger.	Rev. C. Seltzer	Yes.
72	1817	Dungannon	Columbi'na	St. Philip	Second	1851?	65	45	Brick	Wood	Eng. and Ger.	Rev. E. M. Hennessy	No.
73	1834	East Liverpool	"	St. Aloysius	Third	1898	118	52	Brick	Wood	English	Rev. J. P. Carroll	Yes.
74	1880	East Palestine	"	Our Lady of Lourdes	First	1881	60	32	Wood		Eng. and Ger.	*Salem*	No.
75	1865	Edgerton	Williams	St. Mary	First	1866	60	40	Wood	Wood	Eng. and Ger.	Rev. T. S. Major	Yes.
76	1870	Elmore	Ottawa	St. Patrick	Second	1888	40	22	Wood		English	*Genoa*	No.
77	1842	Elyria	Lorain	St. Mary	Second	1886	124	50	Brick	Frame	Eng. and Ger.	Rev. J. T. Schaffeld	Yes.
78	1860	Euclid	Cuyahoga	St. Paul	First [4]	1861	90	34	Wood	Wood	Eng. and Ger.	Rev. A. T. Martin	Yes.
79	1841	Findlay	Hancock	St. Michael	Sec'nd [4]	1858	135	45	Brick	Brick	Eng. and Ger.	Rev. H. Doerner	Yes.

[1] Another church now building. [2] Originally St. Mary's on "Flats." [3] Bought. [4] Enlarged since first built. [5] Succursal to Cathedral.

TABLE III.—CONTINUED.

Number.	Congregation Organized in:	Place.	County.	Church Dedicated to:	Present Church is the:	Present Church Built and First Used:	Size. Exterior Length, Ft.	Size. Exterior Width, Ft.	Church Built of:	Pastoral Residence Built of:	Language of Congregation.	Resident Pastor: Mission Attended From: (In Italic.)	Parochial School?
80	1861	Florence	Williams	St. Joseph	Second	1884	70	40	Brick		Ger. and Eng.	*Edgerton*	No.
81	1834	Fort Jennings	Putnam	St. Joseph	Third	1884	130	55	Brick	Wood	German	Rev. C. Bruschler	Yes[4].
82	1847	Fostoria	Seneca	St. Wendelin	Second	1882	95	45	Brick	Wood	Eng. and Ger.	Rev. J. P. Gloden	Yes.
83	1841	Fremont	Sandusky	St. Ann	First[1]	1844	70	36	Wood	Wood	English	Rev. A. E. Manning	Yes.
84	1857	"	"	St. Joseph	First[1]	1858	95	48	Brick	Brick	German	Rev. S. Bauer	Yes.
85	1842	French Creek	Lorain	Immaculate Conception	Sec'nd[2]	1847	80	35	Wood	Wood	German	Rev. S. Falk	Yes.
86	1850	French Settle't	Wayne	St. Ann	First	1864	40	28	Wood		Eng. and Ger.	*Doylestown*	No.
87	1854	Galion	Crawford	St. Joseph	Third	1881	106	47	Brick	Brick	German	Rev. H. Kaempker	Yes.
88	1869	Galion	Crawford	St. Patrick	First	1871	70	40	Brick		English	*Galion, St. Joseph's*	Yes.
89	1856	Genoa	Ottawa	Our Lady of Lourdes	First	1874	50	30	Wood	Wood	Eng. and Ger.	Rev. J. P. O'Connor	No.
90	1834	Glandorf	Putnam	St. John Baptist	Fourth	1878	175	90	Brick	Brick	German	Rev. F. Nigsch, C.PP.S.	Yes.
91	1865	Grafton	Lorain	Immaculate Conception	Second	1865	80	45	Stone	Wood	Eng. & Polish	Rev. J. Daudet	No.
92	1854	Green Spring	Sandusky	St. Joseph	First	1873	45	30	Wood		English	*Clyde*	No.
93	1887	Hamler	Henry	St. Joseph	First	1887	60	34	Wood		Ger. and Eng.	*Holgate*	No.
94	1845	Harrisburg	Stark	Sacred Heart of Jesus	Second	1876	70	36	Brick	Wood	French	Rev. J. P. Kunnert	No.
95	1888	Haselton	Mahoning	Sacred Heart of Jesus	First	1889	72	32	Wood	Wood	English	Rev. G. Leeming	No.
96	1846	Hicksville	Defiance	St. Michael	First	1890	37	20	Wood		Eng. and Ger.	*Delaware Bend*	No.
97	1886	Holgate	Henry	St. Mary	First	1886	67	33	Wood	Wood	Eng. and Ger.	Rev. W. Panuska	No.
98	1879	Honey Creek	Crawford	Mater Dolorosa	First	1880	70	36	Wood		German	*New Washington*	Yes.
99	1864	Hubbard	Trumbull	St. Patrick	First[2]	1868	82	34	Wood	Wood	English	Rev. N. J. Drohan	Yes.
100	1854	Hudson	Summit	St. Mary	First	1859	50	25	Wood	Wood	English	Rev. F. B. Doherty	No.
101	1890	Huron	Erie	St. Peter	First	1890	58	38	Wood		Ger. and Eng.	*Vermillion*	No.
102	1851	Independence	Cuyahoga	St. Michael	Second	1873	80	40	Brick	Wood	German	Rev. N. Hofstetter	Yes.
103	1858	Jefferson	Ashtabula	St. Joseph, Cal	Sec'nd[3]	1876	62	25	Wood	Frame	English	*Conneaut*	No.
104	1846	Junction	Paulding	St. Mary	First[2]	1866?	65	26	Wood		English	*Antwerp*	No.

105	1861	Kalida	Putnam	St. Michael	Second	1878	65	40	Brick		Ger. and Eng.	*Gland'f, Rev. R. Schuele*	No.
106	1889	Kansas	Seneca	St. James, Apostle	First	1889	50	30	Wood		Ger. and Eng.	*Millersville*	No.
107	1861	Kelley's Island	Erie	St. Michael	First	1861	70	28	Stone	Frame	Eng. and Ger.	Rev. Chas. Reichlin	Yes.
108	1862	Kent	Portage	St. Patrick	First	1868	50	44	Brick	(Rented)	English	Rev. A. Graham	Yes.
109	1865	Kirby	Wyandot	St. Mary	First [1]	1864	50	35	Wood	Wood	Ger. and Eng.	Rev. F. Hultgen	Yes.
110	1856	Landeck	Allen	St. John Baptist	First [2]	1867	80	40	Wood	Brick	German	Rev. J. B. Heiland	Yes.
111	1841	LaPrairie	Sandusky	Immaculate Conception	Second	1860	40	30	Wood		Eng. and Fr.	*Oak Harbor*	No.
112	1889	Latty	Paulding	St. Francis	First	1890	82	32	Wood		English	*Antwerp*	No.
113	1855	Leetonia	Columbi'na	St. Patrick	Second	1881	100	47	Brick	Wood	English	Rev. E. J. Murphy	Yes.
114	1874	Leipsic	Putnam	St. Mary	First	1876	40	22	Wood		Ger. and Eng.	*New Cleveland*	No.
115	1834	Liberty	Seneca	St. Andrew	Third	1889	60	34	Brick		German	*N. Riegel, Rev. E. Glueck*	Yes.
116	1846	Lima	Allen	St. Rose of Lima	Second	1872	117	56	Brick	Wood	English	Rev. J. O'Leary	Yes.
117	1842	Liverpool	Medina	St. Martin of Tours	Third	1861	125	50	Brick	Wood	German	Rev. J. Thein	Yes.
118	1878	Lorain	Lorain	St. Mary	First [4]	1879	80	48	Wood	(Rented)	Eng. and Ger.	Rev. W. Mueller	Yes.
119	1871	Loudonville	Ashland	St. Peter	First	1871	70	34	Brick	Brick	Eng. and Ger.	Rev. J. Sproll	No.
120	1826	Louisville	Stark	St. Louis	Second	1871	132	60	Brick	(Rented)	Fr. and Eng.	Rev. L. Hoffer	Yes.
121	1872	Lowellville	Mahoning	Holy Rosary	First	1884	56	26	Brick		English	*New Bedford, Pa*	No.
122	1863	Madison	Lake	Immaculate Conception	First	1869	55	30	Brick		English	*South Thompson*	No.
123	1844	Mansfield	Richland	St. Peter	Third [3]	1889	125	52	Brick	Brick	Eng. and Ger.	Rev. A. Magenhann	Yes.
124	1864	Mantua	Portage	St. Joseph	First	1871	40	25	Wood		English	*Warren*	No.
125	1842	Marblehead	Ottawa	St. Joseph	Second	1889	60	30	Wood		Eng. and Ger.	*Port Clinton*	Yes.
126	1830	Marshallville	Wayne	St. Joseph	First	1848	75	30	Wood		Eng. and Ger.	*Canal Fulton*	No.
127	1853	Massillon	Stark	St. Joseph	First	1854	60	45	Brick	Frame	English	Rev. J. T. Cahill	Yes.
128	1839	"	"	St. Mary	Third	1890	185	85	Stone	Brick	German	Rev. J. Kuhn	Yes.
129	1838	Maumee	Lucas	St. Joseph	Second	1889	120	55	Brick	Frame	Eng. and Ger.	Rev. J. B. Mertes	Yes.
130	1860	Medina	Medina	St. Francis Xavier	Sec'nd [2]	1877	40	26	Wood		Eng. and Ger.	*Wellington*	No.
131	1867	Mentor	Lake	St. Mary	First	1868	40	20	Wood		English	*Painesville*	No.
132	1863	Milan	Erie	St. Anthony	First	1866	70	40	Wood	Wood	Ger. and Eng.	Rev. G. Schoenemann	Yes.
133	1887	Miller's City	Putnam	St. Nicholas	First	1888	75	35	Wood		Eng. and Ger.	*New Cleveland*	No.
134	1858	Millersville	Sandusky	St. Mary	Sec'nd [2]	1858	83	32	Stone	Frame	German	Rev. M. Dechant	Yes.
135	1853	Mineral Ridge	Trumbull	St. Mary	First	1870	54	28	Wood		English	*Niles*	No.
136	1851	Monroeville	Huron	St. Joseph	Second	1874	124	60	Brick	Brick	Ger. and Eng.	Rev. N. Schmitz	Yes.
137	1866	Mud Creek	Defiance	Immaculate Conception	Second	1875	55	30	Wood		German	*Delaware Bend*	No.
138	1841	Napoleon	Henry	St. Augustine	Second	1883	117	50	Brick	(Rented)	Eng. and Ger.	Rev. M. Pütz	Yes.

[1] Another church now building. [2] Enlarged since first built. [3] Temporary church: second church destroyed by fire, 1889. [4] Catholic District School.

TABLE III.—CONTINUED.

Number.	Congregation Organized in:	Place.	County.	Church Dedicated to:	Present Church is the:	Present Church Built and First Used:	Size. Exterior Length, Ft.	Size. Exterior Width, Ft.	Church Built of:	Pastoral Residence Built of:	Language of Congregation.	Resident Pastor: Mission Attended From: (*In Italic.*)	Parochial School?
139	1832	Navarre	Stark	St. Clement	Sec'nd[2]	1851	100	42	Brick	Frame	Ger. and Eng.	Rev. F. Metternich	Yes.
140	1843	New Bavaria	Henry	Sacred Heart of Jesus	Third	1888	125	53	Brick	Brick	German	Rev. W. A. Harks	Yes.[3]
141	1845	New Berlin	Stark	St. Paul	First	1845	54	40	Brick		Ger. & French.	*Canton, Rev. J. R. Rueckel*	No.
142	1860	New Cleveland	Putnam	Holy Family	First [2]	1861	85	45	Wood	Wood	German	Rev. J. Bertemes	Yes.
143	1887	New Lisbon	Columbi'na	St. George	First	1887	50	30	Brick		English	*Dungannon*	No.
144	1853	New London	Huron	Our Lady of Lourdes	Sec'nd[1]	1875	34	28	Wood		English	*Wellington*	No.
145	1833	New Riegel	Seneca	St. Boniface	Third	1878	140	60	Brick	(Conv. Res.)	German	Rev. B. Russ, C.PP.S.	Yes.
146	1841	N. Washington	Crawford	St. Bernard	Second	1868	100	50	Brick	Brick	Ger. and Eng.	Rev. J. G. Vogt	Yes.
147	1853	Niles	Trumbull	St. Stephen	First [1]	1864	70	38	Wood	Wood	English	Rev. F. M. Scullin	Yes.
148	1864	North Amherst	Lorain	St. Joseph	First [2]	1868	75	30	Wood	Wood	Eng. and Ger.	Rev. J. Romer	Yes.
149	1887	North Creek	Putnam	St. Joseph	First	1887	50	32	Wood		German	*Holgate*	No.
150	1889	No. Lawrence	Stark	St. Patrick	First [1]	1889	75	35	Wood		Eng. and Ger.	*Canal Fulton*	No.
151	1861	North Ridge	Defiance	St. Michael	First [2]	1862	77	28	Wood	Wood	German	(Vacant)	Yes.
152	1875	No. Ridgeville	Lorain	St. Peter	First [2]	1875	100	35	Wood		German	*Avon*	Yes.
153	1856	Norwalk	Huron	St. Mary	First [1]	1859	82	34	Brick	Brick	English	Rev. C. V. Chevraux	Yes.
154	1868	"	"	St. Paul	Sec'nd[1]	1876	90	40	Brick	Brick	German	Rev. J. A. Michenfelder	Yes.
155	1840	"	"	St. Peter	First	1847?	90	40	Wood	Brick	German	Rev. A. Dambach	Yes.
156	1845	Oak Harbor	Ottawa	St. Boniface	First [2]	1872	67	30	Wood	Wood	Ger. and Eng.	Rev. C. Grise	Yes.
157	1854	Olmsted	Cuyahoga	St. Mary	First	1857	60	30	Wood		English	*Berea, St. Mary's*	No.
158	1868	Ottawa	Putnam	Sts. Peter and Paul	First	1870	130	50	Brick		Ger. and Eng.	*Glandorf, Rev. B. Boebner*	Yes.
159	1850	Ottoville	"	Immaculate Conception	Second	1888	175	70	Brick	Wood	German	Rev. M. Mueller	Yes.[3]
160	1845	Painesville	Lake	St. Mary	Second	1856	80	40	Brick	Wood	English	Rev. E. J. Conway	Yes.
161	1872	Parma	Cuyahoga	Holy Family	First	1873	40	20	Wood		German	*Independence*	No.
162	1882	Payne	Paulding	St. John Baptist	First	1883	50	26	Wood		Eng. & French.	*Antwerp*	No.
163	1873	Peninsula	Summit	Mater Dolorosa	First	1882	50	25	Wood		English	*Hudson*	No.

164	1861	Perrysburg	Wood	St. Rose	First [1] [4]	1861	80	30	Brick	Brick	Eng. and Ger.	Rev. G. H. Rieken	Yes.
165	1820	Peru	Huron	St. Alphonse	Second	1851	85	42	Stone	Brick	German	Rev. J. Blaser	Yes.
166	1872	Plymouth	Richland	St. Joseph	First	1872	35	20	Wood		Eng. and Ger.	*Shelby*	No.
167	1843	Port Clinton	Ottawa	Immaculate Conception	First [2]	1860	68	34	Wood	Wood	Eng. and Ger.	Rev. J. Hoerstmann.	No.
168	1860	Prout's Station	Erie	St. Thomas	Second	1876	40	24	Stone		English	*Milan*	No.
169	1848	Providence	Lucas	St. Patrick	First	1845	50	30	Brick	Wood	English	(Vacant)	No.
170	1877	Put in-Bay	Ottawa	Mater Dolorosa	First	1877	40	30	Wood		Ger. and Eng.	*Kelley's Island*	No.
171	1831	Randolph	Portage	St. Joseph	Third [2]	1866	116	50	Wood	Wood	German	Rev. S. Rebholz	Yes.
172	1841	Ravenna	"	Immaculate Conception	First [2]	1862	80	34	Brick	Wood	English	Rev. J. J. Farrell	Yes.
173	1867	Reed	Seneca	Assumption B. V. M	First [2]	1867	81	35	Wood		German	*Thompson*, Rev. X. Mielinger	Yes.
174	1887	Republic	"	St. Aloysius	First [4]	1887	56	38	Wood		Eng. and Ger.	*Shelby*	No.
175	1870	Roachton	Wood	St. Mary	First	1870	50	30	Wood		German	*Perrysburg*	No.
176	1860	Rockport	Cuyahoga	St. Mary	Second	1868	68	40	Brick	Wood	German	Rev. J. F. Kuebler	Yes.
177	1848	"	"	St. Patrick	First	1854	45	30	Wood		English	*Rockport, St. Mary's*	Yes.
178	1865	Rootstown	Portage	St. Peter	First	1868	35	25	Wood		German	*Randolph*	Yes.
179	1857	Royalton	Cuyahoga	Assumption B. V. M.	First [4]	1863	36	16	Wood		English	*Clevel'd*, Rev. J. Te Pas	No.
180	1852	St. Mary's Cor.	Fulton	St. Mary	Second	1880	80	40	Brick	Wood	English	Rev. T. F. McGuire	Yes.
181	1863	S. Patrick's Set.	Seneca	St. Patrick	First	1867?	60	40	Brick	Brick	Eng. and Ger.	*N. Riegel*, Rev. E. Glueck	Yes.
182	1842	S. Stephen's Set.	"	St. Stephen	Second	1889	80	40	Brick	Wood	German	Rev. P. Rist, C. PP. S.	Yes.
183	1853	Salem	Columbi'na	St. Paul	First	1881 [2]	84	50	Wood	(Rented)	Eng. and Ger.	Rev. F. Sinner	No.
184	1866	Salineville	"	St. Patrick	First	1872	75	45	Brick	Frame	English	Rev. C. L. O'Brien	No.
185	1834	Sandusky	Erie	Holy Angels	First	1842	80	46	Stone	Stone	English	Rev. J. Tracy	Yes.
186	1853	"	"	St. Mary	Second	1880	192	74	Stone	Stone and Fr.	German	Rev. J. Heidegger	Yes.
187	1871	"	"	Sts. Peter and Paul	First	1871	145	75	Stone	Stone	English	Rev. R. A. Sidley	Yes.
188	1842	Sheffield	Lorain	St. Teresa	Second	1851	60	40	Frame	Brick	German	Rev. D. Zinsmayer	Yes. [3]
189	1865	Shelby	Richland	Sacred Heart of Mary	First	1866	50	26	Wood	Wood	Eng. and Ger.	Rev. J. F. Smith	Yes.
190	1833	Shelby Settle't.	"	Sacred Heart of Jesus	Second	1851	80	40	Brick	Brick	German	Rev. M. Becker	Yes.
191	1846	Six Mile Woods	Lucas	Immaculate Conception	Third	1880?	93	41	Brick	Wood	Ger. and Eng.	Rev. J. Rosenberg	Yes.
192	1844	S. Thompson	Geauga	St. Patrick	First [2]	1859	58	35	Wood	Wood	English	Rev. F. X. Hroch	No.
193	1858	Spencerville	Allen	St. Patrick	First	1867?	60	36	Wood		English	*Van Wert*	No.
194	1881	Sterling	Wayne	St. Mary	First [4]	1881	45	30	Wood		English	*Wellington*	No.
195	1857	Strasburg	Stark	St. Joseph	First [2]	1857	63	30	Brick		Eng. and Fr.	*Harrisburg*	Yes.
196	1870	Struthers	Mahoning	St. Nicholas	First	1870	40	25	Wood		English	*Hazelton*	No.
197	1861	Stryker	Williams	St. John Evangelist	First	1861	50	30	Wood		Eng. and Ger.	*Archbold*	No.

[1] Another church now building. [2] Enlarged since first built. [3] Catholic district school. [4] Bought.

TABLE III.—CONTINUED.

Number.	Congregation Organized in:	Place.	County.	Church Dedicated to:	Present Church is the:	Present Church Built and First Used:	Size, Exterior: Length, Ft.	Size, Exterior: Width, Ft.	Church Built of:	Pastoral Residence Built of:	Language of Congregation.	Resident Pastor: Mission Attended From: (*In Italic.*)	Parochial School?
198	1842	Summitville	Columbi'na	St. John Evangelist	First	1852	66	40	Brick	Wood	English	Rev. J. Eyler	No.
199	1855	Sylvania	Lucas	St. Joseph	First[1]	1872	60	34	Wood		Eng. and Ger.	*Toledo, Rev. H. Boehmer*	No.
200	1834	Thompson	Seneca	St. Michael	Third	1886	117	50	Brick	(Conv. Res.)	German	Rev. F. X. Griessmayer	Yes.
201	1845	Tiffin	"	St. Joseph	Second	1862	140	60	Brick	Brick	German	Rev. J. M. Puetz	Yes.
202	1831	"	"	St. Mary	Second	1856	100	46	Brick	Brick	English	Rev. M. Healy	Yes.
203	1882	Toledo	Lucas	St. Anthony of Padua	First	1883	160	35	Wood	Wood	Polish	Rev. N. Kolasinski	Yes.
204	1842	"	"	St. Francis de Sales	Second	1870	162	67	Brick	Brick	English	Rev. P. F. Quigley	Yes.
205	1873	"	"	Good Shepherd	First	1873	96	41	Wood	Brick	English	Rev. P. Barry	Yes.
206	1871	"	"	St. Hedwig	First[4]	1886	85	35	Brick	Wood	Polish	Rev. S. J. Wieczorek	Yes.
207	1867	"	"	Immaculate Conception	First	1870	110	54	Wood	Brick	English	Rev. T. P. McCarthy	Yes.
208	1854	"	"	St. Joseph	Sec'nd[1]	1878	136	45	Brick	Wood	French	Rev. L. Braire	Yes.
209	1871	"	"	St. Louis	First	1871	84	48	Brick	Wood	French	Rev. W. J. Smith	Yes.
210	1853	"	"	St. Mary	First[1]	1855	194	65	Brick	(Conv. Res.)	German	Rev. M. Zoeller, S. J.	Yes.
211	1862	"	"	St. Patrick	First	1862	125	56	Brick	Brick	English	Rev. E. Hannin	Yes.
212	1866	"	"	St. Peter	First	1875	145	64	Brick	Brick	German	Rev. P. Danenhoffer	Yes.
213	1883	"	"	Sacred Heart of Jesus	First	1883	100	50	Wood	Wood	German	Rev. A. Eilert	Yes.
214	1842	Toussaint	Ottawa	St. Joseph	First	1861	50	35	Wood	Wood	French	Rev. A. Hamelin	Yes.
215	1883	Tremblayville	Wood	St. Hyacinthe	First	1883	30	20	Wood		Eng. and Fr.	(Vacant.)	No.
216	1857	U. Sandusky	Wyandot	St. Peter	Second	1874	140	60	Brick	Brick	Eng. and Ger.	Rev. A. Huthmacher	Yes.
217	1867	Van Wert	Van Wert	St. Mary	First	1874?	50	35	Brick	Wood	English	Rev. M. J. Clear	No.
218	1842	Vermillion	Erie	St. Mary	First	1860	50	28	Wood	Wood	Eng. and Ger.	Rev. I. J. Wonderly	No.
219	1871	Vienna	Trumbull	St. Joseph	First	1873	45	20	Wood		English	*Hubbard*	No.
220	1886	Wadsworth	Medina	Sacred Heart of Jesus	First	1886	46	26	Wood		Ger. and Eng.	*Wellington*	No.
221	1853	Wakeman	Huron	St. Mary	First	1870	40	30	Wood	Wood	English	Rev. A. Sauvadet	No.
222	1850	Warren	Trumbull	Our Lady of Mt. Carmel	First[1]	1864	70	32	Wood	Wood	Eng. and Ger.	Rev. A. A. Weber	No.

223	1865	Wauseon[3]	Fulton	St. Caspar	First[4]	1872	50	32	Wood		Eng. and Ger.	*Archbold*	No.
224	1849	Wellington	Lorain	St. Patrick	First	1858	30	24	Wood	Wood	English	Rev. N. W. Horst	No.
225	1834	Wellsville	Columbi'na	Immaculate Conception	First	1867	65	57	Brick	Brick	English	Rev. J. C. Desmond	No.
226	1866	W. Brookfield	Stark	St. Barbara	First[1]	1867	60	36	Wood	Wood	German	Rev. H. D. Best	No.
227	1874	Weston	Wood	St. Joseph	First	1874	25	17	Wood		Eng. and Ger.	*Custar*	No.
228	1860	Willoughby	Lake	Immaculate Conception	First	1869	60	26	Wood		English	*Clevel'd, Rev. J. T. O'Connell*	No.
229	1841	Woodville	Sandusky	St. Mary	First	1862	50	33	Brick		Eng. and Ger.	*Genoa*	No.
230	1826	Wooster	Wayne	Immaculate Conception	First[1]	1849	130	40	Brick	Brick	Eng. and Ger.	Rev. F. Ankly	Yes.
231	1826	Youngstown	Mahoning	St. Columba	Second	1861	120	54	Brick	Brick	English	Rev. E. Mears	Yes.
232	1882	"	"	Immaculate Conception	First[2]	1882	100	40	Brick	(Rented)	English	Rev. W. J. Manning	Yes.
233	1869	"	"	St. Joseph	Second	1882	112	57	Brick	Wood	German	Rev. J. Klute	Yes.

[1] Enlarged since first built. [2] Bought. [3] Another church now building. [4] Rebuilt.

TABLE IV.

STATIONS.

April, 1890.

No.	Place.	County.	Attended from.
1	Andover	Ashtabula	Jefferson.
2	Atwater	Portage	Alliance.
3	Aurora	Portage	Warren.
4	Austintown	Mahoning	Niles.
5	Bascom	Seneca	St. Patrick's Settlement.
6	Bass Islands	Ottawa	Kelley's Island.
7	Bedford	Cuyahoga	Hudson.
8	Berlin Heights	Erie	Vermillion.
9	Braceville	Trumbull	Warren.
10	Brecksville	Cuyahoga	Hudson.
11	Brownhelm	Lorain	Vermillion.
12	Burg Hill	Trumbull	Warren.
13	Camden	Lorain	Wakeman.
14	Canfield	Mahoning	Salem.
15	Castalia	Erie	Sandusky.
16	Chagrin Falls	Cuyahoga	Warren.
17	Chardon	Geauga	Painesville.
18	Clarkesville	Defiance	Edgerton.
19	Columbus Grove	Putnam	Lima.
20	Continental	Paulding	Antwerp.
21	Cortland	Trumbull	Warren.
22	Cygnet	Wood	Providence.
23	Dupoint	Putnam	New Bavaria.
24	Emerald	Paulding	Antwerp.
25	Fairfield	Huron	Peru.
26	Fairview	Wayne	Canal Fulton.
27	Farmington	Trumbull	Warren.
28	Flat Rock	Paulding	Antwerp.
29	Fredericksburg	Wayne	Wooster.
30	Garrettsville	Portage	Warren.
31	Geneva	Ashtabula	South Thompson.
32	Girard	Trumbull	Briar Hill.
33	Greenwich	Huron	Wellington.
34	Hessville	Sandusky	Genoa.
35	Homeworth	Columbiana	Alliance.
36	Kingsville	Lake	Jefferson.
37	Kinsman	Trumbull	Warren.
38	Johnsonville	Trumbull	Warren.
39	Lafayette	Allen	Lima.
40	Lakeville	Ashland	Loudonville.
41	Latchie	Wood	Genoa.
42	Leavittsburg	Trumbull	Warren.
43	Limaville	Stark	Alliance.
44	Lindsey	Sandusky	Genoa.
[illegible]	[illegible]andale	Cuyahoga	Rockport.
[illegible]	[illegible]ning	Mahoning	Warren.
[illegible]	[illegible]ary	Wood	Elmore.
[illegible]	[illegible]	Wyandot	Bucyrus.
[illegible]	[illegible]on Falls	Trumbull	Warren.

TABLE IV.

STATIONS.—CONCLUDED.

No.	Place.	County.	Attended From.
50	New Portage	Summit	Wellington.
51	Oberlin	Lorain	Elyria.
52	Orangeville	Trumbull	Warren.
53	Orrville	Wayne	Canal Fulton.
54	Parkham	Summit	Akron.
55	Petersburg	Mahoning	Salem.
56	Portage	Wood	Custar.
57	Robbin's Station	Columbiana	Dungannon.
58	Robertsville	Columbiana	(Vacant.)
59	Rochester	Lorain	Wellington.
60	Rocky Ridge	Ottawa	Toussaint.
61	Shiloh	Richland	Shelby.
62	Solon	Cuyahoga	Warren.
63	Springfield	Mahoning	Briar Hill.
64	Springhills	Williams	Edgerton.
65	Swanton	Fulton	St. Mary's Corners.
66	Talmadge	Summit	Akron.
67	Teegarden	Columbiana	Leetonia.
68	Texas	Henry	Providence.
69	Thomaston	Summit	Akron.
70	Westville	Columbiana	Alliance.
71	Wickliffe	Lake	Euclid.
72	Willshire	Van Wert	Landeck.
73	Windham	Portage	Warren.

TABLE V.

COMMUNITIES AND INSTITUTIONS.

A. MALE RELIGIOUS COMMUNITIES.

April, 1890.

No.	Place.	Communities.	Established.	Superiors.
1	Cleveland	Franciscans	1867	Rev. T. Arentz.
2	"	Jesuits	1880	Rev. H. Knappmeyer.
3	Glandorf	Sanguinists	1848	Rev. F. Nigsch.
4	New Riegel	Sanguinists	1844	Rev. B. Russ.
5	Thompson	Sanguinists	1845	Rev. F. X. Griessmayer.
6	Toledo	Jesuits	1869	Rev. A. Leiter.

TABLE V.—CONTINUED.

B. FEMALE RELIGIOUS COMMUNITIES.

April, 1890.

No.	PLACE.	COMMUNITIES.	ESTABLISHED.	SUPERIORESS.
1	Cleveland	Ursuline Sisters	1850	Mother St. Mary.
2	"	Ladies of Sacred Heart of Mary	1851	Madame Le Masson.
3	"	Sisters of Charity	1851	Mother M. Joseph.
4	"	Sisters of Good Shepherd	1869	Mother M. Baptist.
5	"	Little Sisters of Poor	1870	Mother Noël de St. Louis.
6	"	Sisters of St. Joseph	1872	Mother M. George.
7		Sisters of Notre Dame	1874	Sister M. Modesta (L. S.)*
8	"	Poor Clares	1877	Mother M. Veronica.
9	"	Franciscan Sisters	1884	Sister Leonarda.
10	Glandorf	Sanguinist Sisters	1848	Sister Felicite.
11	N. Bedford ..	Sisters of Humility B. V. M	1864	Mother M. Patrick.
12	New Riegel	Sanguinist Sisters	1844	Sister Cypriana.
13	Thompson	Sanguinist Sisters	1845	Sister M. Dula.
14	Tiffin	Ursuline Sisters	1863	Mother M. Ignatius.
15	"	Franciscan Sisters....	1867	Mother M. Frances.
16	Toledo..	Ursuline Sisters	1854	Mother M. Aloysius.
17	"	Sisters of Charity (Grey Nuns)	1855	Sister Fernand.
18	"	Little Sisters of Poor	1885	Mother M. Louisa.
19	Youngstown	Ursuline Sisters	1874	Mother M. Lawrence.

C. EDUCATIONAL INSTITUTIONS.

April, 1890.

No.	PLACE.	NAME.	ESTABLISHED.	SUPERIORS.
1	Cleveland ...	St. Mary's Theological Seminary...	1848	Rev. N. A. Moes, D. D.
2	" ...	St. Ignatius' College..................	1886	Rev. H. Knappmeyer, S. J.
3	" ...	Ursuline Academy.....................	1850	Mother St. Mary.
4	" ...	Notre Dame Academy................	1874	Sister M. Modesta (L. S.)
5	Nottingham .	Ursuline Academy......................	1877	Mother M. Louis (L. S.)
6	" ..	St. Joseph's Seminary for Boys......	1886	Mother M. Ascension (L. S.)
7	Tiffin	Ursuline Academy.....................	1863	Mother M. Ignatius.
8	"	St. Ignatius' Seminary for Boys....	1888	Mother M. Ignatius.
9	Toledo.......	Ursuline Academy.....................	1854	Mother M. Aloysius.

*Local Superioress.

Charity Hospital and Foundling Asylum, Cleveland, O.

D. CHARITABLE INSTITUTIONS.

April, 1890.

No.	Place.	Name.	Established.	In Charge of	Superior.
1	Cleveland .	Charity Hospital	1865	Sisters of Charity	Sister M. Thomas (L. S.*)
2	"	St. Alexis' Hospital ...	1884	FranciscanSist'rs	Sister Leonarda.
3	"	Lying-in Hospital and Foundling Asylum ..	1873	Sisters of Charity	Sister Mary (L. S.)
4	"	Home for the Aged Poor	1870	Little Sisters of the Poor	Mother M. Noël de St. Louis.
5	"	House of Good Shepherd	1869	Sisters of Good Shepherd	Mother M. Baptist.
6	"	St. Mary's Orphan Asylum for Girls	1851	Ladies of Sacred Heart of Mary.	Madame Le Masson.
7	"	St. Vincent's Orphan Asylum for Boys....	1851	Sisters of Charity	Mother M. Joseph.
	"	St. Joseph's Orphan Asylum for Girls....	1862	Ladies of Sacred Heart of Mary.	Miss Hogan, (L. S.)
	"	Protectory for Girls...	1884	Sisters of Notre Dame	Sister M. Modesta.
10	Louisville .	St. Louis Orphan Asylum for Boys........	1883	Sisters of Charity	Sister M. Patrick (L. S.)
11	N.Bedford.	St. Mary's Orphanage .	1864	Sisters of Humility, B. V. M. ..	Mother M. Patrick.
12	"	St. Mary's Hospital ...	1864	Sisters of Humility, B. V. M. ..	" "
13	Tiffin	St. Francis Orphan Asy. & Home for the Aged	1867	FranciscanSist'rs	Rev. J. L. Bihn.
	Toledo.....	St. Vincent's Orphan Asylum..............	1855	Sisters of Charity	Sister Fernand (L. S.)
	"	St. Vincent's Hospital	1876	" "	" "
16	"	Home for the Aged Poor	1885	Little Sisters of the Poor	Mother M. Louisa.

*Local Superior.

SUMMARY.

Churches with resident pastors.	148	Secular Priests.	171
Mission churches	85	Regulars	38
Total number of churches............	233	Total number of priests	209
Stations (without churches)...............	73	Male Religious Communities..............	6
Seminary	1	Female Religious Communities...........	19
Educational Institutes for boys..........	3	Charitable Institutions	16
Educational Institutes for girls	5	Parochial Schools	127

CATHOLIC PROGRESS

— IN —

Northern Ohio and the Diocese of Cleveland.

The subjoined tabulated statement shows the years when missions, congregations with resident pastors, institutions, as also stations since developed into congregations, were established. It gives a summarized exhibit of the wonderful growth and spread of the Church in Northern Ohio and in the diocese of Cleveland. Steadily, year by year, churches, and religious, charitable and educational institutions have been increasing in number and strength, till the diocese of Cleveland, covering the whole of Northern Ohio, now ranks with the largest and best established dioceses in the United States. The mustard seed of religion, planted by the Dominican Father, Rev. E. Fenwick, near Dungannon in 1817, has grown to a large and vigorous tree under whose shadow rest two hundred and thirty churches and many institutions, spreading their benign influence in behalf of religion, education and charity. The tabulated statement was compiled from various sources and is as accurate as pains-taking care could make it. Places are given alphabetically for each year, and as known at present. Where names of places or churches have been changed in course of time, the names under which they were formerly known are given in parenthesis. Date *after* name of place signifies the year when the *first* church was built, and hence prior to date given such place was attended as a station, with divine service in private houses public halls, or other temporary place of worship. Where no date follows place, a church was built simultaneously with organization of mission or congregation.

1817. Dungannon (St. Paul's Settlement, Hanover,) 1820.

1818.

1819.

1820. Marshallville (Bristol), 1849.

1821.

1822. Consecration of the Rt. Rev. Edward Fenwick as first Bishop of Cincinnati.

1823. Canton, St. John's.

1824.

1825. Canal Fulton (Lawrence, Fulton), 1831.

1826. Louisville (Beechland), 1834; Wooster, 1849; Youngstown, St. Columba's, 1853. Rev. T. H. Martin, O. P., pays the first visit to Cleveland Catholics.

1827. Doylestown (Chippewa), 1837.

1828.

1829. Peru (German Settlement near Norwalk), 1834.

1830. McCutchenville, 1837 [church destroyed by fire in 1871 and not rebuilt.]

1831. Randolph; Tiffin, St. Mary's, 1832.

1832. Navarre (Bethlehem), 1833. Bishop Fenwick died of cholera at Wooster.

1833. Avon, 1844; New Riegel (Wolf's Creek); Shelby Settlement, 1836. Rt. Rev. J. B. Purcell consecrated second Bishop of Cincinnati.

1834. East Liverpool, 1841; Fort Jennings, 1840; Glandorf; Liberty, 1841; Sandusky, Holy Angels', 1842; Thompson, 1839; Wellsville, 1867.

1835. Akron (Cascade), St. Vincent de Paul's, 1844; Bucyrus, 1862; Cleveland, St. Mary's on Flats, [commenced 1838, dedicated 1840, closed 1879, and taken down September, 1888]; La Porte [church removed to Grafton, 1865].

1836.

1837. Marshallville (Bristol), 1865. Toledo (Manhattan, Vistula), St. Francis de Sales', 1842; Rev. E. Thienpont the first priest to visit the Catholics of Toledo, 1837.

1838. Providence, 1845; Maumee (Maumee City, South Toledo), 1841.

1839. Massillon, St. Mary's, 1844.

1840. Abbeyville, 1842 [closed 1859]; Grafton (Rawsonville) 1865; Liverpool, 1842; Norwalk, St. Peter's.

1841. Cuyahoga Falls, 1886; Defiance, St. John's, 1844; Fremont (Lower Sandusky), St. Ann's, 1844; La Prairie; Napoleon, 1856; New Washington, 1846; Ravenna, 1862; Woodville, 1862.

1842. Elyria, 1854; French Creek, 1844; Marblehead, 1868; St. Stephen's Settlement (Bloom); Sheffield; Summitville, 1852; Toussaint, 1861; Vermillion, 1862.

1843. New Bavaria (Poplar Ridge), 1845; Port Clinton, 1860.

1844. Delphos; Findlay, 1856; Mansfield, 1848; New Riegel, Sanguinist Convent; South Thompson, 1859.

1845. Canton, St. Peter's; Harrisburg; New Berlin; Oak Harbor, 1872; Painesville, 1850; Thompson, Sanguinist Convent; Tiffin, St. Joseph's.

1846. Archbold, 1850; Bismarck (Sherman); Delaware Bend, 1848; Hicksville, 1880; Junction, 1860; Lima, 1852; Six Mile Woods, 1848; Toledo, Notre Dame Sisters of Cincinnati open a Convent and select school [closed in 1848].

1847. DIOCESE OF CLEVELAND ERECTED.

Right Rev. Amadeus Rappe consecrated first Bishop of Cleveland. Cleveland, St. Mary's Church on the Flats made the Cathedral church; Fostoria (Rome), 1851. Priests in Diocese, 21; churches, 42; stations, 28; religious communities, 3.

1848. Cleveland—present Cathedral commenced; St. Mary's Theological Seminary opened near Bond street, [transferred in 1850 to frame building "Spring cottage," on Lake street, site of present seminary grounds; enlarged in 1853 by addition of brick building, and in 1856 by a frame building; north wing and middle portion of present building erected in 1859; south wing in 1881]. Glandorf, Sanguinist Convent; Rockport, St. Patrick's, 1853.

1849. Wellington, 1858.

1850. Cleveland, Ursuline Convent and Academy; Ottoville (Section Ten), 1861; Warren, 1864.

1851. Cleveland—St. Mary's Orphan Asylum for Girls; Convent of Ladies of Sacred Heart of Mary; St. Vincent's Asylum for Boys; Convent of Sisters of Charity. Independence.

1852. Alliance, 1860; Cleveland, Cathedral consecrated in November; St. Mary's Corners, 1868.

1853. Ashland, 1863; Cleveland, St. Peter's, 1857; Clyde, 1862; Massillon, St. Joseph's, 1854; Mineral Ridge, 1872; New London, 1872; Niles, 1864; Salem, 1881; Sandusky, St. Mary's; Wakeman, 1872.

1854. Cleveland—West Side (Ohio City), St. Mary's of the Assumption, 1865; St. Patrick's; St. John's College. Crawfordsville, (St. Joseph's, West Salem), 1859; Galion, St. Joseph's, 1855; Green Spring, 1872; Hudson, 1860; Olmsted, 1858; Toledo—St. Joseph's; St. Mary's, 1856; Ursuline Convent and Academy.

1855. Cleveland, St. Joseph's; Sylvania, 1872; Toledo, St. Vincent's Orphan Asylum.

1856. Berea, St. Mary's; Berwick (Frenchtown); Bluffton, 1865; Cleveland, Immaculate Conception; Genoa, 1874; Leetonia, (St. Barbara's 1868–81, St. Patrick's since 1881); Norwalk, St. Mary's, 1858.

1857. Cleveland, St. Bridget's; Conneaut, 1864; Fremont, St. Joseph's, 1858; Royalton, 1864; Strasburg, Upper Sandusky.

1858. Ashtabula, 1860; Big Springs, 1859; Custar, 1866; Jefferson, 1869; Millersville (Greensburg); Spencerville, 1876.

1859. Bellevue; French Settlement, 1864; Cleveland, St. John's College, closed; North Lawrence, 1889.

1860. Cleveland—St. Augustine's; St. Mary's College and Preparatory Seminary opened on Lake street. Convoy, 1864; Euclid, 1861; Medina, 1864; New Cleveland, 1861; Prout's Station; Rockport, St. Mary's; Willoughby, 1869.

1861. Akron, St. Bernard's, 1862; Crestline; Kalida; Kelley's Island; Monroeville, 1862; North Ridge; Perrysburg; Stryker.

1862. Cleveland—(Newburgh), Holy Rosary [since 1881, Holy Name]; St. Joseph's Orphan Asylum for Girls. Kent, 1868; Toledo, St. Patrick's, 1863.

1863. Madison, 1869; Milan, 1865; St. Patrick's Settlement, 1864; Tiffin, Ursuline Convent and Academy.

1864. Antwerp, 1870; Florence; Hubbard, 1867; Mantua, 1871; New Bedford, Convent of Sisters of Humility of Mary; North Amherst, 1869.

1865. Bryan, 1875; Cleveland—St. Malachy's, 1869; Charity Hospital. Edgerton (Clarksville), 1868; Kirby; Shelby, 1866; Wauseon, 1872.

1866. Huron, 1889; Mud Creek; Salineville, 1873; Toledo, St. Peter's, 1873; West Brookfield, 1867.

1867. Cleveland—St. Wenceslas'; Franciscan Monastery. Landeck; Louisville, St. Louis' College [closed 1873]; Mentor, 1868; Reed; Rootstown; Tiffin, St. Francis' Hospital and Orphan Asylum; Toledo, Immaculate Conception, 1868; Van Wert, 1870.

1868. Carey, 1872; Norwalk, St. Paul's; Ottawa, 1872.

1869. Bowling Green, 1881; Briar Hill, 1870. Cleveland—St. Stephen's; Good Shepherd Convent. Galion, St. Patrick's; Youngstown, St. Joseph's.

1870. Bishop Rappe resigned the Episcopal See of Cleveland. Cleveland—Little Sisters of the Poor [Home for the Aged Poor]; St. Mary's of the Annunciation. Elmore, 1873; Roachton, 1872; Struthers, 1872; Vienna, 1874.

1871. Cleveland—St. Columbkill's [discontinued as a congregation in 1872]; Holy Family [St. Edward's since 1886]. Loudonville; Sandusky, Sts. Peter and Paul's; Toledo—St. Hedwig's; St. Louis'. Vienna, 1872.

1872. Cleveland, Convent of Sisters of St. Joseph; Lowellville, 1884; Parma, 1873; Plymouth. Rt. Rev. R. Gilmour consecrated as second Bishop of Cleveland

1873. Berea, St. Adalbert's; Brighton, 1875. Cleveland—St. Stanislas', 1881; House of Maternity and Foundling Asylum. Defiance, Our Lady of Perpetual Help; Peninsula, 1882; Toledo, Good Shepherd's.

1874. Cleveland—St. Procop's; Notre Dame Convent and Academy. Leipsic, 1876; Louisville, Academy for Girls and for Deaf Mutes [discontinued in 1883; building formerly used for a college, then for an academy, is used as an Asylum for Orphan Boys since 1884]; Weston; Youngstown, Ursuline Convent.

1875. Bettsville, 1876; Cecil, 1879; Deshler; North Ridgeville.

1876. Chicago Junction, 1879; Toledo, St. Vincent's Hospital.

1877. Cleveland, Poor Clares' Convent; Collinwood, 1878; Nottingham, Ursuline Convent and Academy; Put-in-Bay. Bishop Rappe died at St. Albans, Vt.

1878. Lorain (Black River), 1879.

1879. Cleveland, Franciscan College [closed 1881]; Honey Creek.

1880. Cleveland—St. Colman's; Holy Trinity. East Palestine.

1881. Sterling (Russell).

1882. Attica; Payne, 1883; Toledo, St. Anthony's; Youngstown, Immaculate Conception.

1883. Big Ditch, 1884. Cleveland—St. Adalbert's; St. Michael's; Our Lady of Lourdes'. Toledo, Sacred Heart; Tremblayville.

1884. Cleveland—St. Alexis' Hospital; St. Mary's Protectory for Girls. Louisville, St. Louis' Asylum for Orphan Boys.

1885. Toledo, Little Sisters of the Poor.

1886. Cleveland, Jesuit College; Holgate; Nottingham, St. Joseph's "Seminary" for Small Boys; Wadsworth.

1887. Cleveland—St. Anthony's; St. Francis'. Hamler; Miller's City; New Lisbon; North Creek; Republic.

1888. Akron, St. Mary's; Ashtabula Harbor, 1889; Cleveland, St. Ladislas'; Haselton; Tiffin, St. Ignatius' "Seminary" for Small Boys. Diocesan School Board and School Inspectors appointed.

1889. Cleveland, Sacred Heart; Kansas; Latty. Rectors and Diocesan Courts, etc., appointed.

ST. MARY'S CHURCH, ON "FLATS," CLEVELAND, O.

[The first Catholic Church erected in Cleveland.]

HISTORICAL SKETCH OF EARLY CATHOLICITY

—AND THE—

FIRST CATHOLIC CHURCH IN CLEVELAND.

In 1793, Augustus Spafford, under the direction of Moses Cleaveland, the General Superintendent of the Connecticut Land Company, began the survey of a portion of the present city of Cleveland. The Hon. Harvey Rice, in his interesting work, *Pioneers of the Western Reserve*, referring to this survey says: "Moses Cleaveland, with the eye of a prophet, foresaw that a great commercial city was here destined to spring into existence at no distant day, and accordingly directed its survey to be made into town lots of so much of the land as was included within the angle formed by the lake and easterly side of the river, and as far southeasterly as seemed requisite for the location of the predicted city. When the survey was completed—October 1, 1796—he felt the importance of selecting a suitable name for the new city, but was perplexed in coming to a satisfactory decision, and hence requested his associates to favor him with their suggestions. They at once baptized the infant city and gave it the name of Cleaveland in honor of their superior in authority. Moses was taken by surprise, blushed and gracefully acknowledged the compliment. The letter 'a,' in the first syllable of his name, was subsequently dropped out by a resident editor of the town, because he could not include it in the headline of his newspaper for want of sufficient space. The public adopted the editor's orthography, which has ever since been retained."*

July, 1800, Cleveland became a part of Trumbull county, which at that time comprised the entire Western Reserve lands, owned and controlled by the above-mentioned company, through whose influence, also, this part of Ohio was

*Pp. 47 and 48.

settled by people from Connecticut and other New England states. They brought with them an intense hatred against Catholics and their Church, which to this day has been perpetuated in their descendants, though gradually in less marked degree.

July 4th, 1825, ground was broken for the Ohio canal, beginning in Cleveland. The ceremony was carried out with much *eclat*, as it was the beginning of a new era for the town which at that time had a population of about five hundred. This number was doubled within a year, because of the canal now in course of construction. With this increase of population in 1826 came the first Catholics—Irish laborers—seeking and finding employment on the canal, which was rapidly pushed to completion. It was during this year also that the first priest came to Cleveland, the Dominican Father, Rev. Thomas Martin, then residing in Perry county, whence he attended a number of missions in Columbiana and Stark counties. He had heard that quite a colony of Catholics were employed on the canal building between Cleveland and Akron, and hence made it his business to visit them and attend to their spiritual wants. The Very Rev. Stephen T. Badin, the proto-priest of the United States, did the same a few times. There is no record of any other priest having come to Cleveland till the advent of

THE REV. JOHN DILLON,

who was sent here by Bishop Purcell in the early part of 1835, as the first resident pastor. He, as his predecessors, said Mass in private houses, as there was no other place to be had then. However, shortly after his arrival Judge Underhill granted him the use of his law office (then located on Spring street, near the present Atwater Block,) in which to say Mass on Sundays. The next place in which Father Dillon assembled his little flock was in a large room, 30x40 feet, known as Shakspeare Hall. It was in the upper story of the Merwin building, on Main street, opposite Union Lane. This hall he fitted up as a temporary place of worship, as best he could with the limited means at his disposal, and in it said Mass for a short time.

Among the regular attendants at the Catholic service held in this hall were several Protestant gentlemen. They were attracted by the eloquence of Father Dillon, for whom they conceived a great regard and admiration because of his talents and amiability. One of these gentlemen was the Hon. Harvey Rice, who is now (1890) over eighty years of age, and one of Cleveland's most distinguished citizens. He settled in Cleveland in 1824, two years before a Catholic priest or layman had come. He is, therefore, a living witness to the wonderful growth of Catholicity in Cleveland, and to him the writer is greatly indebted for much of the information here given. Of Father Dillon he says, that he was a cultivated and scholarly gentleman, polished in manner and an eloquent preacher; that his zeal was limited only by his physical ability, and that he was truly a father to his spiritual children.

When Father Dillon came to Cleveland, he found the Catholics very few in numbers and very poor as to worldly possessions. Added to this he unfortunately found much intemperance, and very little regard for the sacredness of the Sunday. Carousals and free fights were of common occurence, but he set manfully to work to correct these evils and to elevate the moral and social condition of his poor and despised charge.

The next place in which Father Dillon held public service in Cleveland, was in a one-story frame cottage, on the west side of Erie street near Prospect, where it is still standing. In it there were several rooms, the largest serving as a "church," the others as a pastoral residence. A few months later Father Dillon secured Farmers' Hall, in Mechanics Block, at the corner of Prospect and Ontario streets, (now known as the Prospect House,) and transformed it into a temporary church. He continued, however, to reside in the house above mentioned, till his death.

Father Dillon had tired of halls as makeshifts for a church. Besides, the growing number of Catholics made such inconveniently small for their accommodation. But his people were too poor to build a church. He therefore sought help elsewhere and obtained it from kind and generous Protestants. He also went, among other places, to New York city, where his eloquent appeals for assistance resulted in his obtaining about one thousand dollars for the proposed church. But shortly after his return to Cleveland he fell a victim to bilious fever, and died October 16, 1836, at the age of twenty-nine years—a little more than two years after his ordination to the priesthood. His death was a severe blow to his little flock, and was lamented by his own people, as also by those not of the Faith. The Cleveland *Advertiser*, a secular paper, in its issue of October 20, 1836, said of him: "The death of Father Dillon will be deeply felt by his bereaved and afflicted church. He was one of the first of our clergy in point of talent and piety, and though he labored in obscurity, yet he labored faithfully and well." His remains were interred in the Erie street cemetery, but a short distance from the place in which he had resided and died. For eleven months the Catholics of Cleveland were without a resident pastor. Rev. H. D. Juncker came occasionally from Canton, where he was stationed between 1836 and 1837. September, 1837,

THE REV. PATRICK O'DWYER,

a recent arrival from Quebec, was sent as good Father Dillon's successor. His pastoral residence was a small frame cottage, located on the present site of the *Catholic Universe* office, corner of Superior and Muirson streets. During his pastorate he said Mass in the third story of Mechanics Block, already mentioned.

October 24, 1837, Messrs. James S. Clark, Richard Hilliard and Edmund Clark conveyed by land contract to the Rt. Rev. John Baptist Purcell, Bishop of Cincinnati, "In trust for the Roman Catholic Society of Our Lady of the Lake, of said Cleveland, the following piece or parcel of land, to-wit: Lots numbered 218 and 219 [corner Columbus and Girard streets], in the plat of Cleveland centre," subject to the following conditions: "Provided always and these presents are on the express condition, that the said society shall within and during the space of four months from the date of this agreement, erect, build, finish and complete outwardly a respectable and suitable frame house or church building for public worship, and commence regularly holding their meetings therein; to have and to hold the above premises with the appurtenances thereof so long as the same shall be occupied as aforesaid, and so much longer as said church shall own and occupy regularly a respectable lot and house for public worship upon the plat of Cleveland centre." A deed was executed by the above named gentlemen on November 21, 1842, covering the land contract.

Father O'Dwyer at once set to work to increase the building fund already secured by the lamented Father Dillon, and to begin the much needed and long looked for church. In a few months the building was partially erected but could not be completed for lack of means. Meanwhile also, owing to dissensions in the congregation, Father O'Dwyer left Cleveland about June, 1839. The church stood unfinished for months till Bishop Purcell, coming to Cleveland during September of same year, and remaining for three weeks, had it so far pushed towards completion that Mass was said in it for the first time in October, 1839. During his stay in Cleveand at this time, the Bishop also prepared a class of children for first communion, which was administered to them in the new church by Father Henni, who had come from Cincinnati to assist the Bishop.

Although the Catholics of Cleveland now had a church they were without a resident pastor from the time Father O'Dwyer left. On Sundays they assembled in their church, by this time furnished with temporary altar and pews, and there recited the Rosary, one or other of the laity reading from the *Goffine* the epistle and gospel of the day with their explanation.

Meanwhile, through the exertions of the laity, the church was plastered and properly provided with the ordinary requisites, and all were anxiously awaiting its dedication and the appointment of a shepherd for the shepherdless flock.

The former expectation was realized on Sunday, June 7th, 1840, when the solemn and impressive dedicatory ceremonies were performed by the Rt. Rev. Doctor de Forbin-Janson, Bishop of Toule-Nancy, France, then on a visit to the United States. The Rt. Rev. Bishop Purcell assisted at the ceremony and preached an eloquent and appropriate discourse on the occasion. The church was crowded by the joyous Catholics and interested Protestants of the town. The building, 81 by 53 feet, was constructed of frame, had four well-wrought doric columns and was neatly plastered and pewed.* It was also furnished with an altar, considered neat and tasty at the time. The cost of the building, exclusive of furniture, was about $3,000.

The church was dedicated to "Our Lady of the Lake," but by popular usage the name was soon changed to St. Mary's on the "Flats," that part of the city being then and even now so called. The building served as a church for all the Catholics of Cleveland till 1852, and as the first cathedral of Bishop Rappe from October, 1847, till November, 1852, when the present cathedral was opened for divine service. October, 1840,

THE REV. PETER McLAUGHLIN

was appointed Father O'Dwyer's successor. He received a most cordial welcome from the Catholics of Cleveland, who had been without a resident pastor for nearly a year, depending solely on occasional visits of priests from Cincinnati and Dayton. The pastorate of Cleveland was Father McLaughlin's first appointment, he having been ordained by Bishop Purcell only a few weeks previous. He was a man of much energy and an eloquent preacher. Being also conversant to some extent with the German language he satisfied the wants of his "mixed" congregation, quite a number of whom had come from Germany. Under his direction the new church was entirely finished, a choir was organized and a reed organ secured.

With a keen eye to the future growth of Catholicity in Cleveland, and with a view to locating a church in the upper

*Catholic Telegraph, June 20, 1840.

and better portion of the city, and more conveniently situated for his congregation, Father McLaughlin purchased from Thomas May four lots, fronting Superior and Erie streets, the site of the present cathedral. The lots were secured by land contract, dated January 22, 1845, and the purchase price was $4,000. The lots were bought on Father McLaughlin's responsibility, transferred to and assumed by Bishop Purcell, October 15, 1845. Father McLaughlin was much blamed by some of his fault-finding parishioners for buying church lots "in the country." Erie street was at that time the east boundary of the built-up portion of the city. Needless to ask who was the wiser—he or his critics!

The purchasing of these lots was the beginning of an unkind feeling towards Father McLaughlin on the part of a few Catholics; it grew in strength and violence. Finding that he could no longer profitably serve their spiritual interests he asked his bishop to relieve him of the pastorate of St. Mary's. His request was granted, and to the great grief of the better portion of his congregation, and to the sorrow of all the Protestant citizens of Cleveland, who had learnt to respect him for his ability and honesty of purpose, he left in February, 1846, after nearly six years of faithful and disinterested work among his people. A few days before his departure the

THE REV. MAURICE HOWARD

arrived as his successor. Besides attending to St. Mary's congregation, Cleveland, Father Howard also had charge of missions in Lake, Lorain and Geauga counties which had been attended by Father McLaughlin. He had as his assistant for some months the Rev. Michael A. Byrne, who had also shared Father McLaughlin's labors a short time. During his pastorate the Diocese of Cleveland was erected, and

THE RT. REV. AMADEUS RAPPE

consecrated Bishop thereof, October 10, 1847. Bishop Rappe saw the pressing need of better and more ample church facilities for the rapidly increasing number of Catholics of his episcopal city, the church on the Flats having become much too small to accommodate them. Besides, the Germans were clamoring for sermons in their native tongue. The good Bishop secured the aid of the Sanguinist Fathers from Thompson, Seneca county, the Revs. Matthias Kreusch and Jacob Ringele, to minister to the Germans who now received separate services in old St. Mary's.

October 23, 1848, the Bishop purchased from Thomas May, five lots adjoining those secured some years previous by Father McLaughlin, paying for them the sum of $1250. On one of these lots, immediately east of the present cathedral and on the site of the episcopal residence, he had a temporary frame structure erected, known as the church of the Nativity. Mass was celebrated in it for the first time on Christmas, 1848. The building served as a "chapel of ease" to St. Mary's on the Flats, till the completion of the present cathedral, in November, 1852. On week days the sanctuary of this chapel was closed from view by folding doors, and the nave was fitted for a school—the first parochial school in the city and Diocese of Cleveland. An attempt to have a Catholic select school in Cleveland had been made about 1837, but soon failed for lack of an efficient teacher.

January, 1848, the Rev. Louis de Goesbriand succeeded Father Howard in the pastorate of St. Mary's, and was also appointed the vicar-general of Bishop Rappe, retaining the latter position till his consecration as Bishop of Burlington, October, 1853. Father de Goesbriand was assisted during the the time of his pastorate in Cleveland by the Rev. James Conlan, and occasionally by the above mentioned Sanguinist Fathers. The Bishop, when at home, always gave his assistance and had the "lion's share" of the pastoral work, going every morning from his residence (located for a few months near the Haymarket, and from 1848 on Bond street) to his cathedral on the Flats to say Mass, and on Saturday afternoons and eves of feastdays to hear confessions. It is related of him that on one occasion, the day before a great feast of the Church, he went to the confessional immediately after

Mass and remained for thirteen hours, taking but a small collation towards evening. His connection with the parish work seemed to be rather that of a pastor or curate than that of the Bishop of the diocese. He catechised, preached, assisted at marriages, baptised and performed the burial services. He did this so constantly that the good people took it as a matter of course, and often would ask his services in preference to the priests attending the church. From October, 1847, till November 7, 1852,

ST. MARY'S CHURCH ON THE FLATS,

as yet the only Catholic church in Cleveland, served as the first cathedral of the diocese. On last mentioned date the present cathedral, corner of Superior and Erie streets, was finished and *consecrated.* St. Mary's was then assigned to the Germans, who were placed under the pastoral care of the above mentioned Sanguinist Fathers and Rev. N. Roupp, till the advent of the Rev. John H. Luhr, February, 1853. He was appointed their first resident pastor. As the Catholic Germans lived too widely separated to make St. Mary's conveniently located for all, Father Luhr's proposition to have those living east of the river organize as a distinct congregation, was approved by Bishop Rappe, who authorized them to purchase a site for church purposes at the corner of Superior and Dodge streets. This was the beginning of St. Peter's congregation. The Germans living west of the river were formed in November, 1854, as a congregation under the title of St. Mary's of the Assumption, and were given the use of the church on the Flats, till the dedication of their present church, corner Carroll and Jersey streets, in 1865. Revs. J. J. Kramer, F. X. Obermueller, and J. Hamene had successively charge of St. Mary's congregation, till the last mentioned year. From 1865 to 1879 old St. Mary's was the cradle of the following congregations: St. Malachy's, 1865; St. Wenceslas' (Bohemian), 1867; Annunciation (French), 1870. The Catholic Poles of Cleveland were the last to occupy the venerable proto-church of Cleveland, viz.: from 1872 to 1879, when they organized as St. Stanislas' congregation. From 1879 till 1886 the church was practically abandoned, as the Catholics residing in its neighborhood were not sufficient in number to warrant the organization or maintenance of a congregation.

On the Feast of Epiphany, 1886, Bishop Gilmour directed Mgr. Boff, V. G., to celebrate High Mass in it, to prevent, if possible, the church lots from reverting to the heirs of the original grantors, because of the conditional clause in the deed of transfer ; and this all the more, since suit for recovery of title had been threatened. It was a typical winter's day, with plenty of snow and ice covering the interior of the building, open for long to wind and weather. Two years previous a ruthless storm had blown down its much decayed spire, and the cold blasts had full sway in the church through broken roof and almost paneless windows. The forlorn looking edifice was packed to overflowing with an interested audience, composed largely of the old Catholic settlers of Cleveland, who had worshiped within its sacred walls in earlier years, when they were in the prime of life and the church attractive in appearance. Now, the old mother church of Cleveland looked tattered and torn, while her daughters, decked in splendor, were carrying aloft in every part of the city, the Sign of Redemption on graceful spire or lofty tower.

After Mass a general desire was expressed to have the church repaired and put in as good condition as it was when first built—thus to be preserved as a relic for generations of Catholics of Cleveland. An opportunity was offered to put into execution this laudable sentiment, by contributing the money necessary for the proposed expenditure, estimated at about $2,000. A sum less than $100 was contributed, though the list was long open to the Catholic public of Cleveland. Hence this *sentiment* was dismissed as based on *talk*, and the tooth of time was allowed to still further gnaw at the venerable church. Meanwhile the heirs of the original grantors of the lots, on which the church had so long stood, sued for reversal of title to said lots, owing to non-fulfillment of condition, mentioned in the deed of transfer. They based their suit on this fact, that now and for some years past the church had not been used and that there was no Catholic church in use in the part of the city known formerly as Cleveland Centre. The suit was heard in the court of common pleas at its session in the spring of 1888. A compromise decree was issued ordering the sale of the lots, the proceeds to be divided equally between the Diocese of Cleveland and the heirs of the original grantors. To clear the lots preparatory to their sale Bishop Gilmour had the church torn down in September, 1888.

For fifty years old St. Mary's had witnessed Catholicity's wonderful growth in Cleveland. When begun in 1838 there were less than 500 Catholics in Cleveland; in 1888 there were at a fair estimate no less than 60,000. Then there was no church edifice; now twenty-five Catholic churches grace the city, and many of them fit for cathedrals. Then there was neither religious, charitable, nor educational institution; now each of the city churches has a parochial school; a seminary supplies the diocese with priests; a college and two academies afford higher education to our Catholic youth; hospitals nurse the sick, asylums shelter the orphan, wayward, aged, and poor; and devoted religious have charge of institutions of learning and of the homes provided for the wards of our Lord.

And who will recount the many happy recollections centered around the church on the Flats—now no more! Many a joyful scene was witnessed within its sacred inclosure; many a sin-laden heart lightened; many a tear of sorrow and sadness dried by the consoling words of confessor or preacher. In it marriage solemnities were performed, baptismal waters poured, and the last sad rites of burial performed for thousands of Cleveland's Catholics. Though St. Mary's on the Flats is of the past, its sacred memories will remain enshrined in the hearts of the Catholic pioneers of Cleveland and their immediate descendants, for many a year to come—till the last of them shall have passed from mortality to immortality.

HISTORICAL SKETCH OF EARLY CATHOLICITY

—AND THE—

FIRST CATHOLIC CHURCH IN TOLEDO, O.

The site of the present flourishing city, of Toledo covers that of a stockade fort, erected about 1800, near what is now Summit street, and known in the history of Ohio as Fort Industry. Toledo was first settled in 1832 and incorporated in 1836. During the latter year the Wabash and Erie canal was located, and Toledo made its northerly terminus. In 1837 the proposed canal was let by the state authorities. The contractors made every effort to push its construction to an early completion, and to this end secured a large force of laborers.* Many of these laborers were Irish, who were also the first Catholics to come to Toledo. As soon as Bishop Purcell heard that Catholic laborers were engaged on the Wabash canal, he directed the Rev. E. Thienpont, then (1837) stationed at Dayton, to visit them and to attend to their spiritual wants. He was the first priest to visit Toledo. Father Collins, of Cincinnati, was the next, commissioned in like manner, in 1838. Both he and Father Thienpont visited all the Catholic laborers along the canal from Toledo to the Indiana state line, making the journey on horseback. However, owing to the great distance they had to go to reach their temporary charge, their visits were not regular. Hence Bishop Purcell made other arrangements, more satisfactory all around, by appointing the Revs. J. P. Machebeuf and Joseph McNamee, both stationed, at Tiffin, to take pastoral charge of this part of his vast diocese—Toledo and the missions along the Wabash canal. This was done by Father Machebeuf for two

*Howe, Ohio Hist. Collections, pp. 330-332.

ST. FRANCIS DE SALES' CHURCH, TOLEDO, O.
[The first Church used by the Catholics of Toledo.]

months, November and December, 1839, and by Father McNamee from December, 1839, to July, 1841.

They said Mass in the shanties of the laborers along the canal or in the cabins of the few Canadians residing in and near the town of Toledo. In a communication to the *Colorado Catholic*, September 22, 1888, Bishop Machebeuf describes his first visit to Toledo in November, 1839, as follows: "Only a few Catholics were in Toledo at this time. I said Mass in the frame shanty of a poor Canadian. These people having some Catholic acquaintances a short distance up the [Maumee] river, notified them of the opportunity to hear Mass, and all of them attended. There being no suitable house wherein to hold divine service, I rented a room over a drug store, constructed an altar with some boxes, which I covered with calico. This was the first church of good Father Rappe, when he was sent [to Toledo] two years later."

In 1841 Bishop Purcell paid his second episcopal visit to Toledo. In a letter to the *Catholic Telegraph*, of Cincinnati, published August 21st, of that year, he writes of Toledo as follows:

"This place is in all probability destined to be one of the most populous commercial cities in the Northwest. It is, with Maumee and Manhattan in its neighborhood, destined to be the depot of the railroads and canals, especially the Wabash and Erie canal, intersected by the Miami canal and the great Southern Railroad now in active progress all along the southern shore of Lake Erie to Buffalo. It is likewise the only proper point for the termination of the projected railroad from Chicago, to unite with the railroad to New York, and will thereby enjoy the advantages of much, if not all, the trade circuitously carried on between Chicago and Buffalo, by way of the lakes, an interrupted and frequently an unsafe channel of communication. A railroad, thirty-one miles in length, from Adrian, Michigan, is now completed to Toledo. It is contemplated to extend this road to the southern parts of Michigan, thus forming a continuous line of communication between New York and Michigan and Illinois, and the far west generally, by Toledo.

"With such prospects it is not surprising that many of our Catholic brethren from Ireland and Germany should have settled here in the vicinity of the old Catholic Canadian French, who have hitherto attended church at the "Bay Settlement," and at Monroe, Michigan.

"Before the visit of the Bishop of Cincinnati to Rome it was not quite certain whether the tract (formerly claimed by Michigan, but which was finally adjudged by Congress to Ohio,) belonged to his spiritual jurisdiction, or to that of the Bishop of Detroit. But this matter having been decided by the Propaganda in favor of Cincinnati, Rev. Mr. McNamee and Rev. Mr. Machebeuf are the only clergymen who are recognized as pastors, or who have any ordinary jurisdiction in this part of the diocese.

"Church [in Toledo] is at present held in a large room rented for the purpose, but arrangements have been made either for the purchase of a church, under execution for the sum of $2,800, to be paid in installments, or the erection of a new one on either of the two lots offered by agents of proprietors of much of the soil.

"The Bishop and Very Rev. Mr. Henni preached here frequently—the former before very attentive and intelligent audiences in the court house. After one of his sermons a few Protestant gentlemen present came forward and signed their names for between three and four hundred dollars to enable their Catholic brethren to purchase or build a church. The Catholics themselves had subscribed $400 in the forenoon of the same day.

"There are several Indian families in the neighborhood who live among the French, but who have not as yet joined the Church. * * Seven persons were confirmed and a large number partook of the Holy Communion. The erection of a church will give a new impulse to the growth and prosperity of this new city, which has been rather stationary since our former visit, four years ago. Manhattan, about two miles from Toledo, nearer the mouth of the Maumee, contains many families of Catholics, who, in part, attend church at Toledo, but the Bishop could not find time to visit them. * * *"

The Rev. Amadeus Rappe was appointed first pastor of Toledo, where he resided from about September, 1841, till his consecration as Bishop of Cleveland, October, 1847. Shortly after his arrival at Toledo he was urged by the laity either to build a church (a subscription of $1,400 having been raised for that purpose) or to purchase the church mentioned above by Bishop Purcell. It was finally agreed to purchase the church —a Presbyterian (frame) meeting-house, located on Superior street, its present site. The purchase was made about December, 1842. After a few alterations the building was *converted* into a Catholic church—the first in Toledo—and dedicated to St. Francis de Sales. The day of its dedication was one of joy for the Catholics of Toledo, now no longer obliged to worship in cabins, shanties or halls. The church had a basement which Father Rappe had fitted up as a residence for himself, with room enough left for a school to be established eventually.

During Father Rappe's pastorate, in 1845, Toledo was made the terminus of a second canal, (known as the Miami and Erie canal), and was thus connected with Cincinnati. Its construction helped to increase largely the number of Catholic laborers who had been attracted by the employment offered them in the construction of the Wabash and Erie canal.

After the completion of these two important enterprises, many of the employes settled in and near Toledo, and engaged in various avocations. Between 1838 and 1846, Toledo gained an unenviable reputation because of the insidious and destructive *Maumee fever*, which raged with violence, especially in 1838 and 1839, and greatly impeded the work on the canal.

In 1841 the Wabash and Erie canal was still in course of construction. "The Maumee Valley was full of Catholic laborers, and was also literally a land which devoured its inhabitants. The Maumee fever spared no one, and slowly and surely undermined the strongest constitution. Toledo and its environs were full of malaria. At times it was next to impossible to meet a healthy person. Added to this there were many cases of erysipelas, and in 1847 hundreds of ship-fever stricken emigrants landed at the Toledo docks to die a few hours after their arrival among strangers."* Hence the growth of Toledo was greatly checked, as people had no desire to settle where sickness of a maglignant type stared them in the face. But with the proper drainage and grading in the city, and the opening up of the surrounding country, Toledo has long since lost its notoriety as an unhealthy place.

When Father Rappe was elevated to the episcopacy, October, 1847, Rev. Louis de Goesbriand, his faithful co-laborer since January, 1846, was appointed pastor of St. Francis de Sales', Toledo. Four months later he was called to Cleveland and appointed vicar-general.

Rev. Philip Foley was then sent to Toledo, where he resided from February, 1848, till November, 1854. He had as his assistant, in 1848, the Rev. James Moran. In 1849 St. Francis' church was enlarged, to accommodate the Catholic Germans, to whom separate services were given, viz.: by the Rev. Sebastian Sanner, assistant to Rev. Father Foley, 1849-51 ; and by the Rev. Philip Flum, pastor of Maumee, from 1852 till 1854. January, 1854, Rev. Charles Evrard, was appointed first resident pastor of the Catholic Germans, who continued to have separate service in St. Francis' church till the completion of their own (St. Mary's), October, 1856.

November, 1854, Father Foley was succeeded by the Very Rev. A. Campion, who had charge of St. Francis' church till May, 1856. During Father Campion's pastorate (December, 1854) the Ursulines of Cleveland established an academy at Toledo, to succeed the one founded under direction of Father Rappe in 1846, by the Sisters of the Notre Dame, Cincinnati, but which was closed in 1848, for want of support. In 1855 the Grey Nuns of Montreal opened an asylum for orphan boys and girls.

The Rev. Robert A. Sidley was appointed Father Campion's successor in July, 1856, and had charge of St. Francis congregation till April, 1859, when the Rev. Felix M. Boff was appointed pastor. He remained in charge till October, 1872,

*Bishop de Goesbriand's "Reminiscences" in Catholic Universe, December 27, 1888.

when he was called to Cleveland and assigned the pastorate of the cathedral.

From 1854 till 1871, the following priests were assistants at St. Francis de Sales' church, Toledo: Revs. James Monahan, 1854 to April 1, 1855; W. O'Connor, July, 1855 to July, 1858; John Quinn, to December, 1860; Thomas F. Halley, to July, 1861; Thomas P. Thorpe, to May, 1862; Edward Hannin, under whose direction St. Patrick's congregation was founded in December, 1862; and J. B. Couillard, from October, 1869 to February, 1871.

So great was the growth of Catholicity that the formation of St. Patrick's did not seem to lessen the worshipers at St. Francis'. The old fever-breeding canal disappeared from the midst of the city; new streets were opened and old ones improved.

With these changes came new settlers, and hence, during the pastorate of Father Boff, it was found necessary to build a temple larger and more substantial than the proto-church of Toledo. Work was begun in 1862, and in 1870 the present handsome gothic structure, fronting on Cherry street, was ready for dedication. It was a day of rejoicing for pastor and people when Mass was celebrated for the first time in this imposing edifice.

It was also the close of a chapter in the history of the more sacred use of Toledo's first church in which took place scenes similar to those described in the preceding sketch of Cleveland's first House of Sacrifice. But the old and venerable structure still stands as a silent witness to Toledo's phenomenal Catholic growth and progress.* Her beautiful offspring now welcomes the Catholics of St. Francis de Sales' parish; she in turn welcomes their children. For nearly thirty years the walls of the sacred edifice resounded with the word of God and the chant of sacred music; now they re-echo the daily recitations and merry play of the parish school children. Toledo's first Catholic church having well served its purpose, will no doubt soon be sacrificed on the altar of time and disappear forever as the first land mark of Toledo's history of Catholicity.

---

*See List of Churches, etc., p. 224.

REV. EDMUND BURKE IN NORTH-WESTERN OHIO; 1795-96.

LETTER FROM JOHN GILMARY SHEA, LL. D.

[The writer is indebted to the kindness of Mr. John Gilmary Shea, LL. D., the erudite and painstaking historian of the Church in the United States, for the following very interesting letter.—G. F. H.]

ELIZABETH, N. J. Sept. 15, 1887.

REV. DEAR FATHER :—I have just ascertained something which was a surprise to me, and may perhaps be new to you. It fills a gap between the retirement of the Jesuits from their Sandusky mission and the coming of Father Fenwick to Ohio.

A priest, and a man of mark in his day, who became in time a bishop, and Vicar Apostolic of Nova Scotia, was for a time, in 1795-6, a missionary in Northern Ohio. This was the Rev. Edmund Burke, a native of Ireland, and evidently a priest of the Diocese of Dublin, before he came to Canada. He was the last priest of the Diocese of Quebec, and the first English speaking priest in Ohio.

The Rev. Edmund Burke was born in Ireland about 1743. He came to Canada May 16, 1787, according to the Abbe Tanguay, who adds that he was for some years parish priest at Saint Pierre and Saint Laurent, on Isle Orleans, from 1791 to 1794. From his letters he was evidently, in 1794, professor (apparently of mathematics) in the Seminary of Quebec. But he longed for priestly work, and seeing that nothing had been done to continue the work of the Jesuit Fathers among the Indians of the West, after the suppression of the Order, and the retirement of Father Dujaunai, who struggled on alone unaided and hampered for some years, he conceived the project of a great Indian mission in the West, and wrote to Archbishop Troy, of Dublin, to induce him to apply to the Sacred Congregation of the Propaganda. The Prefect, Cardinal Antonelli, wrote to Bishop Hubert, of Quebec, in regard to the matter, and that prelate appointed Rev. Edmund Burke his vicar-general for Upper Canada, with very ample powers, soliciting his attention especially to the French mission on Raisin river, now Monroe, Michigan. He set out from Quebec, September 15, 1795, encouraged by the British authorities in Canada, who were now anxious to avail themselves of the influence of Catholic priests over the western Indians. He reached Detroit, and was at Raisin river, where he dedicated the church to St. Anthony of Padua. But on the 2d of February, 1796, he wrote from the "Miamis" to Archbishop Troy. He says:

"I wrote from Quebec, if I rightly remember, the day before departure for this country; am now distant about five hundred leagues from it, on the western side of Lake Erie, within a few miles of the Miami fort, lately built by the British government. * * * I'm here in the midst of Indians, all heathens. This day a grand council was held in my house by the Ottawas, Chippewas and Pottowatomis. These people receive a certain quantity of Indian corn from the government, and I have been appointed to distribute it. That gives me a consequence among them which I hope will be useful, as soon as I can speak their language, which is not very difficult.

"This (is) the last and most distant parish inhabited by Catholics on this earth; in it is neither law, justice nor subjection. You never meet a man, either Indian or Canadian, without his gun in his hand and his knife at his breast. My house is on the banks of a river which falls into the lake, full of fish and fowl of all sorts; the finest climate in the world, and the most fertile lands. * * * Next summer I go on three hundred leagues towards Mackina, or Lake Superior, where there are some Christian Indians, to see if I can collect them."

He solicited the erection of a Prefecture of the Indian Territory of the West, independent of Quebec, Baltimore and Louisiana, but this was not carried out. This letter, I think, enables us to fix, pretty nearly, the spot where he was. The fort was that erected by the English on the Maumee*, and near which Wayne defeated the Miamis and their confederates. There were probably some Catholics among the soldiers

*Fort Meigs, near the present site of Perrysburg, and opposite the present town of Maumee, Lucas county, Ohio.—H.

in the fort, and his letter shows he had Canadians. His house, where he must have said Mass, was three miles from fort, and evidently surrounded by the Indian camps. He wrote from Detroit in May, but in August, 1796, in a letter from Quebec to Archbishop Troy, says that he received his letter of November 30, 1795, at the Miamis in February—that is, of course, February, 1796. His stay, or visits to Ohio, therefore, extended at least from February, 1795, to February, 1796, and possibly a little longer.

He seems, after some practical experience, to have abandoned his plans of great Indian missions. In 1797 he was at Fort Niagara. In 1803 he was sent by the Bishop of Quebec to Halifax as its first settled pastor. There he erected the Glebe House, which I believe is still the residence of the Archbishop, and he made the plans and laid the foundation of St. Mary's cathedral. He visited Rome in 1816, and the next year (July 4, 1817,) was appointed by Pius VII, Bishop of Sion and Vicar Apostolic of Nova Scotia. He died at Halifax, December 1, 1820, according to Archbishop Hannan's sketch, in his seventy-eighth year.

This gives, I think, Reverend dear friend, another Ohio priest, short as was his stay, and one too conspicuous to be overlooked. I find allusion to his presence in the West, in some letters of Bishop Carroll, and a wandering Dominican Father, Le Deu, and it would seem that when the English finally retired from the posts which they had held in contravention of the treaty of 1783, Rev. Mr. Burke wrote to Bishop Carroll, and may have thought of coming to the Diocese of Baltimore.

I should be most ungrateful if I did not mention that Bishop Maes, of Covington, who has written a sketch of the Church at Monroe, first told me of Bishop Burke's having been at Raisin river; then I found him in the Register at Quebec. * * * Yours most sincerely,

JOHN GILMARY SHEA.

REV. G. F. HOUCK.

CATHOLIC MISCELLANEA

—OF—

Northern Ohio and the Diocese of Cleveland.

For preservation in chronological order of early historical data in connection with the churches, &c., in Northern Ohio and diocese of Cleveland, the result of a careful search of old files of the Cincinnati *Catholic Telegraph* and other papers in which these data were published, is here presented. It is hoped they will prove of interest to the reader, as they will also no doubt be of value to the future historian of the diocese. Omissions supplied, corrections, changed names of places and churches, &c., will be found in brackets.

NORTHERN OHIO.

CORRESPONDENCE, DESCRIPTIVE OF BISHOP FENWICK'S EPISCOPAL VISIT TO NORTHERN OHIO IN 1827.

From U. S. Catholic Miscellany, Charleston, S. C. June 30, 1827.

CANTON, Stark County, June 1, 1827.

* The missionary Fathers, Revs. N. D. Young and J. I. Mullon, traveled through Belmont, Harrison, Jefferson and Columbiana counties to Canton, Stark county. Here they were received by the Rt. Rev. Bishop [he had preceded them from Zanesville to visit the pastor of Canton, Very Rev. John A. Hill, then seriously ill] who was anxiously awaiting their arrival to commence the Jubilee in St. John's Church.

The church is neat, and beautifully situated on an elevation overlooking the village. * * We spent eight days here, as usual, the people attending twice a day with zeal and piety. * * Our two missionaries then proceeded to St. Paul's, in Columbiana county [now St. Philip Neri's, Dungannon]. The building is of brick, not yet finished. * * At the solicitation of some citizens Rev. M. preached to a very numerous and respectable audience in the court house of that place. Considerable prejudice was removed by the discourse.

From U. S. Catholic Miscellany, September 15, 1827.

CORRESPONDENCE.

ST. JOHN'S [CANTON], OHIO, 29th August, 1827.

* * From Canton * * Revs. N. D. Young and J. I. Mullon proceeded to a congregation in Wayne county, [near the present village of Doylestown], consisting of about 15 families. There, according to appointment, they were met by those pious families in one of their houses, the most convenient, for the purpose of obtaining the benefits of religion. Previous to the celebration of the sacred mysteries, one of the missionaries gave a long and satisfactory explanation of the nature of the Holy Sacrifice. * * He also entered upon the explanation of the different vestments used in the celebration of Mass. The Holy Sacrifice having been offered a long and impressive discourse was delivered on the unity of the Church, and concluded by calling the attention of the assembly to the circumstance of the last and general judgment. * * The missioner invited those present to make their objections to anything he had asserted, and said, so far from giving him offense, it would be a source of satisfaction to him in having their objections thus publicly made that he might then have an opportunity of clearing them up before he left the place. Our delay among these good people was short, having been so long from our stations, and having to visit some other places, urged us to leave them

sooner than in other circumstances we could have desired. * * In this settlement a church is now on hand, and we hope will be in readiness for service against the next visit of their worthy pastor [V. Rev. J. A. Hill, of Canton].

WOOSTER, OHIO, September, 1827.

From this settlement [Dungannon] the missionaries went to Wooster, the county town of Wayne county, where, at the request of some of its most respectable citizens, one of them [Rev. Father Mullon] preached in the court house to an audience, chiefly composed of Protestants of the different sects, among whom was the Presbyterian preacher of that place. * * In the vicinity of the place several very respectable Catholic families reside, the most of whom were converts from Presbyterianism. The first priest who visited this part of the state was our present zealous Bishop. About ten years ago he made his first visit to this sequestered part, from Kentucky, where he then resided. Hearing that a Catholic gentleman resided in Wooster, who wished to have the consolations of religion, Doctor Fenwick, whose zeal for the salvation of souls was never dormant since he entered into the sacred ministry, hastened to this part of the state for the purpose, though distant nearly one hundred miles out of his usual route; the fatigues of the journey, the many privations he had to endure, were no obstacles to him. On his arrival he found, as he was informed, only one Catholic in the town, a native of Ireland, who by his industry and correct deportment had become independent, and was at the time engaged in mercantile business. Before Doctor Fenwick left this gentleman's house he had the consolation to receive into the communion of the Church his whole family. * *

From U. S. Catholic Miscellany, February 28, 1828.

CANTON, February, 1828.

Thirty Catholic families arrived from Lorraine, France, at Canton, Stark county. The chief motive that induced these industrious and respectable emigrants to locate themselves in this vicinity was the convenience of having a Catholic church at Canton. They and several congregations, though far asunder, are attended at present by the Very Rev. John A. Hill, V. G.

FROM BISHOP FENWICK'S REPORT OF HIS EPISCOPAL VISIT TO NORTHERN OHIO.

From Catholic Telegraph, October 29, 1831.

* * After a short stay at St. Joseph's [Michigan], the Bishop proceeded to Detroit, and thence to Canton, a flourishing town in Stark county, Ohio. Here he found the congregation much increased under the pastoral care of Rev. Mr. Henni. Three new churches were commenced within twenty miles of Canton, a fourth near Norwalk [Peru], in Huron county, and a fifth [St. Mary's] in Tiffin, a new and flourishing county seat in Seneca. * *

CANTON, OHIO.

From Catholic Telegraph, October 29, 1831.

We learn from a communication to the Bishop of Cincinnati, that the Rev. Mr. Henni, pastor of the Catholic church [St. John's] in Canton, has within the last two years received 21 adult persons into the Church, besides many children who followed their parents; that he administered the Sacrament of Baptism to 269. This truly zealous and indefatigable missionary has been compensated for his toils and hardships, in witnessing the rapid and astonishing increase of his flock.
* *

OBITUARY OF THE RT. REV. EDWARD FENWICK, FIRST BISHOP OF CINCINNATI. DIED AT WOOSTER, OHIO, SEPTEMBER 26, 1832.

From Catholic Telegraph, October 6, 1832.

Our venerated and beloved Bishop has gone to reap the reward of his labors and trials, leaving us the memory of his worth, the example of his virtues, and the odor of his sanctity. He is dead! *Edward Fenwick is no more.*

Where is he whose approving smile was ever ready to cheer us; whose sympathetic heart shared our griefs, and the counsels of whose wisdom was a lamp to our footsteps? Where is he whom we were accustomed to behold at the altar of his God; in the habitations of want and wretchedness; by the bedside of disease and pain; or in the rude cabin of the simple native of the forest; on the errand of mercy and the work of benediction? Alas! those benignant features are stiffened in the rigidity of death; that heart beats no more to human hope, or joy, or feeling; that light is extinguished; and the dank, cold clods of the valley are heaped above that majestic and venerated form.

In the poignancy of the present affliction our only solace is in the consoling hope that his removal is only to an entrance on the happiness of the beatific vision of his God, in those abodes towards which his longing desires were ever directed, and where all his treasures were.

This occasion, and our own feelings, will neither justify nor permit us now and here to dwell, at length, on his character and virtues—they are themes which hereafter througn our pilgrimage we shall recall with delight and gratefully perpend. They will only allow us at this time to record the manner of his decease.

He was on his return homeward from Canton, Stark county, after a long and laborious visitation of the remoter parts of his extensive dioçese, during which his heart was consoled for the disease which weakened his constitution and the fatigue that prostrated his strength, at beholding the fruits of his enlightened charity and zeal. The prevailing epidemic (cholera) arrested his course and terminated his mortal career, at Wooster, in the county of Wayne. * *

We add the following letter, addressed by Rev. M. Henni to Rev. J. I. Mullon, editor of the *Catholic Telegraph:*

WOOSTER, Sept. 27, 1832.

MY DEAR FRIEND.—P. has already advised you of the alarming illness of our good Bishop. A task of most heart-rending character remains to me, to announce to you the event. He is no more! He died yesterday, (Wednesday), at twelve o'clock, and was immediately interred. I witnessed only the mound which covers his remains. *Requiescat in Pace.* Your most affectionate,

M. HENNI.

ST. MARY'S CHURCH, TIFFIN, OHIO.

Catholic Telegraph, May 11, 1833.

The new church at Tiffin, Seneca county, in this state, was opened for divine service on Easter Sunday, on which occasion High Mass was sung, and an appropriate sermon preached by the pastor, the Rev. Edmund Quinn. A few years since there was but one Catholic family in that section of the state, now giving promise of becoming the fairest and most flourishing portion of the diocese.

Through the piety and zeal of the apostolic missionary, who labors in this promising field, a neat and commodious church has been erected, and thus the fertile country around the Sandusky is rendered eligible to Catholic emigrants, who have been hitherto deterred from locating themselves there by the impossibility of enjoying the consolation derivable from a compliance with the duties of their religion, at too great a distance from a church or a resident priest.

REPORT OF BISHOP PURCELL'S VISIT TO NORTHERN OHIO IN 1834.—DUNGANNON, COLUMBIANA COUNTY.

[Extract of letter from Bishop Purcell, dated Hanover, Columbiana county, Ohio, June 16th, 1834.]

Catholic Telegraph, June 27, 1834.

* * After a late Mass on Monday, 9th of June, the Bishop left the house of Mr. Gallagher, * * * and visited the family of Mr. Jeffers, where he had the satisfaction to see ten interesting converts; thence he proceeded, accompanied by Mr. Deloug, (who numbers not fewer than seventy relatives, converted like himself, to the Catholic faith), on the road to St. Paul's church, [now St. Philips,

Dungannon,] in Columbiana county, where he arrived on Saturday, 14th, inst., having visited several Catholic residences in the intervening towns. Rev. Mr. Henni, of Canton, had arrived the day previous at St. Paul's and commenced preparing the attending members of the congregation for the holy sacraments. The interests of this church had been for some time grievously neglected and the ecclesiastical property attached to it misapplied. The exertions of the present pious clergymen and the measures taken during the episcopal visitation, will, it is hoped, efficiently arrest the two-fold evil. The church of St. Paul is a substantial brick edifice, recently much enlarged, but still inadequate to the increasing numbers of the congregation. It is attended by the Catholics of New Lisbon, Hanover, and a thickly settled territory of ten or twelve miles round. The Catholics worshiping at the church are variously estimated at from eight hundred to one thousand souls. They have no resident pastor. There were only six reputed sufficiently well instructed to be admitted to confirmation, and it was truly distressing to observe that many had been suffered to reach their twentieth year without having been imbued with the first elements of a religious education, or received any other sacrament than baptism. * *

ST. JOHN'S, CANTON, STARK COUNTY; VERY REV. JOHN A. HILL; LOUISVILLE, CANAL FULTON, DOYLESTOWN, WOOSTER, ETC.

Bishop Purcell to Catholic Telegraph, July 18, 1834.

MANSFIELD, Richland Co., July 3, 1834.

Our first station, after having left St. Paul's church [near Dungannon], was at Mr. Crevaisier's, in Hanover, where a few persons, unable to attend church, received the holy communion, and one child was baptised. Similar consolations were afforded to the Catholics of Paris, fifteen miles distant, in the house of Mr. James Cassily. Passing by Osnaburg in the public stage, we had not time to visit several Catholic families, chiefly Germans, inhabitants of that town and vicinity. Having rendered our accustomed and solemn homage to the Adorable Sacrament on our arrival in the church of Canton [St. John's], the seat of Stark county, and knelt in the cemetery by the remains of the once animated temples of the Holy Ghost, destined to rise more splendid from their present ruins, we became unconsciously absorbed in reflection at the humble grave of the Rev. Mr. Hill. How many associations, pleasing and melancholy to the soul, did not that sad memorial awaken! What *consistent* testimony did not its peaceful occupant render to the truth! What a contrast between his and the conversion of certain modern proselytes! Willingly did he descend from exalted station, relinquish country, debar himself of the pleasures of a society which he was so eminently qualified to grace and adorn, and sever the dearest ties, to worship at the shrine of that mysterious Catholic religion, always blackened by calumny, but ever bright with holiness, always assaulted by error, but never overcome, and which is now going forth through the New World, as it has gone through the old, "conquering and to conquer." The following epitaph, a tribute of classic as well as sacerdotal piety to the memory and virtues of the deceased ornament of the American priesthood, is inscribed on a plain white slab placed against the south side of the church. It is, we understand, the composition of the Rev. Mr. Henni, associate pastor of the Canton congregation:

D. O. M.
Reverendus Sacerdos Dominus
JOHANNES AUGUSTINUS HILL.

Relictis centuris castris,
Minervæ induit arma
Adscriptis DOMINICI choro
Patris premit vestigia
Patri ignotis in Sylvis:
Pius mitisque animo
Carus et ore facundus
Obiit iii º Non. Sept. MDCCCXXVIII.
Pulveri eheu! fave pulvis
Nova dum silet turba.

On Sunday Rev. V. Raymacher [Dominican] sang Mass, and the Bishop preached in the morning, and again addressed a large audience in the afternoon. The Tuesday following, Feast of St. John Baptist, patron of the church, the sacrament of confirmation was administered to 105 persons, all of whom received the divine Eucharist, on the same day. The order observed during the dispensation of the sacred rite was truly edifying. The progress of Catholicity in this section of the state may be estimated from the fact that there are at present upwards of 2,000 communicants in part of the district, attended by two clergymen, the only priests in Stark county, where, ten years ago, there were scarcely thirty resident Catholic families. This extraordinary increase will appear from the annexed statement, on the correctness of which full reliance can be placed :

Canton, 800 communicants ; Beechland, [Louisville] 7 miles distant, 240 ; Paris, 120 ; Moreck, 15 miles to the east, 100 ; [Canal] Fulton, 130 ; Sugar Creek, 60 ; Randolph, in Portage county, 18 miles north of Canton, 120 ; the remainder are in Medina, Chippewa [Doylestown] and Tuscarawas, where there is, unfortunately, no one to gather the harvest into the barns of the Father of the family, but tenacious Catholic faith alone preserves the love of our holy institutions, cementing the unity of the spirit in the bond of peace. A few only of the congregations did we find time to visit. Beechland [Louisville] is principally a French settlement. Church is held in the house of Mr. Joseph Menegay, which was formerly occupied as a place of meeting by a Baptist minister and his congregation. Bricks to the amount of 120,000, for a new church, are now in the kiln, and a lot of three-fourths of an acre, in an eligible position, near a recently laid off site for a new town, has been given by Mr. Lutzenheizer. The ground for a grave yard is the grant of Mr. Bideau, and forty-nine acres of prime land, generously consecrated[?] by Messrs. James, Richard and Patrick Moffit, to which five others had been added by the good Mr. Menegay, are now recorded in the Bishop's name, as a provision for the support of a pastor.

In the [Canal] Fulton church, a log building fifty by thirty, built on an acre lot presented by Mr. McCue and not yet dedicated, there were fourteen confirmed, of whom five were converts. Messrs. Patton, Bayle, McCadden and Edgington are among the most zealous of the little flock and names which we record with much satisfaction.

In Sugar Creek church, [Marshallville?] Wayne county, likewise a log edifice, small and inconveniently situated, there were fourteen communicants and four confirmed on the 1st of July. The Arnolds, of Allegheny county, Maryland, have planted the mustard seed, and they now cherish its growth in this lonely place. Among the baptized there was one convert.

WOOSTER.

Reaching Wooster late at night, we greatly regretted that we could not sojourn, at least one day, with the excellent Catholics near that town. The dreariness of the hour and the stormy state of the weather were in perfect accord with the feelings inspired by the sight of the room in which the late Bishop died forlorn by every one but his God. Filled with the most serious but salutary impressions of the precarious tenure by which we hold to the present life, we left the town, after a short and broken rest, and proceeded over a wretched road, 33 miles, to Mansfield. There are two English and several German Catholic families in this town, but many more in the neighborhood. They are very irregularly attended. Notwithstanding the briefness of the notice, there were 15 communicants and 4 confirmed in the house of Mr. William Downey. Deprived, for want of time, of the pleasure of visiting Chippewa, [near Doylestown] where Messrs. G. Whitman and Peter Marshall, brother to the Rev. Francis Marshall of Maryland, have lately conveyed eighty acres of good land to the Bishop, towards the support of a priest; and unable, for the same reason, to see the numerous Catholic families newly settled near Bucyrus, Crawford county, of whose attachment to their faith and praiseworthy exertions for the building of a church we have heard much that edified, we left Mansfield on the 3d of July, hoping to reach Paris by Truxville the same day. In this we were disappointed; and after a costly, dangerous and unsuccessful effort to cross the flooded headwaters of the Mohican [Wyandot?], were compelled, with well drenched clothes and broken carriage, to return and think of the patience and joy of the Apostle in greater labors and disasters, while we enjoyed the fireside af our kind host. To-morrow, God willing, we shall renew the effort to reach Norwalk by Sunday, and, we hope, with better success. * *

Catholic Telegraph, August 1, 1834.

EPISCOPAL VISITATION.—NORTHERN OHIO.

LETTER FROM BISHOP PURCELL.

DAYTON, 23d July, 1834.

We shall here conclude our notes of the episcopal visitation. Reports, which, we trust, we shall find to have been exaggerated, having reached us, of the reappearance of cholera, under alarming circumstances, at Cincinnati, induce the Bishop to defer visiting the remaining Catholic stations on his route, and repair promptly to his see, in order to unite with his reverend and, he fears, over-burdened fellow-laborers, in rendering to that beloved portion of his flock, the spiritual consolation and relief of which it may be in need.

From Mansfield to Paris there are many scattered Catholics; we had time to visit none but the numerous and edifying family of Mrs. Trux, residing near the last mentioned, new and rapidly growing town. The number of professors of "the faith once delivered to the saints," increased as we approached

NORWALK,

seat of Huron county. Three miles from the town is a well built frame church under the pastoral care of the Rev. Mr. Tschenhens, of the Holy Order of the Redeemer, founded by the lately canonized Alphonso de Liguori, an Italian bishop. The church, which has been lately erected, was dedicated to the Almighty God, under the invocation of that Holy Prelate and zealous patron of missions. Previously to the ceremony of its benediction the Bishop addressed the congregation (to whom the Rev. Mr. Henni, of Canton, subsequently delivered an eloquent and impressive discourse in the German language) and was obviously much impressed with the necessity of the prayers he preferred to heaven being granted, when he besought the Divine Disposer of every good gift, to cherish and mature the mustard seed, thus sown under the fostering care of the Redemptorists, and thence to diffuse the blessings of the only true and living faith over an extensive territory, where its influence has hitherto been but little felt. Rev. Mr. Tschenhens is now aided by two pious lay brothers, and is soon to be joined by a zealous clergyman of his Order, from Michigan, and a considerable reinforcement from Vienna, who are thought to be now on their voyage to the distant and unknown settlement in the West. After the dedication of the church, the cemetery was blessed, and 19 were confirmed.

At the request of several of the citizens, the Bishop preached in the court house at Norwalk. The day following he was accompanied by Revs. Messrs. Henni and Tschenhens to Lower Sandusky [Fremont] where the divine sacrifice was offered at the residence of Madame Beaugrand. There are not many Catholics settled in the town, but several families have lately arrived in its vicinity. A lot for a church was promised by esteemed friends to the holy cause of truth, and pecuniary assistance will not, it is believed, be withheld when the seasonable time for the commencement of the church shall have arrived.

TIFFIN.

We were much disappointed at finding the church [St. Mary's] of Tiffin still unfinished. It has not yet been dedicated. On Sunday, 13th of July, there were 100 communicants, and on the following Tuesday 26 were confirmed. Exclusive of the Germans, to whom Revs. Messrs. Henni and Tschenhens frequently preached during their stay in the town, there is a large and fervent congregation from the neighborhood of Emmittsburg, Mt. St. Mary's and Westminster, Frederick county, Md. They are the hope of religion and will long continue, as we fondly and devoutly trust, to enhance their Bishop's joy and pastor's crown in the remote and peaceful habitations they have chosen. Rev. Mr. Quinn, who has hitherto attended this congregation, resides at the distance of five [?] miles from Tiffin, and has had to minister to the spiritual wants of the Catholics of a circumference of nearly forty miles, the roads at any season of the year, but particularly in the winter, being of the very worst description.

McCUTCHENVILLE.

In McCutchenville, 10 miles from Tiffin, a charming lot of 2¾ acres has been ceded to the Bishop and his successors in office by Mr. William Arnold, and a considerable sum has been subscribed by Messrs. McLaughlin, Berton, Noel and other Catholics and Protestants for the erection of a church. Two other churches are spoken of and would indeed be necessary, for German congregations, five miles in different directions from Tiffin.

REPORT OF EPISCOPAL VISITATION MADE BY BISHOP PURCELL.

Catholic Telegraph, September 4, 1835.

DUNGANNON.—NEW LISBON.

St. Paul's [near Dungannon] was visited on the first Sunday of August. The Bishop found the congregation much increased and anxious to secure the services of a resident priest. This a favor which it was not in his power to grant. However, on two Sundays of every month, until God is pleased to send more numerous, pious and efficient laborers into His vineyard, the spiritual wants of the congregation will be supplied by the Rev. Mr. Conlan, from Steubenville. The number of Catholics in the town of New Lisbon, six miles from St. Paul's, has likewise been much augmented by the contractors, laborers and men of business attracted to the spot since the commencement of the Sandy and Beaver canal. The divine mysteries were celebrated in the house of a French Catholic, and on Monday evening the Bishop preached in the court house to a large and attentive audience. The Catholics of New Lisbon are anxious for the erection of a church, but it has been recommended to them to enlarge and finish the building at St. Paul's, before they undertake to build another so near it. In time, we trust, there will be a creditable church in either place.

CLEVELAND.

The Catholic congregation of Cleveland has been very recently organized. It consists of not more than three hundred members. They are all poor in this world's wealth, but rich in the faith and hope which ensure their professors those treasures which rust cannot consume, nor earthly distinction affect, and which are forfeited by vice and wilful error. A merchant of Cleveland, Mr. Clark, has presented a lot, in Brooklyn, which is connected and almost identified with Cleveland, by a bridge thrown over the Cuyahoga river. On this lot [not used; first church was built on "Flats" in Cleveland centre.—H.] it is intended to erect a church during the present season and from the friendly and liberal spirit evinced by the Protestant citizens of the town and the spirited exertions which the Catholics are resolved to make, we have no doubt but that the voyager on Lake Erie will soon be cheered, in his approach to this safe harbor, by the aspect of the Sign of our Redemption. We were delighted to hear how greatly the religious, moral and social condition of the Catholics in the vicinity of Cleveland, who had previously enjoyed no means of instruction, has been improved by the unremitting exertions of their pastor, Rev. Mr. Dillon. May the divine blessing continue to remove the obstacles which could mar the projects, or impede the success of this interesting little flock.

CUYAHOGA FALLS.

At this place, which is thirty miles from Cleveland, there are a few Catholics, but many more dispersed through the country around. Many of the influential citizens, who belong to no religion, but who are shocked at the disreputable acts resorted to, for the disparagement of the Catholics among a people who have little opportunity of judging of them but from the caricatures exhibited by sectarians, have strongly urged with promises largely to contribute to the building of a Catholic church. [No church built at C. F. till 1884.—H.] It will be impossible to accede to their request before the completion of the church in Cleveland. Meantime, they shall hear the word of Catholic truth announced at stated visits, by Rev. Mr. Dillon.

RANDOLPH.

The first movement of German Catholics in a new settlement is to build a church and school house of the cheapest and most accessible materials. To improvements in the condition of the country, and their own, they wisely adjourn the construction of more costly and substantial edifices. Within one mile of Randolph [Centre] in Portage county, there is a Catholic German congregation who have raised a small, but remarkably neat log chapel and school house, thereby evincing a laudable attention to the instruction of their children, and a becoming zeal for the religion of their fathers. The congregation consists of forty-five families, and of this little community, it is said, in addition to other praise, that there is not a solitary instance of habitual or occasional intemperance to stain its early and humble history! On the 22d inst. [August, 1835], Rev. Mr. Saenderl [Redemptorist], who accompanied the Bishop, sang High Mass, in which the entire congregation, young and old, joined in admirable accordance; there were fifty-three communicants and twelve confirmed. Several Catholic families, not before heard of, attended from a distance of ten or fifteen miles, or requested through those who were able to come, that they may be visited by a priest. Measures were promptly taken to afford them this consolation. * *

REPORT OF EPISCOPAL VISITATION BY BISHOP PURCELL.

Catholic Telegraph, September 11, 1835.

LOUISVILLE, O.

Beechland [near Louisville], Stark county.—This congregation has suffered from the want of pastoral attention for several months. Still the members of the building committee have not neglected the collection of materials for the erection of a church in the newly located and fast progressing town of Louisville. Eighty-one thousand brick, and much of the gross timber for the construction of the church, are now on the selected site, and the Bishop was cordially seconded in his earnest desire for the completion of, at least, the shell of the building, before the setting in of the winter. The resources of the congregation are fully adequate to the support of a priest, and promises have been given, which it is hoped the Divine Lord of the harvest will enable us to realize, that a worthy laborer shall be speedily placed at their head, to lead them onward in union, strength and piety. The holy mysteries were celebrated in the large dwelling of Mr. Eck, a Catholic lately arrived from Pennsylvania, and many persons were admitted to holy communion and confirmation.

ST. JOHN'S, CANTON.

This healthy and popular town appears destined to enjoy its share of the growing prosperity of the West. Its citizens are now engaged in urging on to completion a cross-cut from the Ohio and Erie, or Sandy and Beaver canal. The church is far too small for the greatly increased numbers of the congregation, and notwithstanding the contemplated formation of several distinct missions in its neighborhood, it will be necessary to erect a new church on, or near, the site of the old one, to accommodate the Catholics and numerous enquirers after religious truth at present residing in the town. At the request of many of the citizens the Bishop preached to an unusually large assemblage in the court house on Sunday evening, August 23d. The Rev. gentleman of the Order of St. Dominic, to whose arduous and untiring efforts for the promotion of faith and morals, during many years, the diocese of Ohio owes a large debt of gratitude, has lately surrendered* the Canton congregation to the care of the Bishop. This measure was exclusively owing to the impossibility, on the part of the Order, of attending to this distant mission, while the congregations of Zanesville, Somerset and Lancaster require more than the time and pains which have been bestowed on their spiritual instruction and improvement in former years. Rev. Mr. Saenderl, Superior of the Redemptorists, and Rev. Mr. O'Bairne have been entrusted by the Bishop with the care of the congregation.

EPISCOPAL VISITATION—NORTHERN OHIO.

Bishop Purcell to Catholic Telegraph, September 15, 1836.

TIFFIN, ST. MARY'S.

Very Rev. S. T. Badin and Rev. H. D. Juncker having reached Tiffin several days before the Bishop, prepared the congregation for the reception of the Sacraments. There were only 23 confirmed. The church is under the care of the Redemptorists [stationed at Peru, Huron Co.] whose number, we regret to say, has not been hitherto large enough to admit of their devoting the necessary time to the instruction and spiritual wants of the diocese. Four clergymen, at least, would be required for Seneca county, in which are five [four?] churches at the present time [Tiffin, Thompson, Wolf's Creek and McCutchenville] in progress of building. Numerous sects, of whose very name the Bishop had never heard before, are swarming through the villages in this and Crawford eounty.

The Tiffin and McCutchenville congregations are comprised of the very best materials; they have been lately much augmented by emigrants from Maryland, Pennsylvania and some parts of Europe. The Germans in their vicinity are

*The Dominicans reassumed charge of St. John's, Canton, about 1837, retaining it till 1842.—H.

peaceful, industrious and full of zeal for the diffusion of our holy religion, for their own edification and the instruction of their children. The Tiffin church, the shell of which, only, has been so long built, will be completed and ready for dedication this fall. * *

FREMONT; LA PRAIRIE.

Lower Sandusky [Fremont] and the French congregation of Muddy Creek [La Prairie], consisting of 20 or 30 families, are still destitute of a church. From the well known liberality, respectability and intelligence of many of the inhabitants, we have no doubt but means will soon be furnished to erect in this interesting vicinity a new and neat little monument to the Faith of ages. We shall look with confidence for its completion by the coming year. * *

CANTON, ST. JOHN'S.

Catholic Telegraph, December 23, 1836.

Rev. Dr. Hoffmann will visit the Catholics of Columbus at the feast of Christmas. He will thence proceed direct to Canton, where, we are happy to announce, will be his future residence as pastor of the Catholic congregation. Cordially do we congratulate our brethren at Canton on their acquisition of so learned and zealous a spiritual guide as Dr. Hoffmann, and we sincerely hope that his pious instructions and edifying manners will soon make them forget their late destitution of pastoral encouragement and succor. We trust some of the prominent members of the congregation will, without delay, prepare the presbytery for his reception.

EAST LIVERPOOL, OHIO.

Catholic Telegraph, May 30 *and June* 6, 1839.

Measures are in progress for the erection of a church in this flourishing village [East Liverpool]. * * A lot has been secured and a subscription commenced. This is owing to the zea. of Rev. James Conlan, pastor of Steubenville, who attends [this and] several neighboring missions. * * Rev. Mr. Conlan is making an appeal to our Catholic brethren in behalf of this infant congregation, to which we hope there will be a liberal response.

DIOCESE OF [CINCINNATI] OHIO.

Bishop Purcell to Catholic Telegraph, February 15, 1840.

It is a subject of no small gratification to the Western Catholics, to observe the sure and steady progress of the Church throughout this extensive portion of our country. About twenty-two years ago there was but one building in this state on which the Sacred Cross was raised, to cheer the heart of the emigrant as he journeyed to some "promised land" in search of home and happiness. Our religion was then associated with a thousand evils in the minds of the inhabitants; truth had a mountain before it, towering to the clouds, which it had to move from the path before it could make further progress on its holy errand. The laborers, however, were not disheartened—"courage mounteth with occasion;"—and they commenced to toil in the good cause, calmly but resolutely, conscious that their duty was being fulfilled, and trusting in the Lord for a successful result. Already have many of their expectations ben realized. * *

We have reason for congratulation, and as we justly entertain a preference for the immediate scene of our labors, we can often see through the parting gloom of the present many bright and cheering vistas of future glory for our diocese. In six years the number of clergy has increased from nineteen to thirty-four. In the almanac for this year Ohio has credit for two charitable institutions, but we have now five in operation. It is also stated therein, that we have 24 churches in Ohio, now the number is 32, and before the ensuing almanac is ready for the press, we hope to have still better news to impart to those who love to see the Church flourishing and prosperous, no matter where it may be planted. * *

DEDICATION OF THE CHURCH OF "OUR LADY OF THE LAKE," [ST. MARY'S ON THE "FLATS"], CLEVELAND, O., JUNE 7, 1840.

Catholic Telegraph, June 20, 1840.

Rt. Rev. Dr. de Forbin-Janson, Bishop of Nancy and Toul, France, and Bishop Purcell of Cincinnati, left Buffalo on the steamboat *Constitution* at 8 P. M. on Friday, 5th of June for Cleveland. At Fairport, 30 miles from the last mentioned place, they were overtaken by a violent storm, during which the vessel, which was very heavily laden, labored a great deal and made but little headway, so that they did not reach their destination for many hours after the usual time employed in making the trip. They were both, as were nearly all their fellow-travelers, gloriously sea-sick and soaked with surf from the swollen waters, and the good Bishop of Nancy was moreover at one moment in imminent danger of serious injury from the falling of a high and heavy pile of cases of merchandise in a sudden lurch of the ship. Finally they disembarked in safety, at 5 A. M., on Sunday morning, *Auspice Maria*.

The Bishop of the diocese was agreeably surprised to find that all the work which he had directed to be done at the new church by Mr. Golden, the architect, had been not only faithfully performed, but that the altar and the plastering, etc., had likewise been very neatly executed. He accordingly resolved not to lose so favorable an occasion of dedicating it. The zealous Bishop of Nancy, who seems to have never known what it is to be weary in well doing, kindly consented to dedicate the church, which he did according to the Roman ritual, and in full pontificals, after which he celebrated High Mass, which was wonderfully well sung in plain chant by the choir. * * * Bishop Purcell preached to a very intelligent and attentive auditory, before and after the ceremony.

The church measures 81 by 53 feet, having four well wrought Doric columns in front, a light but substantial gallery, or organ loft, handsome ceiling, etc., and conveniently

CATHEDRAL SCHOOL, CLEVELAND, O.

situated on Columbus street, between the two [?] congregations of Cleveland and Ohio City [?]. * * * [Church was taken down September, 1888.—H.]*

EPISCOPAL VISITATION.—NORTHERN OHIO.

Bishop Purcell to Catholic Telegraph, July 4, 1840.

LIVERPOOL, Medina Co.,

After his departure from Cleveland [June 8], the Bishop visited two Catholic families near Strongville [Cuyahoga Co.] who had not been favored with the presence of a priest for several years. * * * He was there met by a deputation of German Catholics, of Liverpool, Medina county, by whom he was attended to the residence of Mr. Lawling, in which service is generally held for the neighboring Catholic inhabitants. The next morning a large number of the faithful, living on the east and west banks of Rocky river, assembled on the occasion, in virtue of a previous notice sent there from Cleveland. These formed in procession and proceeded, chanting the *Miserere*, to the graveyard, where the Bishop, in mitre and crosier, blessed the graves of a few persons thus solitarily buried, and gave an instruction to the bystanders on the nature of the ceremony and the circumstances under which one or two of their brethren, who were there interred, had died. Rev. Mr. O'Dwyer then offered the holy sacrifice, and the Bishop preached on the worth of the soul. Many well-inclined Protestants were present. It was thought expedient to recommend the construction of two churches, one at each side of the river, which is often too much swollen to admit of being safely forded. Materials have been prepared for these purposes, and we hope to learn soon that the churches have been built. [In 1842 a log church (St. Mary's) was built east of Rocky river, in the hamlet of Abbeyville, later replaced by a brick structure, but long since abandoned. In the same year a log church was also erected west of same

*See Historical Sketch, "Early Catholicity in Cleveland."

river, one mile from Liverpool Centre. This was replaced in 1861 by the present brick edifice, known as St. Martin's, Liverpool, Medina Co.—H.]

DOYLESTOWN.

About noon the Bishop left [Liverpool] for Chippewa [near Doylestown] in Wayne county, accompanied by five of the congregation on horseback. * * After straying a few miles from the right road, the party reached, before sundown, the residence of Rev. Mr. Schorb, pastor of the congregation. Next day the Bishop visited Mr. Marshall and Mr. Whitman, two zealous Maryland Catholics, who have given a valuable tract of seventy-eight acres of land for the support of a presbytery, and who are now engaged in redeeming a pledge by them voluntarily and generously given to build a church and a dwelling for a priest at their own expense. The cost of the buildings cannot be under seven or eight hundred dollars. Other members of the congregation rival their charity in supplying the church with suitable vestments, and in no other part of the diocese has the Bishop witnessed more zeal, humility and fervor than in this sequestered and delightful spot. Surely the divine mercies are for such a people. The number of communicants has been more than doubled since the arrival of the pastor, being now eighty-five. In [Canal] Fulton, on the canal, nine miles distant, there are eighty-four communicants; in Liverpool, eighty-one; in Randolph, fifty; in Akron, twenty (not including the English-speaking portion, which is considerable); in Wooster, Ashland[?] and Shelby [Settlement], the communicants amount to one hundred and nineteen. All the places are attended [from Chippewa] by Rev. Mr. Schorb, to whom the Bishop promised an assistant, for whose support ample means will be furnished at the glebe-house. The church [at Chippewa], though yet unfinished, is still used for divine service. It was filled on Corpus Christi, when the Bishop and the reverend pastor alternately officiated; the former preached on the great mystery of the divine love in the Adorable Eucharist, and after having praised the zeal and piety of this fine little flock, exhorted all to perseverance and renewed effort to obtain all that is yet wanting for the instruction of the youth of the congregation and the decency and dignity of the worship of God. * *

CANTON, ST. JOHN'S.

On Thursday afternoon [June 11], the Bishop reached Canton in company with Rev. Mr. Schorb. He there witnessed and heard, with inexpressible pleasure, the good done by the indefatigable Rev. Mr. Juncker, and had reason to bless the Almighty's goodness that a constitution, naturally delicate, had not sunken under an accumulation of arduous duties. The new pews, the decent altar, the handsome antependium, speak the man of God, prepared for every good work. He had, up to this date, eighteen hundred and forty-three communicants, [of these there were] in Canton, five hundred and forty-eight; Massillon, seventy-four; Bethlehem [Navarre], seventy-five; Norwalk [Peru], three hundred; Tiffin and German Settlement [New Riegel], five hundred; Sandusky City, twenty-four; Thompson's Settlement [Thompson], eighty-five; Cleveland, twenty-four.

These are not all the Easter communicants in the several places named, but all that Rev. Mr. Juncker was enabled to instruct and otherwise prepare for the reception of the holy sacraments. He was assisted by his Reverend and worthy *confrere*, Mr. Wuertz, in Bethlehem, Norwalk, Tiffin, and the adjacent stations.

Extracts from letter of Bishop Purcell, published in the Catholic Telegraph, July 18, 1840

EAST LIVERPOOL, June 25, 1840.

The town of East Liverpool, Columbiana county, which was laid out nearly thirty years ago, but which began to be improved only a few years past, is one of the healthiest and most agreeably situated on the Ohio river. * * Mr. James Blakely [of East Liverpool, and a convert] with a liberality which we have pleasure in recording, and which we trust will find many imitators in the congregations of the diocese, gave four hundred dollars [for the church just built], and in connection with four other gentlemen, viz.: Messrs. Mitchell, Mausley, Cooke and Smith, presented three town lots for the sacred building. The first two of these four gentlemen have also paid $100 each towards the erection of the church. Mr. John Blakely, a convert like his brother mentioned above, has offered one hundred dollars. Mr. Kerrins, architect of St. Paul's church, Pittsburgh, who resides here, has also given a hundred dollars for a new altar; and his wife, who is a convert, has done and contributed much, in company with the family of another estimable convert, Mr. Bayley, together with Mrs. Blakely, and others, to decorate the sanctuary, if not to build up the very walls of our little Sion. Mr. John J. Murphy has also been a liberal benefactor, and incurred responsibilities towards forwarding the good work. Messrs. Buchheit and Diettrich, German Catholics, the former being the first Catholic who settled here, largely participated in the merit of the forementioned. Many other names might be added, but they do not occur to us at present. The pious pastor, Rev. Mr. [James] Conlan, lodges at the hospitable residence of Mr. Fortune. * * And it is not for ostentation, or any intention of flattering a fondness for even amiable fame, which is very far, we believe, from the minds of all those who have engaged in this pious undertaking, that we have written the foregoing, but only to do as we see done in other places where lists of the benevolent are kept and occasionally published, for the double purpose of acknowledgment and emulation in well doing.

The church is of brick, substantially built, with stone foundation, and water courses, 70x40 ft. in dimensions, and has already cost three thousand dollars. The resources of the committee, and indeed of the congregation, are nearly exhausted, and though the Bishop has come to their assistance as generously as his means and the numberless demands made on him will allow, they are compelled by the hard times to leave the work unfinished for the present. * *

PASTORAL APPOINTMENTS.

Catholic Telegraph, October 10, 1840.

Rev. Peter McLaughlin has been appointed pastor of the congregation of "Our Lady of the Lake," Cleveland, and of the various stations hitherto attended by Rev. Mr. O'Dwyer, in Cuyahoga and the adjoining counties.

Rev. Mr. Louis de Goesbriand succeeds Rev. Mr. Wuertz (removed to Canton in the absence of Rev. Mr. Juncker, who has obtained leave from the Bishop to make a short visit to Europe,) as pastor of St. Louis' Church [Louisville], in Stark county. * *

EPISCOPAL VISITATION.—NORTHERN OHIO.

Bishop Purcell to Catholic Telegraph, December 12, 1840.

McCUTCHENVILLE.

The church of McCutchenville might have been dedicated, as the Bishop and Very Rev. Mr. Henni, on their way from Marion to Crawfordsville had to pass by Tymochtee, which is only a few miles from it, but they were not aware, when they heard that the church was handsomely finished, that they should have to approach so near to that part of Seneca [Wyandot] county during the visitation. This duty devolves on the reverend pastors of Tiffin according to the request made by the Bishop to the Rev. Mr. Machebeuf. * *

FINDLAY.

In Fort Findlay, Hancock county, they [Bishop Purcell and Father Henni,] were agreeably surprised to find more Catholics than they believed to reside there. Church was held at Mr. Engelmann's, a friendly Protestant, married to a Catholic lady from near Emmittsburg, and some children were baptized. [Mr. E. later became a convert.—H.]

GLANDORF.

With much difficulty we [Bishop Purcell and Very Rev. Father Henni] procured a wagon at Findlay to transport us some thirty miles over a very bad road, to Ottawa. We were benighted before we reached the village, but as the rain, which had fallen during the day in torrents, had fortunately ceased, we procured a guide and lantern and ventured to ford the Blanchard river on horseback, that we may [?] reach Glandorf, the settlement of the Rev. Mr. Horstmann, before Sunday morning. We accomplished this task in little more than an hour, and were cordially welcomed by this learned professor, devoted pastor and fervent solitary. Rev. Mr. Horstmann is a native of Prussia. He purchased a section of land in this part of Ohio [Putnam county], in 1834. A few of his compatriots followed him, and a Catholic settlement was commenced. Its increase may be estimated by the following data: In 1835 there were 2 baptisms; in 1836, 20; in 1837, 23; in 1838, 29; in 1839 only 28, and in 1840, to the 30th of October, 33. There were this year 590 communicants, 122 families, 36 confirmed, and 5 deaths in the settlement.

The church, in point of material and style, is well suited to the forest scene around. The pulpit, from which the spiritual Zaccheus not only sees Christ in his law, but also shows him to a faithful people, is formed from the hollow trunk of a sycamore. The dome of the sacred edifice, now canopied only by the firmament, consists, in summer at least, of the arched branches, grapevine, and, for aught we know to the contrary, the ante-deluvian oak.

Near the church, and similarly constructed, stands the school house. The priest was for eighteen months the school master, and it is worthy of record that the common school fund furnished a fair contingent of his salary. We are happy to say that this is not the only instance of such rare justice to the Catholic population of Ohio. In Minster and Wapakoneta we shall have occasion to notice the same honesty and fairness, in giving our people a portion of the education money. * *

From Ottawa [Glandorf?] we started for the Catholic station at Fort Jennings, but the state of the creeks did not admit of our going farther in that direction than Kalida, and during this short journey we had to roll away the fallen timber and make frequent use of the axe to cut down saplings that interrupted our path.

Our next resting place was Lima, in Allen county. Here we could not learn that there were any Catholics. * *

Catholic Telegraph, July 10, 1841.

[EAST] LIVERPOOL, OHIO.

To the Catholic Congregations of Ohio:

With the previously obtained consent of the venerable Bishop of the diocese, the undersigned were appointed to address you, our fellow Catholics, in relation to the difficulties and embarrassments of the Catholic congregation of this place, and to appeal to your liberality and generosity to assist us, in order to enable us to remove the same.

Our church was commenced in the spring of 1837, under the most favorable auspices; being encouraged by the promising state of the times, and the prospect of a considerable increase of our numbers, from a public work then under contract, we were induced to lay out our church on a larger scale than would have been advisable had such a change been contemplated as took place shortly after that period. The building having progressed, however, to that extent that rendered any alteration impossible, we had no alternative left but to abandon the work entirely and lose what had already been expended, or make another effort to finish the building on the plan already begun. The latter course was determined on, and by the most extraordinary exertions, considering our numbers, we have succeeded in raising a beautiful and substantial edifice (40x70 feet, of brick), one that will be an ornament to our town and a credit to our faith. It is in an unfinished state, it is true, but notwithstanding, it will and does answer for public worship, until a change in the times will enable us to complete it. To effect what has been done we have expended $3,000, and unfortunately we have a debt of $1,000, for the payment of which the hammer of the sheriff is now battering at the door. It is to prevent so deplorable a consequence that this appeal is made. Was it for the purpose of building, or raising means to build a church (aware as we are that most if not all the congregations of this diocese have their own difficulties to contend with), we could not expect, nor would we ask at your hands, your assistance; the matter would be local in its nature, and if our circumstances would not permit us to enter into it, we would wait till they were so. But now the case is different; it is not to build a church, but to *save* one, which is already under roof; and these circumstances render its character a general one, affecting every Catholic in the diocese, and in which all must feel a deep interest. A church, on which has been expended upwards of $3,000, is about to be sacrificed for a small remaining debt. This of itself should be an important consideration. But still this would be nothing when compared with the disgrace which must be consequent on such an event, a consequence which we confidently feel you will readily assist us to avert. A small pittance from each individual who will be called on would raise the sum required. We do hope our appeal will not be in vain. We know that it will not. We feel that an appeal made to us under similar circumstances would cause us to contribute a portion which, if equally contributed through the diocese, would much more than raise the amount required in this case.

The different congregations of the diocese will be waited on by our pastor, Rev. James Conlan [attending E. L. from Steubenville,] in a few weeks. We hope none will send him away without contributing something.

JOHN J. MURPHY,
JOSIAH BAGLEY,
JOHN S. BLAKELY.

EPISCOPAL VISITATION.—NORTHERN OHIO.

Bishop Purcell to Catholic Telegraph, July 17, 1841.

PERU; ST. PETER'S, NORWALK, ETC.

* * A clergyman [Rev. Joseph Freygang] from another diocese [Detroit], who had been recently admitted, with much difficulty, into Ohio * * had placed himself at the head of a party [which under his direction left Peru and organized St. Peter's, Norwalk, contrary to the Bishop's positive prohibition] and thus proved the occasion of much disturbance ot the peace and edification, for which this congregation [St. Alphonsus', Peru,] had, with very few exceptions, been at all times remarkable. * * The Bishop experienced great satisfaction at meeting here the former pastor [Rev. F. X. Tschenhens], who had returned [from Pittsburgh] to resume the care of his beloved flock. This zealous priest had been diligently employed for several days in preparing the candidates for confirmation, of whom about twenty-five or thirty received that sacrament [June 20]. The Bishop preached at High Mass on the necessity of obedience to the spiritual authority which Christ has established in His church for the maintenance of good government, happiness and order, and the prevention of the guilt and wretchedness inseparable from schism. * * The church was crowded with a Catholic audience, most of whom were effected even to tears, and all united in addressing the most fervent prayers to heaven for the restoration of the alienated affections of those who had hitherto been of one mind with them in exhibiting the good and pleasant scene of brethren dwelling together in unity. * * After High Mass the Bishop preached in a little grove, near the church, on the sacrament of penance; and the following evening, at the request of the sheriff and a large number of the principal citizens of Norwalk, he preached in the court house. On Tuesday evening [June 22,] the Bishop preached in the school house at New Haven, twelve miles from Norwalk, and on the next

day held "station" at the house of Mr. James Patton, where there were some communicants, and three persons were confirmed. We thence proceeded to

THE CHURCH OF THE SACRED HEART [SHELBY SETTLEMENT].

In this church, attended by about 100 families of German and Irish Catholics, we were kept pretty constantly busy in giving instructions and administering the sacraments. On the evening of the second day, the Bishop preached by request in the Methodist meeting-house at Shelby, four miles from the church. After the sermon the Bishop, accompanied by Rev. Mr. Tschenhens, left Shelby for Bucyrus, 14 miles distant [June 24th]. Very Rev. Mr. Henni, who had arrived at Norwalk from Columbus, where he had officiated the preceding Sunday, returned [from Shelby Settlement] to Norwalk, with the intention of reaching Tiffin for the next Sunday. There are but two or three Catholic families in Bucyrus, although there are many at various distances in the country around. These we could not visit, and therefore we took a stage to Scipio, or Republic, a new and for the present thriving village, being the termination of the finished portion of the Mad River and Lake Erie railroad, commencing at Sandusky City, 26 miles distant. This distance is traveled in the cars, propelled by a locomotive at the rate of about 12 miles an hour

TIFFIN, ST. MARY'S.

The church at Tiffin, which was visited on Sunday, June 27th, is so small that not more than one-third part of the congregation can find place in it. * * The neatness of the church and the piety of the congregation never fail. * * Rev. Mr. McNamee, ordained at Cincinnati, has charge of this interesting flock. He is, through the mercy of God, another happy instance of the devotedness and success with which the alumni of the diocese commence to labor in sowing in tears and garnering in joy the spiritual harvest. Besides Tiffin, the congregations of McCutchenville [ceased to exist since 1870] and the German Settlement in Big Spring township [New Riegel], Attica [St. Stephen's], Maumee, Perrysburg [?], Toledo, Defiance, etc., * * are attended from Tiffin and Norwalk.

McCUTCHENVILLE, WYANDOT COUNTY.

The church of McCutchenville, a neat, frame edifice, wanting but a fraction of the dimensions of the church at Tiffin, was dedicated to God [June 26], under the title of The Visitation. In few places of this, or, as it is believed, of any other diocese, has more been done by a few families than has been accomplished [here] towards the building and decoration of a church.

NEW RIEGEL, SENECA COUNTY.

The church of the German Settlement [then called Wolf's Creek, now New Riegel,] six miles from McCutchenville, is called St. Boniface. It is frequented by 120 families, chiefly Germans—all whose children, planted like young olives on each side of an avenue of trees leading to the church, received on their knees the blessing of the Bishop as he approached the church. Very Rev. Mr. Henni consoled the congregation by one of his eloquent and fervent sermons, after which 16 persons were confirmed. The Easter communicants in all the Tiffin range this year were 662; baptisms from 1st of July, 1840 to 1st of July, 1841, 310; confirmed at Tiffin, 65; marriages, 11; interments, 25.

SANDUSKY.

Rev. Mr. Machebeuf is stationed at Sandusky, on the lake, county seat of the new county of Erie. Church is held in a large hall kindly loaned for this purpose by the proprietor, Judge Mills, an old and tried friend of Catholics, though not himself a Catholic. Five years ago this benevolent man offered the Bishop three lots and a handsome subscription towards a church. The want of a priest, which, thank God, no longer exists, only debarred the acceptance of this liberal offer and the execution of the long cherished prospect. In this city and immediate vicinity there have been 110 communicants, this Easter; 20 baptisms since 1st of January, 20 confirmed, 3 marriages, 3 first communions. After preaching in meeting rooms and in the court house, on Tuesday in the afternoon [June 29,] the Bishop, attended by the Very Rev. Mr. Henni and Rev. Mr. Machebeuf, held a meeting of the congregation, at which he stated that besides the three lots, the sum of $530 in cash was offered by the family of Mr. Mills. The subscriptions of the congregation, very many of whom have not yet been called upon, raised this amount to upwards of $1,600. An estimate hastily drawn up by Mr. Robert Cassidy, stone mason, showed that the walls of a church, 60x46, with basement of 8 ft., and height from principal floor, of due proportions, would require 730 perch of stone. The work can be done here with certainty, for $1.50 per perch, all material, &c., furnished. A building committee to aid the pastor, who must frequently be absent from home, was appointed by the Bishop, and all other preliminary arrangements made, so that the foundations could be blessed and cornerstone placed with one solemnity. The zeal, prudence and piety of the pastor, and the excellent spirit of the flock lead us to hope with confidence that their new church will be covered in before bad weather. The church will be styled "Holy Angels."

EPISCOPAL VISITATION.—NORTHERN OHIO.

Bishop Purcell to Catholic Telegraph, July 31, 1841

SANDUSKY; FREMONT; MAUMEE, &C.

Before leaving Sandusky the Bishop established there a Total Abstinence Society. * * It was at the earnest request of the Rev. Mr. Machebeuf, their devoted pastor, that this effort was made, and the success was such as to leave a strong ground for hope that the example of Cleveland will be here followed. * *

* * Our way [from Sandusky City] to Lower Sandusky [Fremont] lay through the woods profusely adorned with

beautiful wild roses, interspersed with rich clusters of the orange lily. We missed the road, but arrived in good time at our destination. Here, as in Sandusky City, church is kept in a large room, originally built for a store; but a commencement has been made towards the erection of a church on an eligible lot presented for this purpose by Charles Brush, Esq., of Columbus; and an old and faithful friend of the Catholic congregation, Rudolph Dickinson, Esq., at whose hospitable residence the clergy have always found a welcome, has, besides other help, offered all the brick that may be required for the building, The Bishop and Rev. Mr. Henni preached here several times, the former in the court house, where he always finds a large and courteous auditory. In this little congregation, which has greatly improved since it has received more pastoral care than it was possible to bestow on it while there was only one priest for this and the Tiffin missions, 21 were confirmed; and there have been since first January, of this year, 19 baptisms, 102 Easter communions, 16 first communions, 3 marriages and 2 interments. * *

At the French settlement [La Prairie], 9 miles from Lower Sandusky, there was a neat little rural chapel dedicated to St. Philomena. We could not help thinking of the early missionaries, as we approached this sequestered spot in a boat, and again darted by it at our departure, stretched in a light canoe. There is another French settlement [Toussaint] on the Toussaint river, 16 miles from Lower Sandusky, which we had not time to visit. Besides these there are several other stations, such as Marblehead, Port Clinton, &c., which receive as much pastoral care as the extent of the mission will allow. * *

MAUMEE.

From Lower Sandusky to Perrysburg, united by a bridge there over the Maumee river, below Fort Meigs to Maumee City, the road lies through the *Black Swamp*, 31 miles in length. The road is one of the best McAdamized in the Union. * * There were fewer signs of temporal prosperity around Perrysburg [Maumee] since we visited there four years ago than we had anticipated. It is, however, too soon yet to see the beneficial results of the great public works, canals, railroads and turnpikes that terminate or intersect here. * *

The members of the congregation [at Maumee] had, as is everywhere the case, greatly increased; and one of the handsomest churches in the state, owing to the zeal of Rev. Mr. McNamee, the proverbial generosity of the Irish Catholics on the public works, and the kindness of a few citizens of other denominations, belongs to them. It was built in part for the Episcopalians, who for some reason or other, have never occupied it. This church is frame, 65x35 feet, of proportionate height, surmounted by tower and steeple. * * It will be dedicated to God, under the patronage of St. Joseph. We remained here four days, and though we are three in number, viz.: Rev. Messrs. Machebeuf, McNamee and the Bishop, we were constantly employed. We had preaching three or four times a day. On Sunday there was no service in any of the other churches, many of whose people came to ours, as they did during the week, and several among them heard with astonishment what undeniable testimony the Scripture exhibits to sustain those peculiar tenets of our Holy Faith, with which the prejudices of their education had hitherto taught them to consider utterly incompatible.

The Methodist clergyman in charge invited the Bishop to preach a temperance address in his church, but he politely declined, remarking that the Catholic church was large enough, he thought, for any audience that could be collected, and he preferred to see Catholics frequent no church but their own, on any occasion. Indeed, he had stated, in detail, the previous Sunday, many peremptory reasons why, on the subject of temperance, as well as any others, Catholics should go to hear no preacher who could not offer them a sufficient guarantee that he was not likely to rush into the wildest extremes of fanaticism and error. The church was thronged at the temperance address. * *

There were twenty-five confirmed. Three or four priests would have more than enough to do in this part of the diocese. And yet the harvest is rotting for want of laborers!

EPISCOPAL VISITATION.

Bishop Purcell to Catholic Telegraph, December 11, 1841.

CANTON—ST. JOHN'S.

* * We reached Canton at sundown, on Saturday, 6th November. Rarely have we been more consoled than we were at this visitation, seeing and hearing of the peace which reigns throughout this congregation, and of the assiduity of its members in approaching the holy sacraments, under the pastoral care of Rev. Matthias Wuerz. One hundred and twenty were confirmed, and the faithful, after sermons in English and German [in the latter language by Very Rev. Fr. Henni, who accompanied Bishop Purcell on his visitation], were exhorted to build at least one church more for the use of the German Catholics, the present being a great deal too small for either portion of the congregation.

LOUISVILLE.

* * The following Thursday, one hundred and forty persons received the same sacrament [confirmation] at St. Louis' Church, Louisville, Stark county, where Rev. Mr. de Goesbriand is stationed among a flock composed chiefly of French emigrants. * * * It would be impossible, we think, to witness more solemnity and decorum than we here observed in the reception of the sacraments, or in the assistance at the Divine Sacrifice. * *

RANDOLPH.

On Friday morning we attended at St. Martin's [St. Joseph's], near Randolph [Centre], where a beautiful frame church was consumed [?] three years ago, with its furniture, by some base incendiary, whom the spirit of the first schismatic is suspected, we fear but too truly, to have instigated to the sacrilegious deed. Very Rev. Mr. Henni preached a most affecting sermon on the occasion, and all the congregation, with only one or at most two exceptions, knelt down with abundance of tears to ask pardon from God and the grace of repentance for the perpetrators of so deadly a crime. From this place Rev. Mr. Henni went to Hanover, Columbiana county, at the request of the German [?] congregation of St. Paul's [then near Dungannon.]

AKRON.

* * The Bishop proceeded [alone] to Akron, where he said Mass in the house of a German, Mr. Meyer, and with some Irish Catholics and other friends endeavored to provide for the erection of a church for the Catholics of this rapidly growing town, and Cuyahoga Falls, three miles north.

CHIPPEWA [DOYLESTOWN].

* * We were at St. Francis Xavier's Church (Rev. Mr. Schorb's) on the following Sunday [November 14th]. The church was then dedicated and thirty-eight persons were confirmed. We know not if a larger assembly was ever before congregated in so small a space. The building should have been three or four times as large to afford room for all who crowded to the ceremony, and yet the most perfect order was observed during the holy sacrifice and the instruction. * *

WOOSTER.

On Tuesday evening [Nov. 16], the Bishop preached to a crowded audience in the court house at Wooster, standing as it were, according to his own observation, on the grave of his venerated predecessor, whose heroic sacrifices and sublime devotion in the work of an apostle would, he hoped, obtain more than human efficacy for his feeble words. Next morning, after church at Mr. Christian Juncker's, he preached, again by request, in the court house, on the Catholic doctrine of Transubstantiation. We noticed four preachers of different sects taking notes of his sermon.

We heard with exceeding regret of several in this neighborhood who had joined "other religions," because there was none of their own to go to. * * It is confidently hoped that with the generously promised aid of a few Catholics we shall soon have a church in Wooster, where nearly all the sects have anticipated us in the erection of "meeting houses."

After arrangements to this effect the Bishop left in a little carriage, placed, for a week, at his disposal by its proprietor, Mr. John Carroll, a sound-hearted Irish Catholic, and arrived same day at Mt. Eaton. * *

CANAL FULTON ; CANTON ; MASSILLON ; NAVARRE.

* * Next morning [Nov. 19] we reached the church near Fulton [between Canal Fulton and Lawrence] before the congregation was assembled. Here the Bishop preached. * * At early candle-light, same evening, the Bishop preached in the Methodist meeting-house at [Canal] Fulton, and again, in the same place, the following day, after Mass, at which there were many communicants—at Mr. Jesse Patton's. In the evening [November 21] he preached to a very crowded assembly in the court-house at Canton, and proceeded same night to Massillon, where he held service at Mr. Finnegan's, and preached in a large public hall to a respectable and very attentive audience. There should be a church in this place, and we trust there soon will be one worthy of our faith and of the prosperity of this very thriving town. * *

The church of St. Clement at Bethlehem [Navarre] was our next point of labor and rest. * * We shall not exhaust the patience of our readers, already, perhaps, too heavily taxed, by this lengthy communication, by giving utterance to the numerous reflections on the rapid growth, the present urgent necessities and future prospects of the Church in this diocese, which the present visitation has suggested. One thing is certain, it would require the constant attention of two bishops and a hundred priests, as humble, disinterested, patient, healthy, prudent, painstaking, pious and learned as men can be in this world of trial, to preserve the faithful, convert the erring, reclaim the sinful, found schools and build churches necessary over such an extensive spiritual territory. From the depths of our own sense of our insufficiency for the arduous task, we can only implore the Almighty God *to send laborers into His vineyard!*

Catholic Telegraph, February 26, 1842.

REV. MR. RAPPE.

This devoted brother and fellow-laborer sends us [Bishop Purcell] edifying tidings from the north-west of the diocese, under the head of "Toledo, 14th February." He writes as follows: "I have just returned from the state line where I found much work and great consolation. I commence, it seems to me, to be a missionary. I like exceedingly the poverty, the simplicity and the faith of our Irish Catholics. Poor men! Many of them have not been to confession for a long while, and now above all, those who have joined the temperance society are very zealous to approach this sacrament and the Divine Eucharist. I should have two lives to consecrate to such men. They want above everything instruction in their moral duties and the sacraments. But what consoling faith! Last Sunday I celebrated two Masses on the reservoir [in Paulding county], where there are about 600 men, and in the afternoon I was called to the sick. I was followed along the road by a young man who had longed for the occasion of speaking to me. But as the most notable of the place made a circle around me, my good young man was prevented by humility from making his way to me. But on my return from the sick he stopped me as I was about jumping over a ditch, and modestly said to me: 'Sir, I wish to receive the Blessed Sacrament.' 'Very well, my friend, I am going to hear confessions to-morrow; I hope you will have that happiness.' 'But,' he replied, 'it is to-day I wish to do so.' 'My friend,' I added, 'you have dined; you can not communicate now.' 'No, sir, I have neither breakfasted nor dined, because I hoped to receive my Lord to-day.' Blessed are the poor in spirit for surely theirs is the kingdom of heaven.

"I wish to have one hundred medals and two hundred cards, for besides the two hundred persons that I have received into the temperance society, many of the others had taken the pledge in other states, so that they are the majority.

Though I had never been a great friend of the temperance society, I could not refuse to take the pledge myself on seeing the frightful ravages of intemperance among our poor people.

"All the people are very anxious to see the commencing of the foundation of our new church, [in Toledo] but I answer them that I wish first of all to see a great change in their morals; in a word, I wish to put all the whisky bottles and glasses in the bottom of the foundation. Death himself has come to help me in my work, for eighteen or twenty persons have died, Catholics and Protestants, since Christmas, the most part of intemperate habits, so that those who drank to preserve health are now confounded. * *

"My prospects for building a church are encouraging. Fourteen hundred dollars have been subscribed in Toledo, and I reckon upon four hundred more from the public works. Pray that I may have light and grace to know and do the will of God in all things." * *

Extracts from letter sent by Rev. P. J. Machebeuf to the Catholic Telegraph.

SANDUSKY CITY, June 6, 1842.

* * The walls of our new church, the Holy Angels', are entirely finished. They are of cut stone. The most part of the timber for the roof and steeples has been got out, and next week I will give the contract for framing the roof, etc. While I am writing, masons are beginning to build my house, next to the church, of the stone that was left. It will also be all of stone. The people are all very desirous to give me a few days' work, or materials. Mr. Mills [a Protestant], who has done so much already, has been so kind as to give us two acres, not far from the church, for a graveyard. * * The great majority of the congregation, and even the pastor himself, though a Frenchman, now belong to the army of teetotalers; thanks be to God for it. * * I was not at first a friend of total abstinence, but seeing that the prevailing vice, as well as obstacles to all good in this neighborhood, was

intemperance, * * I joined the society, and St. Patrick's day was celebrated with great solemnity. * * The society in this city and neighborhood numbers one hundred and sixty-two members, of whom I had the pleasure of seeing one hundred and fifty make their Easter duty. * *

FREMONT.

We have done nothing so far in Lower Sandusky [Fremont], this season, towards building the new church. If the zeal of a few were imitated by all, the church would soon be raised, and the debts already contracted on the room, temporarily used for the purpose, soon liquidated.

Catholic Telegraph, September 3, 1842.

MASSILLON, ST. MARY'S.

We are happy to announce that our friends at Massillon * * have commenced the good work of erecting a church. The corner-stone was placed on the 20th ult., and a sermon was preached on the occasion by Rev. Matthias Wuertz, pastor of St. John's, Canton. Rev. Mr. de Goesbriand assisted at the edifying ceremony.

Catholic Telegraph.

TOLEDO, DECEMBER, 1842.

The Rev. Mr. Rappe has purchased the Presbyterian meeting house in Toledo [St. Francis de Sales'], in this state. It is a large building, in a handsome part of the town, and after a few alterations, will be used as a Catholic church. Religion has not a more zealous missionary in the West than the reverend gentlemen, through whose exertions the congregations in Toledo and other towns in the neighborhood have been organized.

DIOCESE OF CINCINNATI.

Catholic Telegraph.

December, 1842.—The Catholic Almanac for 1843 has been received * * It is as usual full of interesting statistics. * * The progressive increase in the diocese of Cincinnati will be gratifying to those who take an immediate interest in that portion of the vineyard of Christ. This diocese, which comprises the state of Ohio, was created in the year 1822, and the Rt. Rev. Edward Fenwick appointed its first Bishop. During the administration of the venerable prelate several churches were erected. In the year 1833, when the present Bishop [Purcell] was consecrated, the number of churches in Ohio was sixteen. They were nearly all frame or log buildings and very small, corresponding with the poverty of the Catholic population then scattered throughout the state. The number of priests did not exceed ten or twelve. There are now (1842) forty-five churches in the diocese, some of them equal to any in the United States for solidity, size and beauty.

CLEVELAND.

Catholic Telegraph, January 28, 1843.

The zealous pastor [Rev. P. McLaughlin] of this city and its neighboring missions, is laboring successfully in the good cause of Jesus Christ. * * The marriages during the past year have been eighteen, the baptisms one hundred and eight, deaths, nine. Only two adults of the congregation have died during two years and three months in Cleveland.

REV. P. J. MACHEBEUF.

Catholic Telegraph, January 28, 1843.

We regret to hear that the Rev. Mr. Machebeuf, the pastor of Lower [?] Sandusky [Sandusky City], was shipwrecked on Lake Ontario, whilst on his way to Quebec. The crew and passengers saved their lives with difficulty and landed on an island. They applied for shelter at a farm-house where all were kindly received until the owner discovered that a "popish priest" was among his guests. Our reverend friend, after much solicitation, was graciously permitted to sleep *on the floor*. Such *Christian charity* deserves to be remembered!

REV. AMADEUS RAPPE.

Catholic Telegraph, September 23, 1843.

The Catholics in the northwestern part of the diocese are increasing rapidly under the spiritual guidance of their excellent pastor, the Rev. Mr. Rappe. We learn that two new churches are to be erected, one at Defiance and another in Providence, and that the services of one or two additional clergymen will be required.

REPORT OF REV. AMADEUS RAPPE'S MISSIONS.

Extracts from a letter written by Rev. A. Rappe to Bishop Purcell.

Catholic Telegraph, February 13, 1845.

DEFIANCE.— * * "I went to Defiance the 15th January, [1845] and was very much gratified when I perceived a small frame church erected by the care and sacrifices of a few Catholic families of that place. I hope to celebrate the Holy Mass in it before Easter. I am pleased to tell you that everything has been conducted so well that it will be out of debt when finished. It is not a splendid building, but I hope the Almighty God will have more regard for the good and pious hearts, which built up an humble temple for his glory, with much exertion, than for a monument erected by pride, or without any hard sacrifice. * *

"The example of Defiance has produced a good effect on our Catholic friends of Providence, already animated with a zeal for putting up a handsome church for the benefit of their souls. They feel now a new courage to go on. The stone for the foundation is prepared. We have received a gift of 40,000 brick and 5,000 feet of lumber; an acre of ground for the church and school house, and two acres for a graveyard. * * The work will go on in the spring. The church will be 30x50 feet.

FREMONT, January, 1845.—"The Catholics of Lower Sandusky [Fremont] have opened a subscription to finish the new church. Our generous friend, Mr. Dickinson, has given $50 towards it, and Mr. Rawson $50.

SANDUSKY, January, 1845.—"I passed a few days at Sandusky City, where I found the congregation increasing * * and my good friend, Rev. Mr. Machebeuf, will have occasion to build an addition to his new church after his return. * *

REVS. PEUDEPRAT, RAPPE AND DE GOESBRIAND.

Noticing the publication of the Catholic Almanac for 1846, the *Telegraph* says (December 11, 1845): "Rev. Mr. Peudeprat has succeeded Rev. Mr. de Goesbriand as pastor of St. Louis' congregation, [Louisville], Stark county and Rev. Mr. de Goesbriand and Rev. Mr. Rappe are united in the care of the congregations of Toledo, Maumee, Defiance, Providence, Napoleon and Lower Sandusky [Fremont].

SANDUSKY; HOLY ANGELS'.

Extracts from a letter of Rev. Mr. Machebeuf, Sandusky City, published in the Catholic Telegraph, February 12, 1846.

"Our beautiful little church has been finished since the first Sunday of Advent; and the steeple and spire were completed and the bell hung in time for Christmas. I have never seen our people in better spirits. When I was telling them a few weeks before Xmas that I expected to find a man of good will who would volunteer to go to Toledo for the bell, one of them, by an excess of good will, forgot he was in church, and cried out immediately: 'Say, Priest, I'll go to-morrow:' and he kept his word. As the congregation is increasing daily I have engaged to say Mass in Sandusky every Sunday. * *

"I had the pleasure of seeing Rev. Mr. de Goesbriand on his way to Toledo, and as the ice was good on the bay and the lake shore, we went to "give church" at the Canadian Settlement [Toussaint], on the Toussaint river, and then proceeded together to Toledo, all the way on the ice. But I must say, *en passant*, that we enjoyed somewhat of the comfort our friends, the Baptists, must feel, when, in the heart of winter, they are *dipped;* for, owing to a little forgetfulness of of the track by our guide, we broke in—about fifteen miles from Toledo. But the water in that spot was, fortunately, not more than five feet deep, and had it not been that the vestments and books of my reverend friend were partially injured, everything would have turned out in fun. We made land as soon as we could, and having kindled a fire on the edge of a large prairie, we dried our clothes * * and continued our route to Toledo, where our merry and amiable common friend [Rev. A. Rappe] made us forget our mishap." * *

TOLEDO.

Catholic Telegraph, February 12, 1846.

We learn from Rev. Mr. Rappe that with the aid of his devoted associate, Rev. Mr. de Goesbriand, twenty-five children were prepared to make their first communion at Toledo on the feast of the Epiphany.

The youths of Maumee and La Prairie will be ready to take their place at the Divine Banquet towards the end of Lent. The temperance cause, under the zealous superintendence of these two reverend friends, is well sustained and is doing much good at Toledo.

TOLEDO; SISTERS OF NOTRE DAME [OF CINCINNATI].

Catholic Telegraph, April 30, 1846.

The sisters and scholars are blessed with excellent health, and the school, under such able management, continues to advance in its successful claims to public patronage and esteem. We can not sufficiently admire the heroism with which these Sisters, with the humble but confident hope of being useful to religion and society, disregarded the fears of the "Maumee" fever, from which, through the divine blessing on such devotedness as theirs, they have experienced that there was nothing to fear. * * The Sisters of Notre Dame will not be forgotten in future years when the earliest and most efficient pioneers are commemorated.

BISHOP PURCELL'S EPISCOPAL VISITS.

SANDUSKY; FREMONT, ETC.

Catholic Telegraph, June 18, 1846.

CONFIRMATION.—This sacrament was administered by the Rt. Rev. Bishop of the diocese to 55 persons in the church of the Holy Angels, Sandusky City, [Trinity Sunday, June 7]. Amongst the number were several converts whose entrance into the true fold created quite a sensation in the denominations they had left. The church was blessed on the occasion by the Bishop, assisted by Rev. Messrs. Machebeuf and Byrne. In the chapel of St. Philomena, on the Sandusky river, [La Prairie] there were 36 persons confirmed on Monday, 8th of June, and 45 at Lower Sandusky [St. Ann's, Fremont] where a new church was dedicated [June 8th].

CLEVELAND; TOLEDO; PERU; NORWALK; NEW RIEGEL; TIFFIN, ETC.

Catholic Telegraph, July 2, 1846.

On the feast of Pentecost [May 31] 102 persons were confirmed in St. Mary's Church, Cleveland, and 16 in the church of St. John of the Cross, near Laporte, on the following Tuesday. Forty-one persons were confirmed in the church of St. Francis, at Toledo, on the 14th of June * * and 41 in the church of St. Alphonso [Peru] near Norwalk, on the festival of Corpus Christi [June 11th]. There was a very large and edifying procession in the majestic woods near this church in the forenoon, and in the afternoon the large and beautiful church of St. Peter's, Norwalk, was dedicated.

Sixty-five persons were confirmed at St. Boniface's, Wolf's Creek [New Riegel], where there was also a solemn procession on the Sunday within the octave [of Corpus Christi]. The "old [log] church," so called, though built but a few years ago, has to be taken down, and a new one, larger and to meet the wants of the fast increasing congregation, to be erected in its place.

There were 60 persons confirmed [June 21] in St. Mary's Church, Tiffin, to which an addition [frame] twice the size of the original [brick] building, and in better style of finish, has been recently made.

The Roman Catholic Germans have also built at Tiffin a new, large and beautiful church of brick, which was dedicated to God on the same day [June 21,] in honor of St. Joseph. These two congregations walked in procession through the town to assist at the dedication. The High Mass was sung by the Rev. Matthias Kreusch, [C. PP. S.] and the sermon in German was preached by the Rev. Francis de Sales Brunner, [Provincial of the Sanguinists]. * * The church of St. Bernard, New Washington, is under roof.

BISHOP PURCELL'S EPISCOPAL VISITS.

DUNGANNON, &C.

Catholic Telegraph, July 16, 1846.

EPISCOPAL VISITATION. * * Tuesday, [July 7th,] the Bishop [Purcell] confirmed forty-six at St. Paul's, Columbiana county. The corner-stone of a new church [St. Philip Neri's, Dungannon] one mile from the old one, which is now too small, will be laid on the 15th of August, and also of another [at Summitville?], so much have the Catholics in that vicinity increased under the pastoral care of the Rev. [James] Conlan.

WOOSTER.

Catholic Telegraph, August 26, 1847.

The corner-stone of a new Catholic church was laid on last Friday [August 20], in Wooster, Wayne county, Ohio, by the Rt. Rev. Bishop Purcell, assisted by the pastor, Rev. Philip Foley, and Rev. Messrs. J. H. Luhr and C. Daly. The church * * is to be sixty-five by thirty-eight feet. It will be built of brick, with a solid stone foundation, and situated on a lot of two and one-half acres on the edge of town. A portion of the grounds is to be used as a cemetery.

At the close of the ceremony the Bishop addressed an attentive audience in English, and Rev. Mr. Luhr in German. The pastor and flock are entitled to much credit for their generous exertions to build their church in the thriving town of Wooster, where the number of Catholics is still small, but with the best prospects of increase, both from immigration, conversion, or reversion of many who have forgotten their baptism in the Church, or their having sprung from Catholic parentage.

AKRON, ST. VINCENT'S.

Catholic Telegraph, September 9, 1847.

We are pleased to learn that Rev. Mr. Daly has built a considerable addition to the church of St. Vincent de Paul, of Akron, and that the spirited Catholics of Doylestown, Wayne county, and its vicinity, have resolved to build a new and beautiful church at the last mentioned place, one mile from the site of the church of St. Xavier [at Chippewa], now too small for the congregation.

EPISCOPAL VISITATION BY BISHOP PURCELL.

Catholic Telegraph, September 9, 1847.

MASSILLON.—The new church at Massillon [St. Mary's], a solid stone building, 78x40 feet, was dedicated on the 22d of August. * *

CANAL FULTON, August, 1847.—The church of Canal Fulton, * * a handsome frame, 64x37, was dedicated to Almighty God, in honor of the holy Apostles, Philip and James, on the 24th of the same month [August]. These two churches are under the pastoral care of Rev. Mr. Foley. We are indebted to Judge Griswold, of Canton, agent for the proprietor in New York, for the gift of three lots in [Canal] Fulton, on which the church is eligibly situated.

CANTON.—St. Peter's Church, Canton, was dedicated on the 29th of August. It is of brick, 98x45, a cheap, solid and beautiful building. * *

NEW BERLIN.—The church of New Berlin * * and that of Harrisburgh * * are under roof. There have been *nine* churches built in as many years, within a radius of fourteen miles from Canton.

YOUNGSTOWN.—On the 1st of September [1847] church was held in the house of Mr. James Moore, in Youngstown, Mahoning county. * * We were gratified at the large increase of Catholics near Youngstown, and the size and site, the best in town, given us for a church by the Hon. David Tod.

AKRON.—Mr. James V. Conlan, a student of the diocesan seminary, received tonsure and minor orders in St. Vincent's Church, Akron, on the 2nd of September, Sub-deaconship on the 3d, the holy order of Deacon on the 4th, and on Sunday, the 5th, he will be ordained priest.

DIOCESE OF CLEVELAND.

Catholic Telegraph, October 14, 1847.

CONSECRATION OF BISHOP RAPPE.

This ceremony [of consecration] took place on last Sunday [October 10] in the cathedral of Cincinnati. An immense congregation was present, filling every part of the ample edifice, and preserving throughout the solemn exercises the greatest order and attention. The Rt. Rev. Dr. Purcell was the consecrating prelate, assisted by the Rt. Rev. Dr. Whelan, Bishop of Richmond. * *

BISHOP RAPPE.

The Rt. Rev. Dr. Rappe left town yesterday on his way to Cleveland. The separation of clergymen, heretofore laboring under one bishop, was not without some manifestation of feeling. There has been always such strong attachment between us, and so much friendship in our intercourse with each other, such joy when we met and such regret at parting, that we were not surprised at the emotion with which hands were shaken, when those of the new diocese took farewell of their brethren who remained attached to the diocese of Cincinnati. Henceforth there will be a holy rivalry in working for God. If we can carry into effect only half the good resolutions and promises and pledges which we made at parting, the way the old faith will prosper in Ohio will astonish the "*Evangelical Alliance!*"

BISHOP RAPPE.

Cleveland Daily Herald, March 16, 1848.

* * The Catholic population of our city and immediate vicinity now numbers about 4,000, and the wants of the people require a much larger and more central place of worship than St. Mary's Church [on the Flats]. An effort will be made to build a cathedral the present year, and for this purpose the well known liberality of our citizens will be appealed to. * * A site for the location of the cathedral at the head of Superior, and the corner of Erie and Meadow streets, has been purchased, and we have seen a drawing of the proposed edifice, which will add very much to the good taste and inviting appearance of our beautiful young city.

REPORT OF BISHOP RAPPE'S EPISCOPAL VISITS TO AKRON, RANDOLPH, NAVARRE, WOOSTER, DOYLESTOWN, &c.

Catholic Telegraph, August 9, 1849.

On the 1st of July, Rt. Rev. Bishop Rappe administered the sacrament of confirmation to ten persons in St. Vincent de Paul's, Akron, Summit county, Ohio.

On the 3d he confirmed forty-seven * * at Randolph, Portage county, and dedicated the new church.

He visited Bethlehem [Navarre], Stark county, on the 4th. Here the people have secured the material for a new church, 65x40 feet, to be built of brick.

On the 6th of July the Bishop visited Wooster, Wayne county, where there is a beautiful new church under roof. It was here the first Bishop of Cincinnati, [Rt. Rev. E. Fenwick] "laid down his life for his sheep," having fallen a victim to the cholera in 1832, while engaged in the visitation of his extensive diocese. * *

On the 8th the Bishop laid the corner stone of a new church at Doylestown. * *

On the 9th twenty-eight persons were confirmed in Bristol [Marshallville], Wayne county. Here also, a new church is in process of erection.

The Bishop purchased a church [Protestant frame meeting house,] in Mansfield, where there is a very good prospect for a large congregation.

BISHOP RAPPE'S FIRST VISIT TO EUROPE.

Catholic Telegraph, August 23, 1849.

The Rt. Rev. Bishop Rappe will sail for Europe, on business connected with the interests of religion in his new and flourishing diocese, early in September. We cordially wish the good prelate a prosperous voyage and a safe return. The new cathedral of Cleveland is now in process of erection.

BISHOP RAPPE ON INTEMPERANCE.

March 27, 1851, Bishop Rappe published a pastoral on the vice of intemperance. Commenting on it, the *Catholic Telegraph*, of April 5, 1831, says: "We publish to-day a pastoral of the Rt. Reverend, the Bishop of Cleveland, on a topic which is now creating much excitement. The Bishop, as is well known, is indefatigable in his effort to banish intemperance, and uncompromising in his hostility to the means by which it is perpetuated in the community.

ST. JOHN'S COLLEGE, CLEVELAND.

Under date of August 5, 1855, the *Cincinnati Telegraph* is informed that "St. John's College, an institution which commenced its first session last year deserves particular notice. It has lately undergone several changes and improvements. It is now presided over by Rev. Louis Molon, formerly of Massillon, and has a new faculty whose knowledge and experience as professors in some of the best European establishments guarantee results. It will open this year, the first week of September."

BISHOP RAPPE.—ST. JOHN'S CATHEDRAL, CLEVELAND.

Cincinnati Telegraph, December 6, 1851.

The Rt. Rev. Bishop of Cleveland preached in the cathedral of this city last Sunday. Being now engaged in the erection of a cathedral, he has appealed to the Catholics of Cincinnati to aid him in completing the work. For this purpose a collection will be made at the cathedral on Sunday, and also at the church of St. Francis Xavier. * *

CONSECRATION OF ST. JOHN'S CATHEDRAL, CLEVELAND.

Cleveland Herald, November 8, 1852.

* * The consecration services were witnessed Sunday forenoon [November 7th] by a very large audience. Owing to the rough weather on the lake the Bishops of Boston, Buffalo and Detroit were not present. The cathedral was consecrated by the Most Rev. Archbishop Purcell of Cincinnati. * * The Rt. Rev. M. J. Spalding, Bishop of Louisville, delivered a brief and appropriate discourse, and High Mass was celebrated by the Rt. Rev. Bishop Rappe, of Cleveland; in the afternoon Vespers, and a sermon in German, by the Rev. Mr. Luhr, of Canton.

In the evening Archbishop Purcell delivered an able and eloquent discourse on the progress of the Catholic Church, particularly in the United States and in the West. He referred to the time when the Babe of Bethlehem had not even a stable wherein to lay His head in a village now grown to be the beautiful Forest City; to the first meetings of a feeble band of Catholics in Shakespeare Hall. He made mention of the donation, by liberal citizens, of the site for St. Mary's Church, and of the progress of that church to the splendid sanctuary this day consecrated. The eloquent prelate paid a warm tribute to the self-sacrificing labors of Bishop Rappe; to his devotion in leaving his pleasant home in sunny France on a mission of mercy among the sons of toil on the then sickly Maumee; spoke of his sharing the humblest cabin with the poorest of his flock, and of the high reward which has attended his faithful ministration. * *

LENTEN PASTORAL LETTER OF THE RT. REV. BISHOP RAPPE.

Published in Cincinnati Telegraph, February 2, 1856.

To the Clergy and Laity of the Diocese of Cleveland:

BELOVED CHILDREN IN CHRIST:—We have just terminated the seventh visitation of our new diocese, and it is with feelings of deep gratitude to the God of Mercy that we have witnessed the rapid progress which the faith is making yearly. The number of our zealous clergy, of the faithful, the churches, the schools, and religious institutions has increased to the rate of one in three, in the short period of eight years; and, what is more consoling, is, to see the spirit of piety and zeal prevailing in every congregation, and an invariable calmness and fortitude manifested by our beloved children in this late time of systematic persecution against the Church of God. But we should be unjust in not acknowledging that, after God, this holy growth of religion and Christian virtue has been highly forwarded and developed by the zeal, self-denial, prudence and piety of our brethren in the holy ministry. You have fought a good fight, worthy co-operators, and you already enjoy the fruits of your hard labors. But, in order to secure and increase more and more this consoling improvement in your beloved flocks, continue indefatigable in the care of the youth. Look upon the first communion of your little ones as the groundwork of a holy life. I would exhort you earnestly to set apart five or six weeks, immediately before admitting them to the Holy Table, in order to assemble them twice a day, and, in a familiar and pious manner, explain to them the Christian doctrine, enlighten their minds with a knowledge of the fundamental truths of religion, and lead their innocent hearts to the practice of piety and devotion. Do your best to induce the priests in your vicinity to give a few days' spiritual retreat to them before their general confession and first communion. "Suffer little children to come unto me." By doing so, dearly beloved friends, (and many of you have experienced it) you will create a new generation to replace the old one, which has so nobly and so constantly kept the faith and made the most generous sacrifices for the Catholic church in this country. I need not insist, beloved parents, on the necessity of your seconding the efforts and zeal of your beloved pastors. You will send your children to religious instruction at the time appointed by your clergy; you will edify them at home by your pious example ; you will draw from Heaven by your fervent prayers the graces necessary to secure to them the immense blessings of a good first communion. On that happy day Jesus will hasten to come unto them, to abide with them "He that eateth my flesh and drinketh my blood abideth in me and I in him." He will transform their innocent hearts into delightful temples of piety and zeal. They will live by Jesus and the life of Jesus; but alas! should they receive unworthily, for want of preparation and a sincere confession, then they would eat and drink their own judgment and condemnation. In that case the Bread of Life is changed into a fatal poison which produces in the soul a deadly languor, a disgust of the things of God, a kind of despair, and not unfrequently a total shipwreck of faith and salvation. Such being the awful consequences of a bad communion, would you consent, beloved parents, to neglect anything in your power, to prevent it? O, no! you love your children too dearly to expose their souls to such misfortune and ruin. You love your Church too dearly to see them, by your fault, become her disgrace and her enemies. You have too great a zeal for your salvation to suffer your own children to be your condemnation before the tribunal of God. You know you are bound to secure as far as you can the religious instruction of your family. "He who does not care of his own household," says St. Paul, "hath denied the Faith, and is worse than an infidel." We have full confidence, then, that you will correspond with our exhortations and consult your welfare in sending your children timely and punctually to receive the instructions of their pastors.

†AMADEUS, Bishop of Cleveland.

ST. MARY'S SEMINARY, CLEVELAND.

The main building of St. Mary's Seminary, was begun in the fall of 1859. In relation to the seminary, Bishop Rappe published a pastoral letter, October 29, 1859, from which the following is taken:

"Considering our pecuniary difficulties we should have

postponed the erection of our new seminary, but over-crowded in the old building, and fearing for the health of the professors and students, we have been compelled to begin the new edifice this fall. Trusting in the help of a kind Providence which so frequently has blessed our efforts; trusting also in the generosity of the Catholics of our diocese, we hope to have the work finished before next summer. * * "

OTTOVILLE; FINDLAY.

Catholic Telegraph, October 13, 1860.

The corner stone for a new church at Ottoville, Putnam county, Ohio, was laid on the 9th of September [1860], by Rev. Fr. Westerholt, pastor of Delphos, O. The church is to be 80 by 40 feet; from floor to ceiling 26 feet; height of steeple about 100 feet; style of architecture, Gothic.

A new frame church was dedicated at Findlay, on the 2d of October [1860], by the Very Rev. Father Luhr, V. G. The pastor of this place is the Rev. FatherRoetzer.

FINDLAY, OHIO.

Letter to Cincinnati Catholic Telegraph, February 10, 1869.

"* * * Findlay is a brisk little place of about 4,500 inhabitants, amongst whom * * * about two hundred Catholics, mostly Germans, with the exception of about ten Irish and French families. Eighteen or twenty years ago it contained five or six Catholic families, attending Mass in a small room of a private dwelling, the priest saying Mass on a common table or stand. After a time [1856] Rev. Father O'Sullivan, of Tiffin, built a small [frame] church here, about 20x40 feet in size. Later [1861] Rev. Fr. Roetzer built an addition in front of it, and a school house in the rear, using the old part for the priest's residence. However, it was to stand but a short time, for it was hardly paid for when it caught fire from a defective flue in the school house and burned to the ground. Another site was then obtained, and another church was soon under way, under the supervision of Rev. Father Dechant. But he was destined to see only the foundation completed when he was removed [1867] to another parish, and Rev. Father Vattmann placed in his stead, [June, 1867]. Father Vattmann has the exterior of the church now finished, with the exception of part of tower and the cornice. We have a fine 1,800 lb. bell; * * * the church is 90x45 feet in size, 26 feet from floor to ceiling. The chuch is built of brick, and the tower built up 50 feet of brick, to be continued with frame work. We are much indebted to our non-Catholic friends for their generous donation towards erecting our church. * * *"

RETREAT FOR THE SECULAR CLERGY OF THE DIOCESE OF CLEVELAND.

[Last Official Communication published by Bishop Rappe.]

Cincinnati Catholic Telegraph, July 28, 1869.

An ecclesiastical retreat will be opened in our seminary of Cleveland, on the evening of the 16th of August, and will close on the 23d of the same month. As our seminary has not sufficient accommodation for all the priests of our diocese we invite, first, the clergymen who did not enjoy the blessing of the retreat last year. Should a few rooms remain free they will be given to those who made their retreat last year. Let them apply as soon as possible.

The reverend clergy coming to the retreat are requested to bring along cassock, beretta, etc.

†AMADEUS,
Bishop of Cleveland.

REMINISCENCES OF BISHOP MACHEBEUF'S MISSIONARY LABORS IN NORTHERN OHIO.

[*Published by himself in the Catholic Universe, October* 18, 1888.*]

In the fall of 1838 the young bishop of Cincinnati, the Rt. Rev. J. B. Purcell, made his first visit to Rome, and from Paris wrote to the Very Rev. Father Comfe, his former professor of theology at St. Sulpice, and at this time superior of the seminary of Mont-Ferrand, diocese of Clermont, to procure for him some missionaries for his new diocese. Rev. J. B. Lamy and myself having several times expressed our intention of going to the foreign missions, were notified to be ready to go in the spring with Bishop Purcell to Cincinnati. In the meantime we succeeded in finding three more priests disposed to offer their services to the zealous bishop. They were the Rev. Father Gaçon, who spent his missionary life at St. Martin, Brown county, and died there as chaplain of the Ursuline convent; the Rev. William Cheymol, who succeeded him as chaplain; and the Rev. Father Navarron, who established a mission in Clermont county, and died as pastor of the parish he had organized.

In company with Bishop Purcell, Bishop Flaget, of Bardstown, Ky., Rev. John McGill, afterwards Bishop of Richmond, three priests from some other diocese, and two Sisters, in all fifteen persons, we set sail from Havre May 9, 1839. After a tedious voyage of forty-four days, we landed safely in New York. Traveling by canal and stage coaches, we arrived in Cincinnati August 22d following. Of all my *compagnons de voyage* I am the only one left in this world; all the others have gone to their reward.

After a few days' rest we all received our appointments: Father Lamy, as pastor of Danville, in Knox county, a large settlement of Catholic Americans who had come from Maryland, and a few good German families. I was sent to Tiffin, Seneca county, as assistant to Rev. Joseph M'Namee, a very pious Irish priest, but very sickly. After the Redemptorist

* See also *Catholic Universe*, January 31, 1889.

Fathers of Peru, near Norwalk, had been called away from Ohio (April, 1839), only one Father, the Rev. F. X. Tschenhens, had been left to attend all the missions of the north-west. During the three months I spent in Tiffin, from August to December, I visited the different missions, saying Mass and commencing to speak some broken English, and even to hear confessions. Father M'Namee, unable to undertake distant missions, took pastoral charge of Tiffin and vicinity. In the beginning of November, 1839, I visited for the first time the Irish laborers working on the National or macadamized road, then being built through the "Black Swamp," from Fremont (at that time known as Lower Sandusky) to Perrysburg, on the Maumee river. I first visited Lower Sandusky, where I received the kind hospitality of Mrs. Dickinson and of Mrs. Rawson, very respectable French ladies, married to Protestant gentlemen. In Lower Sandusky I learned that nine or ten miles down the river a good number of Canadian farmers had settled on Mud Creek (in French, *Riviere au Nase*). I went there immediately and found over thirty families, mostly from Detroit and Monroe, Mich. In the few days I spent with them I had the greatest consolation. All of them received the sacraments and showed the best disposition. I appointed some pious ladies to teach catechism on Sundays, and two or three times during the week, to a large number of children. A good widow lady gave a beautiful site on the bank of the river for a church, or rather chapel. * * Before leaving these good and pious people I promised to visit them every month, and in order to facilitate my visits I bought on credit a Canadian pony, borrowed a saddle, and after resting another day at Lower Sandusky, commenced the tedious and long journey through the Black swamp to the Maumee river, traveling only a few miles a day. The National road was graded and partly macadamized, but very rough. I had gone only five or six miles to the river when some good Irishmen, breaking the stone for the road, recognized me as priest. They called me to a large log cabin to attend a sick man; but there was no sick man! It was a pious fraud to keep me for the next day, which was Sunday. Whilst I was warming myself my pony was taken to a stable, and the women were preparing another cabin for me, making a good fire; it was in November, and the weather was wet and cold. Well, I cheerfully resigned myself to spend the Sunday with these good people. Early the next day I put up an altar and prepared everything for Mass. * * * I then said Mass and ventured to address them a few words of broken English. After Mass I had four or five children to baptize, and the generous men were so thankful for having a chance to hear Mass in that wild country and to have their children baptized that they gave me almost enough money to pay for my pony. Promising to visit them again on my return, I started the next day for Perrysburg.

At that time Perrysburg was a poor, little village, on the east side of the Maumee river. There I found only one family, poor Canadians, in a little cabin. How glad I was then that I had been called on Saturday for that sick (?) man.

After Mass in the cabin of the Canadian I crossed the bridgeless river with great difficulty and went to Maumee "City" on the opposite side, where I found two or three Catholics, said Mass for them, and then set foot for Toledo.

Toledo, to-day a beautiful large city, with eleven parishes, Catholic schools, educational and charitable institutions, was then [1839] a real *mud hole*, on the banks of the Maumee river. It comprised a few frame houses, some log cabins, swamps, ponds of muddy water, and worse yet, a number of persons sick with the Maumee fever. There were a very few Catholic families, and five or six single men. I said Mass for eight or ten persons in the frame shanty of a poor Canadian. As they knew of a few families along the river and in the country, I remained at Toledo a few days to give them a chance to hear Mass and go to confession. But there being no suitable house I spent some time looking for a room large enough. This I found over a little drug-store. As Toledo was the town which had the best prospects for future growth and permanency we rented that room, called a "hall," and made up some kind of an altar with dry-goods boxes. A few yards of colored calico served as an antipendium. In my later visits I found a few benches and two brass candlesticks. It was the first "church" of good Father Rappe, when in 1841 he was sent there from Chillicothe, where he had spent some time to learn English in the house of Major Anderson, a pious convert who could speak French. It was in Mr. Anderson's house I met Father Rappe for the first time.

After spending a few days in Toledo I went back to Maumee and kept visiting the little towns along the banks of the Maumee river, *e. g.*, Providence and Napoleon. The most of the Catholics in this section were Irishmen working on the canal, chiefly near Napoleon. As they all lived in miserable tents, crowded and filthy, I could not find any corner for me. I engaged what was called the "parlor," at the village tavern, and on my return at night from saying Mass in the mess-room, and visiting a few sick, was glad to find a quiet room and a good fire.

But I must relate a little anecdote which I mentioned in a meeting of the Catholic circles in Paris. It interested them very much, and gave them an idea of the adventures of missionary life in America. One evening, when I returned as usual to my room, after visiting the camps above and below the town, I found a large number of wagons and horses hitched to the fence, the house and hallway being crowded. I had to go in by the back door, and was told by the landlord, that Napoleon being the county seat, and his house the largest in the town, and my room the most convenient place for holding court, his honor, the judge, was occupying my chair, and the lawyers and jurymen some rough benches and soap boxes—in fact, that court was being held in my room. I had therefore to go to an old log cabin which answered for a dining and sitting room, where I said my office and took supper. But as I was tired, and the court still is session, I passed through the crowd of men into my room. I found my bed occupied by three men setting crossways. I whispered to them that having engaged that room, and slept a few nights in that bed, I had a right to it. They rather hesitated, but as I insisted they got out; and as, fortunately, it had curtains, I closed them carefully and, to the amusement of those who were near by, I undressed, went to bed and slept a few hours till court was over, when the men. with their big boots and loud voices, aroused me from my sleep. The man who was tried, and who had watched me, came to my bed and asked me how I got along. I told him "very well," and asked him what the decision of the court was. He informed me that he got "clear." He then left, and for the rest of the night I had a quiet and undisturbed sleep. The next day I continued my visit, going as far as Independence, near the Indiana State line, where I found a few Catholic families.

Well pleased with my first visit to the public works I returned slowly to Tiffin, where I remained till the end of December. During that month I heard that Bishop Purcell was expected in some town south of Tiffin. I went to meet him there. The good bishop received me very kindly and kept me a few days to help him on the visitation. Before returning he told me that as I was able to get along fairly well in English he appointed me pastor of Sandusky. Here there was neither church nor house, and only a few Catholic families, whose acquaintance I had made whilst attending a sick call there from Tiffin. * * * * *

I went to Sandusky to take pastoral charge of the place on the first day of January, 1840. From Sandusky I continued for some time to visit Lower Sandusky [Fremont], Maumee, Toledo, and all the missions of the north-west. I do not remember exactly when good Father Rappe was sent to Toledo as pastor. I think it was in 1841. We used to visit each other every few weeks. He did not say Mass very long in the room I had rented. He had the good fortune of buying (1842) very cheap, a pretty good-sized Methodist church, all finished and having a good basement. In the latter he had his residence for some time. The bell which belonged to one of the societies was bought also. As there was no town clock, it had been used also for the benefit of the public to strike 6 A. M. 12 noon, and 6 in the evening, for which a compensation was paid by the town. But after it had been bought for the church the town refused to pay for it; adieu clock!

In 1843 there was no pastoral retreat in Cincinnati, and good Father Rappe invited Father Lamy, of Mount Vernon, Father De Goesbriand, of Louisville, Stark Co., and myself, to make a private retreat together. We all accepted his invitation, remaining five days, and enjoying his hospitality, and his zeal and piety as director of the retreat.

In the course of time Father Rappe was made bisbop of Cleveland, afterwards Father Lamy, bishop of Santa Fe; later Father De Goesbriand became bishop of Burlington. You, humble servant was the last to be made bishop.

In 1844 family affairs obliged me to go to France. and Bishop Purcell requested me to procure him some more priests and a community of Sisters for Brown county. As Father Rappe had been for some time chaplain of the large and magnificent convent and academy of the Ursulines at Boulogne sur-Mer, France, he gave me letters of introduction to the Mother Superior of the community. From London I went directly to Boulogne and succeeded in getting two English nuns, both converts, and an Irish nun. In the south of France I found eight more Ursulines, who went to Havre, where we all met, and with three priests formed a goodly party of our own. Before going to France I had applied for an assistant priest. As none was to be had, I was told to bring one from France and keep him as an assistant. I succeeded in procuring a schoolmate of mine, a very good and zealous priest, the Rev. Peter Peudeprat; the other two were left at Pittsburgh, at the request of Bishop Purcell. The priest I brought for my missions was to be pastor of Lower Sandusky. Well, I kept him with me in Sandusky till he could speak some English. It happened at that time that Father Rappe had also asked for an assistant, and was given Father De Goesbriand, then (1846) pastor at Louisville, O. But there being no other priest to take his place, my assistant was sent as pastor to Louisville, to succeed Father De Goesbriand. With no assistant, and with the same number of missions, I told Father Rappe that, as he took away my assistant, he should also take a part of my missions. He did so, and they took charge of the missions of the southwest, leaving to me the east, and for some time, the visiting of the German settlement of Peru, near Norwalk, left without any priest. I visited it one Sunday in each month. * * * *

REMINISCENCES OF THE MISSIONARY LABORS OF BISHOPS RAPPE AND DE GOESBRIAND IN NORTHERN OHIO.

[*Written by Bishop De Goesbriand and published in the Catholic Universe December* 27, 1888.]

Rev. Father Rappe arrived at Cincinnati towards the end of the year 1840, and was immediately sent to Chillicothe by Bishop Purcell to learn English in the house of Mr. Marshall Anderson. This excellent convert to our faith, between whom and the priest there sprung up immediately the most sincere friendship, was admirably qualified to teach English to our future missionary; but Father Rappe's memory was none of the best. His ears could not well catch the sound of words which he had never heard before, and he experienced serious difficulty in learning, though he worked at it long and hard.

In 1841 Toledo was a new place, where there were but few Catholics. They had no church, no priest. At this time, also the State was building the Maumee canal west of Toledo, and the Maumee Valley was full of Catholic laborers. The Maumee Valley at this time was literally a land which devoured its inhabitants. The Maumee fever spared no one; the disease slowly but surely undermined the strongest constitutions, and there was not an old man to be seen then in all that country. Another more dreadful disease reigned amongst the canal men. They earned plenty of money and spent it in drinking; and hence their temporal and spiritual condition was really lamentable.

From 1841, until the beginning of 1846, Father Rappe attended alone to the spiritual wants of the Catholics living along the Maumee canal and river from Toledo to Indiana, and as far south as Section Ten, in Putnam county. His labors and privations must have been extraordinary. The hatred he bore the sin of intemperance owes its origin to the fact that he saw it and its consequences in all its hideousness, along the Maumee Valley. He felt that the only way to save the souls of these poor men from hell was to make them take the pledge of total abstinence. He began the work with a will, and God alone knows how many families he saved from misery, how many souls he reclaimed from sin, who are now in the kingdom of heaven. Hence it is that in those days he was blessed and welcomed as an angel of peace, and the fame of his labors reached far and wide. During the four years that Father Rappe was alone in Toledo he had purchased (1842) a Protestant church in that place and another (1841) at Maumee City. A small church had been erected at Providence and another was being erected at Defiance. Before the beginning of 1846 the canal had been built and was in full operation. The bulk of the canal builders had left, but some of them settled in the Maumee Valley. At this time (1846) Father Rappe had obtained for Toledo a branch of the Sisters of the Congregation of Notre Dame, whose Mother House was at Cincinnati. They had originally come from Namur, Belgium, in 1840.

One priest could not attend to all the work, and it was in January, 1846, that I came to Toledo by direction of the Bishop of Cincinnati. The city, its environs and the whole of the country as far as Indiana were very sickly. At certain seasons it was impossible to meet one healthy-looking person, and frequently entire families were sick and unable to help one another. Apart from the terrible fever, we were occasionally visited by such epidemics as erysipelas, and towards the end of 1847 we saw the ship-fever-stricken immigrants land on the docks to die amongst strangers after a few hours. There were hardly any Catholic families settled on the south side of the Maumee river from Toledo to Defiance. Mass was now said regularly every Sunday at Toledo and frequently at Maumee City. Such settlements as Six-Mile-Woods, Providence, Defiance, and Poplar Ridge [New Bavaria] were visited on week days, and for some time we also had charge of Fremont and LaPrairie. The roads were at times extremely bad, and the mission very extensive, but as the Catholic population was not very large in any settlement, the work would have been pleasant enough, had it not been for the poverty and sickness which prevailed everywhere.

The example of Father Rappe, however, was enough to encourage and comfort any man. He knew every family and all the members thereof, and would bring it about in such a way that every child would be instructed. He had received a particular gift to teach catechism, and he would spend weeks in succession in a settlement to prepare a few children for their first communion. During this time of preparation he would speak to them as many as eight hours every day, and, strange to say, neither he nor the children seemed to be in any way fatigued. As soon as he saw that any neglected the Sunday Mass, or confession, he would go to their houses and remonstrate with them. If he met a stranger who seemed to be a Catholic he would stop him and put him through a course of rather severe questions, if he saw that he did not come to Mass. It was difficult to stand his rebukes, and more difficult yet to resist his entreaties, for he begged of them to have mercy on their own souls. A practice peculiar to Father Rappe, when he visited settlements or public works, was to explain the nature of the Sacraments before administering them, and after they had been received, to make aloud an extemporaneous prayer, imploring the help of God that the effect of the Sacrament might be full and permanent. On such occasions, before saying Mass, he would give a short explanation of it and suggest the dispositions requisite to hear it, and at the end of Mass he would return thanks aloud for the grace of receiving Communion, of hearing Mass, of hearing the word of God, and would in his prayer draw the attention of his hearers to the most practical and salient points of his sermon. The most difficult work had been done, and done by Father Rappe alone, when I arrived at Toledo; but I could well imagine what he did amongst the poor canal men when there were crowds of them in the Maumee Valley.'

The Rt. Rev. A. Rappe was consecrated October 10, 1847, at Cincinnati, by Bishop Purcell, assisted by the Bishop of Wheeling. He came immediately to Cleveland, where Rev. M. Howard was pastor, and left me at Toledo with a young priest whom he had received into the diocese. Rev. M. Howard, having been stationed at Tiffin, I was called to Cleveland in January, 1848, and appointed Vicar General. The only church then in Cleveland was old St. Mary's, on the Flats.

The congregation at that time was large already, and the church much too small. Shortly after his arrival the Bishop had a priest, speaking German, to attend to the spiritual wants of the Catholic Germans, and two High Masses were sung every Sunday in the old building. The Bishop resided first in a hired house south of the Public Square, but moved to the house or block of houses on Bond street, after he had bought it, which was shortly after arriving in Cleveland.

To supply the wants of the growing population he soon erected a frame building, 30x60, on the east part of the cathedral lot. It was named the Church of the Nativity, and here, part of the time, school was taught on week days, a movable partition or folding door being put up to isolate the chancel. There were only fourteen secular priests in the diocese of Cleveland when it was dismembered from Cincinnati. In those days Bishop Rappe used to preach missions in the churches or settlements which he first visited.

The Cathedral was begun in October, 1848. The venerable Administrator of Detroit, Mgr. LeFevre, was present and preached an admirable sermon in the morning at St. Mary's church, on the day of the blessing of the corner stone. We had a procession from the old church, and the crowd, both of Catholics and Protestants, was very great. In the fall of 1849 the Bishop started for Europe. I think it was not long before this time that the venerable Father James Conlan came [October, 1849] to help the clergy of the cathedral.

The Bishop returned in August, 1850, bringing with him four priests, five seminarists, and five or six Ursuline Sisters. The present Ursuline convent property on Euclid avenue had been bought by his direction during his absence.

The brick work and roof of the cathedral were finished before the winter of 1850. All the slates were imported from Wales, and were put on with copper nails. The drawings for the finishing of the interior were made by the now well-known architect, P. C. Keily, who had just finished St. Patrick's church in Newark, N. J., and was then beginning his career as an architect. The cathedral was consecrated November 7, 1852. The Right Rev. Bishop Spalding, of Louisville, preached on the occasion.

Bishop Rappe had arrived in Cleveland at the time of the great immigration from Ireland. Hence his greatest solicitude was to procure for his diocese a sufficient number of priests. This was a very difficult matter. Up to that time there had been but few Catholic schools established in the country. We had no Catholic colleges or seminaries except at very great distances, and among the young men from Europe who offered themselves as candidates for the priesthood many had not the requisite qualifications. The Bishop admitted, however, a few students to his own house, and wished me to instruct them. This was the beginning, and a very imperfect one, of the present flourishing seminary of Cleveland. When Rev. A. Caron arrived in 1848 he was given exclusive charge of the seminary, which continued to improve. When the "Spring Cottage property" on Lake street was purchased in 1850, the seminarists moved thither with their venerable and able director.

Among the seminarists who were admitted, I remember two very saintly young men who died in the house of the Bishop, on Bond street. They were Constant Machen and W. Guilfoyle.

For some years the clergy of the cathedral used to visit regularly once a month, on Sunday, the settlements of Laporte and Painesville, and occasionally on week days, the settlements of Berea, Rockport and Independence. We had also to visit the laborers on the ["C. C." and Lake Shore] railroads when they were building them.

Among the benefactors of the Diocese of Cleveland there is one whose name I have forgotten. The person I refer to [Miss C. Pance] was a lady from Paris who, knowing that there were many orphans in Cleveland to be provided for, volunteered to come, in 1851, and consecrate her fortune to the building of an orphan asylum. With her came two devoted companions, one of whom, Miss Ferec, was well known in Cleveland. The building on Harmon street was erected at the expense of the benefactress I allude to, but she died a few days before it was ready for the reception of orphans. Her coming to Cleveland was very providential, at a time when so many immigrants were carried away by ship-fever or cholera, leaving their children unprovided for.

There is another name which I desire to mention. It is that of Miss C. Bissonette, of LaPrairie, who since became Mother Ursula, the first superioress of the St. Vincent's orphan asylum in Ohio City [now Monroe street, Cleveland], and who died September 11, 1863. During the cholera which did so much havoc in Sandusky City, many children of Catholics had lost both their parents, and some poor widows were left in the greatest distress. At my request this courageous young girl, whose labors at LaPrairie toward the instruction of children I knew, came at once to Sandusky City, at a time when all who could had fled. We made her take possession of a good house which had been deserted. Furniture was obtained by entering a steamboat which lay deserted in the bay. There this devoted soul managed to provide for the wants of orphans and parents till the terrible scourge had passed away. Her vocation to a religious life was undoubtedly the reward for her generosity, in offering her life for the sake of the orphans. I knew of few persons for whom nature and divine grace had done so much as for the venerable Mother Ursula. * * *

THE END.

www.ingramcontent.com/pod-product-compliance
Lightning Source LLC
Chambersburg PA
CBHW030252240426
43673CB00040B/946

* 9 7 8 3 7 4 2 8 3 5 7 0 3 *